Everyman, I will go with thee,
and be thy guide

March 1999

Thomas Hardy

THE HAND OF ETHELBERTA

A COMEDY IN CHAPTERS

Edited by
TORU SASAKI
Kyoto University, Japan

'VITAE POST-SCENIA CELANT'*
−LUCRETIUS

EVERYMAN
J. M. DENT · LONDON
CHARLES E. TUTTLE
VERMONT

Series Editor for the Everyman Thomas Hardy
Norman Page

Introduction and other critical material
© J. M. Dent 1998

This edition first published by Everyman Paperbacks
in 1998

J. M. Dent
Orion Publishing Group
Orion House
5 Upper St Martin's Lane
London
WC2H 9EA
and
Charles E. Tuttle Co. Inc.
28 South Main Street
Rutland, Vermont 05701, USA

Typeset by SetSystems Ltd, Saffron Walden
Printed in Great Britain by
The Guernsey Press Co. Ltd, Guernsey, C. I.

British Library Cataloguing-in-Publication Data
is available upon request.

ISBN 0 460 876457

CONTENTS

NOTE ON THE AUTHOR AND EDITOR

THOMAS HARDY was born in Higher Bockhampton near Dorchester in 1840, the first of four children. His father was a stonemason and builder. At sixteen he trained as an architect and at twenty-two went to work in London. He returned home in 1867. He wrote poetry but failed to get it or his first novel *The Poor Man and the Lady* (1868) published.

Working on the restoration of a church in Cornwall, he met Emma Gifford and they married in 1874. He lost money on his self-financed novel *Desperate Remedies* (1871). *Under the Greenwood Tree* (1872) and *A Pair of Blue Eyes* (1873) followed. *Far From the Madding Crowd* (1874) was his first real success. Settling in Dorchester, he moved into Max Gate, the house he designed, in 1885. He wrote *The Hand of Ethelberta* (1876); *The Return of the Native* (1878) and *The Trumpet-Major* (1880). *A Laodicean* (1881) and *Two on a Tower* (1882) were followed by *The Mayor of Casterbridge* (1886) and *The Woodlanders* (1887). His first collection of short stories, *Wessex Tales* appeared in 1888; three further collections were published between 1891 and 1913. *Tess of the D'Urbervilles* (1891) and *Jude the Obscure* (1896) brought fame, although their hostile reception in some quarters led him to abandon fiction (except *The Well-Beloved*, 1892) and devote himself to poetry.

His first book of verse was *Wessex Poems* (1898), followed by seven further volumes. *The Dynasts*, an epic drama, was published 1904–8. In 1910 he was awarded the Order of Merit. His wife's death in 1912 inspired some of his greatest poems. He married Florence Dugdale in 1914 and died in 1928.

TORU SASAKI is an Associate Professor of Kyoto University, Japan, where he teaches English literature. His publications have appeared in such international journals as the *Dickensian*, *Language and Literature*, and the *Thomas Hardy Journal*.

CHRONOLOGY OF HARDY'S LIFE

Year	Age	Life
1840		Hardy is born 2 June at Higher Bockhampton in the cottage built by his grandfather
1848	8	Attends village school
1849–56	9	Attends school in Dorchester
1856	16	Articled to John Hicks, a Dorchester architect
1858	18	About now writes his first surviving poem, 'Domicilium'

CHRONOLOGY OF HIS TIMES

Year	Literary Context	Historical Events
1840		Great Irish famine Penny Post is introduced
1842		Chartist riots
1846		Repeal of Corn Laws
1847	Charlotte Brontë, *Jane Eyre* Emily Brontë, *Wuthering Heights*	Railway reaches Dorchester
1848	Dickens, *Dombey & Son* Thackeray, *Vanity Fair* Pre-Raphaelite Brotherhood active	
1849	Ruskin, *Seven Lamps of Architecture*	
1850	Death of Wordsworth Tennyson becomes Poet Laureate	
1853	Arnold, *Poems*	1853–6 The Crimean War
1855	Browning, *Men and Women* Elizabeth Gaskell, *North and South*	
1858	George Eliot, *Scenes of Clerical Life*	
1859	Darwin, *The Origin of Species*	
1860	Collins, *The Woman in White*	
1861	Palgrave's anthology, *The Golden Treasury*	American Civil War

Year	Age	Life
1862–7	22	Living in London, working as an architect; writes poetry but fails to get it published
1860s		Throughout this decade Hardy steadily loses his religious faith
1865	25	A short fictional piece called 'How I Built Myself a House' is published
1867	27	Returns to Dorset; begins his first novel, *The Poor Man and the Lady*
1868	28	Romantic affair with his cousin, Tryphena Sparks. *The Poor Man and the Lady* is rejected by publishers
1870	30	Meets and falls in love with Emma Lavinia Gifford while at St Juliot in Cornwall planning the restoration of the church
1871	31	*Desperate Remedies*, published anonymously, is a commercial failure
1872	32	Has minor success with *Under the Greenwood Tree*
1873	33	*A Pair of Blue Eyes*, Hardy's first novel to appear as a serial. Becomes a full-time novelist
1874	34	*Far from the Madding Crowd*, his first real success. Marries Emma Gifford. For next nine years they move from one lodging to another
1876	36	*The Hand of Ethelberta*
1878	38	*The Return of the Native*. Becomes member of London's Savile Club
1879	39	His short story 'The Distracted Preacher' is published
1880	40	*The Trumpet-Major*. Is taken ill for several months
1881	41	*A Laodicean*

Year	Literary Context	Historical Events
1863	Death of Thackeray Mill, *Utilitarianism*	
1864	Newman, *Apologia pro Vita Sua*	
1865	Death of Elizabeth Gaskell	
1866	Swinburne, *Poems and Ballads*	
1867	Ibsen, *Peer Gynt*	Second Reform Bill
1868		Gladstone becomes Prime Minister
1870	Death of Dickens	Franco-Prussian War Education Act brings education for all
1871	Darwin, *The Descent of Man*	Trade Unions legalized
1874		Disraeli becomes Prime Minister The modern bicycle arrives
1876	James, *Roderick Hudson*	
1878		Edison invents the incandescent electric lamp
1879	James Murray becomes editor of what was later to become *The Oxford English Dictionary* Ibsen, *A Doll's House*	
1880	Death of George Eliot Zola, *Nana*	
1881	Revised Version of New Testament	Married Woman's Property Act

Year	Literary Context	Historical Events
1882	Deaths of Darwin, D. G. Rossetti and Trollope	Daimler's petrol engine
1885	Birth of D. H. Lawrence	Salisbury becomes Prime Minister
1886	Death of William Barnes, friend of Hardy, poet, philologist, polymath	
1887	Strindberg, *The Father*	
1888	Death of Arnold; birth of T. S. Eliot About now the works of Kipling and Yeats begin to be published	
1889	Deaths of Browning, G. M. Hopkins and Wilkie Collins	
1890	Death of Newman	First underground railway in London
1891	Shaw, *Quintessence of Ibsenism*	
1892	Death of Tennyson	Gladstone Prime Minister
1893	Pinero, *The Second Mrs Tanqueray*	Independent Labour Party set up
1894	Deaths of Stevenson and Pater	Rosebery becomes Prime Minister
1895	Conrad's first novel, *Almayer's Folly* Wilde, *The Importance of Being Earnest*	Freud's first work on psychoanalysis Marconi's 'wireless' telegraphy
1896	Housman, *A Shropshire Lad*	
1898	Wells, *The War of the Worlds*	The Curies discover radium
1899		The Boer War begins
1900	Deaths of Ruskin and Wilde	

Year	Age	Life
1901	61	*Poems of the Past and the Present* (99 poems)
1904	64	*The Dynasts*, Part I. Death of his mother, Jemima
1905	65	Receives honorary doctorate from Aberdeen University, the first of several
1906	66	*The Dynasts*, Part II. About now meets Florence Dugdale
1908	68	*The Dynasts*, Part III. Edits a selection of Barnes's verse
1909	69	*Time's Laughingstocks* (94 poems)
1910	70	Awarded the Order of Merit
1912	72	Death of his wife, Emma. The Wessex Edition of his works is published by Macmillan
1913	73	*A Changed Man and Other Tales*. Revisits Cornwall and the scenes of his courtship of Emma
1914	74	*Satires of Circumstance* (107 poems). Marries Florence Dugdale
1916	76	*Selected Poems of Thomas Hardy* edited by Hardy himself
1917	77	*Moments of Vision* (159 poems). Begins to write his autobiography with intention that Florence should publish it under her own name after his death
1919–20	79	A de luxe edition of his work, the Mellstock Edition, is published

Year	Literary Context	Historical Events
1901		Death of Queen Victoria, who is succeeded by Edward VII
1903		Wright brothers make first flight in aeroplane with engine
1904	Chekhov, *The Cherry Orchard*	
1906		Liberals win election
1907	Kipling is awarded Nobel Prize	
1908		Asquith becomes Prime Minister
1909	Deaths of Swinburne and Meredith	
1910		Death of Edward VII, who is succeeded by George V
1912		Sinking of *Titanic*
1913	Lawrence, *Sons and Lovers*	First Morris Oxford car
1914	Pound editor of the first anthology of imagist poetry Frost, *North of Boston*	The First World War begins
1916	Death of James Lawrence's *The Rainbow* seized by police	Lloyd George becomes Prime Minister
1917		The Russian Revolution
1918	Sassoon, *Counter-Attack* Hopkins, *Poems*	The war ends Women over thirty given the vote
1919		Treaty of Versailles First woman MP

Year	Age	Life
1920 onwards	80	Max Gate becomes a place of pilgrimage for hundreds of admirers
1922	82	*Late Lyrics and Earlier* (151 poems)
1923	83	*The Queen of Cornwall* (a poetic play)
1924	84	Hardy's adaptation of *Tess* performed in Dorchester
1925	85	*Human Shows* (152 poems)
1928	88	Hardy dies on 11 January; part buried in Westminster Abbey, part at the family church at Stinsford. *Winter Words* (105 poems) is published posthumously. *The Early Life of Thomas Hardy*, his disguised autobiography, is published
1930		*The Later Years of Thomas Hardy*, the second volume of the autobiography, is published. *Collected Poems* (918 poems) followed by *Complete Poems* (947 poems) in 1976

Year	Literary Context	Historical Events
1920	Edward Thomas, *Collected Poems* Owen, *Poems*	First meeting of the League of Nations
1922	Eliot, *The Waste Land* Joyce, *Ulysses*	Mussolini comes to power in Italy Women are given equality in divorce proceedings
1924	Forster, *A Passage to India*	Ramsay MacDonald forms first Labour Government Stalin becomes Soviet Dictator
1926	T. E. Lawrence, *Seven Pillars of Wisdom*	The General Strike
1927		Lindbergh makes first crossing of the Atlantic by air
1928	Lawrence's *Lady Chatterley's Lover* privately printed in Florence	

INTRODUCTION

With *The Hand of Ethelberta: A Comedy in Chapters* (1876) Hardy made 'a plunge in a new and untried direction', for he 'had not the slightest intention of writing for ever about sheepfarming', as he tells us in *The Life and Work of Thomas Hardy*. In 1872 he had published *Under the Greenwood Tree*, aptly subtitled 'A Rural Painting of the Dutch School', which caught the attention of Leslie Stephen, the editor of the *Cornhill*. In the same year he asked Hardy to write a serial story for his magazine, and the novelist responded with *Far from the Madding Crowd*, which turned out to be a popular and critical success, and made his name as a promising writer of rural novels. Pleased with its reception, Stephen asked Hardy for another serial. The result was *The Hand of Ethelberta*, a social satire with a largely urban setting.

Hardy models the novel after a comedy of manners of the kind performed in the Restoration and eighteenth-century theatre. The chapter headings designating the scenes of action, the arch naming of characters (Neigh, Ladywell, Menlove, and so on), and the plot which depends on unexpected arrivals of characters and other similar contrivances, all directly reflect this conception. The subtitle, 'A Comedy in Chapters', is a variation on that of a play, such as 'A Comedy in Five Acts'. It is, then, not surprising that Hardy in the *Life* mentions Congreve and Sheridan in connection with the novel. But it would be a mistake to regard *Ethelberta* as a straight imitation of the stage genre. Ethelberta is by no means a stage-type heroine, and Hardy, with his characteristic iconoclasm, deliberately upsets conventional expectations we may have. The reader is decidedly not given a story in which a proud heroine finally learns her lesson and marries the patient humble hero, on the pattern of *Far from the Madding Crowd*.

In his writing Hardy often takes some elements from his previous work which he then examines in a different light. In

Far from the Madding Crowd there was Bathsheba, and in
Ethelberta he continues his study of a woman of marked
independence, giving a different kind of complexity to the
characterization of the heroine. For one thing, Ethelberta has
strong social ambition. This appears in what she says to
Christopher in a letter: 'the undoubted power you possess will
do you socially no good unless you mix with it the ingredient of
ambition' (Chapter 9). At the same time, however, she can make
an extraordinary declaration like this:

> 'Life is a battle, they say; but it is only so in the sense that a game
> of chess is a battle – there is no seriousness in it; it may be put an
> end to at any inconvenient moment by owning yourself beaten,
> with a careless "Ha-ha!" and sweeping your pieces into the box.
> Experimentally, I care to succeed in society; but at the bottom of
> my heart, I don't care.'
>
> (Chapter 17)

Ambition, then, is not of the utmost importance to Ethelberta:
she is not a social climber in the manner of Thackeray's Becky
Sharp. Indeed, this 'experimental' attitude, here expressed in
terms of the detachment from her own ambition, is a significant
part, and the most interesting feature, of her psychological
make-up. This attitude can be observed in her relationship with
Christopher. To be sure she has a tender regard for the young
man, and when she tells him that they are to remain as friends
only, '[t]ears were in Ethelberta's eyes' (Chapter 24). But later,
when Picotee asks her if she would have married him had it not
been for her, Ethelberta coolly answers: 'It is difficult to say
exactly. It is possible that if I had no relations at all, I might
have married him. And I might not' (Chapter 43). She can cope
with the loss of Christopher, not so much because she knows
that he, signally lacking ambition, is not suited to her, as because
she is at bottom detached from her own emotions – more so
than from her social ambition.

Notice, however, that when the point is reached where, true
to her 'experimental' principle, she should sweep her pieces into
the box with a careless laugh, she does not do so:

> To calmly relinquish the struggle at that point would have been
> the act of a stoic, but not of a woman, particularly when she
> considered the children, the hopes of her mother for them, and

her own condition – though this was least – under the ironical cheers which would greet a slip back into the mire.

(Chapter 28)

The novel hinges on the question: whom will Ethelberta choose for a husband? In making this choice she considers her family, her ambition, and her romantic feelings – in that order. On the whole, her action is not to be regarded as selfishly motivated, for she is admirably concerned about the survival of her family more than anything else. Nevertheless, perhaps because she herself is detached from her emotions, one does not feel involved with Ethelberta, in the way one does, for instance, with Tess. She invites a unique response from us: she is different from Hardy's other heroines in some important respects. Fate has relatively little to do with her: she is too much in control of herself. Crucially, she is not gripped by sexual love, which she substitutes with reason and will-power. Her first marriage, cursorily described in the first paragraph of the novel, is practically non-existent: her 'boy-husband' (Chapter 10) soon dies 'from a chill caught during the wedding tour', and she 'seemed a detached bride rather than a widow'. (Ethelberta is compared to the biblical virgin Abishag in Chapter 45: it is interesting to note Hardy's continued use of female figures associated with King David, following Bathsheba in the immediately preceding novel.) Christopher is plainly not a sexually strong male like Alec d'Urberville, a man to whom Ethelberta might succumb with tragic consequences. He is only a factor among her possible choices, and is unable to affect her seriously. In this regard, he is not much different from other suitors. Hardy was apparently aware of all this, for he says, referring to the subtitle of the novel, in a letter to Stephen (21 May 1875): 'My meaning was simply, as you know, that the story would concern the follies of life rather than the passions, & be told in something of a comedy form, all the people having weaknesses at which the superior lookers-on smile, instead of being ideal characters.' The reader, then, is meant to maintain a sense of distance from the characters, even from Ethelberta. The novelist, another detached 'looker-on', is here being 'experimental' himself, placing the uniquely strong heroine in a comedy without providing sexually dangerous men.

The prevailing detachment, I suspect, is paradoxically related to the fact that *Ethelberta* is a deeply personal novel, with Hardy projecting much of himself, particularly his class anxiety, into the protagonist. For example, Ethelberta's secret marriage ceremony is not unlike Hardy's own, where Emma's uncle was the only guest, since the two families were hostile to one another. Indeed, the novelist and the heroine have the same class background, their family members and relatives consisting of servants, carpenters, and schoolmistresses. On Hardy's mother's side there were people in service. Since his mother's maiden name was Hand, one wonders if Hardy might not have been wryly amused by a private resonance in the novel's title. (Emma Hardy, who probably did not know the whole of her husband's background, disliked the novel, because, she is reported to have said, there is 'too much about servants in it', and the inscribed copy Hardy gave her remained uncut.) With its contrast between the country and the city, the novel centres on Ethelberta's encounter with London society, very much reflecting Hardy's own experience at the time of its composition, when he was just beginning to socialize with the metropolitan literati. The novelist, like the heroine, made his way into this new territory by the profession of writing, also with anxieties about his social background. Their artistic careers follow the same course: Ethelberta starts as a poet, and then becomes a story-teller in order to make a living, while Hardy himself wanted to be a poet, but turned to novel-writing to 'keep base life afoot', as the *Life* informs us. The sense of detachment one may feel in the portrayal of Ethelberta is perhaps partly due to a careful distancing by means of which Hardy objectifies himself, and partly to his 'experimental' attitude towards the novel.

Class awareness, the novel's major preoccupation, is most strongly expressed in Chapter 46, where Sol accuses Ethelberta of being 'a deserter of [her] own lot'. 'Look at my hand,' he says (a pregnant gesture for Hardy?), pointing out that there is something wrong with him, with his ugly hand, becoming a brother to a viscountess. Ethelberta responds with, 'whether you like the peerage or no, they appeal to our historical sense and love of old associations.' Here is a clear symptom of what one might be tempted to call Hardy's 'd'Urberville complex', a conflict between the dignified solidarity with country labourers and the irrepressible yearning for an ancient aristocratic lineage. This conflict appears in many of Hardy's novels in various

forms. He had earlier attempted a class-conscious autobiograph-
ical probing in *A Pair of Blue Eyes*, where a poor architect falls
in love with a social superior, a rector's daughter, but in the
novels up to this time the class issue is nowhere so pronounced
as in *Ethelberta* – except for his very first work of fiction, which
we may surmise had some close links with this one. Hardy's
statement that with *Ethelberta* he made 'a plunge in a new and
untried direction' may need qualification: in a way he went back
to the unpublished *The Poor Man and the Lady* (finished in
1868). The manuscript of this work is lost, and we have no way
of knowing its exact content, but according to the *Life*, it was 'a
striking socialistic novel', the targets of its 'sweeping dramatic
satire' including 'the squirearchy and nobility, London society,
the vulgarity of the middle class', and 'the most important scenes
were laid in London'. *Ethelberta* is by no means a 'socialistic'
novel, but it deals with a serious issue which is of central
importance to Hardy's artistic career. We should not be blinded
by the novel's oddity (the urban setting, comedy, and so on) and
overlook its continuity with his other fiction.

Today Hardy's reputation as a novelist mainly rests upon
what in the 'General Preface to the Wessex Edition of 1912' he
calls the 'Novels of Character and Environment'. His other
novels, however, are by no means negligible. They are undoubtedly stamped with the genius of the great novelist. In different
modes, and with different degrees of commitment, all Hardy
novels deal with his central preoccupations: sexual love and
class. Hardy was intrigued by women, and observing them with
a remarkably keen eye, he depicted the pain and joy of the
relationship between the sexes with deeper penetration than any
other novelist of his day. He belonged to what Merryn and
Raymond Williams call 'the intermediate class', a precariously
mobile group between labourers and the *petite bourgeoisie*,
consisting mainly of farmers, artisans, and tradesmen. The
Wessex novels amply demonstrate the ways in which this class,
both as a sector of the economy and as the bearer of a culture,
was put under pressure in the growing capitalist and industrial
society of nineteenth-century England.

Ethelberta, with *Desperate Remedies* and *A Laodicean*, is put
in the category of 'Novels of Ingenuity', or 'Experiments', which
'show a not infrequent disregard of the probable in the chain of
events' ('General Preface'). The truth, however, is that Hardy

does not care much about probability even in his 'major' novels. These 'Novels of Ingenuity' simply display this attitude in a marked degree. By the same token, the class issue is boldly 'experimented' with in *Ethelberta*, where the novelist presents an extreme case of a marriage between a viscount and a servant's daughter without involving the heroine in sexual complications. When he wrote the novel Hardy was perhaps not yet prepared to grapple with the issue in a more realistic mode. The 'comedy' was in a way a safeguard, whereby he could say, as in the 1895 Preface, that 'there was expected of the reader a certain lightness of mood' in dealing with this 'somewhat frivolous narrative'.

One strong merit of *Ethelberta* as a novel is that it starts very well, and keeps going, without losing much of its narrative momentum, through to the exciting final chapters. This sounds like a blurb, but it is a point worth making: Hardy was fully aware of the importance of narrative interest – 'A story must be worth the telling,' he repeatedly says in the *Life* – and he knew how to arouse and sustain it. The novel also contains powerful and uniquely Hardyan writing. As usual, the novelist's touch is sure in the depiction of country scenery, but here he shows that he can write about the city just as well: the scene in Chapter 18, where Picotee takes a walk across Westminster Bridge as the 'lights along the riverside towards Charing Cross sent an inverted palisade of gleaming swords down into the shaking water', is a case in point. Also strikingly memorable is the horrifying description of Neigh's estate, Fanfield Park, in Chapter 25, with decrepit horses which 'seemed rather to be specimens of some attenuated heraldic animal, scarcely thick enough through the body to throw a shadow: or enlarged castings of the fire-dogs of past times'. The strength of the writing, however, does not lie in these isolated descriptive passages alone. Hardy's is a highly cohesive language which produces echoes and makes thematic connections, thereby creating a richly resonant texture. And the novelist combines this resource with his gift for creating memorable, dramatic scenes.

Consider the title: the 'hand' of Ethelberta. Not only is her 'hand' sought by various suitors, but also the heroine plays her 'hand' in a game of life: 'I have the tale of my own life – to be played as a last card' (Chapter 13); 'I am a rare hand at contrivances' (Chapter 28). It is in keeping with this that Lord Mountclere's brother observes that she 'has played her cards adroitly' (Chapter 45). This series of metaphors energizes seemingly simple gestures in other places. Sol's showing his 'hand' to Ethelberta in Chapter 46, to which I have referred, is one such instance. Also interesting is one involving Ethelberta where, her escape being thwarted, she 'lift[s] her hand for a thrust' in a desperate attempt at pushing Lord Mountclere into a ditch (Chapter 47).

Ethelberta's feet, too, are worth admiring. At the beginning of the novel, when her attention is caught by a wild-duck being chased by a big duck-hawk,

> Ethelberta impulsively started off in a rapid run that would have made a little dog bark with delight and run after, her object being, if possible, to see the end of this desperate struggle for a life so small and unheard-of. Her stateliness went away, and it could be forgiven for not remaining; for her feet suddenly became as quick as fingers, and she raced along over the uneven ground with such force of tread that, being a woman slightly heavier than gossamer, her patent heels punched little D's in the soil with unerring accuracy wherever it was bare, crippled the heather-twigs where it was not, and sucked the swampy places with a sound of quick kisses.
>
> (Chapter 1)

Hardy is often very good at providing a dramatically arresting moment at the start of a novel. Henchard's selling of his wife in *The Mayor of Casterbridge* and Cytherea's witnessing of her father's fall in *Desperate Remedies* readily come to mind. Not so sensational but equally effective is the passage cited above. For here we have, as it were, a microcosm of the whole novel, important themes and metaphors densely combined. The novel is a record of Ethelberta's determined effort for survival, which is here projected in the flight of a duck, and the ensuing Darwinian struggle. That she is a detached, curious observer of this struggle is a reflection of her 'experimental' attitude towards life. The idea of sexual pursuit is suggested also, and not by the use of the word 'kisses' alone. A few pages earlier, a conversation between a hostler and an aged milkman is reported, in which the latter covetously speaks of her beauty, causing the other to reply, 'Michael, a old man like you ought to think about other things, and not be looking two ways at your time of life. Pouncing upon young flesh like a carrion crow – 'tis a vile thing in a old man.' This has prefigured the hawk's chase after the duck, which in turn looks forward to old Mountclere hankering after Ethelberta, who is represented as a small bird: 'Was ever a thrush so safe in a cherry net before!' (Chapter 39).

These metaphorical networks are further extended, via Ladywell's hunting ducks and his voyeuristic spying on Picotee in Chapter 3, to another sexually charged chase scene in the story Ethelberta tells in Chapter 13:

> 'He came forward till he, like myself, was about twenty yards from the edge. I instinctively grasped my useless stiletto. How I longed for the assistance which a little earlier I had so much despised! Reaching the block or boulder upon which I had been sitting, he clasped his arms around from behind; his hands closed upon the empty seat, and he jumped up with an oath. This method of attack told me a new thing with wretched distinctness; he had, as I suppose, discovered my sex; male attire was to serve my turn no longer. The next instant, indeed, made it clear, for he exclaimed, "You don't escape me, masquerading madam," or some such words, and came on. My only hope was that in his excitement he might forget to notice where the grass terminated near the edge of the cliff, though this could be easily felt by a careful walker: to make my own feeling more distinct on this point I hastily bared my feet.'

The focusing upon the feet of the heroine at the end sends us back to Ethelberta's own, treading the ground with the sound of kisses, and the duck's struggle for life which immediately follows. This connection, reinforcing as it does the point made about sexual pursuit in both scenes, leads us to notice that Ethelberta's fantastic story is, again, a reflection of her own situation. The heroine's masquerading as a man corresponds to Ethelberta's concealment of her class origin. Like the man in the story, Lord Mountclere finds out about Ethelberta's humble background underneath the disguise. When at the end Ethelberta is in need of rescue (which she, like her heroine, previously thought unnecessary), Christopher ineffectually comes in, just as he intrudes upon her story-telling at this point, rather foolishly taking the story for an account of a real event.

The heroine's 'baring' her feet, together with the placing of the action on a cliff, reminds us of that erotic scene in *A Pair of Blue Eyes* involving Elfride and Knight. The point about

Ethelberta, however, is that sexuality remains somewhat 'outside' her. It is all there in the eyes of the beholders, such as the milkman, Mountclere, and others. Despite her attractive body, which is 'slightly heavier than gossamer', she is indifferent to her own sexuality and not really troubled by it.

Throughout his career Hardy explores problems of class and sexuality. In *The Hand of Ethelberta* he presents these problems without humanizing them, as he does in *Tess*, for example. No serious suffering is involved here. The novel is essentially an experiment, and the detached treatment of Ethelberta and other characters, and the artificial mode of the whole novel, are deliberate. Whatever the reader might make of it, Hardy knew exactly what he was doing. If this is, as one Victorian reviewer (in the *Morning Post*, 5 August 1876) observes, 'a decidedly clever book', then the novelist himself was not fooled by its cleverness.

TORU SASAKI

NOTE ON THE TEXT

The Hand of Ethelberta was first published serially in the *Cornhill Magazine*, under the editorship of Leslie Stephen, from July 1875 to May 1876, with illustrations by George du Maurier. The division of the novel into instalments was as follows:

1875	Chapters	1876	Chapters
July	1–4	January	31–34
August	5–9	February	35–38
September	10–15	March	39–42
October	16–21	April	43–46
November	22–26	May	47–50
December	27–30		

The serialization also ran in the United States in Sunday issues of the *New York Times* from 20 June 1875 to 9 April 1876.

No manuscript of the novel survives. According to Richard Little Purdy (*Thomas Hardy: A Bibliography Study*, 1954), some portion of it was returned to Hardy by the publisher, Smith, Elder, in 1918, but was subsequently destroyed by him. The *Cornhill* proof-sheets, however, have survived, except for three instalments (February–April), and they are now in the Beinecke Library of Yale University.

Although later in his life Hardy proudly told Virginia Woolf, Leslie Stephen's daughter, that he and her father 'stood shoulder to shoulder against the British public about certain matters dealt with [in *Far from the Madding Crowd*]' (Woolf's diary, 25 July 1926), Stephen's editorial interventions were sometimes motivated by his cautious prudery in the case of that novel. The same can be said of *Ethelberta*, too. This will be seen by putting together Stephen's letters to Hardy and the *Cornhill* proof-sheets, as Simon Gatrell does in his meticulous study, *Hardy the Creator: A Textual Biography* (1988). Stephen wrote to Hardy in May 1875, 'I doubt (to mention the only trifle which occurred

to me) whether a lady ought to call herself or her writings
"amorous". Would not some such word as "sentimental" be
strong enough?' This refers to a conversation between Ethelberta
and her mother-in-law in Chapter 10, where she says, 'It would
be difficult to show that because I have written so-called gay
and amatory verse, I feel amatory and gay.' Originally Hardy
wrote 'amorous and gay', then, after considering Stephen's
suggestion, changed it to 'tender and gay', but in 1912 changed
it again to the present form. Stephen also wrote in August, 'I
may be over particular, but I don't quite like the suggestion of
the very close embrace in the London churchyard.' In Chapter
27, originally Neigh quickly embraces Ethelberta, who is wearing a rose on her bosom, and then is discovered by Ladywell
with rose petals in the breast of his waistcoat.

Stephen also asked Hardy to drop the subtitle, because there
are people who 'understand by Comedy something of the farce
description'. Accordingly it did not appear until Smith, Elder
published the novel in two-volume form in 1876. A single
volume edition followed in 1877.

In 1895 Hardy wrote a Preface for Osgood, McIlvaine's
edition of the Wessex Novels, revised the novel, and reduced it
from the original 50 to the present 48 chapters. Robert Gittings
(*Young Thomas Hardy*, 1975) points out that some autobio-
graphical details were lost in this revision: the description in
Chapter 5 of candles as 'clammy and cadaverous as the fingers
of a corpse' was originally 'as the fingers of a woman who does
nothing' – Hardy had just married a middle-class woman who
never had a proper job; Neigh's being 'a terrible hater of women
. . . particularly of the lower class' (Chapter 25) was originally
stated as caused by his father's 'goings-on', which included
marrying his cook – Hardy's own mother had actually been a
cook in a Dorset vicarage. Excisions were made in Chapters 9
and 12, the remaining material being included in the present
Chapters 8 and 11. What happens in the omitted passages is as
follows. In Chapter 9, Christopher sees Ladywell in a village inn
near Rookington House, and recognizes him as the person he
saw the day before. He then goes to Rookington to show
Ethelberta the music he composed. There he sees Ladywell
again, but to the disappointment of both she is gone. In Chapter
12, Christopher and Faith take a walk in Sandbourne, during
which he picks up a handkerchief and finds that the person who

has dropped it is Picotee. Asking Faith to give it back to her, he leaves. Unknown to him, however, Picotee sees him. From her pained reaction, Faith gathers that she loves him. Later, in a circumspect manner she probes her brother's feelings for Picotee.

Hardy made some minor revision and added a Postscript in 1912 for Macmillan's definitive Wessex Edition, and the present edition is based on that text.

NOTE ON THE PLACE-NAMES OF
THE HAND OF ETHELBERTA

Undoubtedly Hardy based his fictional places upon real ones. This is, however, not to say that there is a clear one-to-one correspondence between the fictional and real places. For example, Casterbridge resembles Dorchester, but they are not identical. Hardy took artistic liberties, for he was a novelist, not a topographer.

The following table indicates this relationship in *The Hand of Ethelberta*:

Aldbrickham	Reading
Anglebury	Wareham
Farnfield	near Farnham, Surrey
Flychett	Lytchett Minster, near Wareham
Havenpool	Poole
Knollsea	Swanage
Melchester	Salisbury
Sandbourne	Bournemouth
Solentsea	Southsea, near Portsmouth

As for more specific place-names, the 'Red Lion' (Chapter 1) was the actual name of the hotel in the centre of Wareham; 'Wyndway House' (Chapter 4) may have been suggested by Upton House, between Poole and Lytchett Minster; 'Rookington Park' (Chapter 5) is based on Hurn (formerly Heron) Court, near Christchurch; 'Enckworth Court' (Chapter 30) on Encombe House, near Kingston; 'Corvsgate Castle' (Chapter 30) on Corfe Castle, between Wareham and Swanage.

More topographical details can be found in, for instance, Hermann Lea's *Thomas Hardy's Wessex* (1913; reprinted by Penguin Books in two volumes, 1986), Denys Kay-Robinson's *Hardy's Wessex Reappraised* (1972), and J. P. Skilling's pamphlet, *The Country of 'The Hand of Ethelberta'* (1976, published by the Thomas Hardy Society).

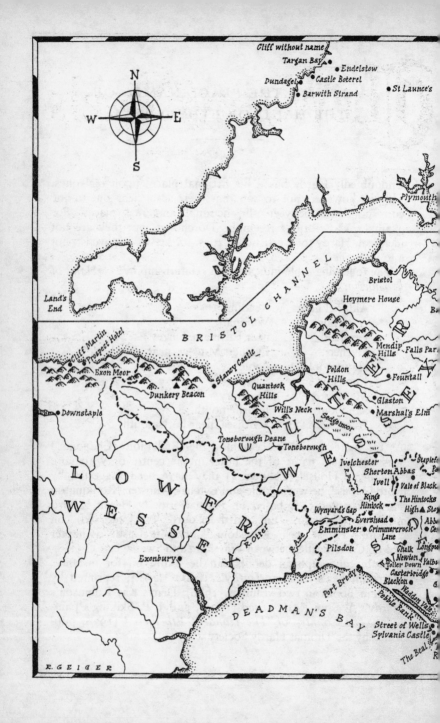

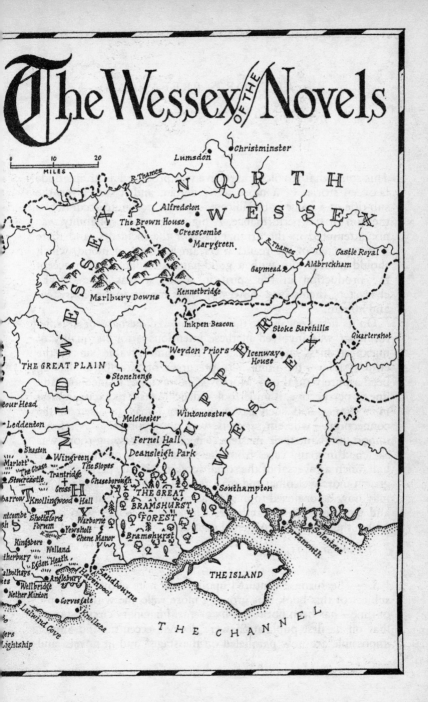

The Wessex of the Novels

0   10   20
MILES

NORTH WESSEX

Christminster
Lumsdon
R. Thames
Alfredston
The Brown House
Cresscombe
Marygreen
R. Thames
Castle Royal
Gaymead
Aldbrickham
Kennetbridge
Marlbury Downs
Inkpen Beacon
Stoke Barehills
Quartershot
Weydon Priors
Icenway House
THE GREAT PLAIN
Stonehenge
MID WESSEX
UPPER WESSEX
cour Head
Leddenton
Melchester
Wintoncester
Shaston
Wingreen
Fernel Hall
Deansleigh Park
Marlott
The Chase
The Slopes
Stourcastle
Trantridge
Cross
Chaseborough
THE GREAT BRAMSHURST FOREST
Southampton
barrow
Knollingwood Hall
ntcombe
Shottsford Forum
Warborne
Yewsholt
Chene Manor
Bramshurst
Portsmouth
Solentsea
Kingsbere
therbury
Welland
Egdon Heath
albothays
kes
Anglebury
Sandbourne
Wellbridge
Nether Minton
Corvesgate
THE ISLAND
Lulwind Cove
gers
Lightship
Knollsea
THE CHANNEL

AUTHOR'S PREFACE

This somewhat frivolous narrative was produced as an interlude between stories of a more sober design, and it was given the sub-title of a comedy to indicate – though not quite accurately – the aim of the performance. A high degree of probability was not attempted in the arrangement of the incidents, and there was expected of the reader a certain lightness of mood, which should inform him with a good-natured willingness to accept the production in the spirit in which it was offered. The characters themselves, however, were meant to be consistent and human.

On its first appearance the novel suffered, perhaps deservedly, for what was involved in these intentions – for its quality of unexpectedness in particular – that unforgivable sin in the critic's sight – the immediate precursor of 'Ethelberta' having been a purely rural tale. Moreover, in its choice of medium, and line of perspective, it undertook a delicate task: to excite interest in a drama – if such a dignified word may be used in the connection – wherein servants were as important as, or more important than, their masters; wherein the drawing-room was sketched in many cases from the point of view of the servants' hall. Such a reversal of the social foreground has, perhaps, since grown more welcome, and readers even of the finer crusted kind may now be disposed to pardon a writer for presenting the sons and daughters of Mr and Mrs Chickerel as beings who come within the scope of a congenial regard.

December 1895.

P.S. – The surmise ventured upon in the note above – that the subject of this book was growing more welcome with the lapse of time – has been borne out by events. Imaginary circumstances that on its first publication were deemed eccentric and almost impossible are now paralleled on the stage* and in novels, and

accepted as reasonable and interesting pictures of life; which
suggests that the comedy (or, more accurately, satire) – issued in
April 1876 – appeared thirty-five years too soon. The artificial
treatment perceptible in many of the pages was adopted for
reasons that seemed good at the date of writing for a story of
that class, and has not been changed.

T. H.

August 1912.

THE HAND OF ETHELBERTA

A Street in Angelbury
A Heath Near It
Inside the 'Red Lion' Inn

I

Young Mrs Petherwin stepped from the door of an old and well-appointed inn in a Wessex town to take a country walk. By her look and carriage she appeared to belong to that gentle order of society which has no worldly sorrow except when its jewellery gets stolen; but, as a fact not generally known, her claim to distinction was rather one of brains than of blood. She was the daughter of a gentleman who lived in a large house not his own, and she began life as a baby christened Ethelberta after an infant of title who does not come into the story at all, having merely furnished Ethelberta's mother with a subject of contemplation. She became teacher in a school, was praised by examiners, admired by gentlemen, not admired by gentlewomen, was touched up with accomplishments by masters who were coaxed into painstaking by her many graces, and, entering a mansion as governess to the daughter thereof, was stealthily married by the son. He, a minor like herself, died from a chill caught during the wedding tour, and a few weeks later was followed into the grave by Sir Ralph Petherwin, his unforgiving father, who had bequeathed his wealth to his wife absolutely.

These calamities were a sufficient reason to Lady Petherwin for pardoning all concerned. She took by the hand the forlorn Ethelberta – who seemed rather a detached bride than a widow – and finished her education by placing her for two or three years in a boarding-school at Bonn. Latterly she had brought the girl to England to live under her roof as daughter and companion, the condition attached being that Ethelberta was never openly to recognize her relations, for reasons which will hereafter appear.

The elegant young lady, as she had a full right to be called if she cared for the definition, arrested all the local attention when she emerged into the summer-evening light with that diadem-and-sceptre bearing – many people for reasons of heredity discovering such graces only in those whose vestibules are lined with ancestral mail, forgetting that a bear may be taught to dance. While this air of hers lasted, even the inanimate objects in the street appeared to know that she was there; but from a way she had of carelessly overthrowing her dignity by versatile moods, one could not calculate upon its presence to a certainty when she was round corners or in little lanes which demanded no repression of animal spirits.

'Well to be sure!' exclaimed a milkman, regarding her. 'We should freeze in our beds if 'twere not for the sun, and, dang me! if she isn't a pretty piece. A man could make a meal between them eyes and chin – eh, hostler? Odd nation dang* my old sides if he couldn't!'

The speaker, who had been carrying a pair of pails on a yoke, deposited them upon the edge of the pavement in front of the inn, and straightened his back to an excruciating perpendicular. His remarks had been addressed to a rickety person, wearing a waistcoat of that preternatural length from the top to the bottom button which prevails among men who have to do with horses. He was sweeping straws from the carriage-way beneath the stone arch that formed a passage to the stables behind.

'Never mind the cursing and swearing, or somebody who's never out of hearing may clap yer name down in his black book,' said the hostler, also pausing, and lifting his eyes to the mullioned and transomed* windows and moulded parapet* above him – not to study them as features of ancient architecture, but just to give as healthful a stretch to the eyes as his acquaintance had done to his back. 'Michael, a old man like you ought to think about other things, and not be looking two ways at your time of life. Pouncing upon young flesh like a carrion crow – 'tis a vile thing in a old man.'

''Tis; and yet 'tis not, for 'tis a natural taste,' said the milkman, again surveying Ethelberta, who had now paused upon a bridge in full view, to look down the river. 'Now, if a poor needy feller like myself could only catch her alone when she's dressed up to the nines for some grand party, and carry her off to some lonely place – sakes, what a pot of jewels and gold things I warrant he'd find about her! 'Twould pay en for his trouble.'

'I don't dispute the picter; but 'tis sly and untimely to think such roguery. Though I've had thoughts like it, 'tis true, about high women – Lord forgive me for't.'

'And that figure of fashion standing there is a widow woman, so I hear?'

'Lady – not a penny less than lady. Ay, a thing of twenty-one or thereabouts.'

'A widow lady and twenty-one. 'Tis a backward age for a body who's so forward in her state of life.'

'Well, be that as 'twill, here's my showings for her age. She was about the figure of two or three-and-twenty when a' got off the carriage last night, tired out wi' boaming* about the country; and nineteen this morning when she came downstairs after a sleep round the clock and a clane-washed face: so I thought to myself, twenty-one, I thought.'

'And what's the young woman's name, make so bold, hostler?'

'Ay, and the house were all in a stoor* with her and the old woman, and their boxes and camp-kettles, that they carry to wash in because hand-basons bain't big enough, and I don't know what all; and t'other folk stopping here were no more than dirt thencefor'ard.'

'I suppose they've come out of some noble city a long way herefrom?'

'And there was her hair up in buckle* as if she'd never seen a clay-cold man at all. However, to cut a long story short, all I know besides about 'em is that the name upon their luggage is Lady Petherwin, and she's the widow of a city gentleman, who was a man of valour in the Lord Mayor's Show.'*

'Who's that chap in the gaiters and pack at his back, come out of the door but now?' said the milkman, nodding towards a figure of that description who had just emerged from the inn and trudged off in the direction taken by the lady – now out of sight.

'Chap in the gaiters? Chok' it all* – why, the father of that nobleman that you call chap in the gaiters used to be hand in glove with half the Queen's court.'

'What d'ye tell o'?'

'That man's father was one of the mayor and corporation of Sandbourne, and was that familiar with men of money, that he'd slap 'em upon the shoulder as you or I or any other poor fool would the clerk of the parish.'

'O, what's my lordlin's name, make so bold, then?'

'Ay, the toppermost class nowadays have left off the use of wheels for the good of their constitutions, so they traipse and walk for many years up foreign hills, where you can see nothing but snow and fog, till there's no more left to walk up; and if they reach home alive, and ha'n't got too old and weared out, they walk and see a little of their own parishes. So they tower about with a pack and a stick and a clane white pocket-handkerchief over their hats just as you see he's got on his. He's been staying here a night, and is off now again. "Young man, young man," I think to myself, "if your shoulders were bent like a bandy* and your knees bowed out as mine be, till there is not an inch of straight bone or gristle in 'ee, th' wouldstn't go doing hard work for play 'a b'lieve."'

'True, true, upon my song.* Such a pain as I have had in my lynes* all this day to be sure; words don't know what shipwreck I suffer in these lynes o' mine – that they do not! And what was this young widow lady's maiden name, then, hostler? Folk have been peeping after her, that's true; but they don't seem to know much about her family.'

'And while I've tended horses fifty year that other folk might straddle 'em, here I be now not a penny the better! Often-times, when I see so many good things about, I feel inclined to help myself in common justice to my pocket.

> 'Work hard and be poor.
> Do nothing and get more.'*

But I draw in the horns of my mind and think to myself, "Forbear, hostler, forbear!" – Her maiden name? Faith, I don't know the woman's maiden name, though she said to me, "Good evening, John;" but I had no memory of ever seeing her afore – no, no more than the dead inside church-hatch* – where I shall soon be likewise – I had not. "Ay, my nabs,'* I think to myself, "more know Tom Fool than Tom Fool knows."'

'More know Tom Fool – what rambling old canticle* is it you say, hostler?' inquired the milkman, lifting his ear. 'Let's have it again – a good saying well spit out is a Christmas fire to my withered heart. More know Tom Fool—'

'Than Tom Fool knows,' said the hostler.

'Ah! That's the very feeling I've felt over and over again, hostler, but not in such gifted language. 'Tis a thought I've had in me for years, and never could lick into shape! – O-ho-ho-ho! Splendid! Say it again, hostler, say it again! To hear my own poor notion that had no name brought into form like that – I wouldn't ha' lost it for the world! More know Tom Fool than – than – h-ho-ho-ho-ho!'

'Don't let your sense o' fitness break out in such uproar, for heaven's sake, or folk will surely think you've been laughing at the lady and gentleman. Well, here's at it again – Night t'ee, Michael.' And the hostler went on with his sweeping.

'Night t'ee, hostler, I must move too,' said the milkman, shouldering his yoke, and walking off; and there reached the inn in a gradual diminuendo, as he receded up the street, shaking his head convulsively, 'More know – Tom Fool – than Tom Fool – ho-ho-ho-ho-ho!'

The 'Red Lion,' as the inn or hotel was called which of late years had become the fashion among tourists, because of the absence from its precincts of all that was fashionable and new, stood near the middle of the town, and formed a corner where in winter the winds whistled and assembled their forces previous to plunging helter-skelter along the streets. In summer it was a fresh and pleasant spot, convenient for such quiet characters as sojourned there to study the geology and beautiful natural features of the country round.

The lady whose appearance had asserted a difference between herself and the Anglebury people, without too clearly showing what that difference was, passed out of the town in a few moments and, following the highway across meadows fed by the Froom, she crossed the railway and soon got into a lonely heath. She had been watching the base of a cloud as it closed down upon the line of a distant ridge, like an upper upon a lower eyelid, shutting in the gaze of the evening sun. She was about to return before dusk came on, when she heard a commotion in the air immediately behind and above her head. The saunterer looked up and saw a wild-duck flying along with the greatest violence, just in its rear being another large bird, which a countryman would have pronounced to be one of the biggest duck-hawks* that he had ever beheld. The hawk neared its intended victim, and the duck screamed and redoubled its efforts.

Ethelberta impulsively started off in a rapid run that would have made a little dog bark with delight and run after, her object

being, if possible, to see the end of this desperate struggle for a
life so small and unheard-of. Her stateliness went away, and it
could be forgiven for not remaining; for her feet suddenly
became as quick as fingers, and she raced along over the uneven
ground with such force of tread that, being a woman slightly
heavier than gossamer, her patent heels punched little D's in the
soil with unerring accuracy wherever it was bare, crippled the
heather-twigs where it was not, and sucked the swampy places
with a sound of quick kisses.

Her rate of advance was not to be compared with that of the
two birds, though she went swiftly enough to keep them well in
sight in such an open place as that around her, having at one
point in the journey been so near that she could hear the whisk
of the duck's feathers against the wind as it lifted and lowered
its wings. When the bird seemed to be but a few yards from its
enemy she saw it strike downwards, and after a level flight of a
quarter of a minute, vanish. The hawk swooped after, and
Ethelberta now perceived a whitely shining oval of still water,
looking amid the swarthy level of the heath like a hole through
to a nether sky.

Into this large pond, which the duck had been making towards
from the beginning of its precipitate flight, it had dived out of
sight. The excited and breathless runner was in a few moments
close enough to see the disappointed hawk hovering and floating
in the air as if waiting for the reappearance of its prey, upon
which grim pastime it was so intent that by creeping along softly
she was enabled to get very near the edge of the pool and
witness the conclusion of the episode. Whenever the duck was
under the necessity of showing its head to breathe, the other
bird would dart towards it, invariably too late, however; for the
diver was far too experienced in the rough humour of the
buzzard family at this game to come up twice near the same
spot, unaccountably emerging from opposite sides of the pool in
succession, and bobbing again by the time its adversary reached
each place, so that at length the hawk gave up the contest and
flew away, a satanic moodiness being almost perceptible in the
motion of its wings.

The young lady now looked around her for the first time, and
began to perceive that she had run a long distance – very much
further than she had originally intended to come. Her eyes had
been so long fixed upon the hawk, as it soared against the bright

and mottled field of sky, that on regarding the heather and plain again it was as if she had returned to a half-forgotten region after an absence, and the whole prospect was darkened to one uniform shade of approaching night. She began at once to retrace her steps, but having been indiscriminately wheeling round the pond to get a good view of the performance, and having followed no path thither, she found the proper direction of her journey to be a matter of some uncertainty.

'Surely,' she said to herself, 'I faced the north at starting:' and yet on walking now with her back where her face had been set, she did not approach any marks on the horizon which might seem to signify the town. Thus dubiously, but with little real concern, she walked on till the evening light began to turn to dusk, and the shadows to darkness.

Presently in front of her Ethelberta saw a white spot in the shade, and it proved to be in some way attached to the head of a man who was coming towards her out of a slight depression in the ground. It was as yet too early in the evening to be afraid, but it was too late to be altogether courageous; and with balanced sensations Ethelberta kept her eye sharply upon him as he rose by degrees into view. The peculiar arrangement of his hat and pugree* soon struck her as being that she had casually noticed on a peg in one of the rooms of the 'Red Lion', and when he came close she saw that his arms diminished to a peculiar smallness at their junction with his shoulders, like those of a doll, which was explained by their being girt round at that point with the straps of a knapsack that he carried behind him. Encouraged by the probability that he, like herself, was staying or had been staying at the 'Red Lion', she said, 'Can you tell me if this is the way back to Anglebury?'

'It is one way; but the nearest is in this direction,' said the tourist – the same who had been criticized by the two old men.

At hearing him speak all the delicate activities in the young lady's person stood still: she stopped like a clock. When she could again fence with the perception which had caused all this she breathed.

'Mr Julian!' she exclaimed. The words were uttered in a way which would have told anybody in a moment that here lay something connected with the light of other days.

'Ah, Mrs Petherwin! – Yes, I am Mr Julian – though that can

matter very little, I should think, after all these years, and what has passed.'

No remark was returned to this rugged reply, and he continued unconcernedly, 'Shall I put you in the path – it is just here?'

'If you please.'

'Come with me, then.'

She walked in silence at his heels, not a word passing between them all the way: the only noises which came from the two were the brushing of her dress and his gaiters against the heather, or the smart rap of a stray flint against his boot.

They had now reached a little knoll, and he turned abruptly: 'That is Anglebury – just where you see those lights. The path down there is the one you must follow; it leads round the hill yonder and directly into the town.'

'Thank you,' she murmured, and found that he had never removed his eyes from her since speaking, keeping them fixed with mathematical exactness upon one point in her face. She moved a little to go on her way; he moved a little less – to go on his.

'Good night,' said Mr Julian.

The moment, upon the very face of it, was critical; and yet it was one of those which have to wait for a future before they acquire a definite character as good or bad.

Thus much would have been obvious to any outsider; it may have been doubly so to Ethelberta, for she gave back more than she had got, replying, 'Good-bye – if you are going to say no more.'

Then in struck Mr Julian: 'What can I say? You are nothing to me ... I could forgive a woman doing anything for spite, except marrying for spite.'

'The connection of that with our present meeting does not appear, unless it refers to what you have done. It does not refer to me.'

'I am not married: you are.'

She did not contradict him, as she might have done. 'Christopher,' she said at last, 'this is how it is: you knew too much of me to respect me, and too little to pity me. A half knowledge of another's life mostly does injustice to the life half known.'

'Then since I can hardly get to know you more, I must do my best to know you less, and elevate my opinion of your nature by forgetting what it consists in,' he said, in a voice from which all feeling was polished away.

'If I did not know that bitterness had more to do with those words than judgment, I – should be – bitter too! You never knew half about me; you only knew me as a governess; you little think what my beginnings were.'

'I have guessed. I have many times told myself that your early life was superior to your position when I first met you. I think I may say without presumption that I recognize a lady by birth when I see her, even under reverses of an extreme kind. And certainly there is this to be said, that the fact of having been bred in a wealthy home does slightly redeem an attempt to attain to such a one again.'

Ethelberta smiled a smile of many meanings.

'However, we are wasting words,' he resumed cheerfully. 'It is better for us to part as we met, and continue to be the strangers that we have become to each other. I owe you an apology for having been betrayed into more feeling than I had a right to show, and let us part friends. Good night, Mrs Petherwin, and success to you. We may meet again, some day, I hope.'

'Good night,' she said, extending her hand. He touched it, turned about, and in a short time nothing remained of him but quick regular brushings against the heather in the deep broad shadow of the moor.

Ethelberta slowly moved on in the direction that he had pointed out. This meeting had surprised her in several ways. First, there was the conjuncture itself; but more than that was the fact that he had not parted from her with any of the tragic resentment that she had from time to time imagined for that scene if it ever occurred. Yet there was really nothing wonderful in this: it is part of the generous nature of a bachelor to be not indisposed to forgive a portionless* sweetheart who, by marrying elsewhere, has deprived him of the bliss of being obliged to marry her himself. Ethelberta would have been disappointed quite had there not been a comforting development of exasperation in the middle part of his talk; but after all it formed a poor substitute for the loving hatred she had expected.

When she reached the hotel the lamp over the door showed a face a little flushed, but the agitation which at first had possessed her was gone to a mere nothing. In the hall she met a slender woman wearing a silk dress of that peculiar black which in sunlight proclaims itself to have once seen better days as a brown, and days even better than those as a lavender, green, or blue.

'Menlove,' said the lady, 'did you notice if any gentleman observed and followed me when I left the hotel to go for a walk this evening?'

The lady's-maid, thus suddenly pulled up in a night forage after lovers, put a hand to her forehead to show that there was no mistake about her having begun to meditate on receiving orders to that effect, and said at last, 'You once told me, ma'am, if you recollect, that when you were dressed, I was not to go staring out of the window after you as if you were a doll I had just manufactured and sent round for sale.'

'Yes, so I did.'

'So I didn't see if anybody followed you this evening.'

'Then did you hear any gentleman arrive here by the late train last night?'

'O no, ma'am – how could I?' said Mrs Menlove – an exclamation which was more apposite than her mistress suspected, considering that the speaker, after retiring from duty, had slipped down her dark skirt to reveal a light, puffed, and festooned one, put on a hat and feather, together with several pennyweights of metal in the form of rings, brooches, and earrings – all in a time whilst one could count a hundred – and enjoyed half-an-hour of prime courtship by an honourable young waiter of the town, who had proved constant as the magnet to the pole for the space of the day and a half that she had known him.

Going at once upstairs, Ethelberta ran down the passage, and after some hesitation softly opened the door of the sitting-room in the best suite of apartments that the inn could boast of.

In this room sat an elderly lady writing by the light of two candles with green shades. Well knowing, as it seemed, who the intruder was, she continued her occupation, and her visitor advanced and stood beside the table. The old lady wore her spectacles low down her cheek, her glance being depressed to about the slope of her straight white nose in order to look through them. Her mouth was pursed up to almost a youthful shape as she formed the letters with her pen, and a slight move of the lip accompanied every downstroke. There were two large antique rings on her forefinger, against which the quill rubbed in moving backwards and forwards, thereby causing a secondary noise rivalling the primary one of the nib upon the paper.

'Mamma,' said the younger lady, 'here I am at last.'

A writer's mind in the midst of a sentence being like a ship at sea, knowing no rest or comfort till safely piloted into the harbour of a full stop, Lady Petherwin just replied with 'What,' in an occupied tone, not rising to interrogation. After signing her name to the letter, she raised her eyes.

'Why, how late you are, Ethelberta, and how heated you look!' she said. 'I have been quite alarmed about you. What do you say has happened?'

The great, chief, and altogether eclipsing thing that had happened was the accidental meeting with an old lover whom she had once quarrelled with; and Ethelberta's honesty would have delivered the tidings at once, had not, unfortunately, all the rest of her attributes been dead against that act, for the old lady's sake even more than for her own.

'I saw a great cruel bird chasing a harmless duck!' she exclaimed innocently. 'And I ran after to see what the end of it would be – much further than I had any idea of going. However, the duck came to a pond, and in running round it to see the end of the fight, I could not remember which way I had come.'

'Mercy!' said her mother-in-law, lifting her large eyelids, heavy as window-shutters, and spreading out her fingers like the horns of a snail. 'You might have sunk up to your knees and got lost in that swampy place – such a time of night, too. What a tomboy you are! And how did you find your way home after all!'

'O, some man showed me the way, and then I had no difficulty, and after that I came along leisurely.'

'I thought you had been running all the way; you look so warm.'

'It is a warm evening . . . Yes, and I have been thinking of old times as I walked along,' she said, 'and how people's positions in life alter. Have I not heard you say that while I was at Bonn, at school, some family that we had known had their household broken up when the father died, and that the children went away you didn't know where?'

'Do you mean the Julians?'

'Yes, that was the name.'

'Why, of course you know it was the Julians. Young Julian

had a day or two's fancy for you one summer, had he not? – just after you came to us, at the same time, or just before it, that my poor boy and you were so desperately attached to each other.'

'O yes, I recollect,' said Ethelberta. 'And he had a sister, I think. I wonder where they went to live after the family collapse.'

'I do not know,' said Lady Petherwin, taking up another sheet of paper. 'I have a dim notion that the son, who had been brought up to no profession, became a teacher of music in some country town – music having always been his hobby. But the facts are not very distinct in my memory.' And she dipped her pen for another letter.

Ethelberta, with a rather fallen countenance, then left her mother-in-law, and went where all ladies are supposed to go when they want to torment their minds in comfort – to her own room. Here she thoughtfully sat down awhile, and some time later she rang for her maid.

'Menlove,' she said, without looking towards a rustle and half a footstep that had just come in at the door, but leaning back in her chair and speaking towards the corner of the looking-glass, 'will you go down and find out if any gentleman named Julian has been staying in this house? Get to know it, I mean, Menlove, not by directly inquiring; you have ways of getting to know things, have you not? If the devoted George were here now, he would help—'

'George was nothing to me, ma'am.'

'James, then.'

'And I only had James for a week or ten days: when I found he was a married man, I encouraged his addresses very little indeed.'

'If you had encouraged him heart and soul, you couldn't have fumed more at the loss of him. But please to go and make that inquiry, will you, Menlove?'

In a few minutes Ethelberta's woman was back again. 'A gentleman of that name stayed here last night, and left this afternoon.'

'Will you find out his address?'

Now the lady's-maid had already been quick-witted enough to find out that, and indeed all about him; but it chanced that a fashionable illustrated weekly paper had just been sent from the bookseller's, and being in want of a little time to look it over before it reached her mistress's hands, Mrs Menlove retired, as if to go and ask the question – to stand meanwhile under the gas-lamp in the passage, inspecting the fascinating engravings. But as time will not wait for tire-women,* a natural length of absence soon elapsed, and she returned again and said,

'His address is, Upper Street, Sandbourne.'

'Thank you, that will do,' replied her mistress.

The hour grew later, and that dreamy period came round when ladies' fancies, that have lain shut up close as their fans during the day, begin to assert themselves anew. At this time a good guess at Ethelberta's thoughts might have been made from her manner of passing the minutes away. Instead of reading, entering notes in her diary, or doing any ordinary thing, she walked to and fro, curled her pretty nether lip within her pretty upper one a great many times, made a cradle of her locked fingers, and paused with fixed eyes where the walls of the room set limits upon her walk to look at nothing but a picture within her mind.

Christopher's House
Sandbourne Town
Sandbourne Moor

2

During the wet autumn of the same year, the postman passed one morning as usual into a plain street that ran through the less fashionable portion of Sandbourne, a modern coast town and watering-place not many miles from the ancient Anglebury. He knocked at the door of a flat-faced brick house, and it was opened by a slight, thoughtful young man, with his hat on, just then coming out. The postman put into his hands a book packet, addressed, 'Christopher Julian, Esq.'

Christopher took the package upstairs, opened it with curiosity, and discovered within a green volume of poems, by an anonymous writer, the title-page bearing the inscription, 'Metres by E.' The book was new, though it was cut,* and it appeared to have been looked into. The young man, after turning it over and wondering where it came from, laid it on the table and went his way, being in haste to fulfil his engagements for the day.

In the evening, on returning home from his occupations, he sat himself down cosily to read the newly-arrived volume. The winds of this uncertain season were snarling in the chimneys, and drops of rain spat themselves into the fire, revealing plainly that the young man's room was not far enough from the top of the house to admit of a twist in the flue, and revealing darkly a little more, if that social rule-of-three* inverse, the higher in lodgings the lower in pocket, were applicable here. However, the aspect of the room, though homely, was cheerful, a somewhat contradictory group of furniture suggesting that the collection consisted of waifs and strays from a former home, the grimy faces of the old articles exercising a curious and subduing effect on the bright faces of the new. An oval mirror of rococo workmanship, and a heavy cabinet-piano with a cornice like that of an Egyptian temple, adjoined a harmonium of yesterday, and a harp that was almost as new. Printed music of the last century, and manuscript music of the previous evening, lay there in such quantity as to endanger the tidiness of a retreat which was indeed only saved from a chronic state of litter by a pair of hands that sometimes played, with the lightness of breezes, about the sewing-machine standing in a remote corner – if any corner could be called remote in a room so small.

Fire lights and shades from the shaking flames struck in a butterfly flutter on the underparts of the mantel-shelf, and upon the reader's cheek as he sat. Presently, and all at once, a much greater intentness pervaded his face: he turned back again, and read anew the subject that had arrested his eyes. He was a man whose countenance varied with his mood, though it kept somewhat in the rear of that mood. He looked sad when he felt almost serene, and only serene when he felt quite cheerful. It is a habit people acquire who have had repressing experiences.

A faint smile and flush now lightened his face, and jumping up he opened the door and exclaimed, 'Faith! will you come here for a moment?'

A prompt step was heard on the stairs, and the young person addressed as Faith entered the room. She was small in figure, and bore less in the form of her features than in their shades when changing from expression to expression the evidence that she was his sister.

'Faith – I want your opinion. But, stop, read this first.' He laid his finger upon a page in the book, and placed it in her hand.

The girl drew from her pocket a little green-leather sheath, worn at the edges to whity-brown, and out of that a pair of spectacles, unconsciously looking round the room for a moment as she did so, as if to ensure that no stranger saw her in the act of using them. Here a weakness was uncovered at once; it was a small, pretty, and natural one; indeed, as weaknesses go in the great world, it might almost have been called a commendable trait. She then began to read, without sitting down.

These 'Metres by E.' composed a collection of soft and marvellously musical rhymes, of a nature known as the *vers de société*.* The lines presented a series of playful defences of the supposed strategy of womankind in fascination, courtship, and marriage – the whole teeming with ideas bright as mirrors and just as unsubstantial, yet forming a brilliant argument to justify the ways of girls to men.* The pervading characteristic of the mass was the means of forcing into notice, by strangeness of contrast, the single mournful poem that the book contained. It was placed at the very end, and under the title of 'Cancelled Words' formed a whimsical and rather affecting love-lament, somewhat in the tone of many of Sir Thomas Wyatt's* poems. This was the piece which had arrested Christopher's attention, and had been pointed out by him to his sister Faith.

'It is very touching,' she said, looking up.

'What do you think I suspect about it – that the poem is addressed to me! Do you remember, when father was alive and we were at Solentsea that season, about a governess who came there with a Sir Ralph Petherwin and his wife, people with a sickly little daughter and a grown-up son?'

'I never saw any of them. I think I remember your knowing something about a young man of that name.'

'Yes, that was the family. Well, the governess there was a very attractive woman, and somehow or other I got more interested in her than I ought to have done (this is necessary to the history), and we used to meet in romantic places – and – and that kind of thing, you know. The end of it was, she jilted me and married the son.'

'You were anxious to get away from Solentsea.'

'Was I? Then that was chiefly the reason. Well, I decided to think no more of her, and I was helped to do it by the troubles that came upon us shortly afterwards; it is a blessed arrangement that one does not feel a sentimental grief at all when additional grief comes in the shape of practical misfortune. However, on the first afternoon of the little holiday I took for my walking tour last summer, I came to Anglebury, and stayed about the neighbourhood for a day or two to see what it was like, thinking we might settle there if this place failed us. The next evening I left, and walked across the heath to Flychett – that's a village about five miles further on – so as to be that distance on my way for next morning; and while I was crossing the heath there I met this very woman. We talked a little, because we couldn't help it – you may imagine the kind of talk it was – and parted as coolly as we had met. Now this strange book comes to me; and I have a strong conviction that she is the writer of it, for that poem sketches a similar scene – or rather suggests it; and the tone generally seems the kind of thing she would write – not that she was a sad woman, either.'

'She seems to be a warm-hearted, impulsive woman, to judge from these tender verses.'

'People who print very warm words have sometimes very cold manners. I wonder if it is really her writing, and if she has sent it to me!'

'Would it not be a singular thing for a married woman to do? Though of course' – (she removed her spectacles as if they hindered her from thinking, and hid them under the timepiece till she should go on reading) – 'of course poets have morals and manners of their own, and custom is no argument with them. I am sure I would not have sent it to a man for the world!'

'I do not see any absolute harm in her sending it. Perhaps she thinks that, since it is all over, we may as well die friends.'

'If I were her husband I should have doubts about the dying. And "all over" may not be so plain to other people as it is to you.'

'Perhaps not. And when a man checks all a woman's finer sentiments towards him by marrying her, it is only natural that it should find a vent somewhere. However, she probably does not know of my downfall since father's death. I hardly think she would have cared to do it had she known that. (I am assuming that it is Ethelberta – Mrs Petherwin – who sends it: of course I am not sure.) We must remember that when I knew her I was a gentleman at ease, who had not the least notion that I should have to work for a living, and not only so, but should have first to invent a profession to work at out of my old tastes.'

'Kit, you have made two mistakes in your thoughts of that lady. Even though I don't know her, I can show you that. Now I'll tell you! the first is in thinking that a married lady would send the book with that poem in it without at any rate a slight doubt as to its propriety: the second is in supposing that, had she wished to do it, she would have given the thing up because of our misfortunes. With a true woman the second reason would have had no effect had she once got over the first. I'm a woman, and that's why I know.'

Christopher said nothing, and turned over the poems.

He lived by teaching music, and, in comparison with starving, thrived; though the wealthy might possibly have said that in comparison with thriving he starved. During this night he hummed airs in bed, thought he would do for the ballad of the fair poetess what other musicians had done for the ballads of other fair poetesses, and dreamed that she smiled on him as her prototype Sappho smiled on Phaon.*

The next morning before starting on his rounds a new circumstance induced him to direct his steps to the bookseller's, and ask a question. He had found on examining the wrapper of the volume that it was posted in his own town.

'No copy of the book has been sold by me,' the bookseller's voice replied from far up the Alpine height of the shop-ladder, where he stood dusting stale volumes, as was his habit of a morning before customers came. 'I have never heard of it – probably never shall'; and he shook out the duster, so as to hit the delicate mean between stifling Christopher and not stifling him.

'Surely you don't live by your shop?' said Christopher, drawing back.

The bookseller's eyes rested on the speaker's; his face changed; he came down and placed his hand on the lapel of Christopher's coat. 'Sir,' he said, 'I starve by it; country bookselling is a miserable, impoverishing, exasperating thing in these days. Can you understand the rest?'

'I can; I forgive a starving man anything,' said Christopher.

'You go a long way very suddenly,' said the bookseller. 'Half as much pity would have seemed better. However, wait a moment.' He looked into a list of new books, and added: 'The work you allude to was only published last week; though, mind you, if it had been published last century I might not have sold a copy.'

Although his time was precious, Christopher had now become so interested in the circumstance that the unseen sender was somebody breathing his own atmosphere, possibly the very writer herself – the book being too new to be known – that he again passed through the blue shadow of the spire which stretched across the street today, and went towards the post-office, animated by a bright intention – to ask the postmaster if he knew the handwriting in which the packet was addressed.

Now the postmaster was an acquaintance of Christopher's, but, as regarded putting that question to him, there was a difficulty. Everything turned upon whether the postmaster at the moment of asking would be in his under-government manner, or in the manner with which mere nature had endowed him. In the latter case his reply would be all that could be wished; in the former, a man who had sunk in society might as well put his tongue into a mousetrap as make an inquiry so obviously outside the pale of legality as was this.

So he postponed his business for the present, and refrained from entering till he passed by after dinner, when pleasant malt liquor, of that capacity for cheering which is expressed by four large letter X's* marching in a row, had refilled the globular trunk of the postmaster and neutralized some of the effects of officiality. The time was well chosen, but the inquiry threatened to prove fruitless: the postmaster had never, to his knowledge, seen the writing before. Christopher was turning away when a clerk in the background looked up and stated that some young lady had brought a packet with such an address upon it into the office two days earlier to get it stamped.

'Do you know her?' said Christopher.

'I have seen her about the neighbourhood. She goes by every morning; I think she comes into the town from two or three miles out, and returns again between four and five in the afternoon.'

'What does she wear?'

'A white wool jacket with zigzags of black braid.'

Christopher left the post-office and went his way. Among his other pupils there were two who lived at some distance from Sandbourne across some meads – one of them in the direction indicated as that habitually taken by the young person; and in the afternoon, as he returned homeward, Christopher loitered and looked around. At first he could see nobody; but when about a mile from the outskirts of the town he discerned a light spot ahead of him, which actually turned out to be the jacket alluded to. In due time he met the wearer face to face; she was not Ethelberta Petherwin – quite a different sort of individual. He had long made up his mind that this would be the case, yet he was in some indescribable way disappointed.

Of the two classes into which gentle young women naturally divide, those who grow red at their weddings, and those who grow pale, the present one belonged to the former class. She was an April-natured, pink-cheeked girl, with eyes that would have made any jeweller in England think of his trade – one who evidently took her day in the daytime, frequently caught the early worm, and had little to do with yawns or candlelight. She came and passed him; he fancied that her countenance changed. But one may fancy anything, and the pair receded each from each without turning their heads. He could not speak to her, plain and simple as she seemed.

It is rarely that a man who can be entered and made to throb by the channel of his ears is not open to a similar attack through the channel of his eyes – for many doors will admit to one mansion – allowance being made for the readier capacity of chosen and practised organs. Hence the beauties, concords, and eloquences of the female form were never without their effect upon Christopher, a born musician, artist, poet, seer, mouthpiece – whichever a translator of Nature's oracles into simple speech may be called. The young girl who had gone by was fresh and pleasant; moreover, she was a sort of mysterious link between himself and the past, which these things were vividly reviving in him.

The following week Christopher met her again. She had not much dignity, he had not much reserve, and the sudden resolution to have a holiday which sometimes impels a plump heart to rise up against a brain that overweights it was not to be resisted. He just lifted his hat, and put the only question he could think of as a beginning: 'Have I the pleasure of addressing the author of a book of very melodious poems that was sent me the other day?'

The girl's forefinger twirled rapidly the loop of braid that it had previously been twirling slowly, and drawing in her breath, she said, 'No, sir.'

'The sender, then?'

'Yes.'

She somehow presented herself as so insignificant by the combined effect of the manner and the words that Christopher lowered his method of address to her level at once. 'Ah,' he said, 'such an atmosphere as the writer of "Metres by E." seems to breathe would soon spoil cheeks that are fresh and round as lady-apples* – eh, little girl? But are you disposed to tell me that writer's name?'

By applying a general idea to a particular case a person with the best of intentions may find himself immediately landed in a quandary. In saying to the country girl before him what would have suited the mass of country lasses well enough, Christopher had offended her beyond the cure of compliment.

'I am not disposed to tell the writer's name,' she replied, with a dudgeon that was very great for one whose whole stock of it was a trifle. And she passed on and left him standing alone.

Thus further conversation was checked; but, through having rearranged the hours of his country lessons, Christopher met her the next Wednesday, and the next Friday, and throughout the following week – no further words passing between them. For a while she went by very demurely, apparently mindful of his offence. But effrontery is not proved to be part of a man's nature till he has been guilty of a second act: the best of men may commit a first through accident or ignorance – may even be betrayed into it by over-zeal for experiment. Some such conclusion may or may not have been arrived at by the girl with the lady-apple cheeks; at any rate, after the lapse of another week a new spectacle presented itself; her redness deepened whenever Christopher passed her by, and embarrassment pervaded her from the lowest stitch to the tip of her feather. She had little chance of escaping him by diverging from the road, for a figure could be seen across the open ground to the distance of half a mile on either side. One day as he drew near as usual, she met him as women meet a cloud of dust – she turned and looked backwards till he had passed.

This would have been disconcerting but for one reason: Christopher was ceasing to notice her. He was a man who often, when walking abroad, and looking as it were at the scene before his eyes, discerned successes and failures, friends and relations, episodes of childhood, wedding feasts and funerals, the landscape suffering greatly by these visions, until it became no more than the patterned wall-tints about the paintings in a gallery; something necessary to the tone, yet not regarded. Nothing but a special concentration of himself on externals could interrupt this habit, and now that her appearance along the way had changed from a chance to a custom he began to lapse again into the old trick. He gazed once or twice at her form without seeing it: he did not notice that she trembled.

He sometimes read as he walked, and book in hand he frequently approached her now. This went on till six weeks had passed from the time of their first encounter. Latterly might have been once or twice heard, when he had moved out of earshot, a sound like a small gasping sigh; but no arrangements were disturbed, and Christopher continued to keep down his eyes as persistently as a saint in a church window.

The last day of his engagement had arrived, and with it the last of his walks that way. On his final return he carried in his hand a bunch of flowers which had been presented to him at the country-house where his lessons were given. He was taking them home to his sister Faith, who prized the lingering blossoms of the seeding season. Soon appeared as usual his fellow-traveller; whereupon Christopher looked down upon his nosegay. 'Sweet simple girl,' he thought, 'I'll endeavour to make peace with her by means of these flowers before we part for good.'

When she came up he held them out to her and said, 'Will you allow me to present you with these?'

The bright colours of the nosegay instantly attracted the girl's hand – perhaps before there had been time for thought to thoroughly construe the position; for it happened that when her arm was stretched into the air she steadied it quickly, and stood with the pose of a statue – rigid with uncertainty. But it was too late to refuse: Christopher had put the nosegay within her fingers. Whatever pleasant expression of thanks may have appeared in her eyes fell only on the bunch of flowers, for during the whole transaction they reached to no higher level than that. To say that he was coming no more seemed scarcely necessary in the circumstances, and wishing her 'Good afternoon' very heartily, he passed on.

He had learnt by this time her occupation, which was that of pupil-teacher* at one of the schools in the town, whither she walked daily from a village rather a long way off. If he had not been poor and the little teacher humble, Christopher might possibly have been tempted to inquire more briskly about her, and who knows how such a pursuit might have ended? But hard externals rule volatile sentiment, and under these untoward influences the girl and the book and the truth about its author were matters upon which he could not afford to expend much time. All Christopher did was to think now and then of the pretty innocent face and round deep eyes, not once wondering if the mind which enlivened them ever thought of him.

Sandbourne Moor (*continued*)

3

It was one of those hostile days of the year when chatterbox ladies remain miserably in their homes to save the carriage and harness, when clerks' wives hate living in lodgings, when vehicles and people appear in the street with duplicates of themselves underfoot, when bricklayers, slaters, and other outdoor journeymen sit in a shed and drink beer, when ducks and drakes play with hilarious delight at their own family game,* or spread out one wing after another in the slower enjoyment of letting the delicious moisture penetrate to their innermost down. The smoke from the flues of Sandbourne had barely strength enough to emerge into the drizzling rain, and hung down the sides of each chimney-pot like the streamer of a becalmed ship; and a troop of rats might have rattled down the pipes from roof to basement with less noise than did the water that day.

On the broad moorland and meadows two or three miles from the town, where Christopher's meetings with the teacher had so regularly occurred, were a stream and some large pools; and beside one of these, near some hatches and a weir, stood a little square building, not much larger inside than the Lord Mayor's coach. It was known simply as 'The Weir House'. On this wet afternoon, which was the one following the day of Christopher's last lesson over the plain, a nearly invisible smoke came from the puny chimney of the hut. Though the door was closed, sounds of chatting and mirth fizzed from the interior, and would have told anybody who had come near – which nobody did – that the usually empty shell was tenanted today.

The scene within was a large fire in a fireplace to which the whole floor of the house was no more than a hearthstone. The occupants were two gentlemanly persons, in shooting costume, who had been traversing the moor for miles in search of wild duck and teal, a waterman, and a small spaniel. In the corner stood their guns, and two or three wild mallards, which represented the scanty product of their morning's labour, the iridescent necks of the dead birds replying to every flicker of the fire. The two sportsmen were smoking, and their man was mostly occupying himself in poking and stirring the fire with a stick: all three appeared to be pretty well wetted.

One of the gentlemen, by way of varying the not very exhilarating study of four brick walls within microscopic distance of his eye, turned to a small square hole which admitted light and air to the hut, and looked out upon the dreary prospect before him. The wide concave of cloud, of the monotonous hue of dull pewter, formed an unbroken hood over the level from horizon to horizon; beneath it, reflecting its wan lustre, was the glazed high-road which stretched, hedgeless and ditchless, past a directing-post where another road joined it, and on to the less regular ground beyond, lying like a riband unrolled across the scene, till it vanished over the furthermost undulation. Beside the pools were occasional tall sheaves of flags and sedge, and about the plain a few bushes, these forming the only obstructions to a view otherwise unbroken.

The sportsman's attention was attracted by a figure in a state of gradual enlargement as it approached along the road.

'I should think that if pleasure can't tempt a native out of doors today, business will never force him out,' he observed. 'There is, for the first time, somebody coming along the road.'

'If business don't drag him out pleasure'll never tempt en, is more like our nater in these parts, sir,' said the man, who was looking into the fire.

The conversation showed no vitality, and down it dropped dead as before, the man who was standing up continuing to gaze into the moisture. What had at first appeared as an epicene shape the decreasing space resolved into a cloaked female under an umbrella: she now relaxed her pace, till, reaching the directing-post where the road branched into two, she paused and looked about her. Instead of coming further she slowly retraced her steps for about a hundred yards.

'That's an appointment,' said the first speaker, as he removed the cigar from his lips; 'and by the lords, what a day and place for an appointment with a woman!'

'What's an appointment?' inquired his friend, a town young man, with a Tussaud complexion* and well-pencilled brows halfway up his forehead, so that his upper eyelids appeared to possess the uncommon quality of tallness.

'Look out here, and you'll see. By that directing-post, where the two roads meet. As a man devoted to art, Ladywell, who has had the honour of being hung higher up on the Academy walls* than any other living painter, you should take out your sketch-book and dash off the scene.'

Where nothing particular is going on, one incident makes a drama; and, interested in that proportion, the art-sportsman put up his eyeglass (a form he adhered to before firing at game that had risen, by which merciful arrangement the bird got safe off), placed his face beside his companion's, and also peered through the opening. The young pupil-teacher – for she was the object of their scrutiny – re-approached the spot whereon she had been accustomed for the last many weeks of her journey home to meet Christopher, now for the first time missing, and again she seemed reluctant to pass the hand-post* for that marked the point where the chance of seeing him ended. She glided backwards as before, this time keeping her face still to the front, as if trying to persuade the world at large, and her own shame-facedness, that she had not yet approached the place at all.

'Query, how long will she wait for him (for it is a man to a certainty)?' resumed the elder of the smokers, at the end of several minutes of silence, when, full of vacillation and doubt, she became lost to view behind some bushes. 'Will she reappear?' The smoking went on, and up she came into open ground as before, and walked by.

'I wonder who the girl is, to come to such a place in this weather? There she is again,' said the young man called Ladywell.

'Some cottage lass, not yet old enough to make the most of the value set on her by her follower, small as that appears to be. Now we may get an idea of the hour named by the fellow for the appointment, for, depend upon it, the time when she first came – about five minutes ago – was the time he should have been there. It is now getting on towards five – half-past four was doubtless the time mentioned.'

'She's not come o' purpose: 'tis her way home from school every day,' said the waterman.

'An experiment on woman's endurance and patience under neglect. Two to one against her staying a quarter of an hour.'

'The same odds against her not staying till five would be nearer probability. What's half-an-hour to a girl in love?'

'On a moorland in wet weather it is thirty perceptible minutes to any fireside man, woman, or beast in Christendom – minutes that can be felt, like the Egyptian plague of darkness.* Now, little girl, go home: he is not worth it.'

Twenty minutes passed, and the girl returned miserably to the hand-post, still to wander back to her retreat behind the sedge, and lead any chance comer from the opposite quarter to believe that she had not yet reached this ultimate point beyond which a meeting with Christopher was impossible.

'Now you'll find that she means to wait the complete half-hour, and then off she goes with a broken heart.'

All three now looked through the hole to test the truth of the prognostication. The hour of five completed itself on their watches; the girl again came forward. And then the three in ambuscade could see her pull out her handkerchief and place it to her eyes.

'She's grieving now because he has not come. Poor little woman, what a brute he must be; for a broken heart in a woman means a broken vow in a man, as I infer from a thousand instances in experience, romance, and history. Don't open the door till she is gone, Ladywell; it will only disturb her.'

As they had guessed, the pupil-teacher, hearing the distant town-clock strike the hour, gave way to her fancy no longer, and launched into the diverging path. This lingering for Christopher's arrival had, as is known, been founded on nothing more of the nature of an assignation than lay in his regular walk along the plain at that time every Monday, Wednesday, and Friday of the six previous weeks. It must be said that he was very far indeed from divining that his injudicious peace-offering of the flowers had stirred into life such a wearing, anxious, hopeful, despairing solicitude as this, which had been latent for some time during his constant meetings with the little stranger.

She vanished in the mist towards the left, and the loiterers in the hut began to move and open the door, remarking, 'Now then for Wyndway House, a change of clothes, and a dinner.'

Sandbourne Pier
Road to Wyndway
Ball-room in Wyndway House

4

The last light of a winter day had gone down behind the houses of Sandbourne, and night was shut close over all. Christopher, about eight o'clock, was standing at the end of the pier with his back towards the open sea, whence the waves were pushing to the shore in frills and flounces that were just rendered visible in all their bleak instability by the row of lights along the sides of the jetty, the rapid motion landward of the wavetips producing upon his eye an apparent progress of the pier out to sea. This pier-head was a spot which Christopher enjoyed visiting on such moaning and sighing nights as the present, when the sportive and variegated throng that haunted the pier on autumn days was no longer there, and he seemed alone with weather and the invincible sea.

Somebody came towards him along the deserted footway, and rays from the nearest lamp streaked the face of his sister Faith.

'O Christopher, I knew you were here,' she said eagerly. 'You are wanted; there's a servant come from Wyndway House for you. He is sent to ask if you can come immediately to play at a little dance they have resolved upon this evening – quite suddenly it seems. If you can come, you must bring with you any assistant you can lay your hands upon at a moment's notice, he says.'

'Wyndway House; why should the people send for me above all other musicians in the town?'

Faith did not know. 'If you really decide to go,' she said, as they walked homeward, 'you might take me as your assistant. I should answer the purpose, should I not, Kit? since it is only a dance or two they seem to want.'

'And your harp I suppose you mean? Yes; you might be competent to take a part. It cannot be a regular ball; they would have had the quadrille band for anything of that sort. Faith – we'll go. However, let us see the man first, and inquire particulars.'

Reaching home, Christopher found at his door a horse and wagonette in charge of a man-servant in livery, who repeated what Faith had told her brother. Wyndway House was a well-known country-seat three or four miles out of the town, and the coachman mentioned that if they were going it would be well that they should get ready to start as soon as they conveniently could, since he had been told to return by ten if possible. Christopher quickly prepared himself, and put a new string or two into Faith's harp, by which time she also was dressed; and, wrapping up herself and her instrument safe from the night air, away they drove at half-past nine.

'Is it a large party?' said Christopher, as they whizzed along.

'No, sir; it is what we call a dance – that is, 'tis like a ball, you know, on a small scale – a ball on a spurt, that you never thought of till you had it. In short, it grew out of a talk at dinner, I believe; and some of the young people present wanted a jig, and didn't care to play themselves, you know, young ladies being an idle class of society at the best of times. We've a house full of sleeping company, you understand – been there a week some of 'em – most of 'em being mistress's relations.'

'They probably found it a little dull.'

'Well, yes – it is rather dull for 'em – Christmastime and all. As soon as it was proposed they were wild for sending post-haste for somebody or other to play to them.'

'Did they name me particularly?' said Christopher.

'Yes; "Mr Christopher Julian," she says. "The gent who's turned music-man?" I said. "Yes, that's him," says she.'

'There were music-men living nearer to your end of the town than I.'

'Yes, but I know it was you particular: though I don't think mistress thought anything about you at first. Mr Joyce – that's the butler – said that your name was mentioned to our old dame, when he was in the room, by a young lady staying with us, and mistress says then, "The Julians have had a downfall, and the son has taken to music." Then when dancing was talked of, they said, "O, let's have him by all means."'

'Was the young lady who first inquired for my family the same one who said, "Let's have him by all means?"'

'O no; but it was on account of her asking that the rest said they would like you to play – at least that's as I had it from Joyce.'

'Do you know that lady's name?'

'Mrs Petherwin.'

'Ah!'

'Cold, sir?'

'O no.'

Christopher did not like to question the man any further, though what he had heard added new life to his previous curiosity; and they drove along the way in silence, Faith's figure, wrapped up to the top of her head, cutting into the sky behind them like a sugar-loaf. Such gates as crossed the roads had been left open by the forethought of the coachman, and, passing the lodge, they proceeded about half-a-mile along a private drive, then ascended a rise, and came in view of the front of the mansion, punctured with windows that were now mostly lighted up.

'What is that?' said Faith, catching a glimpse of something that the carriage-lamp showed on the face of one wall as they passed, a marble bas-relief of some battle-piece, built into the stonework.

'That's the scene of the death of one of the squire's forefathers – Colonel Sir Martin Jones, who was killed at the moment of victory in the battle of Salamanca* but I haven't been here long enough to know the rights of it. When I am in one of my meditations, as I wait here with the carriage sometimes, I think how many more get killed at the moment of victory than at the moment of defeat. This is the entrance for you, sir.' And he turned the corner and pulled up before a side door.

They alighted and went in, Christopher shouldering Faith's harp, and she marching modestly behind, with curly-eared music-books under her arm. They were shown into the house-steward's room, and ushered thence along a badly-lit passage and past a door within which a hum and laughter were audible.

The door next to this was then opened for them, and they entered.

Scarcely had Faith, or Christopher either, ever beheld a more shining scene than was presented by the saloon in which they now found themselves. Coming direct from the gloomy park, and led to the room by that back passage from the servants' quarter, the light from the chandelier and branches against the walls, striking on gilding at all points, quite dazzled their sight for a minute or two; it caused Faith to move forward with her eyes on the floor, and filled Christopher with an impulse to turn back again into some dusky corner where every thread of his not over-new dress suit – rather moth-eaten through lack of feasts for airing it – could be counted less easily.

He was soon seated before a grand piano, and Faith sat down under the shadow of her harp, both being arranged on a daïs within an alcove at one end of the room. A screen of ivy and holly had been constructed across the front of this recess for the games of the children on Christmas Eve, and it still remained there, a small creep-hole being left for entrance and exit.

Then the merry guests tumbled through doors at the further end, and dancing began. The mingling of black-coated men and bright ladies gave a charming appearance to the groups as seen by Faith and her brother, the whole spectacle deriving an unexpected novelty from the accident of reaching their eyes through interstices in the tracery of green leaves, which added to the picture a softness that it would not otherwise have possessed. On the other hand, the musicians, having a much weaker light, could hardly be discerned by the performers in the dance.

The music was now rattling on, and the ladies in their foam-like dresses were busily threading and spinning about the floor, when Faith, casually looking up into her brother's face, was surprised to see that a change had come over it. At the end of the quadrille he leant across to her before she had time to speak, and said quietly, 'She's here!'

'Who?' said Faith, for she had not heard the words of the coachman.

'Ethelberta.'

'Which is she?' asked Faith, peeping through with the keenest interest.

'The one who has the skirts of her dress looped up with convolvulus flowers – the one with her hair fastened in a sort of Venus knot* behind; she has just been dancing with that perfumed piece of a man they call Mr Ladywell – it is he with the high eyebrows arched like a girl's.' He added, with a wrinkled smile, 'I cannot for my life see anybody answering to the character of husband to her, for every man takes notice of her.'

They were interrupted by another dance being called for, and then, his fingers tapping about upon the keys as mechanically as fowls pecking at barleycorns, Christopher gave himself up with a curious and far from unalloyed pleasure to the occupation of watching Ethelberta, now again crossing the field of his vision like a returned comet whose characteristics were becoming purely historical. She was a plump-armed creature, with a white round neck as firm as a fort – altogether a vigorous shape, as refreshing to the eye as the green leaves through which he beheld her. She danced freely, and with a zest that was apparently irrespective of partners. He had been waiting long to hear her speak, and when at length her voice did reach his ears, it was the revelation of a strange matter to find how great a thing that small event had become to him. He knew the old utterance – rapid but not frequent, an obstructive thought causing sometimes a sudden halt in the midst of a stream of words. But the feature by which a cool observer would have singled her out from others in his memory when asking himself what she was like, was a peculiar gaze into imaginary far-away distance when making a quiet remark to a partner – not with contracted eyes like a sea-faring man, but with an open full look – a remark in which little words in a low tone were made to express a great deal, as several single gentlemen afterwards found.

The production of dance-music when the criticizing stage among the dancers has passed, and they have grown full of excitement and animal spirits, does not require much concentration of thought in the producers thereof; and desultory conversation accordingly went on between Faith and her brother from time to time.

'Kit,' she said on one occasion, 'are you looking at the way in which the flowers are fastened to the leaves? – taking a mean advantage of being at the back of the tapestry? You cannot think how you stare at them.'

'I was looking through them – certainly not at them. I have a feeling of being moved about like a puppet in the hands of a person who legally can be nothing to me.'

'That charming woman with the shining bunch of hair and convolvuluses?'

'Yes: it is through her that we are brought here, and through her writing that poem, "Cancelled Words", that the book was sent me, and through the accidental renewal of acquaintance between us on Anglebury Heath, that she wrote the poem. I was, however, at the moment you spoke, thinking more particularly of the little teacher whom Ethelberta must have commissioned to send the book to me; and why that girl was chosen to do it.'

'There may be a hundred reasons. Kit, I have never yet seen her look once this way.'

Christopher had certainly not yet received look or gesture from her; but his time came. It was while he was for a moment outside the recess, and he caught her in the act. She became slightly confused, turned aside, and entered into conversation with a neighbour.

It was only a look, and yet what a look it was! One may say of a look that it is capable of division into as many species, genera, orders, and classes, as the animal world itself. Christopher saw Ethelberta Petherwin's performance in this kind – the well-known spark of light upon the well-known depths of mystery – and felt something going out of him which had gone out of him once before.

Thus continually beholding her and her companions in the giddy whirl, the night wore on with the musicians, last dances and more last dances being added, till the intentions of the old on the matter were thrice exceeded in the interests of the young. Watching the couples whirl and turn, advance and recede as gently as spirits, knot themselves like house-flies and part again, and lullabied by the faint regular beat of their footsteps to the tune, the players sank into the peculiar mesmeric quiet which comes over impressionable people who play for a great length of time in the midst of such scenes; and at last the only noises that Christopher took cognizance of were those of the exceptional kind, breaking above the general sea of sound – a casual smart rustle of silk, a laugh, a stumble, the monosyllabic talk of those who happened to linger for a moment close to the leafy screen – all coming to his ears like voices from those old times when he had mingled in similar scenes, not as servant but as guest.

At the Window
The Road Home

5

The dancing was over at last, and the radiant company had left the room. A long and weary night it had been for the two players, though a stimulated interest had hindered physical exhaustion in one of them for a while. With tingling fingers and aching arms they came out of the alcove into the long and deserted apartment, now pervaded by a dry haze. The lights had burned low, and Faith and her brother were waiting by request till the wagonette was ready to take them home, a breakfast being in course of preparation for them meanwhile.

Christopher had crossed the room to relieve his cramped limbs, and now, peeping through a crevice in the window curtains, he said suddenly, 'Who's for a transformation scene?* Faith, look here!'

He touched the blind, up it flew, and a gorgeous scene presented itself to her eyes. A huge inflamed sun was breasting the horizon beyond a sheet of embayed sea which, to her surprise and delight, the mansion overlooked. The brilliant disc fired all the waves that lay between it and the shore at the bottom of the grounds, where the water tossed the ruddy light from one undulation to another in glares as large and clear as mirrors, incessantly altering them, destroying them, and creating them again; while further off they multiplied, thickened, and ran into one another like struggling armies, till they met the fiery source of them all.

'O, how wonderful it is!' said Faith, putting her hand on Christopher's arm. 'Who knew that whilst we were all shut in here with our puny illumination such an exhibition as this was going on outside! How sorry and mean the grand and stately room looks now!'

Christopher turned his back upon the window, and there

were the hitherto beaming candle-flames shining no more radiantly than tarnished javelin-heads, while the snow-white lengths of wax showed themselves clammy and cadaverous as the fingers of a corpse. The leaves and flowers which had appeared so very green and blooming by the artificial light were now seen to be faded and dusty. Only the gilding of the room in some degree brought itself into keeping with the splendours outside, stray darts of light seizing upon it and lengthening themselves out along fillet,* quirk,* arris,* and moulding, till wasted away.

'It seems,' said Faith, 'as if all the people who were lately so merry here had died: we ourselves look no more than ghosts.' She turned up her weary face to her brother's, which the incoming rays smote aslant, making little furrows of every wrinkle thereon, and shady ravines of every little furrow.

'You are very tired, Faith,' he said. 'Such a heavy night's work has been almost too much for you.'

'O, I don't mind that,' said Faith. 'But I could not have played so long by myself.'

'We filled up one another's gaps; and there were plenty of them towards the morning; but, luckily, people don't notice those things when the small hours draw on.'

'What troubles me most,' said Faith, 'is not that I have worked, but that you should be so situated as to need such miserable assistance as mine. We are poor, are we not, Kit?'

'Yes, we know a little about poverty,' he replied.

While thus lingering

In shadowy thoroughfares of thought,*

Faith interrupted with, 'I believe there is one of the dancers now! – why, I should have thought they had all gone to bed, and wouldn't get up again for days.' She indicated to him a figure on the lawn towards the left, looking upon the same flashing scene as that they themselves beheld.

'It is your own particular one,' continued Faith. 'Yes, I see the blue flowers under the edge of her cloak.'

'And I see her squirrel-coloured* hair,' said Christopher.

Both stood looking at this apparition, who once, and only once, thought fit to turn her head towards the front of the house they were gazing from. Faith was one in whom the meditative somewhat overpowered the active faculties; she went on, with no abundance of love, to theorize upon this gratuitously charming woman, who, striking freakishly into her brother's path, seemed likely to do him no good in her sisterly estimation. Ethelberta's bright and shapely form stood before her critic now, smartened by the motes of sunlight from head to heel: what Faith would have given to see her so clearly within!

'Without doubt she is already a lady of many romantic experiences,' she said dubiously.

'And on the way to many more,' said Christopher. The tone was just of the kind which may be imagined of a sombre man who had been up all night piping that others might dance.

Faith parted her lips as if in consternation at possibilities. Ethelberta, having already become an influence in Christopher's system, might soon become more – an indestructible fascination – to drag him about, turn his soul inside out, harrow him, twist him, and otherwise torment him, according to the stereotyped form of such processes.

They were interrupted by the opening of a door. A servant entered and came up to them.

'This is for you, I believe, sir,' he said. 'Two guineas'; and he placed the money in Christopher's hand. 'Some breakfast will be ready for you in a moment if you like to have it. Would you wish it brought in here; or will you come to the steward's room?'

'Yes, we will come.' And the man then began to extinguish the lights one by one. Christopher dropped the two pounds and two shillings singly into his pocket, and looking listlessly at the footman said, 'Can you tell me the address of that lady on the lawn? Ah, she has disappeared!'

'She wore a dress with blue flowers,' said Faith.

'And remarkable bright in her manner? O, that's the young widow, Mrs – what's that name – I forget for the moment.'

'Widow?' said Christopher, the eyes of his understanding getting wonderfully clear, and Faith uttering a private ejaculation of thanks that after all no commandments* were likely to be broken in this matter. 'The lady I mean is quite a girlish sort of woman.'

'Yes, yes, so she is – that's the one. Coachman says she must have been born a widow, for there is not time for her ever to have been made one. However, she's not quite such a chicken as all that. Mrs Petherwin, that's the party's name.'

'Does she live here?'

'No, she is staying in the house visiting for a few days with her mother-in-law. They are a London family: I don't know her address.'

'Is she a poetess?'

'That I cannot say. She is very clever at verses; but she don't lean over gates to see the sun, and goes to church as regular as you or I, so I should hardly be inclined to say that she's the complete thing. When she's up in one of her vagaries she'll sit with the ladies and make up pretty things out of her head as fast as sticks a-breaking. They will run off her tongue like cotton from a reel, and if she can ever be got in the mind of telling a story she will bring it out that serious and awful that it makes your flesh creep upon your bones; if she's only got to say that she walked out of one door into another, she'll tell it so that there seems something wonderful in it. 'Tis a bother to start her, so our people say behind her back, but, once set going, the house is all alive with her. However, it will soon be dull enough; she and Lady Petherwin are off tomorrow for Rookington, where I believe they are going to stay over New Year's Day.'

'Where do you say they are going?' inquired Christopher, as they followed the footman.

'Rookington Park – about three miles out of Sandbourne, in the opposite direction to this.'

'A widow,' Christopher murmured.

Faith overheard him. 'That makes no difference to us, does it?' she said wistfully.

Forty minutes later they were driving along an open road over a ridge which commanded a view of a small inlet below them, the sands of this nook being sheltered by slopes. Here at once they saw, in the full light of the sun, two women standing side by side, their faces directed over the sea.

'There she is again!' said Faith. 'She has walked along the shore from the lawn where we saw her before.'

'Yes,' said the coachman, 'she's a curious woman seemingly. She'll talk to any poor body she meets. You see she had been out for a morning walk instead of going to bed, and that is some queer mortal or other she has picked up with on her way.'

'I wonder she does not prefer some rest,' Faith observed.

The road then dropped into a hollow, and the women by the

sea were no longer within view from the carriage, which rapidly neared Sandbourne with the two musicians.

The Shore by Wyndway

6

The east gleamed upon Ethelberta's squirrel-coloured hair as she said to her companion, 'I have come, Picotee; but not, as you imagine, from a night's sleep. We have actually been dancing till daylight at Wyndway.'

'Then you should not have troubled to come! I could have borne the disappointment under such circumstances,' said the pupil-teacher, who, wearing a dress not so familiar to Christopher's eyes as had been the little white jacket, had not been recognized by him from the hill. 'You look so tired, Berta. I could not stay up all night for the world!'

'One gets used to these things,' said Ethelberta quietly. 'I should have been in bed certainly, had I not particularly wished to use this opportunity of meeting you before you go home tomorrow. I could not have come to Sandbourne today, because we are leaving to return again to Rookington. This is all that I wish you to take to mother – only a few little things which may be useful to her; but you will see what it contains when you open it.' She handed to Picotee a small parcel. 'This is for yourself,' she went on, giving a small packet besides. 'It will pay your fare home and back, and leave you something to spare.'

'Thank you,' said Picotee docilely.

'Now, Picotee,' continued the elder, 'let us talk for a few minutes before I go back: we may not meet again for some time.' She put her arm round the waist of Picotee, who did the same by Ethelberta; and thus interlaced they walked backwards and forwards upon the firm flat sand with the motion of one body animated by one will.

'Well, what did you think of my poems?'

'I liked them; but naturally, I did not understand all the experience you describe. It is so different from mine. Yet that made them more interesting to me. I thought I should so much like to mix in the same scenes; but that of course is impossible.'

'I am afraid it is. And you posted the book as I said?'

'Yes.' She added hurriedly, as if to change the subject, 'I have told nobody that we are sisters, or that you are known in any way to me or to mother or to any of us. I thought that would be best, from what you said.'

'Yes, perhaps it is best for the present.'

'The box of clothes came safely, and I find very little alteration will be necessary to make the dress do beautifully for me on Sundays. It is quite new-fashioned to me, though I suppose it was old-fashioned to you. O, and Berta, will the title of Lady Petherwin descend to you when your mother-in-law dies?'

'No, of course not. She is only a knight's widow, and that's nothing.'

'The lady of a knight looks as good on paper as the lady of a lord.'

'Yes. And in other places too sometimes. However, about your journey home. Be very careful; and don't make any inquiries at the stations of anybody but officials. If any man wants to be friendly with you, try to find out if it is from a genuine wish to assist you, or from admiration of your fresh face.'

'How shall I know which?' said Picotee.

Ethelberta laughed. 'If Heaven does not tell you at the moment I cannot,' she said. 'But humanity looks with a different eye from love, and upon the whole it is most to be prized by all of us. I believe it ends oftener in marriage than do a lover's flying smiles. So that for this and other reasons love from a stranger is mostly worthless as a speculation; and it is certainly dangerous as a game. Well, Picotee, has any one paid you real attentions yet?'

'No – that is—'

'There is something going on.'

'Only a wee bit.'

'I thought so. There was a dishonesty about your dear eyes which has never been there before, and love-making and dishonesty are inseparable as coupled hounds. Up comes man, and away goes innocence. Are you going to tell me anything about him?'

'I would rather not, Ethelberta; because it is hardly anything.'

'Well, be careful. And mind this, never tell him what you feel.'

'But then he will never know it.'

'Nor must he. He must think it only. The difference between his thinking and knowing is often the difference between your winning and losing. But general advice is not of much use, and I cannot give more unless you tell more. What is his name?'

Picotee did not reply.

'Never mind: keep your secret. However, listen to this: not a kiss – not so much as the shadow, hint, or merest seedling of a kiss!'

'There is no fear of it,' murmured Picotee; 'though not because of me!'

'You see, my dear Picotee, a lover is not a relative; and he isn't quite a stranger; but he may end in being either, and the way to reduce him to whichever of the two you wish him to be is to treat him like the other. Men who come courting are just like bad cooks: if you are kind to them, instead of ascribing it to an exceptional courtesy on your part, they instantly set it down to their own marvellous worth.'

'But I ought to favour him just a little, poor thing? Just the smallest glimmer of a gleam!'

'Only a very little indeed – so that it comes as a relief to his misery, not as adding to his happiness.'

'It is being too clever, all this; and we ought to be harmless as doves.'

'Ah, Picotee! to continue harmless as a dove you must be wise as a serpent,* you'll find – ay, ten serpents, for that matter.'

'But if I cannot get at him, how can I manage him in these ways you speak of?'

'Get at him? I suppose he gets at you in some way, does he not? – tries to see you, or to be near you?'

'No – that's just the point – he doesn't do any such thing, and there's the worry of it!'

'Well, what a silly girl! Then he is not your lover at all?'

'Perhaps he's not. But I am his, at any rate – twice over.'

'That's no use. Supply the love for both sides? Why, it's worse than furnishing money for both. You don't suppose a man will give his heart in exchange for a woman's when he has already got hers for nothing? That's not the way old Adam does business at all.'

Picotee sighed. 'Have you got a young man, too, Berta?'

'A young man?'

'A lover I mean – that's what we call 'em down here.'

'It is difficult to explain,' said Ethelberta evasively. 'I knew one many years ago, and I have seen him again, and – that is all.'

'According to my idea you have one, but according to your own you have not; he does not love you, but you love him – is that how it is?'

'I have not quite considered how it is.'

'Do you love him?'

'I have never seen a man I hate less.'

'A great deal lies covered up there, I expect!'

'He was in that carriage which drove over the hill at the moment we met here.'

'Ah-ah – some great lord or another who has his day by candlelight, and so on. I guess the style. Somebody who no more knows how much bread is a loaf than I do the price of diamonds and pearls.'

'I am afraid he's only a commoner as yet, and not a very great one either. But surely you guess, Picotee? But I'll set you an example of frankness by telling his name. My friend, Mr Julian, to whom you posted the book. Such changes as he has seen! – from affluence to poverty. He and his sister have been playing dances all night at Wyndway – What is the matter?'

'Only a pain!'

'My dear Picotee—'

'I think I'll sit down for a moment, Berta.'

'What – have you over-walked yourself, dear?'

'Yes – and I got up very early, you see.'

'I hope you are not going to be ill, child. You look as if you ought not to be here.'

'O, it is quite trifling. Does not getting up in a hurry cause a sense of faintness sometimes?'

'Yes, in people who are not strong.'

'If we don't talk about being faint it will go off. Faintness is such a queer thing that to think of it is to have it. Let us talk as we were talking before – about your young man and other indifferent matters, so as to divert my thoughts from fainting, dear Berta. I have always thought the book was to be forwarded to that gentleman because he was a connection of yours by marriage, and he had asked for it. And so you have met this – this Mr Julian, and gone for walks with him in evenings, I suppose, just as young men and women do who are courting?'

'No, indeed – what an absurd child you are!' said Ethelberta. 'I knew him once, and he is interesting; a few little things like that make it all up.'

'The love is all on one side, as with me.'

'O no, no: there is nothing like that. I am not attached to any one, strictly speaking – though, more strictly speaking, I am not unattached.'

''Tis a delightful middle mind to be in. I know it, for I was like it once; but I had scarcely been so long enough to know where I was before I was gone past.'

'You should have commanded yourself, or drawn back entirely; for let me tell you that at the beginning of caring for a man – just when you are suspended between thinking and feeling – there is a hair's-breadth of time at which the question of getting into love or not getting in is a matter of will – quite a thing of choice. At the same time, drawing back is a tame dance, and the best of all is to stay balanced awhile.'

'You do that well, I'll warrant.'

'Well, no; for what between continually wanting to love, to escape the blank lives of those who do not, and wanting not to love, to keep out of the miseries of those who do, I get foolishly warm and foolishly cold by turns.'

'Yes – and I am like you as far as the "foolishly" goes. I wish we poor girls could contrive to bring a little wisdom into our love by way of a change!'

'That's the very thing that leading minds in town have begun to do, but there are difficulties. It is easy to love wisely, but the rich man may not marry you; and it is not very hard to reject wisely, but the poor man doesn't care. Altogether it is a precious problem. But shall we clamber out upon those shining blocks of rock, and find some of the little yellow shells that are in the crevices? I have ten minutes longer, and then I must go.'

The Dining-room of a Town House
The Butler's Pantry

7

A few weeks later there was a friendly dinner-party at the house of a gentleman called Doncastle, who lived in a moderately fashionable square of west London. All the friends and relatives present were nice people, who exhibited becoming signs of pleasure and gaiety at being there; but as regards the vigour with which these emotions were expressed, it may be stated that a slight laugh from far down the throat and a slight narrowing of the eye were equivalent as indices of the degree of mirth felt to a Ha-ha-ha! and a shaking of the shoulders among the minor traders of the kingdom; and to a Ho-ho-ho! contorted features, purple face, and stamping foot among the gentlemen in corduroy and fustian who adorn the remoter provinces.

The conversation was chiefly about a volume of musical, tender, and humorous rhapsodies lately issued to the world in the guise of verse, which had been reviewed and talked about everywhere. This topic, beginning as a private dialogue between a young painter named Ladywell and the lady on his right hand, had enlarged its ground by degrees, as a subject will extend on those rare occasions when it happens to be one about which each person has thought something beforehand, instead of, as in the natural order of things, one to which the oblivious listener replies mechanically, with earnest features, but with thoughts far away. And so the whole table made the matter a thing to inquire or reply upon at once, and isolated rills of other chat died out like a river in the sands.

'Witty things, and occasionally Anacreontic:* and they have the originality which such a style must naturally possess when carried out by a feminine hand,' said Ladywell.

'If it is a feminine hand,' said a man near.

Ladywell looked as if he sometimes knew secrets, though he did not wish to boast.

'Written, I presume you mean, in the Anacreontic measure of three feet and a half – spondees and iambics?'* said a gentleman in spectacles, glancing round, and giving emphasis to his inquiry by causing bland glares of a circular shape to proceed from his glasses towards the person interrogated.

The company appeared willing to give consideration to the words of a man who knew such things as that, and hung forward to listen. But Ladywell stopped the whole current of affairs in that direction by saying –

'O no; I was speaking rather of the matter and tone. In fact, the *Seven Days'Review** said they were Anacreontic, you know; and so they are – any one may feel they are.'

The general look then implied a false encouragement, and the man in spectacles looked down again, being a nervous person, who never had time to show his merits because he was so much occupied in hiding his faults.

'Do you know the authoress, Mr Neigh? continued Ladywell.

'Can't say that I do,' he replied.

Neigh was a man who never disturbed the flesh upon his face except when he was obliged to do so, and paused ten seconds where other people only paused one; as he moved his chin in speaking, motes of light from under the candle-shade caught, lost, and caught again the outlying threads of his burnished beard.

'She will be famous some day; and you ought at any rate to read her book.'

'Yes, I ought, I know. In fact, some years ago I should have done it immediately, because I had a reason for pushing on that way just then.'

'Ah, what was that?'

'Well, I thought of going in for Westminster Abbey* myself at that time; but a fellow has so much to do, and—'

'What a pity that you didn't follow it up. A man of your powers, Mr Neigh—'

'Afterwards I found I was too steady for it, and had too much of the respectable householder in me. Besides, so many other men are on the same tack; and then I didn't care about it, somehow.'

'I don't understand high art, and am utterly in the dark on what are the true laws of criticism,' a plain married lady, who wore archæological jewellery, was saying at this time. 'But I know that I have derived an unusual amount of amusement from those verses, and I am heartily thankful to "E." for them.'

'I am afraid,' said a gentleman who was suffering from a bad shirt-front, 'that an estimate which depends upon feeling in that way is not to be trusted as permanent opinion.'

The subject now flitted to the other end.

'Somebody has it that when the heart flies out before the understanding, it saves the judgment a world of pains,' came from a voice in that quarter.

'I, for my part, like something merry,' said an elderly woman, whose face was bisected by the edge of a shadow, which toned her forehead and eyelids to a livid neutral tint, and left her cheeks and mouth like metal at a white heat in the uninterrupted light. 'I think the liveliness of those ballads as great a recommendation as any. After all, enough misery is known to us by our experiences and those of our friends, and what we see in the newspapers, for all purposes of chastening, without having gratuitous grief inflicted upon us.'

'But you would not have wished that *Romeo and Juliet* should have ended happily, or that Othello should have discovered the perfidy of his Ancient* in time to prevent all fatal consequences?'

'I am not afraid to go so far as that,' said the old lady. 'Shakespeare is not everybody, and I am sure that thousands of people who have seen those plays would have driven home more cheerfully afterwards if by some contrivance the characters could all have been joined together respectively. I uphold our anonymous author on the general ground of her levity.'

'Well, it is an old and worn argument – that about the inexpedience of tragedy – and much may be said on both sides. It is not to be denied that the anonymous Sappho's* verses – for it seems that she is really a woman – are clever.'

'Clever!' said Ladywell – the young man who had been one of the shooting-party at Sandbourne – 'they are marvellously brilliant.'

'She is rather warm in her assumed character.'

'That's a sign of her actual coldness; she lets off her feeling in theoretic grooves, and there is sure to be none left for practical ones. Whatever seems to be the most prominent vice, or the most prominent virtue, in anybody's writing is the one thing you are safest from in personal dealings with the writer.'

'O, I don't mean to call her warmth of feeling a vice or virtue exactly—

'I agree with you,' said Neigh to the last speaker but one, in tones as emphatic as they possibly could be without losing their proper character of indifference to the whole matter. 'Warm sentiment of any sort, whenever we have it, disturbs us too much to leave us repose enough for writing it down.'

'I am sure, when I was at the ardent age,' said the mistress of the house, in a tone of pleasantly agreeing with every one, particularly those who were diametrically opposed to each other,' I could no more have printed such emotions and made them public than I – could have helped privately feeling them.'

'I wonder if she has gone through half she says? If so, what an experience!'

'O no – not at all likely,' said Mr Neigh. 'It is as risky to calculate people's ways of living from their writings as their incomes from their way of living.'

'She is as true to nature as fashion is false,' said the painter, in his warmth becoming scarcely complimentary, as sometimes happens with young persons. 'I don't think that she has written a word more than what every woman would deny feeling in a society where no woman says what she means or does what she says. And can any praise be greater than that?'

'Ha-ha! Capital!'

'All her verses seem to me,' said a rather stupid person, 'to be simply –

> "Tral'-la-la-lal'-la-la-la',
> Tral'-la-la-lal'-la-la-lu',
> Tral'-la-la-lal'-la-la-lalla',
> Tral'-la-la-lu'."

When you take away the music there is nothing left. Yet she is plainly a woman of great culture.'

'Have you seen what the *London Light* says about them – one of the finest things I have ever read in the way of admiration?' continued Ladywell, paying no attention to the previous speaker. He lingered for a reply, and then impulsively quoted several lines from the periodical he had named, without aid or hesitation. 'Good, is it not?' added Ladywell.

They assented, but in such an unqualified manner that half as much readiness would have meant more. But Ladywell, though not experienced enough to be quite free from enthusiasm, was too experienced to mind indifference for more than a minute or two. When the ladies had withdrawn, the young man went on –

'Colonel Staff said a funny thing to me yesterday about these very poems. He asked me if I knew her, and—'

'Her? Why, he knows that it is a lady all the time, and we were only just now doubting whether the sex of the writer could be really what it seems. Shame, Ladywell!' said his friend Neigh.

'Ah, Mr Ladywell,' said another, 'now we have found you out. You know her!'

'Now – I say – ha-ha!' continued the painter, with a face expressing that he had not at all tried to be found out as the man possessing incomparably superior knowledge of the poetess. 'I beg pardon really, but don't press me on the matter. Upon my word the secret is not my own. As I was saying, the Colonel said, "Do you know her?" – but you don't care to hear?'

'We shall be delighted!'

'So the Colonel said, "Do you know her?" adding, in a most comic way, "Between U. and E., Ladywell, I believe there is a close affinity" – meaning me, you know, by U. Just like the Colonel – ha-ha-ha!'

The older men did not oblige Ladywell a second time with any attempt at appreciation; but a weird silence ensued, during which the smile upon Ladywell's face became frozen to painful permanence.

'Meaning by E., you know, the "E" of the poems – heh-heh!' he added.

'It was a very humorous incident certainly,' said his friend Neigh, at which there was a laugh – not from anything connected with what he said, but simply because it was the right thing to laugh when Neigh meant you to do so.

'Now don't, Neigh – you are too hard upon me. But, seriously, two or three fellows were there when I said it, and they all began laughing – but, then, the Colonel said it in such a queer way, you know. But you were asking me about her? Well, the fact is, between ourselves, I do know that she is a lady; and I don't mind telling a word—'

'But we would not for the world be the means of making you betray her confidence – would we, Jones?'

'No, indeed; we would not.'

'No, no; it is not that at all – this is really too bad! – you must listen just for a moment—'

'Ladywell, don't betray anybody on our account.'

'Whoever the illustrious young lady may be she has seen a great deal of the world,' said Mr Doncastle blandly, 'and puts her experience of the comedy of its emotions, and of its method of showing them, in a very vivid light.'

'I heard a man say that the novelty with which the ideas are presented is more noticeable than the originality of the ideas themselves,' observed Neigh. 'The woman has made a great talk about herself; and I am quite weary of people asking of her condition, place of abode, has she a father, has she a mother, or dearer one yet than all other.'

'I would have burlesque quotation put down by Act of Parliament, and all who dabble in it placed with him who can cite Scripture for his purposes,'* said Ladywell, in retaliation.

After a pause Neigh remarked half-privately to their host, who was his uncle: 'Your butler Chickerel is a very intelligent man, as I have heard.'

'Yes, he does very well,' said Mr Doncastle.

'But is he not a – very extraordinary man?'

'Not to my knowledge,' said Doncastle, looking up surprised. 'Why do you think that, Alfred?'

'Well, perhaps it was not a matter to mention. He reads a great deal, I dare say?'

'I don't think so.'

'I noticed how wonderfully his face kindled when we began talking about the poems during dinner. Perhaps he is a poet himself in disguise. Did you observe it?'

'No. To the best of my belief he is a very trustworthy and honourable man. He has been with us – let me see, how long? – five months, I think, and he was fifteen years in his last place. It certainly is a new side to his character if he publicly showed any interest in the conversation, whatever he might have felt.'

'Since the matter has been mentioned,' said Mr Jones, 'I may say that I too noticed the singularity of it.'

'If you had not said otherwise,' replied Doncastle somewhat warmly, 'I should have asserted him to be the last man-servant in London to infringe such an elementary rule. If he did so this evening, it is certainly for the first time and I sincerely hope that no annoyance was caused—'

'O no, no – not at all – it might have been a mistake of mine,' said Jones. 'I should quite have forgotten the circumstance if Mr Neigh's words had not brought it to my mind. It was really nothing to notice, and I beg that you will not say a word to him about it on my account.'

'He has a taste that way, my dear uncle, nothing more, depend upon it,' said Neigh. 'If I had such a man belonging to me I should only be too proud. Certainly do not mention it.'

'Of course Chickerel is Chickerel,' Mr Doncastle rejoined. 'We all know what that means. And really, on reflecting, I do remember that he is of a literary turn of mind – not further by an inch than is commendable, you know. I am quite aware as I glance down the papers and prints any morning that Chickerel's eyes have been over the ground before mine, and that he generally forestalls the rest of us by a chapter or so in the last new book sent home; but in these vicious days that particular weakness is really virtue, just because it is not quite a vice.'

'Yes,' said Mr Jones, the reflective man in spectacles, 'positive virtues are getting moved off the stage: negative ones are moved on to the place of positives; we thank bare justice as we used only to thank generosity; call a man honest who steals only by law, and consider him a benefactor if he does not steal at all.'

'Hear, hear!' said Neigh. 'We will decide that Chickerel is even a better trained fellow than if he had shown no interest at all in his face.'

'The action being like those trifling irregularities in art at its vigorous periods, which seemed designed to hide the unpleasant monotony of absolute symmetry,' said Ladywell.

'On the other hand, an affected want of training of that sort would be even a better disguise for an artful man than a perfectly impassable demeanour. He is two removes from discovery in a hidden scheme, whilst a neutral face is only one.'

'You quite alarm me by these subtle theories,' said Mr Doncastle, laughing; and the subject then became compounded with other matters, till the speakers rose to rejoin the charming flock upstairs.

In the basement story at this hour Mr Chickerel the butler, who had formed the subject of discussion on the floor above, was busily engaged in looking after his two subordinates as they bustled about in the operations of clearing away. He was a man of whom, if the shape of certain bones and muscles of the face is ever to be taken as a guide to the character, one might safely have predicated conscientiousness in the performance of duties, a thorough knowledge of all that appertained to them, a general desire to live on without troubling his mind about anything which did not concern him. Any person interested in the matter would have assumed without hesitation that the estimate his employer had given of Chickerel was a true one – more, that not only would the butler under all ordinary circumstances resolutely prevent his face from showing curiosity in an unbecoming way, but that, with the soul of a true gentleman, he would, if necessary, equivocate as readily as the noblest of his betters to remove any stain upon his honour in such trifles. Hence it is apparent that if Chickerel's countenance really appeared, as Neigh had asserted, full of curiosity with regard to the gossip that was going on, the feelings which led to the exhibition must have been of a very unusual and irrepressible kind.

His hair was of that peculiar bluish-white which is to be observed when the oncoming years, instead of singling out special locks of a man's head for operating against, advance uniformly over the whole field, and enfeeble the colour at all points before absolutely extinguishing it anywhere; his nose was of the knotty shape in the gristle and earthward tendency in the flesh which is commonly said to carry sound judgment above it, his eyes were thoughtful, and his face was thin – a contour which, if it at once abstracted from his features that cheerful assurance of single-minded honesty which adorns the exteriors of so many of his brethren, might have raised a presumption in the minds of some beholders that perhaps in this case the quality might not be altogether wanting within.

The coffee having been served to the people upstairs, one of the footmen rushed into his bedroom on the lower floor, and in a few minutes emerged again in the dress of a respectable clerk who had been born for better things, with the trifling exceptions that he wore a low-crowned hat, and instead of knocking his heels on the pavement walked with a gait as delicate as a lady's. Going out of the area-door* with a cigar in his mouth, he mounted the steps hastily to keep an appointment round the corner – the keeping of which as a private gentleman necessitated the change of the greater part of his clothes twice within a quarter of an hour – the limit of his time of absence. The other footman was upstairs, and the butler, finding that he had a few minutes to himself, sat down at the table and wrote:

MY DEAR ETHELBERTA, – I did not intend to write to you for some few days to come, but the way in which you have been talked about here this evening makes me anxious to send a line or two at once, though I have very little time to spare, as usual. We have just had a dinner-party – indeed the carriages have not yet been brought round – and the talk at dinner was about your verses, of course. The thing was brought up by a young fellow named Ladywell – do you know him? He is a painter by profession, but he has a pretty good private income beyond what he gets by practising his line of business among the nobility, and that I expect is not little, for he is well known, and encouraged because he is young, and good-looking, and so forth. His family own a good bit of land somewhere out Aldbrickham way. However, I am before my story. From what they all said it is pretty clear that you are thought a great deal of in fashionable society as a poetess – but perhaps you know this as well as I – moving in it as you do yourself, my dear.

The ladies afterwards got very curious about your age, so curious, in fact, and so full of certainty that you were thirty-five and a blighted existence, if an hour, that I felt inclined to rap out there and then, and hang what came of it: 'My daughter, ladies, was to my own and her mother's certain knowledge only twenty-one last birthday, and has as bright a heart as anybody in London.' One of them actually said that you must be fifty to have got such an experience. Her guess was a very shrewd one in the bottom of it, however, for it was grounded upon the way you use those strange experiences of mine in the society that I tell you of, and dress them up as if they were yours; and, as you see, she hit off my own age to a year. I thought it was very sharp of her to be so right, although so wrong.

I do not want to influence your plans in any way about things which your school learning fits you to understand much better than I, who never had such opportunities, but I think that if I were in your place, Berta, I would not let my name be known just yet, for people always want what's kept from them, and don't value what's given. I am not sure, but I think that after the women had gone upstairs the others turned their thoughts upon you again; what they said about you I don't know, for if there's one thing I hate 'tis hanging about the doors when the men begin to get moved by their wine, which they did to a large extent tonight, and spoke very loud. They always do here, for old Don is a hearty giver in his way. However, as you see these people from their own level now, it is not much that I can tell you in seeing them only from the under side, though I see strange things sometimes, and of course –

> 'What great ones do the less will prattle of,'*

as it says in that book of select pieces that you gave me.

Well, my dear girl, I hope you will prosper. One thing above all others you'll have to mind, and it is that folk must continually strain to advance in order to remain where they are: and you particularly. But as for trying too hard, I wouldn't do it. Much lies in minding this, that your best plan for lightness of heart is to raise yourself a little higher than your old mates, but not so high as to be quite out of their reach. All human beings enjoy themselves from the outside, and so getting on *a little* has this good in it, you still keep in your old class where your feelings are, and are thoughtfully treated by this class: while by getting on *too much* you are sneered at by your new acquaintance, who don't know the skill of your rise, and you are parted from and forgot by the old ones who do. Whatever happens, don't be too quick to feel. You will surely get some hard blows when you are found out, for if the great can find no excuse for hitting with a mind, they'll do it and say 'twas in fun. But you are young and healthy, and youth and health are power. I wish I could have a decent footman here with me, but I suppose it is no use trying. It is such men as these that provoke the contempt we get. Well, thank God a few years will see the end of me, for I am growing ashamed of my company – so different as they are to the servants of old times. – Your affectionate father,

R. CHICKEREL

P.S. – Do not press Lady Petherwin any further to remove the rules on which you live with her. She is quite right: she cannot keep us, and to recognize us would do you no good, nor us either. We are content to see you secretly, since it is best for you.

Christopher's Lodgings
The Grounds about Rookington

8

Meanwhile, in the distant town of Sandbourne, Christopher Julian had recovered from the weariness produced by his labours at the Wyndway evening-party where Ethelberta had been a star. Instead of engaging his energies to clear encumbrances from the tangled way of his life, he now set about reading the popular 'Metres by E.' with more interest and assiduity than ever; for though Julian was a thinker by instinct, he was a worker by effort only; and the higher of these kinds being dependent upon the lower for its exhibition, there was often a lamentable lack of evidence of his power in either. It is a provoking correlation, and has conduced to the obscurity of many a genius.

'Kit,' said his sister, on reviving at the end of the bad headache which had followed the dance, 'those poems seem to have increased in value with you. The lady, lofty as she appears to be, would be flattered if she only could know how much you study them? Have you decided to thank her for them? Now let us talk it over – I like having a chat about such a pretty new subject.'

'I would thank her in a moment if I were absolutely certain that she had anything to do with sending them, or even writing them. I am not quite sure of that yet.'

'How strange that a woman could bring herself to write those verses!'

'Not at all strange – they are natural outpourings.'

Faith looked critically at the remoter caverns of the fire.

'Why strange?' continued Christopher. 'There is no harm in them.'

'O no – no harm. But I cannot explain to you – unless you see it partly of your own accord – that to write them she must be rather a fast lady – not a bad fast lady; a nice fast lady, I mean, of course. There, I have said it now, and I daresay you are vexed with me, for your interest in her has deepened to what it originally was, I think. I don't mean any absolute harm by "fast", Kit.'

'Bold, forward, you mean, I suppose?'

Faith tried to hit upon a better definition which should meet all views; and, on failing to do so, looked concerned at her brother's somewhat grieved appearance, and said, helplessly, 'Yes, I suppose I do.'

'My idea of her is quite the reverse. A poetess must intrinsically be sensitive, or she could never feel: but then, frankness is a rhetorical necessity even with the most modest, if their inspirations are to do any good in the world. You will, for certain, not be interested in something I was going to tell you, which I thought would have pleased you immensely; but it is not worth mentioning now.'

'If you will not tell me, never mind. But don't be crabbed, Kit! You know how interested I am in all your affairs.'

'It is only that I have composed an air to one of the prettiest of her songs, "When tapers tall" – but I am not sure about the power of it. This is how it begins – I threw it off in a few minutes, after you had gone to bed.'

He went to the piano and lightly touched over an air, the manuscript copy of which he placed in front of him, and listened to hear her opinion, having proved its value frequently; for it was not that of a woman merely, but impersonally human. Though she was unknown to fame, this was a great gift in Faith, since to have an unsexed judgment is as precious as to be an unsexed being is deplorable.

'It is very fair indeed,' said the sister, scarcely moving her lips in her great attention. 'Now again, and again, and again. How could you do it in the time!'

Kit knew that she admired his performance: passive assent was her usual praise, and she seldom insisted vigorously upon any view of his compositions unless for purposes of emendation.

'I was thinking that, as I cannot very well write to her, I may as well send her this,' said Christopher, with lightened spirits, voice to correspond, and eyes likewise; 'there can be no objection to it, for such things are done continually. Consider while I am gone, Faith. I shall be out this evening for an hour or two.'

When Christopher left the house shortly after, instead of going into the town on some errand, as was customary whenever he went from home after dark, he ascended a back street, passed over the hills behind, and walked at a brisk pace inland along the road to Rookington Park, where, as he had learnt, Ethelberta and Lady Petherwin were staying for a time, the day or two which they spent at Wyndway having formed a short break in the middle of this visit. The moon was shining tonight, and Christopher sped onwards over the pallid high-road as readily as he could have done at noonday. In three-quarters of an hour he reached the park gates; and entering now upon a tract which he had never before explored, he went along more cautiously and with some uncertainty as to the precise direction that the road would take. A frosted expanse of even grass, on which the shadow of his head appeared with an opal halo round it, soon allowed the house to be discovered beyond, the other portions of the park abounding with timber older and finer than that of any other spot in the neighbourhood. Christopher withdrew into the shade, and wheeled round to the front of the building that contained his old love. Here he gazed and idled, as many a man has done before him – wondering which room the fair poetess occupied, waiting till lights began to appear in the upper windows – which they did as uncertainly as glow-worms blinking up at eventide – and warming with currents of revived feeling in perhaps the sweetest of all conditions. New love is brightest, and long love is greatest; but revived love is the tenderest thing known upon earth.

Occupied thus, Christopher was greatly surprised to see, on casually glancing to one side, another man standing close to the shadowy trunk of another tree, in a similar attitude to his own, gazing, with arms folded, as blankly at the windows of the house as Christopher himself had been gazing. Not willing to be discovered, Christopher stuck closer to his tree. While he waited thus, the stranger began murmuring words, in a slow soft voice. Christopher listened till he heard the following: –

'Pale was the day and rayless, love,
    That had an eve so dim.'

Two well-known lines from one of Ethelberta's poems.

Jealousy is a familiar kind of heat which disfigures, licks playfully, clouds, blackens, and boils a man as a fire does a pot; and on recognizing these pilferings from what he had grown to regard as his own treasury, Christopher's fingers began to nestle with great vigour in the palms of his hands. Three or four minutes passed, when the unknown rival gave a last glance at the windows, and walked away. Christopher did not like the look of that walk at all – there was grace enough in it to suggest that his antagonist had no mean chance of finding favour in a woman's eyes. A sigh, too, seemed to proceed from the stranger's breast; but as their distance apart was too great for any such sound to be heard by any possibility, Christopher set down that to imagination, or to the brushing of the wind over the trees.

The lighted windows went out one by one, and all the house was in darkness. Julian then walked off himself, with a vigour that was spasmodic only, and with much less brightness of mind than he had experienced on his journey hither. The stranger had gone another way, and Christopher saw no more of him. When he reached Sandbourne, Faith was still sitting up.

'But I told you I was going to take a long walk,' he said.

'No, Christopher: really you did not. How tired and sad you do look – though I always know beforehand when you are in that state: one of your feet has a drag about it as you pass along the pavement outside the window.'

'Yes, I forgot that I did not tell you.'

He could not begin to describe his pilgrimage: it was too silly a thing even for her to hear of.

'It does not matter at all about my staying up,' said Faith assuringly; 'that is, if exercise benefits you. Walking up and down the sands, I suppose?'

'No; not walking up and down the sands.'

'The turnpike-road to Rookington is pleasant.'

'Faith, that is really where I have been. How came you to know?'

'I only guessed. Verses and an accidental meeting produce a special journey.'

'Ethelberta is a fine woman, physically and mentally, both. I wonder people do not talk about her twice as much as they do.'

'Then surely you are getting attached to her again. You think you discover in her more than anybody else does; and love begins with a sense of superior discernment.'

'No, no. That is only nonsense,' he said hurriedly. 'However, love her or love her not, I can keep a corner of my heart for you, Faith. There is another brute after her too, it seems.'

'Of course there is: I expect there are many. Her position in society is above ours, so that it is an unwise course to go troubling yourself more about her.'

'No. If a needy man must be so foolish as to fall in love, it is

best to do so where he cannot double his foolishness by marrying
the woman.'

'I don't like to hear you talk so slightingly of what poor father
did.'

Christopher fixed his attention on the supper. That night, late
as it was, when Faith was in bed and sleeping, he sat before a
sheet of music-paper, neatly copying his composition upon it.
The manuscript was intended as an offering to Ethelberta at the
first convenient opportunity.

'Well, after all my trouble to find out about Ethelberta, here
comes the clue unasked for,' said the musician to his sister a few
days later.

She turned and saw that he was reading the *Wessex Reflector*.

'What is it?' asked Faith.

'The secret of the true authorship of the book is out at last,
and it is Ethelberta of course. I am so glad to have it proved
hers.'

'But can we believe – ?'

'O yes. Just hear what "Our London Correspondent" says. It
is one of the nicest bits of gossip that he has furnished us with
for a long time.'

'Yes: now read it, do.'

' " The author of 'Metres by E.',"' Christopher began, ' "a
book of which so much has been said and conjectured, and one,
in fact, that has been the chief talk for several weeks past of the
literary clubs to which I belong, is a young lady who was a
widow before she reached the age of nineteen, and is now not
far beyond her fourth lustrum.* I was additionally informed by
a friend whom I met yesterday on his way to the House of
Lords, that her name is Mrs Petherwin – Christian name
Ethelberta; and that she resides with her mother-in-law at their
house in Exonbury Crescent. She is, moreover, the daughter of
the late Bishop of Silchester (if report may be believed), whose
active benevolence, as your readers know, left his family in
comparatively straightened circumstances at his death. The
marriage was a secret one, and much against the wish of her
husband's friends, who are wealthy people on all sides. The
death of the bridegroom two or three weeks after the wedding
led to a reconciliation; and the young poetess was taken to the
home which she still occupies, devoted to the composition of

such brilliant effusions as those the world has lately been favoured with from her pen."'

'If you want to send her your music, you can do so now,' said Faith.

'I might have sent it before, but I wanted to deliver it personally. However, it is all the same now, I suppose, whether I send it or not. I always knew that our destinies would lie apart, though she was once temporarily under a cloud. Her momentary inspiration to write that "Cancelled Words" was the worst possible omen for me. It showed that, thinking me no longer useful as a practical chance, she would make me ornamental as a poetical regret. But I'll send the manuscript of the song.'

'In the way of business, as a composer only; and you must say to yourself, "Ethelberta, as thou art but woman, I dare; but as widow I fear thee."'

Notwithstanding Christopher's affected carelessness, that evening saw a great deal of nicety bestowed upon the operation of wrapping up and sending off the song. He dropped it into the box and heard it fall, and with the curious power which he possessed of setting his wisdom to watch any particular folly in himself that it could not hinder, speculated as he walked on the result of this first tangible step of return to his old position as Ethelberta's lover.

A Lady's Drawing-rooms
Ethelberta's Dressing-room

9

It was a house on the north side of Hyde Park, between ten and eleven in the evening, and several intelligent and courteous people had assembled there to enjoy themselves as far as it was possible to do so in a neutral way – all carefully keeping every variety of feeling in a state of solution, in spite of any attempt such feelings made from time to time to crystallize on interesting subjects in hand.

'Neigh, who is that charming woman with her head built up in a novel way even for hair architecture – the one with her back towards us?' said a man whose coat fitted doubtfully to a friend whose coat fitted well.

'Just going to ask for the same information,' said Mr Neigh, determining the very longest hair in his beard to an infinitesimal nicety by drawing its lower portion through his fingers. 'I have quite forgotten – cannot keep people's names in my head at all; nor could my father either – nor any of my family – a very odd thing. But my old friend Mrs Napper knows for certain.' And he turned to one of a small group of middle-aged persons near, who, instead of skimming the surface of things in general, like the rest of the company, were going into the very depths of them.

'O – that is the celebrated Mrs Petherwin, the woman who makes rhymes and prints 'em,' said Mrs Napper, in a detached sentence, and then continued talking again to those on the other side of her.

The two loungers went on with their observations of Ethelberta's headdress, which, though not extraordinary or eccentric, did certainly convey an idea of indefinable novelty. Observers were sometimes half inclined to think that her cuts and modes were acquired by some secret communication with the mysterious clique which orders the livery of the fashionable world, for – and it affords a parallel to cases in which clever thinkers in other spheres arrive independently at one and the same conclusion – Ethelberta's fashion often turned out to be the coming one.

'O, is that the woman at last?' said Neigh, diminishing his broad general gaze at the room to a close criticism of Ethelberta.

'"The rhymes," as Mrs Napper calls them, are not to be despised,' said his companion. 'They are not quite *virginibus puerisque*,* and the writer's opinions of life and society differ very materially from mine, but I cannot help admiring her in the more reflective pieces; the songs I don't care for. The method in which she handles curious subjects, and at the same time impresses us with a full conviction of her modesty, is very adroit, and somewhat blinds us to the fact that no such poems were demanded of her at all.'

'I have not read them,' said Neigh, secretly wrestling with his jaw, to prevent a yawn; 'but I suppose I must. The truth is, that I never care much for reading what one ought to read; I wish I did, but I cannot help it. And, no doubt, you admire the lady immensely for writing them: I don't. Everybody is so talented nowadays that the only people I care to honour as deserving real distinction are those who remain in obscurity. I am myself hoping for a corner in some biographical dictionary when the time comes for those works only to contain lists of the exceptional individuals of whom nothing is known but that they lived and died.'

'Ah – listen. They are going to sing one of her songs,' said his friend, looking towards a bustling movement in the neighbourhood of the piano. 'I believe that song, "When tapers tall", has been set to music by three or four composers already.'

'Men of any note?' said Neigh, at last beaten by his yawn, which courtesy nevertheless confined within his person to such an extent that only a few unimportant symptoms, such as reduced eyes and a certain rectangular manner of mouth in speaking, were visible.

'Scarcely,' replied the other man. Established writers of music do not expend their energies upon new verse until they find that such verse is likely to endure; for should the poet be soon forgotten, their labour is in some degree lost.'

'Artful dogs – who would have thought it?' said Neigh, just as an exercise in words; and they drew nearer to the piano, less to become listeners to the singing than to be spectators of the scene in that quarter. But among some others the interest in the songs seemed to be very great; and it was unanimously wished that the young lady who had practised the different pieces of music privately would sing some of them now in the order of their composers' reputations. The musical persons in the room unconsciously resolved themselves into a committee of taste.

One and another had been tried, when, at the end of the third, a lady spoke to Ethelberta.

'Now, Mrs Petherwin,' she said, gracefully throwing back her face, 'your opinion is by far the most valuable. In which of the cases do you consider the marriage of verse and tune to have been most successful?'

Ethelberta, finding these and other unexpected calls made upon herself, came to the front without flinching.

'The sweetest and the best that I like by far,' she said, 'is none of these. It is one which reached me by post only this morning from a place in Wessex, and is written by an unheard-of man who lives somewhere down there – a man who will be, nevertheless, heard a great deal of some day, I hope – think. I have only practised it this afternoon; but, if one's own judgment is worth anything, it is the best.'

'Let us have your favourite, by all means,' said another friend of Ethelberta's who was present – Mrs Doncastle.

'I am so sorry that I cannot oblige you, since you wish to hear it,' replied the poetess regretfully; 'but the music is at home. I had not received it when I lent the others to Miss Belmaine, and it is only in manuscript like the rest.'

'Could it not be sent for?' suggested an enthusiast who knew that Ethelberta lived only in the next street, appealing by a look to her, and then to the mistress of the house.

'Certainly, let us send for it,' said that lady. A footman was at once quietly despatched with precise directions as to where Christopher's sweet production might be found.

'What – is there going to be something interesting?' asked a young married friend of Mrs Napper, who had returned to her original spot.

'Yes – the best song she has written is to be sung in the best manner to the best air that has been composed for it. I should not wonder if she were going to sing it herself.'

'Did you know anything of Mrs Petherwin until her name leaked out in connection with these ballads?'

'No; but I think I recollect seeing her once before. She is one of those people who are known, as one may say, by subscription: everybody knows a little, till she is astonishingly well known altogether; but nobody knows her entirely. She was the orphan child of some clergyman, I believe. Lady Petherwin, her mother-in-law, has been taking her about a great deal latterly.'

'She has apparently a very good prospect.'

'Yes; and it is through her being of that curious undefined character which interprets itself to each admirer as whatever he would like to have it. Old men like her because she is so girlish; youths because she is womanly; wicked men because she is good in their eyes; good men because she is wicked in theirs.'

'She must be a very anomalous sort of woman, at that rate.'

'Yes. Like the British Constitution, she owes her success in practice to her inconsistencies in principle.'

'These poems must have set her up. She appears to be quite the correct spectacle. Happy Mrs Petherwin!'

The subject of their dialogue was engaged in a conversation

with Mrs Belmaine upon the management of households – a theme provoked by a discussion that was in progress in the pages of some periodical of the time. Mrs Belmaine was very full of the argument, and went on from point to point till she came to servants.

The face of Ethelberta showed caution at once.

'I consider that Lady Plamby pets her servants by far too much,' said Mrs Belmaine. 'O, you do not know her? Well, she is a woman with theories; and she lends her maids and men books of the wrong kind for their station, and sends them to picture exhibitions which they don't in the least understand – all for the improvement of their taste, and morals, and nobody knows what besides. It only makes them dissatisfied.'

The face of Ethelberta showed venturesomeness. 'Yes, and dreadfully ambitious!' she said.

'Yes, indeed. What a turn the times have taken! People of that sort push on, and get into business, and get great warehouses, until at last, without ancestors, or family, or name, or estate—'

'Or the merest scrap of heirloom or family jewel.'

'Or heirlooms, or family jewels, they are thought as much of as if their forefathers had glided unobtrusively through the peerage—'

'Ever since the first edition.'

'Yes.' Mrs Belmaine, who really sprang from a good old family, had been going to say, 'for the last seven hundred years', but fancying from Ethelberta's addendum that she might not date back more than a trifling century or so, adopted the suggestion with her usual well-known courtesy, and blushed down to her locket at the thought of the mistake that she might have made. This sensitiveness was a trait in her character which gave great gratification to her husband, and, indeed, to all who knew her.

'And have you any theory on the vexed question of servant-government?' continued Mrs Belmaine, smiling. 'But no – the subject is of far too practical a nature for one of your bent, of course.'

'O no – it is not at all too practical. I have thought of the matter often,' said Ethelberta. 'I think the best plan would be for somebody to write a pamphlet, "The Shortest Way with the Servants", just as there was once written a terribly stinging one'

"The Shortest Way with the Dissenters",* which had a great effect.'

'I have always understood that that was written by a dissenter as a satire upon the Church?'

'Ah – so it was: but the example will do to illustrate my meaning.'

'Quite so – I understand – so it will,' said Mrs Belmaine, with clouded faculties.

Meanwhile Christopher's music had arrived. An accomplished gentleman, who had every musical talent except that of creation, scanned the notes carefully from top to bottom, and sat down to accompany the singer. There was no lady present of sufficient confidence or skill to venture into a song she had never seen before, and the only one who had seen it was Ethelberta herself; she did not deny having practised it the greater part of the afternoon, and was very willing to sing it now if anybody would derive pleasure from the performance. Then she began, and the sweetness of her singing was such that even the most unsympathetic honoured her by looking as if they would be willing to listen to every note the song contained if it were not quite so much trouble to do so. Some were so interested that, instead of continuing their conversation, they remained in silent consideration of how they would continue it when she had finished; while the particularly civil people arranged their countenances into every attentive form that the mind could devise. One emotional gentleman looked at the corner of a chair as if, till that moment, such an object had never crossed his vision before; the movement of his finger to the imagined tune was, for a deaf old clergyman, a perfect mine of interest; whilst a young man from the country was powerless to put an end to an enchanted gaze at nothing at all in the exact middle of the room before him. Neigh, and the general phalanx of cool men and celebrated club yawners, were so much affected that they raised their chronic look of great objection to things, to an expression of scarcely any objection at all.

'What makes it so interesting,' said Mrs Doncastle to Ethelberta, when the song was over and she had retired from the focus of the company, 'is, that it is played from the composer's own copy, which has never met the public eye, or any other than his own before today. And I see that he has actually sketched in the lines by hand, instead of having ruled paper –

just as the great old composers used to do. You must have been as pleased to get it fresh from the stocks like that as he probably was pleased to get your thanks.'

Ethelberta became reflective. She had not thanked Christopher; moreover, she had decided, after some consideration, that she ought not to thank him. What new thoughts were suggested by that remark of Mrs Doncastle's, and what new inclination resulted from the public presentation of his tune and her words as parts of one organic whole, are best explained by describing her doings at a later hour, when, having left her friends somewhat early, she had reached home and retired from public view for that evening.

Ethelberta went to her room, sent away the maid who did double duty for herself and Lady Petherwin, walked in circles about the carpet till the fire had grown haggard and cavernous, sighed, took a sheet of paper and wrote: –

DEAR MR JULIAN, – I have said I would not write: I have said it twice; but discretion, under some circumstances, is only another name for unkindness. Before thanking you for your sweet gift, let me tell you in a few words of something which may materially change an aspect of affairs under which I appear to you to deserve it.

With regard to my history and origin you are altogether mistaken; and how can I tell whether your bitterness at my previous silence on those points may not cause you to withdraw your act of courtesy now? But the gratification of having at last been honest with you may compensate even for the loss of your respect.

The matter is a small one to tell, after all. What will you say on learning that I am not the trodden-down "lady by birth" that you have supposed me? That my father is not dead, as you probably imagine; that he is working for his living as one among a peculiarly stigmatized and ridiculed multitude?

Had he been a brawny cottager, carpenter, mason, blacksmith, well-digger, navvy, tree-feller – any effective and manly trade, in short, a worker in which can stand up in the face of the noblest and daintiest, and bare his gnarled arms and say, with a consciousness of superior power, "Look at a real man!" I should have been able to show you antecedents which, if not intensely romantic, are not altogether antagonistic to romance. But the present fashion of associating with one particular class everything that is ludicrous and bombastic overpowers me when I think of it in relation to myself and your known sensitiveness. When the well-born poetess of good report melts into . . .

Having got thus far, a faint-hearted look, which had begun to show itself several sentences earlier, became pronounced. She threw the writing into the dull fire, poked and stirred it till a red inflammation crept over the sheet, and then started anew: –

DEAR MR JULIAN, – Not knowing your present rank as composer – whether on the very brink of fame, or as yet a long way off – I cannot decide what form of expression my earnest acknowledgments should take. Let me simply say in one short phrase, I thank you infinitely!

I am no musician, and my opinion on music may not be worth much: yet I know what I like (as everybody says, but I do not use the words as a form to cover a hopeless blank on all connected with the subject), and this sweet air I love. You must have glided like a breeze about me – seen into a heart not worthy of scrutiny, jotted down words that cannot justify attention – before you could have apotheosized the song in so exquisite a manner. My gratitude took the form of wretchedness when, on hearing the effect of the ballad in public this evening, I thought that I had not power to withhold a reply which might do us both more harm than good. Then I said, 'Away with all emotion – I wish the world was drained dry of it – I will take no notice,' when a lady whispered at my elbow to the effect that of course I had expressed my gratification to you. I ought first, to have mentioned that your creation has been played tonight to full drawing-rooms, and the original tones cooled the artificial air like a fountain almost.

I prophesy great things of you. Perhaps, at the time when we are each but a row of bones in our individual graves, your genius will be remembered, while my mere cleverness will have been long forgotten.

But – you must allow a woman of experience to say this – the undoubted power that you possess will do you socially no good unless you mix with it the ingredient of ambition – a quality in which I fear you are very deficient. It is in the hope of stimulating you to a better opinion of yourself that I write this letter.

Probably I shall never meet you again. Not that I think circumstances to be particularly powerful to prevent such a meeting, rather it is that I shall energetically avoid it. There can be no such thing as strong friendship between a man and a woman not of one family.

More than that there must not be, and this is why we will not meet. You see that I do not mince matters at all; but it is hypocrisy to avoid touching upon a subject which all men and women in our position inevitably think of, no matter what they say. Some women might have written distantly, and wept at the repression of their real feeling; but it is better to be more frank, and keep a dry eye. – Yours,

ETHELBERTA

Her feet felt cold and her heart weak as she directed the letter, and she was overpowered with weariness. But murmuring, 'If I let it stay till the morning I shall not send it, and a man may be lost to fame because of a woman's squeamishness – it shall go,' she partially dressed herself, wrapped a large cloak around her, descended the stairs, and went out to the pillar-box at the corner, leaving the door not quite close. No gust of wind had realized her misgivings that it might be blown shut on her return, and she re-entered as softly as she had emerged.

It will be seen that Ethelberta had said nothing about her family after all.

Lady Petherwin's House

10

The next day old Lady Petherwin, who had not accompanied Ethelberta the night before, came into the morning-room, with a newspaper in her hand.

'What does this mean, Ethelberta?' she inquired in tones from which every shade of human expressiveness was extracted by some awful and imminent mood that lay behind. She was pointing to a paragraph under the heading of 'Literary Notes' which contained in a few words the announcement of Ethelberta's authorship that had more circumstantially appeared in the *Wessex Reflector*.

'It means what it says,' said Ethelberta quietly.

'Then it is true?'

'Yes. I must apologize for having kept it such a secret from you. It was not done in the spirit that you may imagine: it was merely to avoid disturbing your mind that I did it so privately.'

'But surely you have not written every one of those ribald verses?'

Ethelberta looked inclined to exclaim most vehemently against this; but what she actually did say was, ' "Ribald" – what do you mean by that? I don't think that you are aware what "ribald" means.'

'I am not sure that I am. As regards some words as well as some persons, the less you are acquainted with them the more it is to your credit.'

'I don't quite deserve this, Lady Petherwin.'

'Really, one would imagine that women wrote their books during those dreams in which people have no moral sense, to see how improper some, even virtuous, ladies become when they get into print.'

'I might have done a much more unnatural thing than write those poems. And perhaps I might have done a much better thing, and got less praise. But that's the world's fault, not mine.'

'You might have left them unwritten, and shown more fidelity.'

'Fidelity! it is more a matter of humour than principle. What has fidelity to do with it?'

'Fidelity to my dear boy's memory.'

'It would be difficult to show that because I have written so-called gay and amatory verse, I feel amatory and gay. It is too often assumed that a person's fancy is a person's real mind. I believe that in the majority of cases one is fond of imagining the direct opposite of one's principles in sheer effort after something fresh and free; at any rate, some of the lightest of those rhymes were composed between the deepest fits of dismals I have ever known. However, I did expect that you might judge in the way you have judged, and that was my chief reason for not telling you what I had done.'

'You don't deny that you tried to escape from recollections you ought to have cherished? There is only one thing that women of your sort are as ready to do as to take a man's name, and that is, drop his memory.'

'Dear Lady Petherwin – don't be so unreasonable as to blame

a live person for living! No woman's head is so small as to be filled for life by a memory of a few months. Over three years have passed since I last saw my boy-husband. We were mere children; see how I have altered since in mind, substance, and outline – I have even grown half an inch taller since his death. Two years will exhaust the regrets of widows who have long been faithful wives; and ought I not to show a little new life when my husband died in the honeymoon?'

'No. Accepting the protection of your husband's mother was, in effect, an avowal that you rejected the idea of being a widow to prolong the idea of being a wife; and the sin against your conventional state thus assumed is almost as bad as would have been a sin against the married state itself. If you had gone off when he died, saying, "Thank heaven, I am free!" you would, at any rate, have shown some real honesty.'

'I should have been more virtuous by being more unfeeling. That often happens.'

'I have taken to you, and made a great deal of you – given you the inestimable advantages of foreign travel and good society to enlarge your mind. In short, I have been like a Naomi to you in everything, and I maintain that writing these poems saps the foundation of it all.'

'I do own that you have been a very good Naomi to me thus far; but Ruth* was quite a fast widow in comparison with me, and yet Naomi never blamed her. You are unfortunate in your illustration. But it is dreadfully flippant of me to answer you like this, for you have been kind. But why will you provoke me!'

'Yes, you are flippant, Ethelberta. You are too much given to that sort of thing.'

'Well, I don't know how the secret of my name has leaked out; and I am not ribald, or anything you say,' said Ethelberta, with a sigh.

'Then you own you do not feel so ardent as you seem in your book?'

'I do own it.'

'And that you are sorry your name has been published in connection with it?'

'I am.'

'And you think the verses may tend to misrepresent your character as a gay and rapturous one, when it is not?'

'I do fear it.'

'Then, of course, you will suppress the poems instantly. That is the only way in which you can regain the position you have hitherto held with me.'

Ethelberta said nothing; and the dull winter atmosphere had far from light enough in it to show by her face what she might be thinking.

'Well?' said Lady Petherwin.

'I did not expect such a command as that,' said Ethelberta 'I have been obedient for nearly four years, and would continue so – but I cannot suppress the poems. They are not mine now to suppress.'

'You must get them into your hands. Money will do it, I suppose?'

'Yes, I suppose it would – a thousand pounds.'

'Very well; the money shall be forthcoming,' said Lady Petherwin, after a pause. 'You had better sit down and write about it at once.'

'I cannot do it,' said Ethelberta; 'and I will not. I don't wish them to be suppressed. I am not ashamed of them; there is nothing to be ashamed of in them; and I shall not take any steps in the matter.'

'Then you are an ungrateful woman, and wanting in natural affection for the dead! Considering your birth—'

'That's an intolerable—'

Lady Petherwin crashed out of the room in a wind of indignation, and went upstairs and heard no more. Adjoining her chamber was a smaller one called her study, and, on reaching this, she unlocked a cabinet, took out a small deed-box, removed from it a folded packet, unfolded it, crumpled it up, and turning round suddenly flung it into the fire. Then she stood and beheld it eaten away word after word by the flames, 'Testament' – 'all that freehold' – 'heirs and assigns' appearing occasionally for a moment only to disappear for ever. Nearly half the document had turned into a glossy black when the lady clasped her hands.

'What have I done!' she exclaimed. Springing to the tongs she seized with them the portion of the writing yet unconsumed, and dragged it out of the fire. Ethelberta appeared at the door.

'Quick, Ethelberta!' said Lady Petherwin. 'Help me to put this out!' And the two women went tramping wildly upon the document and smothering it with a corner of the hearth-rug.

'What is it?' said Ethelberta.

'My will!' said Lady Petherwin. 'I have kept it by me lately, for I have wished to look over it at leisure—'

'Good heavens!' said Ethelberta. 'And I was just coming in to tell you that I would always cling to you, and never desert you, ill-use me how you might!'

'Such an affectionate remark sounds curious at such a time,' said Lady Petherwin, sinking down in a chair at the end of the struggle.

'But,' cried Ethelberta, 'you don't suppose—'

'Selfishness, my dear, has given me such crooked looks that I can see it round a corner.'

'If you mean that what is yours to give may not be mine to take, it would be as well to name it in an impersonal way, if you must name it at all,' said the daughter-in-law, with wet eyelids. 'God knows I had no selfish thought in saying that. I came upstairs to ask you to forgive me, and knew nothing about the will. But every explanation distorts it all the more!'

'We two have got all awry, dear – it cannot be concealed – awry – awry. Ah, who shall set us right again? However, now I must send for Mr Chancerly – no, I am going out on other business; and I will call upon him. There, don't spoil your eyes: you may have to sell them.'

She rang the bell and ordered the carriage; and half-an-hour later Lady Petherwin's coachman drove his mistress up to the door of her lawyer's office in Lincoln's Inn Fields.

Sandbourne and its Neighbourhood
Some London Streets

11

While this was going on in town, Christopher, at his lodgings in Sandbourne, had been thrown into rare old visions and dreams by the appearance of Ethelberta's letter. Flattered and encouraged to ambition as well as to love by her inspiriting sermon, he put off now the last remnant of cynical doubt upon the genuineness of his old mistress, and once and for all set down as disloyal a belief he had latterly acquired that 'Come, woo me, woo me; for I am like enough to consent,'* was all a young woman had to tell.

All the reasoning of political and social economists would not have convinced Christopher that he had a better chance in London than in Sandbourne of making a decent income by reasonable and likely labour; but a belief in a far more improbable proposition, impetuously expressed, warmed him with the idea that he might become famous there. The greater is frequently more readily credited than the less, and an argument which will not convince on a matter of halfpence appears unanswerable when applied to questions of glory and honour.

The regulation wet towel and strong coffee of the ambitious and intellectual student floated before him in visions; but it was with a sense of relief that he remembered that music, in spite of its drawbacks as a means of sustenance, was a profession happily unencumbered with those excruciating preliminaries to greatness.

Christopher talked about the new move to his sister, and he was vexed that her hopefulness was not roused to quite the pitch of his own. As with others of his sort, his too general habit of accepting the most clouded possibility that chances offered was only transcended by his readiness to kindle with a fitful excitement now and then. Faith was much more equable. 'If you were not the most melancholy man God ever created,' she said, kindly looking at his vague deep eyes and thin face, which was but a few degrees too refined and poetical to escape the epithet of lantern-jawed from any one who had quarrelled with him, 'you would not mind my coolness about this. It is a good thing of course to go; I have always fancied that we were mistaken in coming here. Mediocrity stamped "London" fetches more than talent marked "provincial". But I cannot feel so enthusiastic.'

'Still, if we are to go, we may as well go by enthusiasm as by calculation; it is a sensation pleasanter to the nerves, and leads to just as good a result when there is only one result possible.'

'Very well,' said Faith. 'I will not depress you. If I had to describe you I should say you were a child in your impulses, and an old man in your reflections. Have you considered when we shall start?'

'Yes.'

'What have you thought?'

'That we may very well leave the place in six weeks if we wish.'

'We really may?'

'Yes. And what is more, we will.'

Christopher and Faith arrived in London on an afternoon at the end of winter, and beheld from one of the river bridges snow-white scrolls of steam from the tall chimneys of Lambeth, rising against the livid sky behind, as if drawn in chalk on toned cardboard.

The first thing he did that evening, when settled in their apartments near the British Museum, before applying himself to the beginning of the means by which success in life might be attained, was to go out in the direction of Ethelberta's door, leaving Faith unpacking the things, and sniffing extraordinary smoke-smells which she discovered in all nooks and crannies of the rooms. It was some satisfaction to see Ethelberta's house, although the single feature in which it differed from the other houses in the Crescent was that no lamp shone from the fanlight over the entrance – a speciality which, if he cared for omens, was hardly encouraging. Fearing to linger near lest he might be detected, Christopher stole a glimpse at the door and at the steps, imagined what a trifle of the depression worn in each step her feet had tended to produce, and strolled home again.

Feeling that his reasons for calling just now were scarcely sufficient, he went next day about the business that had brought him to town, which referred to a situation as organist in a large church in the north-west district. The post was half ensured already, and he intended to make of it the nucleus of a professional occupation and income. Then he sat down to think of the preliminary steps towards publishing the song that had so pleased her, and had also, as far as he could understand from her letter, hit the popular taste very successfully; a fact which, however little it may say for the virtues of the song as a composition, was a great recommendation to it as a property. Christopher was delighted to perceive that out of this position he could frame an admissible, if not an unimpeachable, reason for calling upon Ethelberta. He determined to do so at once, and obtain the required permission by word of mouth.

He was greatly surprised, when the front of the house appeared in view on this spring afternoon, to see what a white and sightless aspect pervaded all the windows. He came close:

the eyeball blankness was caused by all the shutters and blinds being shut tight from top to bottom. Possibly this had been the case for some time – he could not tell. In one of the windows was a card bearing the announcement, 'This House to be let Furnished'.

Here was a merciless clash between fancy and fact. Regretting now his faint-heartedness in not letting her know beforehand by some means that he was about to make a new start in the world, and coming to dwell near her, Christopher rang the bell to make inquiries. A gloomy caretaker appeared after a while, and the young man asked whither the ladies had gone to live. He was beyond measure depressed to learn that they were in the south of France – Arles, the man thought the place was called – the time of their return to town being very uncertain; though one thing was clear, they meant to miss the forthcoming London season altogether.

As Christopher's hope to see her again had brought a resolve to do so, so now resolve led to dogged patience. Instead of attempting anything by letter, he decided to wait; and he waited well, occupying himself in publishing a 'March' and a 'Morning and Evening Service in E flat'. Some four-part songs, too, engaged his attention when the heavier duties of the day were over – these duties being the giving of lessons in harmony and counterpoint, in which he was aided by the introductions of a man well known in the musical world, who had been acquainted with young Julian as a promising amateur long before he adopted music as the staff of his pilgrimage.

It was the end of summer when he again tried his fortune at the house in Exonbury Crescent. Scarcely calculating upon finding her at this stagnant time of the town year, and only hoping for information, Julian was surprised and excited to see the shutters open, and the house wearing altogether a living look, its neighbours having decidedly died off meanwhile.

'The family here,' said a footman in answer to his inquiry, 'are only temporary tenants of the house. It is not Lady Petherwin's people.'

'Do you know the Petherwins' present address?'

'Underground, sir, for the old lady. She died some time ago in Switzerland, and was buried there, I believe.'

'And Mrs Petherwin – the young lady,' said Christopher, starting.

'We are not acquainted personally with the family,' the man replied. 'My master has only taken the house for a few months, whilst extensive alterations are being made in his own on the other side of the park, which he goes to look after every day. If you want any further information about Lady Petherwin, Mrs Petherwin will probably give it. I can let you have her address.'

'Ah, yes; thank you,' said Christopher.

The footman handed him one of some cards which appeared to have been left for the purpose. Julian, though tremblingly anxious to know where Ethelberta was, did not look at it till he could take a cool survey in private. The address was 'Arrowthorne Lodge, Upper Wessex'.

'Dear me!' said Christopher to himself, 'not far from Melchester; and not dreadfully far from Sandbourne.'

Arrowthorne Park and Lodge

12

Summer was just over when Christopher Julian found himself rattling along in the train to Sandbourne on some trifling business appertaining to his late father's affairs, which would afford him an excuse for calling at Arrowthorne about the song of hers that he wished to produce. He alighted in the afternoon at a little station some twenty miles short of Sandbourne, and leaving his portmanteau behind him there, decided to walk across the fields, obtain if possible the interview with the lady, and return then to the station to finish the journey to Sandbourne, which he could thus reach at a convenient hour in the evening, and, if he chose, take leave of again the next day.

It was an afternoon which had a fungous smell out of doors, all being sunless and stagnant overhead and around. The various species of trees had begun to assume the more distinctive colours of their decline, and where there had been one pervasive green were now twenty greenish yellows, the air in the vistas between them being half opaque with blue exhalation. Christopher in his walk overtook a countryman, and inquired if the path they were following would lead him to Arrowthorne Lodge.

''Twill take 'ee into Arr'thorne Park,' the man replied. 'But you won't come anigh the Lodge, unless you bear round to the left as might be.'

'Mrs Petherwin lives there, I believe?'

'No, sir. Leastwise unless she's but lately come. I have never heard of such a woman.'

'She may possibly be only visiting there.'

'Ah, perhaps that's the shape o't. Well, now you tell o't, I have seen a strange face thereabouts once or twice lately. A young good-looking maid enough, seemingly.'

'Yes, she's considered a very handsome lady.'

'I've heard the woodmen say, now that you tell o't, that they meet her every now and then, just at the closing in of the day, as they come home along with their nitches* of sticks; ay, stalking about under the trees by herself – a tall black martel,* so long-legged and awful-like that you'd think 'twas the old feller himself* a-coming, they say. Now a woman must be a queer body to my thinking, to roam about by night so lonesome and that? Ay, now that you tell o't, there is such a woman, but 'a never have showed in the parish; sure I never thought who the body was – no, not once about her, nor where 'a was living and that – not I, till you spoke. Well, there, sir, that's Arr'thorne Lodge; do you see they three elms?' He pointed across the glade towards some confused foliage a long way off.

'I am not sure about the sort of tree you mean,' said Christopher, 'I see a number of trees with edges shaped like edges of clouds.'

'Ay, ay, they be oaks; I mean the elms to the left hand.'

'But a man can hardly tell oaks from elms at that distance, my good fellow!'

'That 'a can very well – leastwise, if he's got the sense.'

'Well, I think I see what you mean,' said Christopher. 'What next?'

'When you get there, you bear away smart to nor'-west, and you'll come straight as a line to the Lodge.'

'How the deuce am I to know which is north-west in a strange place, with no sun to tell me?'

'What, not know nor'-west? Well, I should think a boy could never live and grow up to be a man without knowing the four quarters. I knowed 'em when I was a mossel of a chiel.* We be no great scholars here, that's true, but there isn't a Tom-rig or Jack-straw* in these parts that don't know where they lie as

well as I. Now I've lived, man and boy, these eight-and-sixty
years, and never met a man in my life afore who hadn't learnt
such a common thing as the four quarters.'

Christopher parted from his companion and soon reached a
stile, clambering over which he entered a park. Here he threaded
his way, and rounding a clump of aged trees the young man
came in view of a light and elegant country-house in the half-
timbered Gothic style of the late revival,* apparently only a few
years old. Surprised at finding himself so near, Christopher's
heart fluttered unmanageably till he had taken an abstract view
of his position, and, in impatience at his want of nerve, adopted
a sombre train of reasoning to convince himself that, far from
indulgence in the passion of love bringing bliss, it was a folly,
leading to grief and disquiet – certainly one which would do
him no good. Cooled down by this, he stepped into the drive
and went up to the house.

'Is Mrs Petherwin at home?' he said modestly.

'Who did you say, sir?'

He repeated the name.

'Don't know the person.'

'The lady may be a visitor – I call on business.'

'She is not visiting in this house, sir.'

'Is not this Arrowthorne Lodge?'

'Certainly not.'

'Then where is Arrowthorne Lodge, please?'

'Well, it is nearly a mile from here. Under the trees by the
high-road. If you go across by that footpath it will bring you
out quicker than by following the bend of the drive.'

Christopher wondered how he could have managed to get
into the wrong park; but, setting it down to his ignorance of the
difference between oak and elm, he immediately retraced his
steps, passing across the park again, through the gate at the end
of the drive, and into the turnpike road. No other gate, park, or
country seat of any description was within view.

'Can you tell me the way to Arrowthorne Lodge?' he inquired
of the first person he met, who was a little girl.

'You are just coming away from it, sir,' said she. 'I'll show
you; I am going that way.'

They walked along together. Getting abreast the entrance of
the park he had just emerged from, the child said, 'There it is,
sir; I live there too.'

Christopher, with a dazed countenance, looked towards a cottage which stood nestling in the shrubbery and ivy like a mushroom among grass. 'Is that Arrowthorne Lodge?' he repeated.

'Yes! and if you go up the drive, you come to Arrowthorne House.'

'Arrowthorne Lodge – where Mrs Petherwin lives, I mean.'

'Yes. She lives there along wi' mother and we. But she don't want anybody to know it, sir, cause she's celebrate,* and 'twouldn't do at all.'

Christopher said no more, and the little girl became interested in the products of the bank and ditch by the wayside. He left her, pushed open the heavy park-gate, and tapped at the Lodge door.

The latch was lifted. 'Does Mrs Petherwin,' he began, and, determined that there should be no mistake, repeated, 'Does Mrs Ethelberta Petherwin, the poetess, live here?' turning full upon the person who opened the door.

'She does, sir,' said a faltering voice; and he found himself face to face with the pupil-teacher of Sandbourne.

The Lodge (*continued*)
The Copse Behind

13

'This is indeed a surprise; I – am glad to see you!' Christopher stammered, with a wire-drawn, radically different smile from the one he had intended – a smile not without a tinge of ghastliness.

'Yes – I am home for the holidays,' said the blushing maiden; and, after a critical pause, she added, 'If you wish to speak to my sister, she is in the plantation with the children.'

'O no – no, thank you – not necessary at all,' said Christopher, in haste. 'I only wish for an interview with a lady called Mrs Petherwin.'

'Yes; Mrs Petherwin – my sister,' said Picotee. 'She is in the plantation. That little path will take you to her in five minutes.'

The amazed Christopher persuaded himself that this discovery was very delightful, and went on persuading so long that at last he felt it to be so. Unable, like many other people, to enjoy being satirized in words because of the irritation it caused him as aimed-at victim, he sometimes had philosophy enough to appreciate a satire of circumstance, because nobody intended it. Pursuing the path indicated, he found himself in a thicket of scrubby undergrowth, which covered an area enclosed from the park proper by a decaying fence. The boughs were so tangled that he was obliged to screen his face with his hands, to escape the risk of having his eyes filliped out by the twigs that impeded his progress. Thus slowly advancing, his ear caught, between the rustles, the tones of a voice in earnest declamation; and, pushing round in that direction, he beheld through some beech boughs an open space about ten yards in diameter, floored at the bottom with deep beds of curled old leaves, and cushions of furry moss. In the middle of this natural theatre was the stump of a tree that had been felled by a saw, and upon the flat stool thus formed stood Ethelberta, whom Christopher had not beheld since the ball at Wyndway House.

Round her, leaning against branches or prostrate on the ground, were five or six individuals. Two were young mechanics – one of them evidently a carpenter. Then there was a boy about thirteen, and two or three younger children. Ethelberta's appearance answered as fully as ever to that of an English lady skilfully perfected in manner, carriage, look, and accent; and the incongruity of her present position among lives which had had many of Nature's beauties stamped out of them, and few of the beauties of Art stamped in, brought him, as a second feeling, a pride in her that almost equalled his first sentiment of surprise. Christopher's attention was meanwhile attracted from the constitution of the group to the words of the speaker in the centre of it – words to which her auditors were listening with still attention.

It appeared to Christopher that Ethelberta had lately been undergoing some very extraordinary experiences. What the beginning of them had been he could not in the least understand, but the portion she was describing came distinctly to his ears, and he wondered more and more.

'He came forward till he, like myself, was about twenty yards from the edge. I instinctively grasped my useless stiletto. How I longed for the assistance which a little earlier I had so much despised! Reaching the block or boulder upon which I had been sitting, he clasped his arms around from behind; his hands closed upon the empty seat, and he jumped up with an oath. This method of attack told me a new thing with wretched distinctness; he had, as I suppose, discovered my sex; male attire was to serve my turn no longer. The next instant, indeed, made it clear, for he exclaimed, "You don't escape me, masquerading madam," or some such words, and came on. My only hope was that in his excitement he might forget to notice where the grass terminated near the edge of the cliff, though this could be easily felt by a careful walker: to make my own feeling more distinct on this point I hastily bared my feet.'

The listeners moistened their lips, Ethelberta took breath, and then went on to describe the scene that ensued, 'A dreadful variation on the game of Blindman's buff,'* being the words by which she characterized it.

Ethelberta's manner had become so impassioned at this point that the lips of her audience parted, the children clung to their elders, and Christopher could control himself no longer. He thrust aside the boughs, and broke in upon the group.

'For Heaven's sake, Ethelberta,' he exclaimed with great excitement, 'where did you meet with such a terrible experience as that?'

The children shrieked, as if they thought that the interruption was in some way the catastrophe of the events in course of narration. Every one started up; the two young mechanics stared, and one of them inquired, in return, 'What's the matter, friend?'

Christopher had not yet made reply when Ethelberta stepped from her pedestal down upon the crackling carpet of deep leaves.

'Mr Julian!' said she, in a serene voice, turning upon him eyes of such a disputable stage of colour, between brown and grey, as would have commended itself to a gallant duellist of the last century as a point on which it was absolutely necessary to take some friend's life or other. But the calmness was artificially done, and the astonishment that did not appear in Ethelberta's tones was expressed by her gaze. Christopher was not in a mood to draw fine distinctions between recognized and unrecognized organs of speech. He replied to the eyes.

'I own that your surprise is natural,' he said, with an anxious look into her face, as if he wished to get beyond this interpolated scene to something more congenial and understood. 'But my concern at such a history of yourself since I last saw you is even more natural than your surprise at my manner of breaking in.'

'That history would justify any conduct in one who hears it—'

'Yes, indeed.'

'If it were true,' added Ethelberta, smiling. 'But it is as false as—' She could name nothing notoriously false without raising an image of what was disagreeable, and she continued in a better manner: 'The story I was telling is entirely a fiction, which I am getting up for a particular purpose – very different from what appears at present.'

'I am sorry there was such a misunderstanding,' Christopher stammered, looking upon the ground uncertain and ashamed. 'Yet I am not, either, for I am very glad you have not undergone such trials, of course. But the fact is, I – being in the neighbour-hood – I ventured to call on a matter of business, relating to a poem which I had the pleasure of setting to music at the beginning of the year.'

Ethelberta was only a little less ill at ease than Christopher showed himself to be by this way of talking.

'Will you walk slowly on?' she said gently to the two young men, 'and take the children with you; this gentleman wishes to speak to me on business.'

The biggest young man caught up a little one under his arm, and plunged amid the boughs; another little one lingered behind for a few moments to look shyly at Christopher, with an oblique manner of hiding her mouth against her shoulder and her eyes behind her pinafore. Then she vanished, the boy and the second young man followed, and Ethelberta and Christopher stood within the wood-bound circle alone.

'I hope I have caused no inconvenience by interrupting the proceedings,' said Christopher softly; 'but I so very much wished to see you!'

'Did you, indeed – really wish to see me?' she said gladly. 'Never mind inconvenience then; it is a word which seems shallow in meaning under the circumstances. I surely must say that a visit is to my advantage, must I not? I am not as I was, you see, and may receive as advantages what I used to consider as troubles.'

'Has your life really changed so much?'

'It has changed. But what I first meant was that an interesting visitor at a wrong time is better than a stupid one at a right time.'

'I had been behind the trees for some minutes, looking at you, and thinking of you; but what you were doing rather interrupted my first meditation. I had thought of a meeting in which we should continue our intercourse at the point at which it was broken off years ago, as if the omitted part had not existed at all; but something, I cannot tell what, has upset all that feeling, and—'

'I can soon tell you the meaning of my extraordinary perform-ance,' Ethelberta broke in quickly, and with a little trepidation. 'My mother-in-law, Lady Petherwin, is dead; and she has left me nothing but her house and furniture in London – more than I deserve, but less than she had distinctly led me to expect; and so I am somewhat in a corner.'

'It is always so.'

'Not always, I think. But this is how it happened. Lady Petherwin was very capricious; when she was not foolishly kind she was unjustly harsh. A great many are like it, never thinking what a good thing it would be, instead of going on tacking from side to side between favour and cruelty, to keep to a mean line of common justice. And so we quarrelled, and she, being absolute mistress of all her wealth, destroyed her will that was in my favour, and made another, leaving me nothing but the fag-end of the lease of the town-house and the furniture in it. Then, when we were abroad, she turned to me again, forgave everything, and, becoming ill afterwards, wrote a letter to the brother, to whom she had left the bulk of her property, stating that I was to have £20,000 of the £100,000 she had bequeathed to him – as in the original will – doing this by letter in case anything should happen to her before a new will could be considered, drawn, and signed, and trusting to his honour quite that he would obey her expressed wish should she die abroad. Well, she did die, in the full persuasion that I was provided for; but her brother (as I secretly expected all the time) refused to be morally bound by a document which had no legal value, and the result is that he has everything, except, of course, the furniture and the lease. It would have been enough to break the heart of a person who had calculated upon getting a fortune, which I never did; for I felt always like an intruder and a bondswoman, and had wished myself out of the Petherwin family a hundred times, with my crust of bread and liberty. For one thing, I was always forbidden to see my relatives, and it pained me much. Now I am going to move for myself, and consider that I have a good chance of success in what I may undertake, because of an indifference I feel about succeeding which gives the necessary coolness that any great task requires.'

'I presume you mean to write more poems?'

'I cannot – that is, I can write no more that satisfy me. To blossom into rhyme on the sparkling pleasures of life, you must be under the influence of those pleasures, and I am at present quite removed from them – surrounded by gaunt realities of a very different description.'

'Then try the mournful. Trade upon your sufferings: many do, and thrive.'

'It is no use to say that – no use at all. I cannot write a line of verse. And yet the others flowed from my heart like a stream. But nothing is so easy as to seem clever when you have money.'

'Except to seem stupid when you have none,' said Christopher, looking at the dead leaves.

Ethelberta allowed herself to linger on that thought for a few seconds; and continued, 'Then the question arose, what was I to do? I felt that to write prose would be an uncongenial occupation, and altogether a poor prospect for a woman like me. Finally I have decided to appear in public.'

'Not on the stage?'

'Certainly not on the stage. There is no novelty in a poor lady turning actress, and novelty is what I want. Ordinary powers exhibited in a new way effect as much as extraordinary powers exhibited in an old way.'

'Yes – so they do. And extraordinary powers, and a new way too, would be irresistible.'

'I don't calculate upon both. I had written a prose story by request, when it was found that I had grown utterly inane over verse. It was written in the first person, and the style was modelled after De Foe's.* The night before sending it off, when I had already packed it up, I was reading about the professional story-tellers of Eastern countries, who devoted their lives to the telling of tales. I unfastened the manuscript and retained it, convinced that I should do better by *telling* the story.'

'Well thought of!' exclaimed Christopher, looking into her face. 'There is a way for everybody to live, if they can only find it out.'

'It occurred to me,' she continued, blushing slightly, 'that tales of the weird kind were made to be told, not written. The action of a teller is wanted to give due effect to all stories of incident; and I hope that a time will come when, as of old, instead of an unsocial reading of fiction at home alone, people will meet together cordially, and sit at the feet of a professed romancer. I am going to tell my tales before a London public.* As a child, I had a considerable power in arresting the attention of other children by recounting adventures which had never happened; and men and women are but children enlarged a little. Look at this.'

She drew from her pocket a folded paper, shook it abroad, and disclosed a rough draft of an announcement to the effect that Mrs Petherwin, Professed Story-teller, would devote an evening to that ancient form of the romancer's art, at a well-known fashionable hall in London. 'Now you see,' she continued, 'the meaning of what you observed going on here. That you heard was one of three tales I am preparing, with a view of selecting the best. As a reserved one, I have the tale of my own life – to be played as a last card. It was a private rehearsal before my brothers and sisters – not with any view of obtaining their criticism, but that I might become accustomed to my own voice in the presence of listeners.'

'If I only had had half your enterprise, what I might have done in the world!'

'Now did you ever consider what a power De Foe's manner would have if practised by word of mouth? Indeed, it is a style which suits itself infinitely better to telling than to writing, abounding as it does in colloquialisms that are somewhat out of place on paper in these days, but have a wonderful power in making a narrative seem real. And so, in short, I am going to talk De Foe on a subject of my own. Well?'

The last word had been given tenderly, with a long-drawn sweetness, and was caused by a look that Christopher was bending upon her at the moment, in which he revealed that he was thinking less of the subject she was so eagerly and hopefully descanting upon than upon her aspect in explaining it. It is a fault of manner particularly common among men newly imported into the society of bright and beautiful women; and we will hope that, springing as it does from no unworthy source, it is as soon forgiven in the general world as it was here.

'I was only following a thought,' said Christopher: – 'a thought of how I used to know you, and then lost sight of you, and then discovered you famous, and how we are here under these sad autumn trees, and nobody in sight.'

'I think it must be tea-time,' she said suddenly. 'Tea is a great meal with us here – you will join us, will you not?' And Ethelberta began to make for herself a passage through the boughs. Another rustle was heard a little way off, and one of the children appeared.

'Emmeline wants to know, please, if the gentleman that come to see 'ee will stay to tea; because, if so, she's agoing to put in another spoonful for him and a bit of best green.'

'O Georgina – how candid! Yes, put in some best green.'

Before Christopher could say any more to her, they were emerging by the corner of the cottage, and one of the brothers drew near them. 'Mr Julian, you'll bide and have a cup of tea wi' us?' he inquired of Christopher. 'A' old friend of yours, is he not, Mrs Petherwin? Dan and I be going back to Sandbourne tonight, and we can walk with 'ee as far as the station.'

'I shall be delighted,' said Christopher; and they all entered the cottage. The evening had grown clearer by this time; the sun was peeping out just previous to departure, and sent gold wires of light across the glades and into the windows, throwing a pattern of the diamond quarries, and outlines of the geraniums in pots, against the opposite wall. One end of the room was polygonal, such a shape being dictated by the exterior design; in this part the windows were placed as at the east end of continental churches. Thus, from the combined effects of the ecclesiastical lancet lights and the apsidal* shape of the room, it occurred to Christopher that the sisters were all a delightful set of pretty saints, exhibiting themselves in a lady chapel, and backed up by unkempt major prophets, as represented by the forms of their big brothers.

Christopher sat down to tea as invited, squeezing himself in between two children whose names were almost as long as their persons, and whose tin cups discoursed primitive music by means of spoons rattled inside them until they were filled. The tea proceeded pleasantly, notwithstanding that the cake, being a little burnt, tasted on the outside like the latter plums in snapdragon.* Christopher never could meet the eye of Picotee, who continued in a wild state of flushing all the time, fixing her looks upon the sugar-basin, except when she glanced out of the window to see how the evening was going on, and speaking no word at all unless it was to correct a small sister of somewhat crude manners as regards filling the mouth, which Picotee did in a whisper, and a gentle inclination of her mouth to the little one's ear, and a still deeper blush than before.

Their visitor next noticed that an additional cup-and-saucer and plate made their appearance occasionally at the table, were silently replenished, and then carried off by one of the children to an inner apartment.

'Our mother is bedridden,' said Ethelberta, noticing Christopher's look at the proceeding. 'Emmeline attends to the household, except when Picotee is at home, and Joey attends to the gate; but our mother's affliction is a very unfortunate thing for the poor children. We are thinking of a plan of living which will, I hope, be more convenient than this is; but we have not yet decided what to do.'

At this minute a carriage and pair of horses became visible through one of the angular windows of the apse, in the act of turning in from the highway towards the park gate. The boy who answered to the name of Joey sprang up from the table with the promptness of a Jack-in-the-box, and ran out at the door. Everybody turned as the carriage passed through the gate, which Joey held open, putting his other hand where the brim of his hat would have been if he had worn one, and lapsing into a careless boy again the instant that the vehicle had gone by.

'There's a tremendous large dinner-party at the House tonight,' said Emmeline methodically, looking at the equipage over the edge of her teacup, without leaving off sipping. 'That was Lord Mountclere. He's a wicked old man, they say.'

'Lord Mountclere?' said Ethelberta musingly 'I used to know some friends of his. In what way is he wicked?'

'I don't know,' said Emmeline, with simplicity. 'I suppose it is because he breaks the commandments. But I wonder how a big rich lord can want to steal anything.' Emmeline's thoughts of breaking commandments instinctively fell upon the eighth, as being in her ideas the only case wherein the gain could be considered as at all worth the hazard.

Ethelberta said nothing; but Christopher thought that a shade of depression passed over her.

'Hook back the gate, Joey,' shouted Emmeline, when the carriage had proceeded up the drive. 'There's more to come.'

Joey did as ordered, and by the time he got indoors another carriage turned in from the public road – a one-horse brougham* this time.

'I know who that is: that's Mr Ladywell,' said Emmeline, in the same matter-of-fact tone. 'He's been here afore: he's a distant relation of the squire's, and he once gave me sixpence for picking up his gloves.'

'What shall I live to see?' murmured the poetess, under her breath, nearly dropping her teacup in an involuntary trepidation, from which she made it a point of dignity to recover in a moment. Christopher's eyes, at that exhibition from Ethelberta, entered her own like a pair of lances. Picotee, seeing Christopher's quick look of jealousy, became involved in her turn, and grew pale as a lily in her endeavours to conceal the complications to which it gave birth in her poor little breast likewise.

'You judge me very wrongly,' said Ethelberta, in answer to Christopher's hasty look of resentment.

'In supposing Mr Ladywell to be a great friend of yours?' said Christopher, who had in some indescribable way suddenly assumed a right to Ethelberta as his old property.

'Yes: for I hardly know him, and certainly do not value him.'

After this there was something in the mutual look of the two, though their words had been private, which did not tend to remove the anguish of fragile Picotee. Christopher, assured that Ethelberta's embarrassment had been caused by nothing more than the sense of her odd social subsidence, recovered more bliss than he had lost, and regarded calmly the profile of young Ladywell between the two windows of his brougham as it passed the open cottage door, bearing him along unconscious as the dead of the nearness of his beloved one, and of the sad buffoonery that fate, fortune, and the guardian angels had been playing with Ethelberta of late. He recognized the face as that of the young man whom he had encountered when watching Ethelberta's window from Rookington Park.

'Perhaps you remember seeing him at the Christmas dance at Wyndway?' she inquired. 'He is a good-natured fellow. After-wards he sent me that portfolio of sketches you see in the corner.

He might possibly do something in the world as a painter if he were obliged to work at the art for his bread, which he is not.' She added with bitter pleasantry: 'In bare mercy to his self-respect I must remain unseen here.'

It impressed Christopher to perceive how, under the estrangement which arose from differences of education, surroundings, experience, and talent, the sympathies of close relationship were perceptible in Ethelberta's bearing towards her brothers and sisters. At a remark upon some simple pleasure wherein she had not participated because absent and occupied by far more comprehensive interests, a gloom as of banishment would cross her face and dim it for awhile, showing that the free habits and enthusiasms of country life had still their charm with her, in the face of the subtler gratifications of abridged bodices, candle-light, and no feelings in particular, which prevailed in town. Perhaps the one condition which could work up into a permanent feeling the passing revival of his fancy for a woman whose chief attribute he had supposed to be sprightliness was added now by the romantic ubiquity of station that attached to her. A discovery which might have grated on the senses of a man wedded to conventionality was a positive pleasure to one whose faith in society had departed with his own social ruin.

The room began to darken, whereupon Christopher arose to leave; and the brothers Sol and Dan offered to accompany him.

A Turnpike Road

14

'We be thinking of coming to London ourselves soon,' said Sol, a carpenter and joiner by trade, as he walked along at Christopher's left hand. 'There's so much more chance for a man up the country. Now, if you was me, how should you set about getting a job, sir?'

'What can you do?' said Christopher.

'Well, I am a very good staircase hand; and I have been called neat at sash-frames; and I can knock together doors and shutters very well; and I can do a little at the cabinet-making. I don't mind framing a roof, neither, if the rest be busy; and I am always ready to fill up my time at planing floor-boards by the foot.'

'And I can mix and lay flat tints,'* said Dan, who was a house painter, 'and pick out mouldings, and grain in every kind of wood you can mention – oak, maple, walnut, satinwood, cherry-tree—'

'You can both do too much to stand the least chance of being allowed to do anything in a city, where limitation is all the rule in labour. To have any success, Sol, you must be a man who can thoroughly look at a door to see what ought to be done to it, but as to looking at a window, that's not your line; or a person who, to the remotest particular, understands turning a screw, but who does not profess any knowledge of how to drive a nail. Dan must know how to paint blue to a marvel, but must be quite in the dark about painting green. If you stick to some such principle of speciality as this, you may get employment in London.'

'Ha-ha-ha' said Dan, striking at a stone in the road with the stout green hazel he carried. 'A wink is as good as a nod:* thank'ee – we'll mind all that now.'

'If we do come,' said Sol, 'we shall not mix up with Mrs Petherwin at all.'

'O indeed!'

'O no. (Perhaps you think it odd that we call her "Mrs Petherwin", but that's by agreement as safer and better than Berta, because we be such rough chaps you see, and she's so lofty.) 'Twould demean her to claim kin wi' her in London – two journeymen like us, that know nothing besides our trades.'

'Not at all,' said Christopher, by way of chiming in in the friendliest manner. 'She would be pleased to see any straight-forward honest man and brother, I should think, notwithstanding that she has moved in other society for a time.'

'Ah, you don't know Berta!' said Dan, looking as if he did.

'How – in what way do you mean?' said Christopher uneasily.

'So lofty – so very lofty! Isn't she, Sol? Why she'll never stir out from mother's till after dark, and then her day begins; and she'll traipse about under the trees, and never go into the high-road, so that nobody in the way of gentle-people shall run up against her and know her living in such a small hut after biding in a big manshion-place. There, we don't find fault wi' her about it: we like her just the same, though she don't speak to us in the street; for a feller must be a fool to make a piece of work about a woman's pride, when 'tis his own sister, and hang upon her and bother her when he knows 'tis for her good that he should not. Yes, her life has been quare enough. I hope she enjoys it, but for my part I like plain sailing. None of your ups and downs for me. There, I suppose 'twas her nater to want to look into the world a bit.'

'Father and mother kept Berta to school, you understand, sir,' explained the more thoughtful Sol, 'because she was such a quick child, and they always had a notion of making a governess of her. Sums? If you said to that child, "Berta, 'levenpence-three-farthings a day, how much a year?" she would tell 'ee in three seconds out of her own little head. And that hard sum about the herrings she had done afore she was nine.'

'True, she had,' said Dan. 'And we all know that to do that is to do something that's no nonsense.'

'What is the sum?' Christopher inquired.

'What – not know the sum about the herrings?' said Dan, spreading his gaze all over Christopher in amazement.

'Never heard of it,' said Christopher.

'Why down in these parts just as you try a man's soul by the Ten Commandments, you try his head by that there sum – hey, Sol?'

'Ay, that we do.'

'A herring and a half for three-halfpence, how many can ye get for 'levenpence: that's the feller; and a mortal teaser he is, I assure 'ee. Our parson, who's not altogether without sense o' week days, said one afternoon, "If cunning can be found in the multiplication table at all, Chickerel, 'tis in connection with that sum." Well, Berta was so clever in arithmetic that she was asked to teach summing at Miss Courtley's, and there she got to like foreign tongues more than ciphering,* and at last she hated ciphering, and took to books entirely. Mother and we were very proud of her at that time: not that we be stuck-up people at all – be we, Sol?'

'Not at all; nobody can say that we be that, though there's more of it in the country than there should be by all account.'

'You'd be surprised to see how vain the girls about here be getting. Little rascals, why they won't curtsey to the loftiest lady in the land; no, not if you were to pay 'em to do it. Now, the men be different. Any man will touch his hat for a pint of beer. But then, of course, there's some difference between the two. Touching your hat is a good deal less to do than bending your knees, as Berta used to say, when she was blowed up for not doing it. She was always one of the independent sort – you never saw such a maid as she was! Now, Picotee was quite the other way.'

'Has Picotee left Sandbourne entirely?'

'O no; she is home for the holidays. Well, Mr Julian, our road parts from yours just here, unless you walk into the next town along with us. But I suppose you get across to this station and go by rail?'

'I am obliged to go that way for my portmanteau,' said Christopher, 'or I should have been pleased to walk further. Shall I see you in Sandbourne tomorrow? I hope so.'

'Well, no. 'Tis hardly likely that you will see us – hardly. We know how unpleasant it is for a high sort of man to have rough chaps like us hailing him, so we think it best not to meet you – thank you all the same. So if you should run up against us in the street, we should be just as well pleased by your taking no notice, if you wouldn't mind. 'Twill save so much awkwardness – being in our working clothes. 'Tis always the plan that Mrs Petherwin and we agree to act upon, and we find it best for both. I hope you take our meaning right, and as no offence, Mr Julian.'

'And do you do the same with Picotee?'

'O Lord, no – 'tisn't a bit of use to try. That's the worst of Picotee – there's no getting rid of her. The more in the rough we be the more she'll stick to us; and if we say she shan't come, she'll bide and fret about it till we be forced to let her.'

Christopher laughed, and promised, on condition that they would retract the statement about their not being proud; and then he wished his friends good night.

An Inner Room at the Lodge

15

At the Lodge at this time a discussion of some importance was in progress. The scene was Mrs Chickerel's bedroom, to which, unfortunately, she was confined by some spinal complaint; and here she now appeared as an interesting woman of five-and-forty, properly dressed as far as visible, and propped up in a bed covered with a quilt which presented a field of little squares in many tints, looking altogether like a bird's-eye view of a market garden.

Mrs Chickerel had been nurse in a nobleman's family until her marriage, and after that she played the part of wife and mother, upon the whole, affectionately and well. Among her minor differences with her husband had been one about the naming of the children; a matter that was at last compromised by an agreement under which the choice of the girls' names became her prerogative, and that of the boys' her husband's, who limited his field of selection to strict historical precedent as a set-off to Mrs Chickerel's tendency to stray into the regions of romance.

The only grown-up daughters at home, Ethelberta and Picotee, with their brother Joey, were sitting near her; the two youngest children, Georgina and Myrtle, who had been strutting in and out of the room, and otherwise endeavouring to walk, talk, and speak like the gentleman just gone away, were packed off to bed. Emmeline, of that transitional age which causes its exponent to look wistfully at the sitters when romping and at the rompers when sitting, uncertain whether her position in the household is that of child or woman, was idling in a corner. The two absent brothers and two absent sisters – eldest members of the family – completed the round ten whom Mrs Chickerel with thoughtless readiness had presented to a crowded world, to cost Ethelberta many wakeful hours at night while she revolved schemes how they might be decently maintained.

'I still think,' Ethelberta was saying, 'that the plan I first proposed is the best. I am convinced that it will not do to attempt to keep on the Lodge. If we are all together in town, I can look after you much better than when you are far away from me down here.'

'Shall we not interfere with you – your plans for keeping up your connections?' inquired her mother, glancing up towards Ethelberta by lifting the flesh of her forehead, instead of troubling to raise her face altogether.

'Not nearly so much as by staying here.'

'But,' said Picotee, 'if you let lodgings, won't the gentlemen and ladies know it?'

'I have thought of that,' said Ethelberta, 'and this is how I shall manage. In the first place, if mother is there, the lodgings can be let in her name, all bills will be receipted by her, and all tradesmen's orders will be given as from herself. Then, we will take no English lodgers at all; we will advertise the rooms only in Continental newspapers, as suitable for a French or German gentleman or two, and by this means there will be little danger of my acquaintance discovering that my house is not entirely a private one, or of any lodger being a friend of my acquaintance. I have thought over every possible way of combining the dignified social position I must maintain to make my story-telling attractive, with my absolute lack of money, and I can see no better one.'

'Then if Gwendoline is to be your cook, she must soon give notice at her present place?'

'Yes. Everything depends upon Gwendoline and Cornelia. But there is time enough for them to give notice – Christmas will be soon enough. If they cannot or will not come as cook and housemaid, I am afraid the plan will break down. A vital condition is that I do not have a soul in the house (beyond the lodgers) who is not one of my own relations. When we have put Joey into buttons, he will do very well to attend to the door.'

'But s'pose,' said Joey, after a glassy look at his future appearance in the position alluded to, 'that any of your gentle-people come to see ye, and when I opens the door and lets 'em in a swinging big lodger stalks downstairs. What will 'em think? Up will go their eye-glasses at one another till they glares each other into holes. My gracious!'

'The one who calls will only think that another visitor is leaving, Joey. But I shall have no visitors, or very few. I shall let it be well known among my late friends that my mother is an invalid, and that on this account we receive none but the most intimate friends. These intimate friends not existing, we receive nobody at all.'

'Except Sol and Dan, if they get a job in London? They'll have to call upon us at the back door, won't they, Berta?' said Joey.

'They must go down the area steps. But they will not mind that; they like the idea.'

'And father, too, must he go down the steps?'

'He may come whichever way he likes. He will be glad enough to have us near at any price. I know that he is not at all happy at leaving you down here, and he away in London. You remember that he has only taken the situation at Mr Doncastle's on the supposition that you all come to town as soon as he can see an opening for getting you there; and as nothing of the sort has offered itself to him, this will be the very thing. Of course, if I succeed wonderfully well in my schemes for story-tellings, readings of my ballads and poems, lectures on the art of versification, and what not, we need have no lodgers; and then we shall all be living a happy family – all taking our share in keeping the establishment going.'

'Except poor me!' sighed the mother.

'My dear mother, you will be necessary as a steadying power – a flywheel, in short, to the concern. I wish that father could live there, too.'

'He'll never give up his present way of life – it has grown to be a part of his nature. Poor man, he never feels at home except in somebody else's house, and is nervous and quite a stranger in his own. Sich is the fatal effects of service!'

'O mother, don't!' said Ethelberta tenderly, but with her teeth on edge; and Picotee curled up her toes, fearing that her mother was going to moralize.

'Well, what I mean is, that your father would not like to live upon your earnings, and so forth. But in town we shall be near him – that's one comfort, certainly.'

'And I shall not be wanted at all,' said Picotee, in a melancholy tone.

'It is much better to stay where you are,' her mother said. 'You will come and spend the holidays with us, of course, as you do now.'

'I should like to live in London best,' murmured Picotee, her head sinking mournfully to one side. 'I *hate* being in Sandhourne now!'

'Nonsense!' said Ethelberta severely. 'We are all contriving how to live most comfortably, and it is by far the best thing for you to stay at the school. You used to be happy enough there.'

Picotee sighed, and said no more.

A Large Public Hall

16

It was the second week in February, Parliament had just met, and Ethelberta appeared for the first time before an audience in London.

There was some novelty in the species of entertainment that the active young woman had proposed to herself, and this doubtless had due effect in collecting the body of strangers that greeted her entry, over and above those friends who came to listen to her as a matter of course. Men and women who had become totally indifferent to new actresses, new readers, and new singers, once more felt the freshness of curiosity as they considered the promise of the announcement. But the chief inducement to attend lay in the fact that here was to be seen in the flesh a woman with whom the tongue of rumour had been busy in many romantic ways – a woman who, whatever else might be doubted, had certainly produced a volume of verses which had been the talk of the many who had read them, and of the many more who had not, for several consecutive weeks.

What was her story to be? Persons interested in the inquiry – a small proportion, it may be owned, of the whole London public, and chiefly young men – answered this question for themselves by assuming that it would take the form of some pungent and gratifying revelation of the innermost events of her own life, from which her gushing lines had sprung as an inevitable consequence, and which being once known, would cause such musical poesy to appear no longer wonderful.

The front part of the room was well filled, rows of listeners showing themselves like a drilled-in* crop of which not a seed has failed. They were listeners of the right sort, a majority having noses of the prominent and dignified type, which when viewed in oblique perspective ranged as regularly as bow-windows at a watering-place.* Ethelberta's plan was to tell

her pretended history and adventures while sitting in a chair –
as if she were at her own fireside, surrounded by a circle of
friends. By this touch of domesticity a great appearance of truth
and naturalness was given, though really the attitude was at first
more difficult to maintain satisfactorily than any one wherein
stricter formality should be observed. She gently began her
subject, as if scarcely knowing whether a throng were near her
or not, and, in her fear of seeming artificial, spoke too low. This
defect, however, she soon corrected, and ultimately went on in
a charmingly colloquial manner. What Ethelberta relied upon
soon became evident. It was not upon the intrinsic merits of her
story as a piece of construction, but upon her method of telling
it. Whatever defects the tale possessed – and they were not a few
– it had, as delivered by her, the one pre-eminent merit of
seeming like truth. A modern critic* has well observed of De
Foe that he had the most amazing talent on record for telling
lies; and Ethelberta, in wishing her fiction to appear like a real
narrative of personal adventure, did wisely to make De Foe her
model. His is a style even better adapted for speaking than for
writing, and the peculiarities of diction which he adopts to give
verisimilitude to his narratives acquired enormous additional
force when exhibited as *vivâ-voce** mannerisms. And although
these artifices were not, perhaps, slavishly copied from that
master of feigning, they would undoubtedly have reminded her
hearers of him, had they not mostly been drawn from an easeful
section in society which is especially characterized by the mental
condition of knowing nothing about any author a week after
they have read him. The few there who did remember De Foe
were impressed by a fancy that his words greeted them anew in
a winged auricular form, instead of by the weaker channels of
print and eyesight. The reader may imagine what an effect this
well-studied method must have produced when intensified by a
clear, living voice, animated action, and the brilliant and expres-
sive eye of a handsome woman – attributes which of themselves
almost compelled belief. When she reached the most telling
passages, instead of adding exaggerated action and sound,
Ethelberta would lapse to a whisper and a sustained stillness,
which were more striking than gesticulation. All that could be
done by art was there, and if inspiration was wanting nobody
missed it.

It was in performing this feat that Ethelberta seemed first to discover in herself the full power of that self-command which further onward in her career more and more impressed her as a singular possession, until at last she was tempted to make of it many fantastic uses, leading to results that affected more households than her own. A talent for demureness under difficulties without the cold-bloodedness which renders such a bearing natural and easy, a face and hand reigning unmoved outside a heart by nature turbulent as a wave, is a constitutional arrangement much to be desired by people in general; yet, had Ethelberta been framed with less of that gift in her, her life might have been more comfortable as an experience, and brighter as an example, though perhaps duller as a story.

'Ladywell, how came this Mrs Petherwin to think of such a queer trick as telling romances, after doing so well as a poet?' said a man in the stalls to his friend, who had been gazing at the Story-teller with a rapt face.

'What – don't you know? – everybody did, I thought,' said the painter.

'A mistake. Indeed, I should not have come here at all had I not heard the subject mentioned by accident yesterday at Grey's; and then I remembered her to be the same woman I had met at some place – Belmaine's I think it was – last year, when I thought her just getting on for handsome and clever, not to put it too strongly.'

'Ah! naturally you would not know much,' replied Ladywell, in an eager whisper. 'Perhaps I am judging others by myself a little more than – but, as you have heard, she is an acquaintance of mine. I know her very well, and, in fact, I originally suggested the scheme to her as a pleasant way of adding to her fame. "Depend upon it, dear Mrs Petherwin," I said, during a pause in one of our dances together some time ago, "any public appearance of yours would be successful beyond description."'

'O, I had no idea that you knew her so well! Then it is quite through you that she has adopted this course?'

'Well, not entirely – I could not say entirely. She said that some day, perhaps, she might do such a thing; and, in short, I reduced her vague ideas to form.'

'I should not mind knowing her better – I must get you to throw us together in some way,' said Neigh, with some interest. 'I had no idea that you were such an old friend. You could do it, I suppose?'

'Really, I am afraid – hah-hah – may not have the opportunity of obliging you. I met her at Wyndway, you know, where she was visiting with Lady Petherwin. It was some time ago, and I cannot say that I have ever met her since.'

'Or before?' said Neigh.

'Well – no; I never did.'

'Ladywell, if I had half your power of going to your imagination for facts, I would be the greatest painter in England.'

'Now Neigh – that's too bad – but with regard to this matter, I do speak with some interest,' said Ladywell, with a pleased sense of himself.

'In love with her? – Smitten down? – Done for?'

'Now, now! However, several other fellows chaff me about her. It was only yesterday that Jones said—'

'Do you know why she cares to do this sort of thing?'

'Merely a desire for fame, I suppose.'

'I should think she has fame enough already.'

'That I can express no opinion upon. I am thinking of getting her permission to use her face in a subject I am preparing, It is a fine face for canvas. Glorious contour – glorious. Ah, here she is again, for the second part.'

'Dream on, young fellow. You'll make a rare couple!' said Neigh, with a flavour of superciliousness unheeded by his occupied companion.

Further back in the room were a pair of faces whose keen interest in the performance contrasted much with the languidly permissive air of those in front. When the ten minutes' break occurred, Christopher was the first of the two to speak. 'Well, what do you think of her, Faith?' he said, shifting restlessly on his seat.

'I like the quiet parts of the tale best, I think,' replied the sister; 'but, of course, I am not a good judge of these things. How still the people are at times! I continually take my eyes from her to look at the listeners. Did you notice the fat old lady in the second row, with her cloak a little thrown back? She was absolutely unconscious, and stayed with her face up and lips parted like a little child of six.'

'She well may! the thing is a triumph. That fellow Ladywell is here, I believe – yes, it is he, busily talking to the man on his right. If I were a woman I would rather go donkey-driving than stick myself up there, for gaping fops to quiz* and say what they like about! But she had no choice, poor thing; for it was that or nothing with her.'

Faith, who had secret doubts about the absolute necessity of Ethelberta's appearance in public, said, with remote meanings, 'Perhaps it is not altogether a severe punishment to her to be looked at by well-dressed men. Suppose she feels it as a blessing, instead of an affliction?'

'She is a different sort of woman, Faith, and so you would say if you knew her. Of course, it is natural for you to criticize her severely just now, and I don't wish to defend her.'

'I think you do a little, Kit.'

'No; I am indifferent about it all. Perhaps it would have been better for me if I had never seen her; and possibly it might have been better for her if she had never seen me. She has a heart, and the heart is a troublesome encumbrance when great things have to be done. I wish you knew her: I am sure you would like each other.'

'O yes,' said Faith, in a voice of rather weak conviction. 'But, as we live in such a plain way, it would be hardly desirable at present.'

Ethelberta being regarded, in common with the latest conjurer, spirit-medium, aëronaut, giant, dwarf, or monarch, as a new sensation, she was duly criticized in the morning papers, and even obtained a notice in some of the weekly reviews.

'A handsome woman,' said one of these, 'may have her own reasons for causing the flesh of the London public to creep upon its bones by her undoubtedly remarkable narrative powers; but we question if much good can result from such a form of entertainment. Nevertheless, some praise is due. We have had the novel-writer among us for some time, and the novel-reader has occasionally appeared on our platforms; but we believe that this is the first instance on record of a Novel-teller – one, that is to say, who relates professedly as fiction a romantic tale which has never been printed – the whole owing its chief interest to the method whereby the teller identifies herself with the leading character in the story.'

Another observed: 'When once we get away from the magic influence of the story-teller's eye and tongue, we perceive how improbable, even impossible, is the tissue of events to which we have been listening with so great a sense of reality, and we feel almost angry with ourselves at having been the victims of such utter illusion.'

'Mrs Petherwin's personal appearance is decidedly in her favour,' said another. 'She affects no unconsciousness of the fact that form and feature are no mean vehicles of persuasion, and she uses the powers of each to the utmost. There spreads upon her face when in repose an air of innocence which is charmingly belied by the subtlety we discover beneath it when she begins her tale; and this amusing discrepancy between her physical presentment, and the inner woman is further illustrated by the misgiving, which seizes us on her entrance, that so impressionable a lady will never bear up in the face of so trying an audience ... The combinations of incident which Mrs Petherwin persuades her hearers that she has passed through are not a little marvellous; and if what is rumoured be true, that the tales are to a great extent based upon her own experiences, she has proved herself to be no less daring in adventure than facile in her power of describing it.'

Ethelberta's House

17

After such successes as these, Christopher could not forego the seductive intention of calling upon the poetess and romancer at her now established town residence in Exonbury Crescent. One wintry afternoon he reached the door – now for the third time – and gave a knock which had in it every tender refinement that could be thrown into the somewhat antagonistic vehicle of noise. Turning his face down the street he waited restlessly on the step. There was a strange light in the atmosphere: the glass of the street-lamps, the varnished back of a passing cab, a milkwoman's cans, and a row of church-windows glared in his eyes like new-rubbed copper and on looking the other way he beheld a bloody sun* hanging among the chimneys at the upper end, as a danger-lamp to warn him off.

By this time the door was opened, and before him stood Ethelberta's young brother Joey, thickly populated with little buttons, the remainder of him consisting of invisible green.

'Ah, Joseph!' said Christopher, instantly recognizing the boy. 'What, are you here in office? Is your—'

Joey lifted his forefinger and spread his mouth in a genial manner, as if to signify particular friendliness mingled with general caution.

'Yes, sir, Mrs Petherwin is my mistress. I'll see if she is at home, sir,' he replied, raising his shoulders and winking a wink of strategic meanings by way of finish – all which signs showed, if evidence were wanted, how effectually this pleasant young page understood, though quite fresh from Wessex, the duties of his peculiar position. Mr Julian was shown to the drawing-room, and there he found Ethelberta alone.

She gave him a hand so cool and still that Christopher, much as he desired the contact, was literally ashamed to let her see and feel his own, trembling with unmanageable excess of feeling. It was always so, always had been so, always would be so, at these meetings of theirs: she was immeasurably the stronger; and the deep-eyed young man fancied, in the chagrin which the perception of this difference always bred in him, that she triumphed in her superior control. Yet it was only in little things that their sexes were thus reversed: Christopher would receive quite a shock if a little dog barked at his heels, and be totally unmoved when in danger of his life.

Certainly the most self-possessed woman in the world, under pressure of the incongruity between their last meeting and the present one, might have shown more embarrassment than Ethelberta showed on greeting him today. Christopher was only a man in believing that the shyness which she did evince was chiefly the result of personal interest. She might or might not have been said to blush – perhaps the stealthy change upon her face was too slow an operation to deserve that name: but, though pale when he called, the end of ten minutes saw her colour high and wide. She soon set him at his ease, and seemed to relax a long-sustained tension as she talked to him of her arrangements, hopes, and fears.

'And how do you like London society?' said Ethelberta.

'Pretty well, as far as I have seen it: to the surface of its front door.'

'You will find nothing to be alarmed at if you get inside.'

'O no – of course not – except my own shortcomings,' said

the modest musician. 'London society is made up of much more refined people than society anywhere else.'

'That's a very prevalent opinion; and it is nowhere half so prevalent as in London society itself. However, come and see my house – unless you think it a trouble to look over a house?'

'No; I should like it very much.'

The decorations tended towards the artistic gymnastics prevalent in some quarters at the present day.[1]* Upon a general flat tint of duck's-egg green appeared quaint patterns of conventional foliage, and birds, done in bright auburn, several shades nearer to redbreast-red than was Ethelberta's hair, which was thus thrust further towards brown by such juxtaposition – a possible reason for the choice of tint. Upon the glazed tiles within the chimney-piece were the forms of owls, bats, snakes, frogs, mice, spiders in their webs, moles, and other objects of aversion and darkness, shaped in black and burnt in after the approved fashion.

'My brothers Sol and Dan did most of the actual work,' said Ethelberta, 'though I drew the outlines, and designed the tiles round the fire. The flowers, mice, and spiders are done very simply, you know: you only press a real flower, mouse, or spider out flat under a piece of glass, and then copy it, adding a little more emaciation and angularity at pleasure.'

'In that "at pleasure" is where all the art lies,' said he.

'Well, yes – that is the case,' said Ethelberta thoughtfully; and preceding him upstairs, she threw open a door on one of the floors, disclosing Dan in person, engaged upon a similar treatment of this floor also. Sol appeared bulging from the door of a closet, a little further on, where he was fixing some shelves; and both wore workmen's blouses. At once coming down from the short ladder he was standing upon, Dan shook Christopher's hand with some velocity.

'We do a little at a time, you see,' he said, 'because Colonel down below, and Mrs Petherwin's visitors, shan't smell the turpentine.'

'We be pushing on today to get it out of the way,' said Sol, also coming forward and greeting their visitor, but more reluctantly than his brother had done. 'Now I'll tell ye what – you two,' he added, after an uneasy pause, turning from Christopher

[1] Written in 1875.

to Ethelberta and back again in great earnestness; 'you'd better not bide here, talking to us rough ones, you know, for folks might find out that there's something closer between us than workmen and employer and employer's friend. So Berta and Mr Julian, if you'll go on and take no more notice o' us, in case of visitors, it would be wiser – else, perhaps, if we should be found out intimate with ye, and bring down your gentility, you'll blame us for it. I get as nervous as a cat when I think I may be the cause of any disgrace to ye.'

'Don't be so silly, Sol,' said Ethelberta, laughing.

'Ah, that's all very well,' said Sol, with an unbelieving smile; 'but if we bain't company for you out of doors, you bain't company for us within – not that I find fault with ye or mind it, and shan't take anything for painting your house, nor will Dan neither, any more for that – no, not a penny; in fact, we are glad to do it for 'ee. At the same time, you keep to your class, and we'll keep to ours. And so, good afternoon, Berta, when you like to go, and the same to you, Mr Julian. Dan, is that your mind?'

'I can't but own it,' said Dan.

The two brothers then turned their backs upon their visitors, and went on working, and Ethelberta and her lover left the room. 'My brothers, you perceive,' said she, 'represent the respectable British workman in his entirety, and a touchy individual he is, I assure you, on points of dignity, after imbibing a few town ideas from his leaders. They are painfully off-hand with me, absolutely refusing to be intimate, from a mistaken notion that I am ashamed of their dress and manners; which, of course, is absurd.'

'Which, of course, is absurd,' said Christopher.

'Of course it is absurd!' she repeated with warmth, and looking keenly at him. But, finding no harm in his face, she continued as before: 'Yet, all the time, they will do anything under the sun that they think will advance my interests. In our hearts we are one. All they ask me to do is to leave them to themselves, and therefore I do so. Now, would you like to see some more of your acquaintance?'

She introduced him to a large attic; where he found himself in the society of two or three persons considerably below the middle height, whose manners were of that gushing kind some-times called Continental, their ages ranging from five years to eight. These were the youngest children, presided over by Emmeline, as professor of letters, capital and small.

'I am giving them the rudiments of education here,' said Ethelberta; 'but I foresee several difficulties in the way of keeping them here, which I must get over as best I can. One trouble is, that they don't get enough air and exercise.'

'Is Mrs Chickerel living here as well?' Christopher ventured to inquire, when they were downstairs again.

'Yes; but confined to her room as usual, I regret to say. Two more sisters of mine, whom you have never seen at all, are also here. They are older than any of the rest of us, and had, broadly speaking, no education at all, poor girls. The eldest, Gwendoline, is my cook, and Cornelia is my housemaid. I suffer much sadness, and almost misery sometimes, in reflecting that here are we, ten brothers and sisters, born of one father and mother, who might have mixed together and shared all in the same scenes, and been properly happy, if it were not for the strange accidents that have split us up into sections as you see, cutting me off from them without the compensation of joining me to any others. They are all true as steel in keeping the secret of our kin, certainly; but that brings little joy, though some satisfaction perhaps.'

'You might be less despondent, I think. The tale-telling has been one of the successes of the season.'

'Yes, I might; but I may observe that you scarcely set the example of blitheness.'

'Ah – that's not because I don't recognize the pleasure of being here. It is from a more general cause: simply an underfeeling I have that at the most propitious moment the distance to the possibility of sorrow is so short that a man's spirits must not rise higher than mere cheerfulness out of bare respect to his insight.

> "As long as skies are blue, and fields are green,
>   Evening must usher night, night urge the morrow,
> Month follow month with woe, and year wake year to sorrow."*

Ethelberta bowed uncertainly; the remark might refer to her past conduct or it might not. 'My great cause of uneasiness is the children,' she presently said, as a new page of matter. 'It is my duty, at all risk and all sacrifice of sentiment, to educate and provide for them. The grown-up ones, older than myself, I cannot help much, but the little ones I can. I keep my two French lodgers for the sake of them.'

'The lodgers, of course, don't know the relationship between yourself and the rest of the people in the house?'

'O no! – nor will they ever. My mother is supposed to let the ground and first floors to me – a strange lady – as she does the second and third floors to them. Still, I may be discovered.'

'Well – if you are?'

'Let me be. Life is a battle, they say; but it is only so in the sense that a game of chess is a battle – there is no seriousness in it; it may be put an end to at any inconvenient moment by owning yourself beaten, with a careless "Ha-ha!" and sweeping your pieces into the box. Experimentally, I care to succeed in society; but at the bottom of my heart, I don't care.'

'For that very reason you are likely to do it. My idea is, make ambition your business and indifference your relaxation, and you will fail; but make indifference your business and ambition your relaxation, and you will succeed. So impish are the ways of the gods.'

'I hope that you at any rate will succeed,' she said, at the end of a silence.

'I never can – if success means getting what one wants.'

'Why should you not get that?'

'It has been forbidden to me.'

Her complexion changed just enough to show that she knew what he meant. 'If you were as bold as you are subtle, you would take a more cheerful view of the matter,' she said, with a look signifying innermost things.

'I will instantly! Shall I test the truth of my cheerful view by a word of question?'

'I deny that you are capable of taking that view, and until you prove that you are, no question is allowed,' she said, laughing, and still warmer in the face and neck. 'Nothing but melancholy, gentle melancholy, now as in old times when there was nothing to cause it.'

'Ah – you only tease.'

'You will not throw aside that bitter medicine of distrust, for the world. You have grown so used to it, that you take it as food, as some invalids do their mixtures.'

'Ethelberta, you have my heart – my whole heart. You have

had it ever since I first saw you. Now you understand me, and no pretending that you don't, mind, this second time.'

'I understood you long ago; you have not understood me.'

'You are mysterious,' he said lightly; 'and perhaps if I disentangle your mystery I shall find it to cover – indifference. I hope it does – for your sake.'

'How can you say so!' she exclaimed reproachfully. 'Yet I wish it did too – I wish it did cover indifference – for yours. But you have all of me that you care to have, and may keep it for life if you wish to. Listen, surely there was a knock at the door? Let us go inside the room: I am always uneasy when anybody comes, lest any awkward discovery should be made by a visitor of my miserable contrivances for keeping up the establishment.'

Joey met them before they had left the landing.

'Please, Berta,' he whispered, 'Mr Ladywell has called, and I've showed him into the liberry. You know, Berta, this is how it was, you know: I thought you and Mr Julian were in the drawing-room, and wouldn't want him to see ye together, and so I asked him to step into the liberry a minute.'

'You must improve your way of speaking,' she said, with quick embarrassment, whether at the mention of Ladywell's name before Julian, or at the way Joey coupled herself with Christopher, was quite uncertain. 'Will you excuse me for a few moments?' she said, turning to Christopher. 'Pray sit down; I shall not be long.' And she glided downstairs.

They had been standing just by the drawing-room door, and Christopher turned back into the room with no very satisfactory countenance. It was very odd, he thought, that she should go down to Ladywell in that mysterious manner, when he might have been admitted to where they were talking without any trouble at all. What could Ladywell have to say, as an acquaintance calling upon her for a few minutes, that he was not to hear? Indeed, if it came to that, what right had Ladywell to call upon her at all, even though she were a widow, and to some extent chartered to live in a way which might be considered a trifle free if indulged in by other young women. This was the first time that he himself had ventured into her house on that very account – a doubt whether it was quite proper to call, considering her youth, and the fertility of her position as ground for scandal. But no sooner did he arrive than here was Ladywell blundering in, and, since this conjunction had occurred on his first visit the chances were that Ladywell came very often.

Julian walked up and down the room, every moment expanding itself to a minute in his impatience at the delay and vexation at the cause. After scrutinizing for the fifth time every object on the walls as if afflicted with microscopic closeness of sight, his hands under his coat-tails, and his person jigging up and down upon his toes, he heard her coming up the stairs. When she entered the apartment her appearance was decidedly that of a person subsiding after some little excitement.

'I did not calculate upon being so long,' she said sweetly, at the same time throwing back her face and smiling. 'But I – was longer than I expected.'

'It seemed rather long,' said Christopher gloomily; 'but I don't mind it.'

'I am glad of that,' said Ethelberta.

'As you asked me to stay, I was very pleased to do so, and always should be; but I think that now I will wish you good-bye.'

'You are not vexed with me?' she said, looking quite into his face. 'Mr Ladywell is nobody, you know.'

'Nobody?'

'Well, he is not much, I mean. The case is, that I am sitting to him for a subject in which my face is to be used – otherwise than as a portrait – and he called about it.'

'May I say,' said Christopher, 'that if you want yourself painted, you are ill-advised not to let it be done by a man who knows how to use the brush a little?'

'O, he can paint!' said Ethelberta rather warmly. 'His last picture was excellent, I think. It was greatly talked about.'

'I imagined you to say that he was a mere nobody!'

'Yes, but – how provoking you are! – nobody, I mean, to talk to. He is a true artist, nevertheless.'

Christopher made no reply. The warm understanding between them had quite ended now, and there was no fanning it up again. Sudden tiffs had been the constant misfortune of their courtship in days gone by, had been the remote cause of her marriage to another; and the familiar shadows seemed to be rising again to cloud them with the same persistency as ever. Christopher went downstairs with well-behaved moodiness, and left the house forthwith. The postman came to the door at the same time.

Ethelberta opened a letter from Picotee – now at Sandbourne again; and, stooping to the fire-light, she began to read: –

MY DEAR ETHELBERTA, – I have tried to like staying at Sandbourne because you wished it, but I can't endure the town at all, dear Berta; everything is so wretched and dull! O, I only wish you knew how dismal it is here, and how much I would give to come to London! I cannot help thinking that I could do better in town. You see, I should be close to you, and should have the benefit of your experience. I would not mind what I did for a living could I be there where you all are. It is so like banishment to be here. If I could not get a pupil-teachership in some London school (and I believe I could by advertising) I could stay with you, and be governess to Georgina and Myrtle, for I am sure you cannot spare time enough to teach them as they ought to be taught, and Emmeline is not old enough to have any command over them. I could also assist at your dress-making, and you must require a great deal of that to be done if you continue to appear in public. Mr Long read in the papers the account of your first evening, and afterwards I heard two ladies of our committtee talking about it; but of course not one of them knew my personal interest in the discussion. Now will you, Ethelberta, think if I may not come: Do, there's a dear sister! I will do anything you set me about if I may only come. – Your ever affectionate,

PICOTEE

'Great powers above – what worries do beset me!' cried Ethelberta, jumping up. 'What can possess the child so suddenly? – she used to like Sandbourne well enough!' She sat down, and hastily scribbled the following reply: –

MY DEAR PICOTEE, – There is only a little time to spare before the post goes, but I will try to answer your letter at once. Whatever is the reason of this extraordinary dislike to Sandbourne? It is a nice healthy place, and you are likely to do much better than either of our elder sisters, if you follow straight on in the path you have chosen. Of course, if such good fortune should attend me that I get rich by my contrivances of public story-telling and so on, I shall share everything with you and the rest of us, in which case you shall not work at all. But (although I have been

unexpectedly successful so far) this is problematical; and it would
be rash to calculate upon all of us being able to live, or even us
seven girls only, upon the fortune I am going to make that way.
So, though I don't mean to be harsh, I must impress upon you the
necessity of going on as you are going just at present. I know the
place must be dull, but we must all put up with dulness sometimes.
You, being next to me in age, must aid me as well as you can in
doing something for the younger ones: and if anybody at all comes
and lives here otherwise than as a servant, it must be our father –
who will not, however, at present hear of such a thing when I
mention it to him. Do think of all this, Picotee, and bear up!
Perhaps we shall all be happy and united some day. Joey is waiting
to run to the post-office with this at once. All are well. Sol and
Dan have nearly finished the repairs and decorations of my house
– but I will tell you of that another time. – Your affectionate sister,

                                                    BERTA

Near Sandbourne
London Streets
Ethelberta's

18

When this letter reached its destination the next morning,
Picotee, in her over-anxiety, could not bring herself to read it in
anybody's presence, and put it in her pocket till she was on her
walk across the moor. She still lived at the cottage out of the
town, though at some inconvenience to herself, in order to teach
at a small village night-school whilst still carrying on her larger
occupation of pupil-teacher in Sandbourne.

So she walked and read, and was soon in tears. Moreover,
when she thought of what Ethelberta would have replied had
that keen sister known the wildness of her true reason in wishing
to go, she shuddered with misery. To wish to get near a man
only because he had been kind to her, and had admired her
pretty face, and had given her flowers, to nourish a passion all
the more because of its hopeless impracticability, were things to
dream of, not to tell.* Picotee was quite an unreasoning animal.

Her sister arranged situations for her, told her how to conduct herself in them, how to make up anew, in unobtrusive shapes, the valuable wearing apparel she sent from time to time – so as to provoke neither exasperation in the little gentry, nor superciliousness in the great. Ethelberta did everything for her, in short; and Picotee obeyed orders with the abstracted ease of mind which people show who have their thinking done for them, and put out their troubles as they do their washing. She was quite willing not to be clever herself, since it was unnecessary while she had a much-admired sister, who was clever enough for two people and to spare.

This arrangement, by which she gained an untroubled existence in exchange for freedom of will, had worked very pleasantly for Picotee until the anomaly of falling in love on her own account created a jar in the machinery. Then she began to know how wearing were miserable days, and how much more wearing were miserable nights. She pictured Christopher in London calling upon her dignified sister (for Ethelberta innocently mentioned his name sometimes in writing) and imagined over and over again the mutual signs of warm feeling between them. And now Picotee resolved upon a noble course. Like Juliet, she had been troubled with a consciousness that perhaps her love for Christopher was a trifle forward and unmaidenly, even though she had determined never to let him or anybody in the whole world know of it.* To set herself to pray that she might have strength to see him without a pang the lover of her sister, who deserved him so much more than herself, would be a grand penance and corrective.

After uttering petitions to this effect for several days, she still felt very bad; indeed, in the psychological difficulty of striving for what in her soul she did not desire, rather worse, if anything. At last, weary of walking the old road and never meeting him, and blank in a general powerlessness, she wrote the letter to Ethelberta, which was only the last one of a series that had previously been written and torn up.

Now this hope had been whirled away like thistledown, and the case was grievous enough to distract a greater stoic than Picotee. The end of it was that she left the school on insufficient notice, gave up her cottage home on the plea – true in the letter – that she was going to join a relative in London, and went off thither by a morning train, leaving her things packed ready to be sent on when she should write for them.

Picotee arrived in town late on a cold February afternoon, bearing a small bag in her hand. She crossed Westminster Bridge on foot, just after dusk, and saw a luminous haze hanging over each well-lighted street as it withdrew into distance behind the nearer houses, showing its direction as a train of morning mist shows the course of a distant stream when the stream itself is hidden. The lights along the riverside towards Charing Cross sent an inverted palisade of gleaming swords down into the shaking water, and the pavement ticked to the touch of pedestrians' feet, most of whom tripped along as if walking only to practise a favourite quick step, and held handkerchiefs to their mouths to strain off the river mist from their lungs. She inquired her way to Exonbury Crescent, and between five and six o'clock reached her sister's door.

Two or three minutes were passed in accumulating resolution sufficient to ring the bell, which when at last she did, was not performed in a way at all calculated to make the young man Joey hasten to the door. After the lapse of a certain time he did, however, find leisure to stroll and see what the caller might want, out of curiosity to know who there could be in London afraid to ring a bell twice.

Joey's delight exceeded even his surprise, the ruling maxim of his life being the more the merrier, under all circumstances. The beaming young man was about to run off and announce her upstairs and downstairs, left and right, when Picotee called him hastily to her. In the hall her quick young eye had caught sight of an umbrella with a peculiar horn handle – an umbrella she had been accustomed to meet on Sandbourne Moor on many happy afternoons. Christopher was evidently in the house.

'Joey,' she said, as if she were ready to faint, 'don't tell Berta I am come. She has company, has she not?'

'O no – only Mr Julian!' said the brother. 'He's quite one of the family!'

'Never mind – can't I go down into the kitchen with you?' she inquired. There had been bliss and misery mingled in those tidings, and she scarcely knew for a moment which way they affected her. What she did know was that she had run her dear fox to earth, and a sense of satisfaction at that feat prevented her just now from counting the cost of the performance.

'Does Mr Julian come to see her very often?' said she.

'O yes – he's always a-coming – a regular bore to me.'

'A regular what?'

'Bore! – Ah, I forgot, you don't know our town words. However, come along.'

They passed by the doors on tiptoe, and their mother upstairs being, according to Joey's account, in the midst of a nap, Picotee was unwilling to disturb her; so they went down at once to the kitchen, when forward rushed Gwendoline the cook, flourishing her floury hands, and Cornelia the housemaid, dancing over her brush; and these having welcomed and made Picotee comfortable, who should ring the area-bell, and be admitted down the steps, but Sol and Dan. The workman-brothers, their day's duties being over, had called to see their relations, first, as usual, going home to their lodgings in Marylebone and making themselves as spruce as bridegrooms, according to the rules of their newly-acquired town experience. For the London mechanic is only nine hours a mechanic, though the country mechanic works, eats, drinks, and sleeps a mechanic throughout the whole twenty-four.

'God bless my soul – Picotee!' said Dan, standing fixed. 'Well – I say, this is splendid! ha-ha!'

'Picotee – what brought you here?' said Sol, expanding the circumference of his face in satisfaction. 'Well, come along – never mind so long as you be here.'

Picotee explained circumstances as well as she could without stating them, and, after a general conversation of a few minutes, Sol interrupted with – 'Anybody upstairs with Mrs Petherwin?'

'Mr Julian was there just now,' said Joey; 'but he may be gone. Berta always lets him slip out how he can, the form of ringing me up not being necessary with him. Wait a minute – I'll see.'

Joseph vanished up the stairs; and, the question whether Christopher were gone or not being an uninteresting one to the majority, the talking went on upon other matters. When Joey crept down again a minute later, Picotee was sitting aloof and silent, and he accordingly singled her out to speak to.

'Such a lark, Picotee!' he whispered. 'Berta's a-courting of her young man. Would you like to see how they carries on a bit?'

'Dearly I should!' said Picotee, the pupils of her eyes dilating.

Joey conducted her to the top of the basement stairs, and told her to listen. Within a few yards of them was the morning-room door, now standing ajar; and an intermittent flirtation in soft male and female tones could be heard going on inside. Picotee's lips parted at thus learning the condition of things, and she leant against the stair-newel.

'My? What's the matter?' said Joey.

'If this is London, I don't like it at all!' moaned Picotee.

'Well – I never see such a girl – fainting all over the stairs for nothing in the world.'

'O – it will soon be gone – it is – it is only indigestion.'

'Indigestion? Much you simple country people can know about that! You should see what devils of indigestions we get in high life – eating 'normous great dinners and suppers that require clever physicians to carry 'em off, or else they'd carry us off with gout next day; and waking in the morning with such a splitting headache, and dry throat, and inward cusses about human nature, that you feel all the world like some great lord. However, now let's go down again.'

'No, no, no!' said the unhappy maiden imploringly. 'Hark!'

They listened again. The voices of the musician and poetess had changed: there was a decided frigidity in their tone – then came a louder expression – then a silence.

'You needn't be afeard,' said Joey. 'They won't fight; bless you, they busts out quarrelling like this times and times when they've been over-friendly, but it soon gets straight with 'em again.'

There was now a quick walk across the room, and Joey and his sister drew down their heads out of sight. Then the room door was slammed, quick footsteps went along the hall, the front door closed just as loudly, and Christopher's tread passed into nothing along the pavement.

'That's rather a wuss one than they mostly have; but Lord, 'tis nothing at all.'

'I don't much like biding here listening!' said Picotee.

'O, 'tis how we do all over the West End,' said Joey. ''Tis yer ignorance of town life that makes it seem a good deal to 'ee.'

'You can't make much boast about town life; for you haven't left off talking just as they do down in Wessex.'

'Well, I own to that – what's fair is fair, and 'tis a true charge; but if I talk the Wessex way 'tisn't for want of knowing better;

'tis because my staunch nater makes me bide faithful to our old
ancient institutions. You'd soon own 'twasn't ignorance in me,
if you knowed what large quantities of noblemen I gets mixed
up with every day. In fact 'tis thoughted here and there that I
shall do very well in the world.'

'Well, let us go down,' said Picotee. 'Everything seems so
overpowering here.'

'O, you'll get broke in soon enough. I felt just the same when
I first entered into society.'

'Do you think Berta will be angry with me? How does she
treat you?'

'Well, I can't complain. You see she's my own flesh and blood,
and what can I say? But, in secret truth, the wages are terrible
low, and barely pays for the tobacco I consooms.'

'O Joey, you wicked boy! If mother only knew that you
smoked!'

'I don't mind the wickedness so much as the smell. And Mrs
Petherwin has got such a nose for a fellow's clothes. 'Tis one of
the greatest knots* in service – the smoke question. 'Tis
thoughted that we shall make a great stir about it in the
mansions of the nobility soon.'

'How much more you know of life than I do – you only
fourteen and me seventeen!'

'Yes, that's true. You see, age is nothing – 'tis opportunity.
And even I can't boast, for many a younger man knows more.'

'But don't smoke, Joey – there's a dear!'

'What can I do? Society hev its rules, and if a person wishes
to keep himself up, he must do as the world do. We be all
Fashion's slave – as much a slave as the meanest in the land!'

They got downstairs again; and when the dinner of the French
lady and gentleman had been sent up and cleared away, and
also Ethelberta's evening tea (which she formed into a genuine
meal, making a dinner of luncheon, when nobody was there, to
give less trouble to her servant-sisters), they all sat round the
fire. Then the rustle of a dress was heard on the staircase, and
squirrel-haired Ethelberta appeared in person. It was her custom
thus to come down every spare evening, to teach Joey and her
sisters something or other – mostly French, which she spoke
fluently; but the cook and housemaid showed more ambition
than intelligence in acquiring that tongue, though Joey learnt it
readily enough.

There was consternation in the camp for a moment or two, on account of poor Picotee, Ethelberta being not without firmness in matters of discipline. Her eye instantly lighted upon her disobedient sister, now looking twice as disobedient as she really was.

'O, you are here, Picotee? I am glad to see you,' said the mistress of the house quietly.

This was altogether to Picotee's surprise, for she had expected a round rating at least, in her freshness hardly being aware that this reserve of feeling was an acquired habit of Ethelberta's, and that civility stood in town for as much vexation as a tantrum represented in Wessex.

Picotee lamely explained her outward reasons for coming, and soon began to find that Ethelberta's opinions on the matter would not be known by the tones of her voice. But innocent Picotee was as wily as a religionist in sly elusions* of the letter whilst infringing the spirit of a dictum; and by talking very softly and earnestly about the wondrous good she could do by remaining in the house as governess to the children, and playing the part of lady's-maid to her sister at show times, she so far coaxed Ethelberta out of her intentions that she almost accepted the plan as a good one. It was agreed that for the present, at any rate, Picotee should remain. Then a visit was made to Mrs Chickerel's room, where the remainder of the evening was passed; and harmony reigned in the household.

Ethelberta's Drawing-room

19

Picotee's heart was fitfully glad. She was near the man who had enlarged her capacity from girl's to woman's, a little note or two of young feeling to a whole diapason*; and though nearness was perhaps not in itself a great reason for felicity when viewed beside the complete realization of all that a woman can desire in such circumstances, it was much in comparison with the outer darkness of the previous time.

It became evident to all the family that some misunderstanding had arisen between Ethelberta and Mr Julian. What Picotee hoped in the centre of her heart as to the issue of the affair it would be too complex a thing to say. If Christopher became cold towards her sister he would not come to the house; if he continued to come it would really be as Ethelberta's lover – altogether, a pretty game of perpetual check for Picotee.

He did not make his appearance for several days. Picotee, being a presentable girl, and decidedly finer-natured than her sisters below stairs* was allowed to sit occasionally with Ethelberta in the afternoon, when the teaching of the little ones had been done for the day; and thus she had an opportunity of observing Ethelberta's emotional condition with reference to Christopher, which Picotee did with an interest that the elder sister was very far from suspecting.

At first Ethelberta seemed blithe enough without him. One more day went, and he did not come, and then her manner was that of apathy. Another day passed, and from fanciful elevations of the eyebrow, and long breathings, it became apparent that Ethelberta had decidedly passed the indifferent stage, and was getting seriously out of sorts about him. Next morning she looked all hope. He did not come that day either, and Ethelberta began to look pale with fear.

'Why don't you go out?' said Picotee timidly.

'I can hardly tell: I have been expecting some one.'

'When she comes I must run up to mother at once, must I not?' said clever Picotee.

'It is not a lady,' said Ethelberta blandly. She came then and stood by Picotee, and looked musingly out of the window. 'I may as well tell you, perhaps,' she continued. 'It is Mr Julian. He is – I suppose – my lover, in plain English.'

'Ah!' said Picotee.

'Whom I am not going to marry until he gets rich.'

'Ah – how strange! If I had him – such a lover, I mean – I would marry him if he continued poor.'

'I don't doubt it, Picotee; just as you come to London without caring about consequences, or would do any other crazy thing and not mind in the least what came of it. But somebody in the family must take a practical view of affairs, or we should all go to the dogs.'

Picotee recovered from the snubbing which she felt that she deserved, and charged gallantly by saying, with delicate showings of indifference, 'Do you love this Mr What's-his-name of yours?'

'Mr Julian? O, he's a very gentlemanly man. That is, except when he is rude, and ill-uses me, and will not come and apologize!'

'If I had him – a lover, I would ask him to come if I wanted him to.'

Ethelberta did not give her mind to this remark; but, drawing a long breath, said, with a pouting laugh, which presaged unreality, 'The idea of his getting indifferent now! I have been intending to keep him on until I got tired of his attentions, and then put an end to them by marrying him; but here is he, before he has hardly declared himself, forgetting my existence as much as if he had vowed in church to love and cherish me for life. 'Tis an unnatural inversion of the manners of society.'

'When did you first get to care for him, dear Berta?'

'O – when I had seen him once or twice.'

'Goodness – how quick you were!'

'Yes – if I am in the mind for loving I am not to be hindered by shortness of acquaintanceship.'

'Nor I neither!' sighed Picotee.

'Nor any other woman. We don't need to know a man well in order to love him. That's only necessary when we want to leave off.'

'O Berta – you don't believe that!'

'If a woman did not invariably form an opinion of her choice before she has half seen him, and love him before she has half formed an opinion, there would be no tears and pining in the whole feminine world, and poets would starve for want of a topic. I don't believe it, do you say? Ah, well, we shall see.'

Picotee did not know what to say to this; and Ethelberta left the room to see about her duties as public story-teller, in which capacity she had undertaken to appear again this very evening.

The Neighbourhood of the Hall
The Road Home

London was illuminated by the broad full moon. The pavements looked white as if mantled with snow; ordinary houses were sublimated to the rank of public buildings, public buildings to palaces, and the faces of women walking the streets to those of calendared saints* and guardian-angels, by the pure bleaching light from the sky.

In the quiet little street where opened the private door of the Hall chosen by Ethelberta for her story-telling, a brougham was waiting. The time was about eleven o'clock; and presently a lady came out from the building, the moonbeams forthwith flooding her face, which they showed to be that of the Story-teller herself. She hastened across to the carriage, when a second thought arrested her motion: telling the manservant and a woman inside the brougham to wait for her, she wrapped up her features and glided round to the front of the house, where she paused to observe the carriages and cabs driving up to receive the fashionable crowd stepping down from the doors. Standing here in the throng which her own talent and ingenuity had drawn together, she appeared to enjoy herself by listening for a minute or two to the names of several persons of more or less distinction as they were called out, and then regarded attentively the faces of others of lesser degree: to scrutinize the latter was, as the event proved, the real object of the journey from round the corner. When nearly every one had left the doors, she turned back disappointed. Ethelberta had been fancying that her alienated lover Christopher was in the back rows tonight, but, as far as could now be observed, the hopeful supposition was a false one.

When she got round to the back again, a man came forward. It was Ladywell, whom she had spoken to already that evening. 'Allow me to bring you your note-book, Mrs Petherwin: I think you had forgotten it,' he said. 'I assure you that nobody has handled it but myself.'

Ethelberta thanked him, and took the book. 'I use it to look into between the parts, in case my memory should fail me,' she explained. 'I remember that I did lay it down, now you remind me.'

Ladywell had apparently more to say, and moved by her side towards the carriage; but she declined the arm he offered, and said not another word till he went on, haltingly:

'Your triumph tonight was very great, and it was as much a triumph to me as to you; I cannot express my feeling – I cannot say half that I would. If I might only—'

'Thank you much,' said Ethelberta, with dignity. 'Thank you for bringing my book, but I must go home now. I know that you will see that it is not necessary for us to be talking here.'

'Yes – you are quite right,' said the repressed young painter, struck by her seriousness. 'Blame me; I ought to have known better. But perhaps a man – well, I will say it – a lover without indiscretion is no lover at all. Circumspection and devotion are a contradiction in terms. I saw that, and hoped that I might speak without real harm.'

'You calculated how to be uncalculating, and are natural by art!' she said, with the slightest accent of sarcasm. 'But pray do not attend me further – it is not at all necessary or desirable. My maid is in the carriage.' She bowed, turned, and entered the vehicle, seating herself beside Picotee.

'It was harsh!' said Ladywell to himself, as he looked after the retreating carriage. 'I was a fool; but it was harsh. Yet what man on earth likes a woman to show too great a readiness at first? She is right: she would be nothing without repulse!' And he moved away in an opposite direction.

'What man was that?' said Picotee, as they drove along.

'O – a mere Mr Ladywell: a painter of good family, to whom I have been sitting for what he calls an Idealization. He is a dreadful simpleton.'

'Why did you choose him?'

'I did not: he chose me. But his silliness of behaviour is a hopeful sign for the picture. I have seldom known a man cunning with his brush who was not simple with his tongue; or, indeed, any skill in particular that was not allied to general stupidity.'

'Your own skill is not like that, is it, Berta?'

'In men – in men. I don't mean in women. How childish you are!'

The slight depression at finding that Christopher was not present, which had followed Ethelberta's public triumph that evening, was covered over, if not removed, by Ladywell's declaration, and she reached home serene in spirit. That she had not the slightest notion of accepting the impulsive painter made little difference; a lover's arguments being apt to affect a lady's mood as much by measure as by weight. A useless declaration, like a rare china teacup with a hole in it, has its ornamental value in enlarging a collection.

No sooner had they entered the house than Mr Julian's card was discovered; and Joey informed them that he had come particularly to speak with Ethelberta, quite forgetting that it was her evening for tale-telling.

This was real delight, for between her excitements Ethelberta had been seriously sick-hearted at the horrible possibility of his never calling again. But alas! for Christopher. There being nothing like a dead silence for getting one's off-hand sweetheart into a corner, there is nothing like prematurely ending it for getting into that corner one's self.

'Now won't I punish him for daring to stay away so long!' she exclaimed as soon as she got upstairs. 'It is as bad to show constancy in your manners as fickleness in your heart at such a time as this.'

'But I thought honesty was the best policy?' said Picotee.

'So it is, for the man's purpose. But don't you go believing in sayings, Picotee: they are all made by men, for their own advantages. Women who use public proverbs as a guide through events are those who have not ingenuity enough to make private ones as each event occurs.'

She sat down, and rapidly wrote a line to Mr Julian: –

EXONBURY CRESCENT

I return from Mayfair Hall to find you have called. You will, I know, be good enough to forgive my saying what seems an unfriendly thing, when I assure you that the circumstances of my peculiar situation make it desirable, if not necessary. It is that I beg you not to give me the pleasure of a visit from you for some little time, for unhappily the frequency of your kind calls has been noticed; and I am now in fear that we may be talked about – invidiously – to the injury of us both. The town, or a section of it, has turned its bull's-eye* upon me with a brightness which I did not in the least anticipate; and you will, I am sure, perceive how indispensable it is that I should be circumspect. – Yours sincerely,

E. PETHERWIN

As soon as Ethelberta had driven off from the Hall, Ladywell turned back again; and, passing the front entrance, overtook his acquaintance Mr Neigh, who had been one of the last to emerge. The two were going in the same direction, and they walked a short distance together.

'Has anything serious happened?' said Neigh, noticing an abstraction in his companion. 'You don't seem in your usual mood tonight.'

'O, it is only that affair between us,' said Ladywell.

'Affair? Between you and whom?'

'Her and myself, of course. It will be in every fellow's mouth now, I suppose!'

'But – not anything between yourself and Mrs Petherwin?'

'A mere nothing. But surely you started, Neigh, when you suspected it just this moment?'

'No – you merely fancied that.'

'Did she not speak well tonight! You were in the room, I believe?'

'Yes, I just turned in for half-an-hour: it seems that everybody does, so I thought I must. But I had no idea that you were feeble that way.'

'It is very kind of you, Neigh – upon my word it is – very kind; and of course I appreciate the delicacy which – which – '

'What's kind?'

'I mean your well-intentioned plan for making me believe that nothing is known of this. But stories will of course get wind; and if our attachment has made more noise in the world than I intended it should, and causes any public interest, why – ha-ha! – it must. There is some little romance in it perhaps, and people will talk of matters of that sort between individuals of any repute – little as that is with one of the pair.'

'Of course they will – of course. You are a rising man, remember, whom some day the world will delight to honour.'

'Thank you for that, Neigh. Thank you sincerely.'

'Not at all. It is merely justice to say it, and one must be generous to deserve thanks.'

'Ha-ha! – that's very nicely put, and undeserved I am sure. And yet I need a word of that sort sometimes!'

'Genius is proverbially modest.'

'Pray don't, Neigh – I don't deserve it, indeed. Of course it is well meant in you to recognize any slight powers, but I don't deserve it. Certainly, my self-assurance was never too great. 'Tis the misfortune of all children of art that they should be so dependent upon any scraps of praise they can pick up to help them along.'

'And when that child gets so deep in love that you can only see the whites of his eyes—'

'Ah – now, Neigh – don't, I say!'

'But why did—'

'Why did I love her?'

'Yes, why did you love her?'

'Ah, if I could only turn self-vivisector, and watch the operation of my heart, I should know!'

'My dear fellow, you must be very bad indeed to talk like that. A poet himself couldn't be cleaner gone.'

'Now, don't chaff, Neigh; do anything, but don't chaff. You know that I am the easiest man in the world for taking it at most times. But I can't stand it now; I don't feel up to it. A glimpse of paradise, and then perdition. What would you do, Neigh?'

'She has refused you, then?'

'Well – not positively refused me; but it is so near it that a dull man couldn't tell the difference. I hardly can myself.'

'How do you really stand with her?' said Neigh, with an anxiety ill-concealed.

'Off and on – neither one thing nor the other. I was deter-mined to make an effort the last time she sat to me, and so I met her quite coolly, and spoke only of technicalities with a forced smile – you know that way of mine for drawing people out, eh, Neigh?'

'Quite, quite.'

'A forced smile, as much as to say, "I am obliged to entertain you, but as a mere model for art purposes." But the deuce a bit did she care. And then I frequently looked to see what time it was, as the end of the sitting drew near – rather a rude thing to do, as a rule.'

'Of course. But that was your, *finesse*. Ha-ha! – capital! Yet why not struggle against such slavery? It is regularly pulling you down. What's a woman's beauty, after all?'

'Well you may say so! A thing easier to feel than define,' murmured Ladywell. 'But it's no use, Neigh – I can't help it as long as she repulses me so exquisitely! If she would only care for me a little, I might get to trouble less about her.'

'And love her no more than one ordinarily does a girl by the time one gets irrevocably engaged to her. But I suppose she keeps you back so thoroughly that you carry on the old adoration with as much vigour as if it were a new fancy every time?'

'Partly yes, and partly no! It's very true, and it's not true!'

''Tis to be hoped she won't hate you outright, for then you would absolutely die of idolizing her.'

'Don't, Neigh! – Still there's some truth in it – such is the perversity of our hearts. Fancy marrying such a woman!'

'We should feel as eternally united to her after years and years of marriage as to a dear new angel met at last night's dance.'

'Exactly – just what I should have said. But did I hear you say "We", Neigh? You didn't say "*We* should feel"?'

'Say "we"? – yes – of course – putting myself in your place just in the way of speaking, you know.'

'Of course, of course; but one is such a fool at these times that one seems to detect rivalry in every trumpery sound! Were you never a little touched?'

'Not I. My heart is in the happy position of a country which has no history or debt.'*

'I suppose I should rejoice to hear it,' said Ladywell. 'But the consciousness of a fellow-sufferer being in just such another hole is such a relief always, and softens the sense of one's folly so very much.'

'There's less Christianity in that sentiment than in your confessing to it, old fellow. I know the truth of it nevertheless, and that's why married men advise others to marry. Were all the world tied up, the pleasantly tied ones would be equivalent to those at present free. But what if your fellow-sufferer is not only in another such a hole, but in the same one?'

'No, Neigh – never! Don't trifle with a friend who—'

'That is, refused like yourself, as well as in love.'

'Ah, thanks, thanks! It suddenly occurred to me that we might be dead against one another as rivals, and a friendship of many long – days be snapped like a – like a reed.'

'No – no – only a jest,' said Neigh, with a strangely accelerated speech. 'Love-making is an ornamental pursuit that matter-of-fact fellows like me are quite unfit for. A man must have courted at least half-a-dozen women before he's a match for one; and since triumph lies so far ahead, I shall keep out of the contest altogether.'

'Your life would be pleasanter if you were engaged. It is a nice thing, after all.'

'It is. The worst of it would be that, when the time came for breaking it off, a fellow might get into an action for breach* – women are so fond of that sort of thing now; and I hate love-affairs that don't end peaceably!'

'But end it by peaceably marrying, my dear fellow!'

'It would seem so singular. Besides, I have a horror of antiquity: and you see, as long as a man keeps single, he belongs in a measure to the rising generation, however old he may be; but as soon as he marries and has children, he belongs to the last generation, however young he may be. Old Jones's son is a deal younger than young Brown's father, though they are both the same age.'

'At any rate, honest courtship cures a man of many evils he had no power to stem before.'

'By substituting an incurable matrimony!'

'Ah – two persons must have a mind for that before it can happen!' said Ladywell, sorrowfully shaking his head.

'I think you'll find that if one has a mind for it, it will be quite sufficient. But here we are at my rooms. Come in for half-an-hour?'

'Not tonight, thanks!'

They parted, and Neigh went in. When he got upstairs he murmured in his deepest chest note, 'O, lords, that I should come to this! But I shall never be such a fool as to marry her! What a flat* that poor young devil was not to discover that we were tarred with the same brush. O, the deuce, the deuce!' he continued, walking about the room as if passionately stamping, but not quite doing it because another man had rooms below.

Neigh drew from his pocket-book an envelope embossed with

the name of a fashionable photographer and out of this pulled a portrait of the lady who had, in fact, enslaved his secret self equally with his frank young friend the painter. After contemplating it awhile with a face of cynical adoration, he murmured, shaking his head, 'Ah, my lady; if you only knew this, I should be snapped up like a snail! Not a minute's peace for me till I had married you. I wonder if I shall! – I wonder.'

Neigh was a man of five-and-thirty – Ladywell's senior by ten years; and, being of a phlegmatic temperament, he had glided thus far through the period of eligibility with impunity. He knew as well as any man how far he could go with a woman and yet keep clear of having to meet her in church without her bonnet;* but it is doubtful if his mind that night were less disturbed with the question how to guide himself out of the natural course which his passion for Ethelberta might tempt him into, than was Ladywell's by his ardent wish to secure her.

About the time at which Neigh and Ladywell parted company, Christopher Julian was entering his little place in Bloomsbury. The quaint figure of Faith, in her bonnet and cloak, was kneeling on the hearth-rug endeavouring to stir a dull fire into a bright one.

'What – Faith! you have never been out alone?' he said.

Faith's soft, quick-shutting eyes looked unutterable things, and she replied, 'I have been to hear Mrs Petherwin's story-telling again.'

'And walked all the way home through the streets at this time of night, I suppose!'

'Well, nobody molested me, either going or coming back.'

'Faith, I gave you strict orders not to go into the streets after two o'clock in the day, and now here you are taking no notice of what I say at all!'

'The truth is, Kit, I wanted to see with my spectacles what this woman was really like, and I went without them last time. I slipped in behind, and nobody saw me.'

'I don't think much of her after what I have seen tonight,' said Christopher, moodily recurring to a previous thought.

'Why? What is the matter?'

'I thought I would call on her this afternoon, but when I got there I found she had left early for the performance. So in the evening, when I thought it would be all over, I went to the private door of the Hall to speak to her as she came out, and ask her flatly a question or two which I was fool enough to think I must ask her before I went to bed. Just as I was drawing near she came out, and, instead of getting into the brougham that was waiting for her, she went round the corner. When she came back a man met her and gave her something, and they stayed talking together two or three minutes. The meeting may certainly not have been intentional on her part; but she has no business to be going on so coolly when – when – in fact, I have come to the conclusion that a woman's affection is not worth having. The only feeling which has any dignity or permanence or worth is family affection between close blood-relations.'

'And yet you snub me sometimes, Mr Kit.'

'And, for the matter of that, you snub me. Still you know what I mean – there's none of that off-and-on humbug between us. If we grumble with one another we are united just the same: if we don't write when we are parted, we are just the same when we meet – there has been some rational reason for silence; but as for lovers and sweethearts, there is nothing worth a rush in what they feel!'

Faith said nothing in reply to this. The opinions she had formed upon the wisdom of her brother's pursuit of Ethelberta would have come just then with an ill grace. It must, however, have been evident to Christopher, had he not been too preoccupied for observation, that Faith's impressions of Ethelberta were not quite favourable as regarded her womanhood, notwithstanding that she greatly admired her talents.

Ethelberta's House

22

Ethelberta came indoors one day from the University boat-race,* and sat down, without speaking, beside Picotee, as if lost in thought.

'Did you enjoy the sight?' said Picotee.

'I scarcely know. We couldn't see at all from Mrs Belmaine's carriage, so two of us – very rashly – agreed to get out and be rowed across to the other side where the people were quite few.

But when the boatman had us in the middle of the river he declared he couldn't land us on the other side because of the barges; so there we were in a dreadful state – tossed up and down like corks upon great waves made by steamers till I made up my mind for a drowning. Well, at last we got back again, but couldn't reach the carriage for the crowd; and I don't know what we should have done if a gentleman hadn't come – sent by Mrs Belmaine, who was in a great fright about us; then he was introduced to me, and – I wonder how it will end!'

'Was there anything so wonderful in the beginning, then?'

'Yes. One of the coolest and most practised men in London was ill-mannered towards me from sheer absence of mind – and could there be higher flattery? When a man of that sort does not give you the politeness you deserve, it means that in his heart he is rebelling against another feeling which his pride suggests that you do not deserve. O, I forgot to say that he is a Mr Neigh, a nephew of Mr Doncastle's, who lives at ease about Piccadilly and Pall Mall, and has a few acres somewhere – but I don't know much of him. The worst of my position now is that I excite this superficial interest in many people and a deep friendship in nobody. If what all my supporters feel could be collected into the hearts of two or three they would love me better than they love themselves; but now it pervades all and operates in none.'

'But it must operate in this gentleman?'

'Well, yes – just for the present. But men in town have so many contrivances for getting out of love that you can't calculate upon keeping them in for two days together. However, it is all the same to me. There's only – but let that be.'

'What is there only?' said Picotee coaxingly.

'Only one man,' murmured Ethelberta, in much lower tones. 'I mean, whose wife I should care to be; and the very qualities I like in him will, I fear, prevent his ever being in a position to ask me.'

'Is he the man you punished the week before last by forbidding him to come?'

'Perhaps he is: but he does not want civility from me. Where there's much feeling there's little ceremony.'

'It certainly seems that he does not want civility from you to make him attentive to you,' said Picotee, stifling a sigh; 'for here is a letter in his handwriting, I believe.'

'You might have given it to me at once,' said Ethelberta, opening the envelope hastily. It contained very few sentences: they were to the effect that Christopher had received her letter forbidding him to call; that he had therefore at first resolved not to call or even see her more, since he had become such a shadow in her path. Still, as it was always best to do nothing hastily, he had on second thoughts decided to ask her to grant him a last special favour, and see him again just once, for a few minutes only that afternoon, in which he might at least say Farewell. To avoid all possibility of compromising her in anybody's eyes, he would call at half-past six, when other callers were likely to be gone, knowing that from the peculiar constitution of the household the hour would not interfere with her arrangements. There being no time for an answer, he would assume that she would see him, and keep the engagement; the request being one which could not rationally be objected to.

'There – read it!' said Ethelberta, with glad displeasure. 'Did you ever hear such audacity? Fixing a time so soon that I cannot reply, and thus making capital out of a pretended necessity, when it is really an arbitrary arrangement of his own. That's real rebellion – forcing himself into my house when I said strictly he was not to come; and then, that it cannot rationally be objected to – I don't like his "rationally".'

'Where there's much love there's little ceremony, didn't you say just now?' observed innocent Picotee.

'And where there's little love, no ceremony at all. These manners of his are dreadful, and I believe he will never improve.'

'It makes you care not a bit about him, does it not, Berta?' said Picotee hopefully.

'I don't answer for that,' said Ethelberta. 'I feel, as many others do, that a want of ceremony which is produced by abstraction of mind is no defect in a poet or musician, fatal as it may be to an ordinary man.'

'Mighty me! You soon forgive him.'

'Picotee, don't you be so quick to speak. Before I have finished, how do you know what I am going to say? I'll never tell you anything again, if you take me up so. Of course I am going to punish him at once, and make him remember that I am a lady, even if I do like him a little.'

'How do you mean to punish him?' said Picotee, with interest.

'By writing and telling him that on no account is he to come.'

'But there is not time for a letter—'

'That doesn't matter. It will show him that I did not *mean* him to come.'

At hearing the very merciful nature of the punishment, Picotee sighed without replying; and Ethelberta despatched her note. The hour of appointment drew near, and Ethelberta showed symptoms of unrest. Six o'clock struck and passed. She walked here and there for nothing, and it was plain that a dread was filling her: her letter might accidentally have had, in addition to the moral effect which she had intended, the practical effect which she did not intend, by arriving before, instead of after, his purposed visit to her, thereby stopping him in spite of all her care.

'How long are letters going to Bloomsbury?' she said suddenly.

'Two hours, Joey tells me,' replied Picotee, who had already inquired on her own private account.

'There!' exclaimed Ethelberta petulantly. 'How I dislike a man to misrepresent things! He said there was not time for a reply!'

'Perhaps he didn't know,' said Picotee, in angel tones; 'and so it happens all right, and he has got it, and he will not come after all.'

They waited and waited, but Christopher did not appear that night; the true case being that his declaration about insufficient time for a reply was merely an ingenious suggestion to her not to be so cruel as to forbid him. He was far from suspecting when the letter of denial did reach him – about an hour before the time of appointment – that it was sent by a refinement of art, of which the real intention was futility, and that but for his own misstatement it would have been carefully delayed.

The next day another letter came from the musician, decidedly short and to the point. The irate lover stated that he would not be made a fool of any longer: under any circumstances he meant to come that self-same afternoon, and should decidedly expect her to see him.

'I will not see him!' said Ethelberta. 'Why did he not call last night?'

'Because you told him not to,' said Picotee.

'Good gracious, as if a woman's words are to be translated as literally as Homer! Surely he is aware that more often that not "No" is said to a man's importunities because it is traditionally the correct modest reply, and for nothing else in the world. If all men took words as superficially as he does, we should die of decorum in shoals.'

'Ah, Berta! how could you write a letter that you did not mean should be obeyed?'

'I did in a measure mean it, although I could have shown Christian forgiveness if it had not been. Never mind; I will not see him. I'll plague my heart for the credit of my sex.'

To ensure the fulfilment of this resolve, Ethelberta determined to give way to a headache that she was beginning to be aware of, go to her room, disorganize her dress, and ruin her hair by lying down; so putting it out of her power to descend and meet Christopher on any momentary impulse.

Picotee sat in the room with her, reading, or pretending to read, and Ethelberta pretended to sleep. Christopher's knock came up the stairs, and with it the end of the farce.

'I'll tell you what,' said Ethelberta in the prompt and broadly-awake tone of one who had been concentrated on the expectation of that sound for a length of time, 'it was a mistake in me to do this! Joey will be sure to make a muddle of it.'

Joey was heard coming up the stairs. Picotee opened the door, and said, with an anxiety transcending Ethelberta's, 'Well?'

'O, will you tell Mrs Petherwin that Mr Julian says he'll wait.'

'You were not to ask him to wait,' said Ethelberta, within.

'I know that,' said Joey, 'and I didn't. He's doing that out of his own head.'

'Then let Mr Julian wait, by all means,' said Ethelberta. 'Allow him to wait if he likes, but tell him it is uncertain if I shall be able to come down.'

Joey then retired, and the two sisters remained in silence.

'I wonder if he's gone,' Ethelberta said, at the end of a long time.

'I thought you were asleep,' said Picotee. 'Shall we ask Joey? I have not heard the door close.'

Joey was summoned, and after a leisurely ascent, interspersed by various gymnastic performances over the handrail here and there, appeared again.

'He's there jest the same: he don't seem to be in no hurry at all,' said Joey.

'What is he doing?' inquired Picotee solicitously.

'O, only looking at his watch sometimes, and humming tunes,

and playing rat-a-tat-tat upon the table. He says he don't mind waiting a bit.'

'You must have made a mistake in the message,' said Ethelberta, within.

'Well, no. I am correct as a jineral thing. I jest said perhaps you would be engaged all the evening, and perhaps you wouldn't.'

When Joey had again retired, and they had waited another ten minutes, Ethelberta said, 'Picotee, do you go down and speak a few words to him. I am determined he shall not see me. You know him a little; you remember when he came to the Lodge?'

'What must I say to him?'

Ethelberta paused before replying. 'Try to find out if – if he is much grieved at not seeing me, and say – give him to understand that I will forgive him, Picotee.'

'Very well.'

'And Picotee—'

'Yes.'

'If he says he *must* see me – I think I will get up. But only if he says *must*: you remember that.'

Picotee departed on her errand. She paused on the staircase trembling, and thinking between the thrills how very far would have been the conduct of her poor slighted self from proud recalcitration had Mr Julian's gentle request been addressed to her instead of to Ethelberta; and she went some way in the painful discovery of how much more tantalizing it was to watch an envied situation that was held by another than to be out of sight of it altogether. Here was Christopher waiting to bestow love, and Ethelberta not going down to receive it: a commodity unequalled in value by any other in the whole wide world was being wantonly wasted within that very house. If she could only have stood tonight as the beloved Ethelberta, and not as the despised Picotee, how different would be this going down! Thus she went along, red and pale moving in her cheeks as in the Northern Lights* at their strongest time.

Meanwhile Christopher had sat waiting minute by minute till the evening shades grew browner, and the fire sank low. Joey, finding himself not particularly wanted upon the premises after the second inquiry, had slipped out to witness a nigger perform-ance* round the corner, and Julian began to think himself forgotten by all the household. The perception gradually cooled his emotions and enabled him to hold his hat quite steadily.

When Picotee gently thrust open the door she was surprised to find the room in darkness, the fire gone completely out, and the form of Christopher only visible by a faint patch of light, which, coming from a lamp on the opposite side of the way and falling upon the mirror, was thrown as a pale nebulosity upon his shoulder. Picotee was too flurried at sight of the familiar outline to know what to do, and, instead of going or calling for a light, she mechanically advanced into the room. Christopher did not turn or move in any way, and then she perceived that he had begun to doze in his chair.

Instantly, with the precipitancy of the timorous, she said, 'Mr Julian!' and touched him on the shoulder – murmuring then, 'O, I beg pardon, I – I will get a light.'

Christopher's consciousness returned, and his first act, before rising, was to exclaim, in a confused manner, 'Ah – you have come – thank you, Berta!' then impulsively to seize her hand, as it hung beside his head, and kiss it passionately. He stood up, still holding her fingers.

Picotee gasped out something, but was completely deprived of articulate utterance, and in another moment, being unable to control herself at this sort of first meeting with the man she had gone through fire and water to be near, and more particularly by the overpowering kiss upon her hand, burst into hysterical sobbing. Julian, in his inability to imagine so much emotion – or at least the exhibition of it – in Ethelberta, gently drew Picotee further forward by the hand he held, and utilized the solitary spot of light from the mirror by making it fall upon her face. Recognizing the childish features, he at once, with an exclamation, dropped her hand and started back. Being in point of fact a complete bundle of nerves and nothing else, his thin figure shook like a harp-string in painful excitement at a contretemps which would scarcely have quickened the pulse of an ordinary man.

Poor Picotee, feeling herself in the wind of a civil d——,* started back also, sobbing more than ever. It was a little too much that the first result of his discovery of the mistake should be absolute repulse. She leant against the mantelpiece, when Julian, much bewildered at her superfluity of emotion, assisted her to a seat in sheer humanity. But Christopher was by no means pleased when he again thought round the circle of circumstances.

'How could you allow such an absurd thing to happen?' he said, in a stern, though trembling voice. 'You knew I might mistake. I had no idea you were in the house: I thought you were miles away, at Sandbourne or somewhere! But I see: it is just done for a joke, ha-ha!'

This made Picotee rather worse still. 'O-O-O-O!' she replied, in the tone of pouring from a bottle. 'What shall I do-o-o-o! It is – not done for a – joke at all-l-l-l!'

'Not done for a joke? Then never mind – don't cry, Picotee. What was it done for, I wonder?'

Picotee, mistaking the purport of his inquiry, imagined him to refer to her arrival in the house, quite forgetting, in her guilty sense of having come on his account, that he would have no right or thought of asking questions about a natural visit to a sister, and she said: 'When you – went away from – Sandbourne, I – I – I didn't know what to do, and then I ran away, and came here, and then Ethelberta – was angry with me; but she says I may stay; but she doesn't know – that I know you, and how we used to meet along the road every morning – and I am afraid to tell her – O, what shall I do!'

'Never mind it,' said Christopher, a sense of the true state of her case dawning upon him with unpleasant distinctness, and bringing some irritation at his awkward position; though it was impossible to be long angry with a girl who had not reasoning foresight enough to perceive that doubtful pleasure and certain pain must be the result of any meeting whilst hearts were at cross purposes in this way.

'Where is your sister?' he asked.

'She wouldn't come down, unless she *must*,' said Picotee. 'You have vexed her, and she has a headache besides that, and I came instead.'

'So that I mightn't be wasted altogether. Well, it's a strange business between the three of us. I have heard of one-sided love, and reciprocal love, and all sorts, but this is my first experience of a concatenated affection. You follow me, I follow Ethelberta, and she follows – Heaven knows who!'

'Mr Ladywell!' said the mortified Picotee.

'Good God, if I didn't think so!' said Christopher, feeling to the soles of his feet like a man in a legitimate drama.*

'No, no, no!' said the frightened girl hastily. 'I am not sure it is Mr Ladywell. That's altogether a mistake of mine!'

'Ah, yes, you want to screen her,' said Christopher, with a withering smile at the spot of light. 'Very sisterly, doubtless; but none of that will do for me. I am too old a bird* by far – by very far! Now are you sure she does not love Ladywell?'

'Yes!'

'Well, perhaps I blame her wrongly. She may have some little good faith – a woman has, here and there. How do you know she does not love Ladywell?'

'Because she would prefer Mr Neigh to him, any day.'

'Ha!'

'No, no – you mistake, sir – she doesn't love either at all – Ethelberta doesn't. I meant that she cannot love Mr Ladywell because he stands lower in her opinion than Mr Neigh, and him she certainly does not care for. She only loves you. If you only knew how true she is you wouldn't be so suspicious about her, and I wish I had not come here – yes, I do!'

'I cannot tell what to think of it. Perhaps I don't know much of this world after all, or what girls will do. But you don't excuse her to me, Picotee.'

Before this time Picotee had been simulating haste in getting a light; but in her dread of appearing visibly to Christopher's eyes, and showing him the precise condition of her tear-stained face, she put it off moment after moment, and stirred the fire, in hope that the faint illumination thus produced would be sufficient to save her from the charge of stupid conduct as entertainer.

Fluttering about on the horns of this dilemma, she was greatly relieved when Christopher, who read her difficulty, and the general painfulness of the situation, said that since Ethelberta was really suffering from a headache he would not wish to disturb her till tomorrow, and went off downstairs and into the street without further ceremony.

Meanwhile other things had happened upstairs. No sooner had Picotee left her sister's room, than Ethelberta thought it would after all have been much better if she had gone down herself to speak to this admirably persistent lover. Was she not drifting somewhat into the character of coquette, even if her ground of offence – a word of Christopher's about somebody else's mean parentage, which was spoken in utter forgetfulness of her own position, but had wounded her to the quick nevertheless – was to some extent a tenable one? She knew what facilities in suffering Christopher always showed; how a touch to other people was a blow to him, a blow to them his deep wound, although he took such pains to look stolid and unconcerned under those inflictions, and tried to smile as if he had no feelings whatever. It would be more generous to go down to him, and be kind. She jumped up with that alertness which comes so spontaneously at those sweet bright times when desire and duty run hand in hand.

She hastily set her hair and dress in order – not such matchless order as she could have wished them to be in, but time was precious – and descended the stairs. When on the point of pushing open the drawing-room door, which wanted about an inch of being closed, she was astounded to discover that the room was in total darkness, and still more to hear Picotee sobbing inside. To retreat again was the only action she was capable of at that moment: the clash between this picture and the anticipated scene of Picotee and Christopher sitting in frigid propriety at opposite sides of a well-lighted room was too great. She flitted upstairs again with the least possible rustle, and flung herself down on the couch as before, panting with excitement at the new knowledge that had come to her.

There was only one possible construction to be put upon this in Ethelberta's rapid mind, and that approximated to the true one. She had known for some time that Picotee once had a lover, or something akin to it, and that he had disappointed her in a way which had never been told. No stranger, save in the capacity of the one beloved, could wound a woman sufficiently to make her weep, and it followed that Christopher was the man of Picotee's choice. As Ethelberta recalled the conversations, conclusion after conclusion came like pulsations in an aching head. 'O, how did it happen, and who is to blame?' she exclaimed. 'I cannot doubt his faith, and I cannot doubt hers; and yet how can I keep doubting them both?'

It was characteristic of Ethelberta's jealous motherly guard over her young sisters that, amid these contending inquiries, her foremost feeling was less one of hope for her own love than of championship for Picotee's.

Ethelberta's House (*continued*)

23

Picotee was heard on the stairs: Ethelberta covered her face.

'Is he waiting?' she said faintly, on finding that Picotee did not begin to speak.

'No; he is gone,' said Picotee.

'Ah, why is that?' came quickly from under the handkerchief. 'He has forgotten me – that's what it is!'

'O no, he has not!' said Picotee, just as bitterly.

Ethelberta had far too much heroism to let much in this strain escape her, though her sister was prepared to go any lengths in the same. 'I suppose,' continued Ethelberta, in the quiet way of one who had only a headache the matter with her, 'that he remembered you after the meeting at Anglebury?'

'Yes, he remembered me.'

'Did you tell me you had seen him before that time?'

'I had seen him at Sandbourne. I don't think I told you.'

'At whose house did you meet him?'

'At nobody's. I only saw him sometimes,' replied Picotee, in great distress.

Ethelberta, though of all women most miserable, was brimming with compassion for the throbbing girl so nearly related to her, in whom she continually saw her own weak points without the counterpoise of her strong ones. But it was necessary to repress herself awhile: the intended ways of her life were blocked and broken up by this jar of interests, and she wanted time to ponder new plans. 'Picotee, I would rather be alone now, if you don't mind,' she said. 'You need not leave me any light; it makes my eyes ache, I think.'

Picotee left the room. But Ethelberta had not long been alone and in darkness when somebody gently opened the door, and entered without a candle.

'Berta,' said the soft voice of Picotee again, 'may I come in?'

'O yes,' said Ethelberta. 'Has everything gone right with the house this evening?'

'Yes; and Gwendoline went out just now to buy a few things, and she is going to call round upon father when he has got his dinner cleared away.'

'I hope she will not stay and talk to the other servants. Some day she will let drop something or other before father can stop her.'

'O Berta!' said Picotee, close beside her. She was kneeling in front of the couch, and now flinging her arm across Ethelberta's shoulder and shaking violently, she pressed her forehead against her sister's temple, and breathed out upon her cheek:

'I came in again to tell you something which I ought to have told you just now, and I have come to say it at once because I am afraid I shan't be able to tomorrow. Mr Julian was the young man I spoke to you of a long time ago, and I should have told you all about him, but you said he was your young man too, and – and I didn't know what to do then, because I thought it was wrong in me to love your young man; and Berta, he didn't mean me to love him at all, but I did it myself, though I did not want to do it, either; it would come to me! And I didn't know he belonged to you when I began it, or I would not have let him meet me at all; no I wouldn't!'

'Meet you? You don't mean to say he used to meet you?' whispered Ethelberta.

'Yes,' said Picotee; 'but he could not help it. We used to meet on the road, and there was no other road unless I had gone ever so far round. But it is worse than that, Berta! That was why I couldn't bide in Sandbourne, and, and ran away to you up here; it was not because I wanted to see you, Berta, but because I – I wanted –'

'Yes, yes, I know,' said Ethelberta hurriedly.

'And then when I went downstairs he mistook me for you for a moment, and that caused – a confusion!'

'O, well, it does not much matter,' said Ethelberta, kissing Picotee soothingly. 'You ought not of course to have come to London in such a manner; but, since you have come, we will make the best of it. Perhaps it may end happily for you and for him. Who knows?'

'Then don't you want him, Berta?'

'O no; not at all!'

'What – and don't you *really* want him, Berta?' repeated Picotee, starting up.

'I would much rather he paid his addresses to you. He is not the sort of man I should wish to – think it best to marry, even if I were to marry, which I have no intention of doing at present. He calls to see me because we are old friends, but his calls do not mean anything more than that he takes an interest in me. It is not at all likely that I shall see him again! and I certainly never shall see him unless you are present.'

'That will be very nice.'

'Yes. And you will be always distant towards him, and go to leave the room when he comes, when I will call you back; but suppose we continue this tomorrow? I can tell you better then what to do.'

When Picotee had left her the second time, Ethelberta turned over upon her breast and shook in convulsive sobs which had little relationship with tears. This abandonment ended as suddenly as it had begun – not lasting more than a minute and a half altogether – and she got up in an unconsidered and unusual impulse to seek relief from the stinging sarcasm of this event – the unhappy love of Picotee – by mentioning something of it to another member of the family, her eldest sister Gwendoline, who was a woman full of sympathy.

Ethelberta descended to the kitchen, it being now about ten o'clock. The room was empty, Gwendoline not having yet returned, and Cornelia being busy about her own affairs upstairs. The French family had gone to the theatre, and the house on that account was very quiet tonight. Ethelberta sat down in the dismal place without turning up the gas, and in a few minutes admitted Gwendoline.

The round-faced country cook floundered in, untying her bonnet as she came, laying it down on a chair, and talking at the same time. 'Such a place as this London is, to be sure!' she exclaimed, turning on the gas till it whistled. 'I wish I was down in Wessex again. Lord-a-mercy, Berta, I didn't see it was you! I thought it was Cornelia. As I was saying, I thought that, after biding in this underground cellar all the week, making up messes for them French folk, and never pleasing 'em, and never shall, because I don't understand that line, I thought I would go out and see father, you know.'

'Is he very well?' said Ethelberta.

'Yes; and he is going to call round when he has time. Well, as I was a-coming home-along I thought, "Please the Lord I'll have some chippols for supper just for a plain treat," and I went round to the late greengrocer's for 'em; and do you know they sweared me down that they hadn't got such things as chippols in the shop, and had never heard of 'em in their lives. At last I

said, "Why, how can you tell me such a brazen story? – here
they be, heaps of 'em!" It made me so vexed that I came away
there and then, and wouldn't have one – no, not at a gift.'

'They call them young onions here,' said Ethelberta quietly;
'you must always remember that. But, Gwendoline, I wanted—'

Ethelberta felt sick at heart, and stopped. She had come down
on the wings of an impulse to unfold her trouble about Picotee
to her hard-headed and much older sister, less for advice than
to get some heart-ease by interchange of words; but alas, she
could proceed no further. The wretched homeliness of Gwendoline's mind seemed at this particular juncture to be absolutely
intolerable, and Ethelberta was suddenly convinced that to
involve Gwendoline in any such discussion would simply be
increasing her own burden, and adding worse confusion to her
sister's already confused existence.

'What were you going to say?' said the honest and unsuspect-
ing Gwendoline.

'I will put it off until tomorrow,' Ethelberta murmured
gloomily; 'I have a bad headache, and I am afraid I cannot stay
with you after all.'

As she ascended the stairs, Ethelberta ached with an added
pain not much less than the primary one which had brought her
down. It was that old sense of disloyalty to her class and kin by
feeling as she felt now which caused the pain, and there was no
escaping it. Gwendoline would have gone to the ends of the
earth for her: she could not confide a thought to Gwendoline!

'If she only knew of that unworthy feeling of mine, how she
would grieve,' said Ethelberta miserably.

She next went up to the servants' bedrooms, and to where
Cornelia slept. On Ethelberta's entrance Cornelia looked up
from a perfect wonder of a bonnet, which she held in her hands.
At sight of Ethelberta the look of keen interest in her work
changed to one of gaiety.

'I am so glad – I was just coming down,' Cornelia said in a
whisper; whenever they spoke as relations in this house it was
in whispers. 'Now, how do you think this bonnet will do? May
I come down, and see how I look in your big glass?' She clapped
the bonnet upon her head. 'Won't it do beautiful for Sunday
afternoon?'

'It looks very attractive, as far as I can see by this light,' said
Ethelberta. 'But is it not rather too brilliant in colour – blue and

red together, like that? Remember, as I often tell you, people in town never wear such bright contrasts as they do in the country.'

'O Berta!' said Cornelia, in a deprecating tone; 'don't object. If there's one thing I do glory in it is a nice flare-up about my head o' Sundays – of course if the family's not in mourning, I mean.' But, seeing that Ethelberta did not smile, she turned the subject, and added docilely: 'Did you come up for me to do anything? I will put off finishing my bonnet if I am wanted.'

'I was going to talk to you about family matters, and Picotee,' said Ethelberta. 'But, as you are busy, and I have a headache, I will put it off till tomorrow.'

Cornelia seemed decidedly relieved, for family matters were far from attractive at the best of times; and Ethelberta went down to the next floor, and entered her mother's room.

After a short conversation Mrs Chickerel said, 'You say you want to ask me something?'

'Yes: but nothing of importance, mother. I was thinking about Picotee, and what would be the best thing to do—'

'Ah, well you may, Berta. I am so uneasy about this life you have led us into, and full of fear that your plans may break down; if they do, whatever will become of us? I know you are doing your best; but I cannot help thinking that the coming to London and living with you was wild and rash, and not well weighed afore we set about it. You should have counted the cost first, and not advised it. If you break down, and we are all discovered living so queer and unnatural, right in the heart of the aristocracy, we should be the laughing-stock of the country: it would kill me, and ruin us all – utterly ruin us!'

'O mother, I know all that so well!' exclaimed Ethelberta, tears of anguish filling her eyes. 'Don't depress me more than I depress myself by such fears, or you will bring about the very thing we strive to avoid! My only chance is in keeping in good spirits; and why don't you try to help me a little by taking a brighter view of things?'

'I know I ought to, my dear girl, but I cannot. I do so wish that I never let you tempt me and the children away from the Lodge. I cannot think why I allowed myself to be so persuaded – cannot think! You are not to blame – it is I. I am much older than you, and ought to have known better than listen to such a scheme. This undertaking seems too big – the bills frighten me. I have never been used to such wild adventure, and I can't sleep at night for fear that your tale-telling will go wrong, and we shall all be exposed and shamed. A story-teller seems such an impossible castle-in-the-air sort of a trade for getting a living by – I cannot think how ever you came to dream of such an unheard-of thing.'

'But it is *not* a castle in the air, and it *does* get a living!' said Ethelberta, her lip quivering.

'Well, yes, while it is just a new thing; but I am afraid it cannot last – that's what I fear. People will find you out as one of a family of servants, and their pride will be stung at having gone to hear your romancing; then they will go no more, and what will happen to us and the poor little ones?'

'We must all scatter again!'

'If we could get as we were once, I wouldn't mind that. But we shall have lost our character as simple country folk who know nothing, which are the only class of poor people that squires will give any help to; and I much doubt if the girls would get places after such a discovery – it would be so awkward and unheard-of.'

'Well, all I can say is,' replied Ethelberta, 'that I will do my best. All that I have is theirs and yours as much as mine, and these arrangements are simply on their account. I don't like my relations being my servants; but if they did not work for me, they would have to work for others, and my service is much lighter and pleasanter than any other lady's would be for them, so the advantages are worth the risk. If I stood alone, I would go and hide my head in any hole, and care no more about the world and its ways. I wish I was well out of it, and at the bottom of a quiet grave – anybody might have the world for me then! But don't let me disturb you longer; it is getting late.'

Ethelberta then wished her mother good-night, and went away. To attempt confidences on such an ethereal matter as love was now absurd; her hermit spirit was doomed to dwell apart* as usual; and she applied herself to deep thinking without aid and alone. Not only was there Picotee's misery to disperse; it became imperative to consider how best to overpass a more general catastrophe.

Mrs Chickerel, in deploring the risks of their present speculative
mode of life, was far from imagining that signs of the foul future
so much dreaded were actually apparent to Ethelberta at the
time the lament was spoken. Hence the daughter's uncommon
sensitiveness to prophecy. It was as if a dead-reckoner* poring
over his chart should predict breakers ahead to one who already
beheld them.

That her story-telling would prove so attractive Ethelberta
had not ventured to expect for a moment; that having once
proved attractive there should be any falling-off until such time
had elapsed as would enable her to harvest some solid fruit was
equally a surprise. Future expectations are often based without
hesitation upon one happy accident, when the only similar
condition remaining to subsequent sets of circumstances is that
the same person forms the centre of them. Her situation was so
peculiar, and so unlike that of most public people, that there
was hardly an argument explaining this triumphant opening
which could be used in forecasting the close; unless, indeed,
more strategy were employed in the conduct of the campaign
than Ethelberta seemed to show at present.

There was no denying that she commanded less attention than
at first: the audience had lessened, and, judging by appearances,
might soon be expected to be decidedly thin. In excessive
lowness of spirit, Ethelberta translated these signs with the bias
that a lingering echo of her mother's dismal words naturally
induced, reading them as conclusive evidence that her adventure
had been chimerical in its birth. Yet it was very far less
conclusive than she supposed. Public interest might without
doubt have been renewed after a due interval, some of the
falling-off being only an accident of the season. Her novelties
had been hailed with pleasure, the rather that their freshness
tickled than that their intrinsic merit was appreciated; and, like
many inexperienced dispensers of a unique charm, Ethelberta,
by bestowing too liberally and too frequently, was destroying

the very element upon which its popularity depended. Her entertainment had been good in its conception, and partly good in its execution; yet her success had but little to do with that goodness. Indeed, what might be called its badness in a histrionic sense – that is, her look sometimes of being out of place, the sight of a beautiful woman on a platform, revealing tender airs of domesticity which showed her to belong by character to a quiet drawing-room – had been primarily an attractive feature. But alas, custom was staling this by improving her up to the mark of an utter impersonator, thereby eradicating the pretty abashments of a poetess out of her sphere; and more than one well-wisher who observed Ethelberta from afar feared that it might some day come to be said of her that she had

> Enfeoffed herself to popularity:
> That, being daily swallowed by men's eyes,
> They surfeited with honey, and began
> To loathe the taste of sweetness, whereof a little
> More than a little is by much too much.*

But this in its extremity was not quite yet.

We discover her one day, a little after this time, sitting before a table strewed with accounts and bills from different tradesmen of the neighbourhood, which she examined with a pale face, collecting their totals on a blank sheet. Picotee came into the room, but Ethelberta took no notice whatever of her. The younger sister, who subsisted on scraps of notice and favour, like a dependent animal, even if these were only an occasional glance of the eye, could not help saying at last, 'Berta, how silent you are. I don't think you know I am in the room.'

'I did not observe you,' said Ethelberta. 'I am very much engaged: these bills have to be paid.'

'What, and cannot we pay them?' said Picotee, in vague alarm.

'O yes, I can pay them. The question is, how long shall I be able to do it?'

'That is sad; and we are going on so nicely, too. It is not true that you have really decided to leave off story-telling now the people don't crowd to hear it as they did?'

'I think I shall leave off.'

'And begin again next year?'

'That is very doubtful.'

'I'll tell you what you might do,' said Picotee, her face kindling with a sense of great originality. 'You might travel about to country towns and tell your story splendidly.'

'A man in my position might perhaps do it with impunity; but I could not without losing ground in other domains. A woman may drive to Mayfair from her house in Exonbury Crescent, and speak from a platform there, and be supposed to do it as an original way of amusing herself; but when it comes to starring in the provinces she establishes herself as a woman of a different breed and habit. I wish I were a man! I would give up this house, advertise it to be let furnished, and sally forth with confidence. But I am driven to think of other ways to manage than that.'

Picotee fell into a conjectural look, but could not guess.

'The way of marriage,' said Ethelberta. 'Otherwise perhaps the poetess may live to become what Dryden called himself when he got old and poor – a rent-charge on Providence* ... Yes, I must try that way,' she continued, with a sarcasm towards people out of hearing. 'I must buy a "Peerage" for one thing, and a "Baronetage" and a "House of Commons",* and a "Landed Gentry",* and learn what people are about me. I must go to Doctors' Commons* and read up wills of the parents of any likely gudgeons* I may know. I must get a Herald* to invent an escutcheon* of my family, and throw a genealogical tree into the bargain in consideration of my taking a few second-hand heirlooms of a pawnbroking friend of his. I must get up sham ancestors, and find out some notorious name to start my pedigree from. It does not matter what his character was; either villain or martyr will do, provided that he lived five hundred years ago. It would be considered far more creditable to make good my descent from Satan in the age when he went to and fro on the earth* than from a ministering angel* under Victoria.'

'But, Berta, you are not going to marry any stranger who may turn up?' said Picotee, who had creeping sensations of dread when Ethelberta talked like this.

'I had no such intention. But, having once put my hand to the plough, how shall I turn back?'

'You might marry Mr Ladywell,' said Picotee, who preferred to look at things in the concrete.

'Yes, marry him villainously; in cold blood, without a moment to prepare himself.'

'Ah, you won't!'

'I am not so sure about that. I have brought mother and the children to town against her judgment and against my father's; they gave way to my opinion as to one who from superior education has larger knowledge of the world than they. I must prove my promises, even if Heaven should fall upon me for it, or what a miserable future will theirs be! We must not be poor in London. Poverty in the country is a sadness, but poverty in town is a horror. There is something not without grandeur in the thought of starvation on an open mountain or in a wide wood, and your bones lying there to bleach in the pure sun and rain; but a back garret in a rookery,* and the other starvers in the room insisting on keeping the window shut – anything to deliver us from that!'

'How gloomy you can be, Berta! It will never be so dreadful. Why, I can take in plain sewing, and you can do translations, and mother can knit stockings, and so on. How much longer will this house be yours?'

'Two years. If I keep it longer than that I shall have to pay rent at the rate of three hundred a year. The Petherwin estate provides me with it till then, which will be the end of Lady Petherwin's term.'

'I see it; and you ought to marry before the house is gone, if you mean to marry high,' murmured Picotee, in an inadequate voice, as one confronted by a world so tragic that any hope of her assisting therein was out of the question.

It was not long after this exposition of the family affairs that Christopher called upon them; but Picotee was not present, having gone to think of superhuman work on the spur of Ethelberta's awakening talk. There was something new in the way in which Ethelberta received the announcement of his name; passion had to do with it, so had circumspection; the latter most, for the first time since their reunion.

'I am going to leave this part of England,' said Christopher, after a few gentle preliminaries. 'I was one of the applicants for the post of assistant-organist at Melchester Cathedral when it became vacant, and I find I am likely to be chosen, through the interest of one of my father's friends.'

'I congratulate you.'

'No, Ethelberta, it is not worth that. I did not originally mean to follow this course at all; but events seemed to point to it in the absence of a better.'

'I too am compelled to follow a course I did not originally mean to take.' After saying no more for a few moments, she added, in a tone of sudden openness, a richer tincture creeping up her cheek, 'I want to put a question to you boldly – not exactly a question – a thought. Have you considered whether the relations between us which have lately prevailed are – are the best for you – and for me?'

'I know what you mean,' said Christopher, hastily anticipating all that she might be going to say; 'and I am glad you have given me the opportunity of speaking upon that subject. It has been very good and considerate in you to allow me to share your society so frequently as you have done since I have been in town, and to think of you as an object to exist for and strive for. But I ought to have remembered that, since you have nobody at your side to look after your interests, it behoved me to be doubly careful. In short, Ethelberta, I am not in a position to marry, nor can I discern when I shall be, and I feel it would be an injustice to ask you to be bound in any way to one lower and less talented than you. You cannot, from what you say, think it desirable that the engagement should continue. I have no right to ask you to be my betrothed, without having a near prospect of making you my wife. I don't mind saying this straight out – I have no fear that you will doubt my love; thank Heaven, you know what that is well enough! However, as things are, I wish you to know that I cannot conscientiously put in a claim upon your attention.'

A second meaning was written in Christopher's look, though he scarcely uttered it. A woman so delicately poised upon the social globe could not in honour be asked to wait for a lover who was unable to set bounds to the waiting period. Yet he had privily dreamed of an approach to that position – an unreserved, ideally perfect declaration from Ethelberta that time and practical issues were nothing to her; that she would stand as fast without material hopes as with them; that love was to be an end with her henceforth, having utterly ceased to be a means. Therefore this surreptitious hope of his, founded on no reasonable expectation, was like a guilty thing surprised* when Ethelberta answered, with a predominance of judgment over passion still greater than before:

'It is unspeakably generous in you to put it all before me so nicely, Christopher. I think infinitely more of you for being so unreserved, especially since I too have been thinking much on the indefiniteness of the days to come. We are not numbered among the blest few who can afford to trifle with the time. Yet to agree to anything like a positive parting will be quite unnecessary. You did not mean that, did you? for it is harsh if you did.' Ethelberta smiled kindly as she said this, as much as to say that she was far from really upbraiding him. 'Let it be only that we will see each other less. We will bear one another in mind as deeply attached friends if not as definite lovers, and keep up friendly remembrances of a sort which, come what may, will never have to be ended by any painful process termed breaking off. Different persons, different natures; and it may be that marriage would not be the most favourable atmosphere for our old affection to prolong itself in. When do you leave London?'

The disconnected query seemed to be subjoined to disperse the crude effect of what had gone before.

'I hardly know,' murmured Christopher. 'I suppose I shall not call here again.'

Whilst they were silent somebody entered the room softly, and they turned to discover Picotee.

'Come here, Picotee,' said Ethelberta.

Picotee came with an abashed bearing to where the other two were standing, and looked down steadfastly.

'Mr Julian is going away,' she continued, with determined firmness. 'He will not see us again for a long time.' And Ethelberta added, in a lower tone, though still in the unflinching manner of one who had set herself to say a thing, and would say it – 'He is not to be definitely engaged to me any longer. We are not thinking of marrying, you know, Picotee. It is best that we should not.'

'Perhaps it is,' said Christopher hurriedly, taking up his hat. 'Let me now wish you good-bye; and, of course, you will always know where I am, and how to find me.'

It was a tender time. He inclined forward that Ethelberta might give him her hand, which she did; whereupon their eyes met. Mastered by an impelling instinct she had not reckoned with, Ethelberta presented her cheek. Christopher kissed it faintly. Tears were in Ethelberta's eyes now, and she was heartfull of many emotions. Placing her arm round Picotee's waist, who had never lifted her eyes from the carpet, she drew the slight girl forward, and whispered quickly to him – 'Kiss her, too. She is my sister, and I am yours.'

It seemed all right and natural to their respective moods and the tone of the moment that free old Wessex manners should prevail, and Christopher stooped and dropped upon Picotee's cheek likewise such a farewell kiss as he had imprinted upon Ethelberta's.

'Care for us both equally!' said Ethelberta.

'I will,' said Christopher, scarcely knowing what he said.

When he had reached the door of the room, he looked back and saw the two sisters standing as he had left them, and equally tearful. Ethelberta at once said, in a last futile struggle against letting him go altogether, and with thoughts of her sister's heart:

'I think that Picotee might correspond with Faith; don't you, Mr Julian?'

'My sister would much like to do so,' said he.

'And you would like it too, would you not, Picotee?'

'O yes,' she replied. 'And I can tell them all about you.'

'Then it shall be so, if Miss Julian will.' She spoke in a settled way, as if something intended had been set in train; and Christopher having promised for his sister, he went out of the house with a parting smile of misgiving.

He could scarcely believe as he walked along that those late words, yet hanging in his ears, had really been spoken, that still visible scene enacted. He could not even recollect for a minute or two how the final result had been produced. Did he himself first enter upon the long-looming theme, or did she? Christopher had been so nervously alive to the urgency of setting before the hard-striving woman a clear outline of himself, his surroundings and his fears, that he fancied the main impulse to this consummation had been his, notwithstanding that a faint initiative had come from Ethelberta. All had completed itself quickly, unceremoniously, and easily. Ethelberta had let him go a second time; yet on foregoing mornings and evenings, when contemplating the necessity of some such explanation, it had seemed that nothing less than Atlantean* force could overpower their mutual gravitation towards each other.

On his reaching home Faith was not in the house, and, in the restless state which demands something to talk at, the musician went off to find her, well knowing her haunt at this time of the day. He entered the spiked and gilded gateway of the Museum hard by, turned to the wing devoted to sculptures, and descended to a particular basement room, which was lined with bas-reliefs from Nineveh.* The place was cool, silent, and soothing; it was empty, save of a little figure in black, that was standing with its face to the wall in an innermost nook. This spot was Faith's own temple; here, among these deserted antiques, Faith was always happy. Christopher looked on at her for some time before she noticed him, and dimly perceived how vastly differed her homely suit and unstudied contour – painfully unstudied to fastidious eyes – from Ethelberta's well-arranged draperies, even from Picotee's clever bits of ribbon, by which she made herself look pretty out of nothing at all. Yet this negligence was his sister's essence; without it she would have been a spoilt product. She had no outer world, and her rusty black was as appropriate to Faith's unseen courses as were Ethelberta's correct lights and shades to her more prominent career.

'Look, Kit,' said Faith, as soon as she knew who was approaching. 'This is a thing I never learnt before; this person is really Sennacherib,* sitting on his throne; and these with fluted beards and hair like plough-furrows, and fingers with no bones in them, are his warriors – really carved at the time, you know. Only just think that this is not imagined of Assyria, but done in Assyrian times by Assyrian hands. Don't you feel as if you were actually in Nineveh; that as we now walk between these slabs, so walked Ninevites between them once?'

'Yes . . . Faith, it is all over. Ethelberta and I have parted.'

'Indeed. And so my plan is to think of verses in the Bible about Sennacherib and his doings, which resemble these; this verse, for instance, I remember: "Now in the fourteenth year of King Hezekiah did Sennacherib, King of Assyria, come up against all the fenced cities of Judah and took them. And Hezekiah, King of Judah, sent to the King of Assyria to Lachish," and so on. Well, there it actually is, you see. There's Sennacherib, and there's Lachish. Is it not glorious to think that this is a picture done at the time of those very events?'

'Yes. We did not quarrel this time, Ethelberta and I. If I may so put it, it is worse than quarrelling. We felt it was no use going on any longer, and so – Come, Faith, hear what I say, or else tell me that you won't hear, and that I may as well save my breath!'

'Yes, I will really listen,' she said, fluttering her eyelids in her concern at having been so abstracted, and excluding Sennacherib there and then from Christopher's affairs by the first settlement of her features to a present-day aspect, and her eyes upon his face. 'You said you had seen Ethelberta. Yes, and what did she say?'

'Was there ever anybody so provoking! Why, I have just told you!'

'Yes, yes; I remember now. You have parted. The subject is too large for me to know all at once what I think of it, and you must give me time, Kit. Speaking of Ethelberta reminds me of what I have done. I just looked into the Academy* this morning – I thought I would surprise you by telling you about it. And what do you think I saw? Ethelberta – in the picture painted by Mr Ladywell.'

'It is never hung?' said he, feeling that they were at one as to a topic at last.

'Yes. And the subject is an Elizabethan knight parting from a lady of the same period – the words explaining the picture being –

> "Farewell! thou art too dear for my possessing,
> And like enough thou know'st thy estimate."*

The lady is Ethelberta, to the shade of a hair – her living face; and the knight is—'

'Not Ladywell?'

'I think so; I am not sure.'

'No wonder I am dismissed! And yet she hates him. Well, come along, Faith. Women allow strange liberties in these days.'

Ethelberta was a firm believer in the kindly effects of artistic education upon the masses. She held that defilement of mind often arose from ignorance of eye; and her philanthropy being, by the simple force of her situation, of that sort which lingers in the neighbourhood of home, she concentrated her efforts in this kind upon Sol and Dan. Accordingly, the Academy exhibition having now just opened, she ordered the brothers to appear in their best clothes at the entrance to Burlington House just after noontide on the Saturday of the first week, this being the only day and hour at which they could attend without 'losing a half',* and therefore it was necessary to put up with the inconvenience of arriving at a crowded and enervating time.

When Ethelberta was set down in the quadrangle she perceived the faithful pair, big as the Zamzummims* of old time, standing like sentinels in the particular corner that she had named to them: for Sol and Dan would as soon have attempted petty larceny as broken faith with their admired lady-sister Ethelberta. They welcomed her with a painfully lavish exhibition of large new gloves, and chests covered with broad triangular areas of padded blue silk, occupying the position that the shirt-front had occupied in earlier days, and supposed to be lineally descended from the tie of a neckerchief.

The dress of their sister for today was exactly that of a respectable workman's relative who had no particular ambition in the matter of fashion – a black stuff gown, a plain bonnet to match. A veil she wore for obvious reasons: her face was getting well known in London, and it had already appeared at the private view in an uncovered state, when it was scrutinized more than the paintings around. But now homely and useful labour was her purpose.

Catalogue in hand she took the two brothers through the galleries, teaching them in whispers as they walked, and occasionally correcting them – first, for too reverential a bearing towards the well-dressed crowd, among whom they persisted in walking with their hats in their hands and with the contrite bearing of meek people in church; and, secondly, for a tendency which they too often showed towards straying from the contemplation of the pictures as art to indulge in curious speculations on the intrinsic nature of the delineated subject, the gilding of the frames, the construction of the skylights overhead, or admiration for the bracelets, lockets, and lofty eloquence of persons around them.

'Now,' said Ethelberta, in a warning whisper, 'we are coming near the picture which was partly painted from myself. And, Dan, when you see it, don't you exclaim "Hullo!" or "That's Berta to a T," or anything at all. It would not matter were it not dangerous for me to be noticed here today. I see several people who would recognize me on the least provocation.'

'Not a word,' said Dan. 'Don't you be afeard about that. I feel that I baint upon my own ground today; and wouldn't do anything to cause an upset, drown me if I would. Would you, Sol?'

In this temper they all pressed forward, and Ethelberta could not but be gratified at the reception of Ladywell's picture, though it was accorded by critics not very profound. It was an operation of some minutes to get exactly opposite, and when side by side the three stood there they overheard the immediate reason of the pressure. 'Farewell, thou art too dear for my possessing' had been lengthily discoursed upon that morning by the Coryphæus* of popular opinion; and the spirit having once been poured out sons and daughters could prophesy.* But, in truth, Ladywell's work, if not emphatically original, was happily centred on a middle stratum of taste, and apart from this adventitious help commanded, and deserved to commend, a wide area of appreciation.

While they were standing here in the very heart of the throng Ethelberta's ears were arrested by two male voices behind her, whose words formed a novel contrast to those of the other speakers around.

'Some men, you see, with extravagant expectations of themselves, coolly get them gratified, while others hope rationally and are disappointed. Luck, that's what it is. And the more easily a man takes life the more persistently does luck follow him.'

'Of course; because, if he's industrious he does not want luck's assistance. Natural laws will help him instead.'

'Well, if it is true that Ladywell has painted a good picture he has done it by an exhaustive process. He has painted every possible bad one till nothing more of that sort is left for him. You know what lady's face served as the original to this, I suppose?'

'Mrs Petherwin's, I hear.'

'Yes, Mrs Alfred Neigh that's to be.'

'What, that elusive fellow caught at last?'

'So it appears; but she herself is hardly so well secured as yet, it seems, though he takes the uncertainty as coolly as possible. I knew nothing about it till he introduced the subject as we were standing here on Monday, and said, in an off-hand way, "I mean to marry that lady." I asked him how. "Easily," he said; "I will have her if there are a hundred at her heels." You will understand that this was quite in confidence.'

'Of course, of course.' Then there was a slight laugh, and the companions proceeded to other gossip.

Ethelberta, calm and compressed in manner, sidled along to extricate herself, not daring to turn round, and Dan and Sol followed, till they were all clear of the spot. The brothers, who had heard the words equally well with Ethelberta, made no remark to her upon them, assuming that they referred to some peculiar system of courtship adopted in high life, with which they had rightly no concern.

Ethelberta ostensibly continued her business of tutoring the young workmen just as before, though every emotion in her had been put on the alert by this discovery. She had known that Neigh admired her; yet his presumption in uttering such a remark as he was reported to have uttered, confidentially or otherwise, nearly took away her breath. Perhaps it was not altogether disagreeable to have her breath so taken away.

'I mean to marry that lady.' She whispered the words to herself twenty times in the course of the afternoon. Sol and Dan were left considerably longer to their private perceptions of the false and true in art than they had been earlier in the day.

When she reached home Ethelberta was still far-removed in her reflections; and it was noticed afterwards that about this time in her career her openness of manner entirely deserted her. She mostly was silent as to her thoughts, and she wore an air of unusual stillness. It was the silence and stillness of a starry sky, where all is force and motion. This deep undecipherable habit sometimes suggested, though it did not reveal, Ethelberta's busy brain to her sisters, and they said to one another, 'I cannot think what's coming to Berta: she is not so nice as she used to be.'

The evening under notice was passed desultorily enough after the discovery of Neigh's self-assured statement. Among other things that she did after dark, while still musingly examining the probabilities of the report turning out true, was to wander to the large attic where the children slept, a frequent habit of hers at night, to learn if they were snug and comfortable. They were talking now from bed to bed, the person under discussion being herself. Herself seemed everywhere today.

'I know that she is a fairy,' Myrtle was insisting, 'because she must be, to have such pretty things in her house, and wear silk dresses such as mother and we and Picotee haven't got, and have money to give us whenever we want it.'

'Emmeline says perhaps she knows the fairy's god-mother, and is not a fairy herself, because Berta is too tall for a real fairy.'

'She must be one; for when there was a notch burnt in the hem of my pretty blue frock she said it should be gone in the morning if I would go to bed and not cry; and in the morning it was gone, and all nice and straight as new.'

Ethelberta was recalling to mind how she had sat up and repaired the damage alluded to by cutting off half an inch of the skirt all round and hemming it anew, when the breathing of the children became regular, and they fell asleep. Here were bright little minds ready for a training, which without money and influence she could never give them. The wisdom which knowledge brings, and the power which wisdom may bring, she had always assumed would be theirs in her dreams for their social elevation. By what means were these things to be ensured to them if her skill in bread-winning should fail her? Would not a well-contrived marriage be of service? She covered and tucked in one more closely, lifted another upon the pillow and straightened the soft limbs to an easy position; then sat down by the window and looked out at the flashing stars. Thoughts of Neigh's audacious statement returned again upon Ethelberta. He had said that he meant to marry her. Of what standing was the man who had uttered such an intention respecting one to whom a politic marriage had become almost a necessity of existence?

She had often heard Neigh speak indefinitely of some estate –
'my little place' he had called it – which he had purchased no
very long time ago. All she knew was that its name was
Farnfield, that it lay thirty or forty miles out of London in a
south-westerly direction, a railway station in the district bearing
the same name, so that there was probably a village or small
town adjoining. Whether the dignity of this landed property was
that of domain, farmstead, allotment, or garden-plot, Ethelberta
had not the slightest conception. She was almost certain that
Neigh never lived there, but that might signify nothing. The
exact size and value of the estate would, she mused, be curious,
interesting, and almost necessary information to her who must
become mistress of it were she to allow him to carry out his
singularly cool and crude, if tender, intention. Moreover, its
importance would afford a very good random sample of his
worldly substance throughout, from which alone, after all, could
the true spirit and worth and seriousness of his words be
apprehended. Impecuniosity may revel in unqualified vows and
brim over with confessions as blithely as a bird of May, but
such careless pleasures are not for the solvent, whose very
dreams are negotiable, and are expressed with due care
accordingly.

That Neigh had used the words she had far more than *primâ-
facie** appearances for believing. Neigh's own conduct towards
her, though peculiar rather than devoted, found in these words
alone a reasonable key. But, supposing the estate to be such a
verbal hallucination as, for instance, hers had been at Arrowthorne, when her poor, unprogressive, hopelessly impracticable
Christopher came there to visit her, and was so wonderfully
undeceived about her social standing: what a *fiasco*, and what a
cuckoo-cry would his utterances about marriage seem then.
Christopher had often told her of his expectations from 'Arrowthorne Lodge', and of the blunders that had resulted in consequence. Had not Ethelberta's affection for Christopher partaken
less of lover's passion than of old-established tutelary tenderness
she might have been reminded by this reflection of the transcendent fidelity he had shown under that trial – as severe a trial,
considering the abnormal, almost morbid, development of the
passion for position in present-day society, as can be prepared
for men who move in the ordinary, unheroic channels of life.

By the following evening the consideration of this possibility, that Neigh's position might furnish scope for such a disillusive discovery by herself as hers had afforded to Christopher, decoyed Ethelberta into a curious little scheme. She was piqued into a practical undertaking by the man who could say to his friend with such *sangfroid*,* 'I mean to marry that lady.'

Merely telling Picotee to prepare for an evening excursion, of which she was to talk to no one, Ethelberta made ready likewise, and they left the house in a cab about half-an-hour before sunset, and drove to the Waterloo Station.

With the decline and departure of the sun a fog gathered itself out of the low meadow-land that bordered the railway as they went along towards the west, stretching over it like a placid lake, till, at the end of the journey, the mist became generally pervasive, though not dense. Avoiding observation as much as they conveniently could, the two sisters walked from the long wooden shed which formed the station here, into the rheumy air and along the road to the open country. Picotee occasionally questioned Ethelberta on the object of the strange journey; she did not question closely, being satisfied that in such sure hands as Ethelberta's she was safe.

Deeming it unwise to make any inquiry just yet beyond the simple one of the way to Farnfield, Ethelberta led her companion along a newly-fenced road across a heath. In due time they came to an ornamental gate with a curved sweep of wall on each side, signifying the entrance to some enclosed property or other. Ethelberta, being quite free from any digested plan for encouraging Neigh in his resolve to wive, was startled to find a hope in her that this very respectable beginning before their eyes was the entrance to the Farnfield property: that she hoped it was nevertheless unquestionable. Just beyond lay a turnpike-house, where was dimly visible a woman in the act of putting up a shutter to the front window.

Compelled by this time to come to special questions, Ethelberta instructed Picotee to ask of this person if the place they had just passed was the entrance to Farnfield Park. The woman replied that it was. Directly she had gone indoors Ethelberta turned back again towards the park gate.

'What have we come for, Berta?' said Picotee, as she turned also.

'I'll tell you some day,' replied her sister.

It was now much past eight o'clock, and, from the nature of

the evening, dusk. The last stopping up-train was about ten, so
that half-an-hour could well be afforded for looking round.
Ethelberta went to the gate, which was found to be fastened by
a chain and padlock.

'Ah, the London season,'* she murmured.

There was a wicket at the side, and they entered. An avenue
of young fir trees three or four feet in height extended from the
gate into the mist, and down this they walked. The drive was
not in very good order, and the two women were frequently
obliged to walk on the grass to avoid the rough stones in the
carriage-way. The double line of young firs now abruptly
terminated, and the road swept lower, bending to the right,
immediately in front being a large lake, calm and silent as a
second sky. They could hear from somewhere on the margin the
purl of a weir, and around were clumps of shrubs, araucarias
and deodars* being the commonest.

Ethelberta could not resist being charmed with the repose of
the spot, and hastened on with curiosity to reach the other side
of the pool, where, by every law of manorial topography, the
mansion would be situate. The fog concealed all objects beyond
a distance of twenty yards or thereabouts, but it was nearly full
moon, and though the orb was hidden, a pale diffused light
enabled them to see objects in the foreground. Reaching the
other side of the lake the drive enlarged itself most legitimately
to a large oval, as for a sweep before a door, a pile of rockwork
standing in the midst.

But where should have been the front door of a mansion was
simply a rough rail fence, about four feet high. They drew near
and looked over.

In the enclosure, and on the site of the imaginary house, was
an extraordinary group. It consisted of numerous horses in the
last stage of decrepitude, the animals being such mere skeletons
that at first Ethelberta hardly recognized them to be horses at
all; they seemed rather to be specimens of some attenuated
heraldic animal, scarcely thick enough through the body to
throw a shadow: or enlarged castings of the fire-dog of past
times. These poor creatures were endeavouring to make a meal
from herbage so trodden and thin that scarcely a wholesome
blade remained; the little that there was consisted of the sourer
sorts common on such sandy soils, mingled with tufts of heather
and sprouting ferns.

'Why have we come here, dear Berta?' said Picotee, shuddering.

'I hardly know,' said Ethelberta.

Adjoining this enclosure was another and smaller one, formed of high boarding, within which appeared to be some sheds and outhouses. Ethelberta looked through the crevices, and saw that in the midst of the yard stood trunks of trees as if they were growing, with branches also extending, but these were sawn off at the points where they began to be flexible, no twigs or boughs remaining. Each torso was not unlike a huge hat-stand, and suspended to the pegs and prongs were lumps of some substance which at first she did not recognize; they proved to be a chronological sequel to the previous scene. Horses' skulls, ribs, quarters, legs, and other joints were hung thereon, the whole forming a huge open-air larder emitting not too sweet a smell.

But what Stygian* sound was this? There had arisen at the moment upon the mute and sleepy air a varied howling from a hundred tongues. It had burst from a spot close at hand – a low wooden building by a stream which fed the lake – and reverberated for miles. No further explanation was required.

'We are close to a kennel of hounds,' said Ethelberta, as Picotee held tightly to her arm. 'They cannot get out, so you need not fear. They have a horrid way of suddenly beginning thus at different hours of the night, for no apparent reason: though perhaps they hear us. These poor horses are waiting to be killed for their food.'

The experience altogether, from its intense melancholy, was very depressing, almost appalling to the two lone young women, and they quickly retraced their footsteps. The pleasant lake, the purl of the weir, the rudimentary lawns, shrubberies, and avenue, had changed their character quite. Ethelberta fancied at that moment that she could not have married Neigh, even had she loved him, so horrid did his belongings appear to be. But for many other reasons she had been gradually feeling within this hour that she would not go out of her way at a beck from a man whose interest was so unimpassioned.

Thinking no more of him as a possible husband she ceased to be afraid to make inquiries about the peculiarities of his possessions. In the high-road the came upon a local man, resting from wheeling a wheelbarrow, and Ethelberta asked him, with the air of a country-woman, who owned the estate across the road.

'The man owning that is one of the name of Neigh,' said the native, wiping his face. ''Tis a family that have made a very large fortune by the knacker* business and tanning, though they be only sleeping partners in it now, and live like lords. Mr Neigh was going to pull down the old huts here, and improve the place and build a mansion – in short, he went so far as to have the grounds planted, and the roads marked out, and the fish-pond made, and the place christened Farnfield Park; but he did no more. "I shall never have a wife," he said, "so why should I want a house to put her in?" He is a terrible hater of women, I hear, particularly the lower class.'

'Indeed!'

'Yes; and since then he has let half the land to the Honourable Mr Mountclere, a brother of Lord Mountclere's. Mr Mountclere wanted the spot for a kennel, and as the land is too poor and sandy for cropping, Mr Neigh let him have it. 'Tis his hounds that you hear howling.'

They passed on. 'Berta, why did we come down here?' said Picotee.

'To see the nakedness of the land.* It was a whim only, and as it will end in nothing, it is not worth while for me to make further explanation.'

It was with a curious sense of renunciation that Ethelberta went homeward. Neigh was handsome, grim-natured, rather wicked, and an indifferentist;* and these attractions interested her as a woman. But the news of this evening suggested to Ethelberta that herself and Neigh were too nearly cattle of one colour for a confession on the matter of lineage to be well received by him; and without confidence of every sort on the nature of her situation, she was determined to contract no union at all. The sympathy of unlikeness might lead the scion of some family, hollow and fungous with antiquity, and as yet unmarked by a mésalliance, to be won over by her story; but the antipathy of resemblance would be ineradicable.

Ethelberta's Drawing-room

While Ethelberta during the next few days was dismissing that
evening journey from her consideration, as an incident
altogether foreign to the organized course of her existence, the
hidden fruit thereof was rounding to maturity in a species
unforeseen.

Inferences unassailable as processes are, nevertheless, to be
suspected, from the almost certain deficiency of particulars on
some side or other. The truth in relation to Neigh's supposed
frigidity was brought before her at the end of the following
week, when Dan and Sol had taken Picotee, Cornelia, and the
young children to Kew* for the afternoon.

Early that morning, hours before it was necessary, there had
been such a chatter of preparation in the house as was seldom
heard there. Sunday hats and bonnets had been retrimmed with
such cunning that it would have taken a milliner's apprentice at
least to discover that any thread in them was not quite new.
There was an anxious peep through the blind at the sky at
daybreak by Georgina and Myrtle, and the perplexity of these
rural children was great at the weather-signs of the town, where
atmospheric effects had nothing to do with clouds, and fair days
and foul came apparently quite by chance. Punctually at the
hour appointed two friendly human shadows descended across
the kitchen window, followed by Sol and Dan, much to the
relief of the children's apprehensions that they might forget the
day.

The brothers were by this time acquiring something of the
airs and manners of London workmen; they were less spon-
taneous and more comparative; less genial, but smarter; in
obedience to the usual law by which the emotion that takes the
form of humour in country workmen becomes transmuted to
irony among the same order in town. But the fixed and dogged
fidelity to one another under apparent coolness, by which this
family was distinguished, remained unshaken in these members
as in all the rest, leading them to select the children as companions in their holiday in preference to casual acquaintance. At
last they were ready, and departed, and Ethelberta, after chatting
with her mother awhile, proceeded to her personal duties.

The house was very silent that day, Gwendoline and Joey being the only ones left below stairs. Ethelberta was wishing that she had thrown off her state and gone to Kew to have an hour of childhood over again in a romp with the others, when she was startled by the announcement of a male visitor – none other than Mr Neigh.

Ethelberta's attitude on receipt of this information sufficiently expressed a revived sense that the incidence of Mr Neigh on her path might have a meaning after all. Neigh had certainly said he was going to marry her, and now here he was come to her house – just as if he meant to do it forthwith. She had mentally discarded him; yet she felt a shock which was scarcely painful, and a dread which was almost exhilarating. Her flying visit to Farnfield she thought little of at this moment. From the fact that the mind prefers imaginings to recapitulation, conjecture to history, Ethelberta had dwelt more upon Neigh's possible plans and anticipations than upon the incidents of her evening journey; and the former assumed a more distinct shape in her mind's eye than anything on the visible side of the curtain.

Neigh was perhaps not quite so placidly nonchalant as in ordinary; still, he was by far the most trying visitor that Ethelberta had lately faced, and she could not get above the stage – not a very high one for the mistress of a house – of feeling her personality to be inconveniently in the way of his eyes. He had somewhat the bearing of a man who was going to do without any fuss what gushing people would call a philanthropic action.

'I have been intending to write a line to you,' said Neigh; 'but I felt that I could not be sure of writing my meaning in a way which might please you. I am not bright at a letter – never was. The question I mean is one that I hope you will be disposed to answer favourably, even though I may show the awkwardness of a fellow – person who has never put such a question before. Will you give me a word of encouragement – just a hope that I may not be unacceptable as a husband to you? Your talents are very great; and of course I know that I have nothing at all in that way. Still people are happy together sometimes in spite of such things. Will you say "Yes," and settle it now?'

'I was not expecting you had come upon such an errand as this,' said she, looking up a little, but mostly looking down. 'I cannot say what you wish, Mr Neigh.'

'Perhaps I have been too sudden and presumptuous. Yes, I know I have been that. However, directly I saw you I felt that nobody ever came so near my idea of what is desirable in a lady, and it occurred to me that only one obstacle should stand in the way of the natural results, which obstacle would be your refusal. In common kindness consider. I daresay I am judged to be a man of inattentive habits – I know that's what you think of me; but under your influence I should be very different; so pray do not let your dislike to little matters influence you.'

'I would not indeed. But believe me there can be no discussion of marriage between us,' said Ethelberta decisively.

'If that's the case I may as well say no more. To burden you with my regrets would be out of place, I suppose,' said Neigh, looking calmly out of the window.

'Apart from personal feeling, there are considerations which would prevent what you contemplated,' she murmured. 'My affairs are too lengthy, intricate, and unpleasant for me to explain to anybody at present. And that would be a necessary first step.'

'Not at all. I cannot think that preliminary to be necessary at all. I would put my lawyer in communication with yours, and we would leave the rest to them: I believe that is the proper way. You could say anything in confidence to your family-man; and you could inquire through him anything you might wish to know about my – about me. All you would need to say to myself are just the two little words – "I will," in the church here at the end of the Crescent.'

'I am sorry to pain you, Mr Neigh – so sorry,' said Ethelberta. 'But I cannot say them.' She was rather distressed that, despite her discouraging words, he still went on with his purpose, as if he imagined what she so distinctly said to be no bar, but rather a stimulant, usual under the circumstances.

'It does not matter about paining me,' said Neigh. 'Don't take that into consideration at all. But I did not expect you to leave me so entirely without help – to refuse me absolutely as far as words go – after what you did. If it had not been for that I should never have ventured to call. I might otherwise have supposed your interest to be fixed in another quarter, but your acting in that manner encouraged me to think you could listen to a word.'

'What do you allude to?' said Ethelberta. 'How have I acted?'

Neigh appeared reluctant to go any further; but the allusion soon became suffficiently clear. 'I wish my little place at Farnfield had been worthier of you,' he said brusquely. 'However, that's a matter of time only. It is useless to build a house there yet. I wish I had known that you would be looking over it at that time of the evening. A single word, when we were talking about it the other day, that you were going to be in the neighbourhood, would have been sufficient. Nothing could have given me so much delight as to have driven you round.'

He knew that she had been to Farnfield: that knowledge was what had inspired him to call upon her today! Ethelberta breathed a sort of exclamation, not right out, but stealthily, like a parson's damn. Her face did not change, since a face must be said not to change while it preserves the same pleasant lines in the mobile parts as before; but anybody who has preserved his pleasant lines under the half-minute's peer of the invidious camera, and found what a wizened, starched kind of thing they stiffen to towards the end of the time, will understand the tendency of Ethelberta's lovely features now.

'Yes; I walked round,' said Ethelberta faintly.

Neigh was decidedly master of the position at last; but he spoke as if he did not value that. His knowledge had furnished him with grounds for calling upon her, and he hastened to undeceive her from supposing that he could think ill of any motive of hers which gave him those desirable grounds.

'I supposed you, by that, to give some little thought to me occasionally,' he resumed, in the same slow and orderly tone. 'How could I help thinking so? It was your doing that which encouraged me. Now, was it not natural – I put it to you?'

Ethelberta was almost exasperated at perceiving the awful extent to which she had compromised herself with this man by her impulsive visit. Lightly and philosophically as he seemed to take it – as a thing, in short, which every woman would do by nature unless hindered by difficulties – it was no trifle to her as long as he was ignorant of her justification; and this she determined that he should know at once, at all hazards.

'It was through you in the first place that I did look into your grounds!' she said excitely. 'It was your presumption that caused me to go there. I should not have thought of such a thing else. If you had not said what you did say I never should have thought of you or Farnfield either – Farnfield might have been in Kamtschatka* for all I cared.'

'I hope sincerely that I never said anything to disturb you?'

'Yes, you did – not to me, but to somebody,' said Ethelberta, with her eyes over-full of retained tears.

'What have I said to somebody that can be in the least objectionable to you?' inquired Neigh, with much concern.

'You said – you said, you meant to marry me – just as if I had no voice in the matter! And that annoyed me, and made me go there out of curiosity.'

Neigh changed colour a little. 'Well, I did say it: I own that I said it,' he replied at last. Probably he knew enough of her nature not to feel long disconcerted by her disclosure, however she might have become possessed of the information. The explanation was certainly a great excuse to her curiosity; but if Ethelberta had tried she could not have given him a better ground for making light of her objections to his suit. 'I felt that I must marry you, that we were predestined to marry ages ago, and I feel it still!' he continued, with listless ardour. 'You seem to regret your interest in Farnfield; but to me it is a charm, and has been ever since I heard of it.'

'If you only knew all!' she said helplessly, showing, without perceiving it, an unnecessary humility in the remark, since there was no more reason just then that she should go into details about her life than that he should about his. But melancholy and mistaken thoughts of herself as a counterfeit had brought her to this.

'I do not wish to know more,' said Neigh.

'And would you marry any woman off-hand, without being thoroughly acquainted with her circumstances?' she said, looking at him curiously, and with a little admiration, for his unconscionably phlegmatic treatment of her motives in going to Farnfield had a not unbecoming daring about it in Ethelberta's eye.

'I would marry a woman off-hand when that woman is you. I would make you mine this moment did I dare; or, to speak with absolute accuracy, within twenty-four hours. Do assent to it, dear Mrs Petherwin, and let me be sure of you for ever. I'll drive to Doctors' Commons this minute, and meet you tomorrow morning at nine in the church just below. It is a simple impulse, but I would adhere to it in the coolest moment. Shall it be arranged in that way, instead of our waiting through the ordinary routine of preparation? I am not a youth now, but I can see the bliss of such an act as that, and the contemptible nature of methodical proceedings beside it!'

He had taken her hand. Ethelberta gave it a subtle movement backwards to imply that he was not to retain the prize, and said, 'One whose inner life is almost unknown to you, and whom you have scarcely seen except at other people's houses!'

'We know each other far better than we may think at first,' said Neigh. 'We are not people to love in a hurry, and I have not done so in this case. As for worldly circumstances, the most important items in a marriage contract are the persons themselves, and, as far as I am concerned, if I get a lady fair and wise I care for nothing further. I know you are beautiful, for all London owns it; I know you are gifted, for I have read your poetry and heard your romances; and I know you are politic and discreet – '

'For I have examined your property,' said she, with a weak smile.

Neigh bowed. 'And what more can I wish to know? Come, shall it be?'

'Certainly not tomorrow.'

'I would be entirely in your hands in that matter. I will not urge you to be precipitate – I could not expect you to be ready yet. My suddenness perhaps offended you; but, having thought deeply of this bright possibility, I was apt to forget the forbearance that one ought to show at first in mentioning it. If I have done wrong forgive me.'

'I will think of that,' said Ethelberta, with a cooler manner. 'But seriously, all these words are nothing to the purpose. I must remark that I prize your friendship, but it is not for me to marry now. You have convinced me of your goodness of heart and freedom from unworthy suspicions; let that be enough. The best way in which I in my turn can convince you of my goodness of heart is by asking you to see me in private no more.'

'And do you refuse to think of me as—. Why do you treat me like that, after all?' said Neigh, surprised at this want of harmony with his principle that one convert to matrimony could always find a second ready-made.

'I cannot explain, I cannot explain,' said she, impatiently. 'I would and I would not – explain, I mean, not marry. I don't love anybody, and I have no heart left for beginning. It is only honest in me to tell you that I am interested in watching another man's career, though that is not to the point either, for no close relationship with him is contemplated. But I do not wish to speak of this any more. Do not press me to it.'

'Certainly I will not,' said Neigh, seeing that she was distressed and sorrowful. 'But do consider me and my wishes; I have a right to ask it, for it is only asking a continuance of what you have already begun to do. Tomorrow I believe I shall have the happiness of seeing you again.'

She did not say no, and long after the door had closed upon him she remained fixed in thought. 'How can he be blamed for his manner,' she said, 'after knowing what I did!'

Ethelberta as she sat felt herself much less a Petherwin than a Chickerel, much less a poetess richly freighted with fancy than an adventuress with a nebulous prospect. Neigh was one of the few men whose presence seemed to attenuate her dignity in some mysterious way to its very least proportions; and that act of espial, which had so quickly and inexplicably come to his knowledge, helped his influence still more. She knew little of the nature of the town bachelor; there were opaque depths in him which her thoughts had never definitely plumbed. Notwithstanding her exaltation to the atmosphere of the Petherwin family, Ethelberta was very far from having the thoroughbred London woman's knowledge of sets, grades, coteries, cliques, forms, glosses, and niceties, particularly on the masculine side. Setting the years from her infancy to her first look into town against those linking that epoch with the present, the former period covered not only the greater time, but contained the mass of her most vivid impressions of life and its ways. But in recognizing her ignorance of the ratio between words to women and deeds to women in the ethical code of the bachelor of the club, she forgot that human nature in the gross differs little with situation, and that a gift which, if the germs were lacking, no amount of training in clubs and coteries could supply, was mother-wit like her own.

Neigh's remark that he believed he should see Ethelberta again the next day referred to a contemplated pilgrimage of an unusual sort which had been arranged for that day by Mrs Belmaine upon the ground of an incidental suggestion of Ethelberta's. One afternoon in the week previous they had been chatting over tea at the house of the former lady, Neigh being present as a casual caller, when the conversation was directed upon Milton by somebody opening a volume of the poet's works that lay on a table near.

> Milton! thou shouldst be living at this hour:
> England hath need of thee — *

said Mrs Belmaine with the degree of flippancy which is considered correct for immortal verse, the Bible, God, etc., in these days. And Ethelberta replied, lit up by a quick remembrance, 'It is a good time to talk of Milton; for I have been much impressed by reading the "Life",* and I have decided to go and see his tomb. Could we not all go? We ought to quicken our memories of the great, and of where they lie, by such a visit occasionally.'

'We ought,' said Mrs Belmaine.

'And why shouldn't we?' continued Ethelberta, with interest.

'To Westminster Abbey?' said Mr Belmaine, a common man of thirty, younger than his wife, who had lately come into the room.

'No; to where he lies comparatively alone – Cripplegate Church.'

'I always thought that Milton was buried in Poet's Corner,' said Mr Belmaine.

'So did I,' said Neigh; 'but I have such an indifferent head for places that my thinking goes for nothing.'

'Well, it would be a pretty thing to do,' said Mrs Belmaine, 'and instructive to all of us. If Mrs Petherwin would like to go, I should. We can take you in the carriage and call round for Mrs Doncastle on our way, and set you both down again coming back.'

'That would be excellent,' said Ethelberta. 'There is nowhere I like going to so much as the depths of the city. The absurd narrowness of world-renowned streets is so surprising – so crooked and shady as they are too, and full of the quaint smells of old cupboards and cellars. Walking through one of them reminds me of being at the bottom of some crevasse or gorge, the proper surface of the globe being the tops of the houses.'

'You will come to take care of us, John? And you, Mr Neigh, would like to come? We will tell Mr Ladywell that he may join us if he cares to,' said Mrs Belmaine.

'O yes,' said her husband quietly; and Neigh said he should like nothing better, after a faint aspect of apprehension at the remoteness of the idea from the daily track of his thoughts. Mr Belmaine observing this, and mistaking it for an indication that Neigh had been dragged into the party against his will by his over-hasty wife, arranged that Neigh should go independently and meet them there at the hour named if he chose to do so, to give him an opportunity of staying away. Ethelberta also was by this time doubting if she had not been too eager with her proposal. To go on such a sentimental errand might be thought by her friends to be simply troublesome, their adherence having been given only in the regular course of complaisance. She was still comparatively an outsider here, her life with Lady Petherwin having been passed chiefly in alternations between English watering-places and continental towns. However, it was too late now to muse on this, and it may be added that from first to last Ethelberta never discovered from the Belmaines whether her proposal had been an infliction or a charm, so perfectly were they practised in sustaining that complete divorce between thinking and saying which is the hall-mark of high civilization.

But, however she might doubt the Belmaines, she had no doubt as to Neigh's true sentiments: the time had come when he, notwithstanding his air of being oppressed by almost every lively invention of town and country for charming griefs to rest, would not be at all oppressed by a quiet visit to the purlieus of St Giles's, Cripplegate, since she was the originator, and was going herself.

It was a bright hope-inspiring afternoon in this mid-May time when the carriage containing Mr and Mrs Belmaine, Mrs Doncastle, and Ethelberta, crept along the encumbered streets towards Barbican; till turning out of that thoroughfare into Redcross Street they beheld the bold shape of the old tower they sought, clothed in every neutral shade, standing clear against the sky, dusky and grim in its upper stage, and hoary grey below, where every corner of every stone was completely rounded off by the waves of wind and storm.

All people were busy here: our visitors seemed to be the only idle persons the city contained; and there was no dissonance – there never is – between antiquity and such beehive industry; for pure industry, in failing to observe its own existence and aspect, partakes of the unobtrusive nature of material things. This intramural stir was a flywheel transparent by excessive motion, through which Milton and his day could be seen as if nothing intervened. Had there been ostensibly harmonious accessories, a crowd of observing people in search of the poetical, conscious of the place and the scene, what a discord would have arisen there! But everybody passed by Milton's grave except Ethelberta and her friends, and for the moment the city's less invidious conduct appeared to her more respectful as a practice than her own.

But she was brought out of this rumination by the halt at the church door, and completely reminded of the present by finding the church open, and Neigh – the, till yesterday, unimpassioned Neigh – waiting in the vestibule to receive them, just as if he lived there. Ladywell had not arrived. It was a long time before Ethelberta could get back to Milton again, for Neigh was continuing to impend over her future more and more visibly. The objects along the journey had distracted her mind from him; but the moment now was as a direct renewal and prolongation of the declaration-time yesterday, and as if in furtherance of the conclusion of the episode.

They all alighted and went in, the coachman being told to take the carriage to a quiet nook further on, and return in half an hour. Mrs Belmaine and her carriage some years before had accidentally got jammed cross-wise in Cheapside through the clumsiness of the man in turning up a side street, blocking that great artery of the civilized world for the space of a minute and a half, when they were pounced upon by half-a-dozen police-men and forced to back ignominiously up a little slit between the houses where they did not mean to go, amid the shouts of the hindered drivers; and it was her nervous recollection of that event which caused Mrs Belmaine to be so precise in her directions now.

By the time that they were grouped around the tomb the visit had assumed a much more solemn complexion than any one among them had anticipated. Ashamed of the influence that she discovered Neigh to be exercising over her, and opposing it steadily, Ethelberta drew from her pocket a small edition of Milton, and proposed that she should read a few lines from 'Paradise Lost'. The responsibility of producing a successful afternoon was upon her shoulders; she was, moreover, the only one present who could properly manage blank verse, and this was sufficient to justify the proposal.

She stood with her head against the marble slab just below the bust, and began a selected piece, Neigh standing a few yards off on her right looking into his hat in order to listen accurately, Mr and Mrs Belmaine and Mrs Doncastle seating themselves in a pew directly facing the monument.[1] The ripe warm colours of afternoon came in upon them from the west, upon the sallow piers and arches, and the infinitely deep brown pews beneath, the aisle over Ethelberta's head being in misty shade through which glowed a lurid light from a dark-stained window behind. The sentences fell from her lips in a rhythmical cadence one by one, and she could be fancied a priestess of him before whose image she stood, when with a vivid suggestiveness she delivered here, not many yards from the central money-mill of the world, yet out from the very tomb of their author, the passage containing the words:

> Mammon led them on;
> Mammon, the least erected spirit that fell
> From heaven.*

When she finished reading Ethelberta left the monument, and then each one present strayed independently about the building, Ethelberta turning to the left along the passage to the south door. Neigh – from whose usually apathetic face and eyes there had proceeded a secret smouldering light as he listened and regarded her – followed in the same direction and vanished at her heels into the churchyard, whither she had now gone. Mr and Mrs Belmaine exchanged glances, and instead of following

[1] There have been changes since this was written.*

the pair they went with Mrs Doncastle into the vestry to inquire
of the person in charge for the register of the marriage of Oliver
Cromwell,* which was solemnized here. The church was now
quite empty, and its stillness was as a vacuum into which an
occasional noise from the street overflowed and became rarefied
away to nothing.

Something like five minutes had passed when a hansom
stopped outside the door, and Ladywell entered the porch. He
stood still, and, looking inquiringly round for a minute or two,
sat down in one of the high pews, as if under the impression
that the others had not yet arrived.

While he sat here Neigh reappeared at the south door
opposite, and came slowly in. Ladywell, in rising to go to him,
saw that Neigh's attention was engrossed by something he held
in his hand. It was his pocket-book, and Neigh was looking at a
few loose flower petals which had been placed between the
pages. When Ladywell came forward Neigh looked up, started,
and closed the book quickly, so that some of the petals fluttered
to the ground between the two men. They were striped, red and
white, and appeared to be leaves of the Harlequin rose.

'Ah! here you are, Ladywell,' he said, recovering himself. 'We
had given you up: my aunt said that you would not care to
come. They are all in the vestry.' How it came to pass that
Neigh designated those in the vestry as 'all', when there was one
in the churchyard, was a thing that he himself could hardly have
explained, so much more had it to do with instinct than with
calculation.

'Never mind them – don't interrupt them,' said Ladywell.
'The plain truth is that I have been very greatly disturbed in
mind; and I could not appear earlier by reason of it. I had some
doubt about coming at all.'

'I am sorry to hear that.'

'Neigh – I may as well tell you and have done with it. I have
found that a lady of my acquaintance has two strings to her
bow, or I am very much in error.'

'What – Mrs Petherwin?' said Neigh uneasily. 'But I thought
that – that fancy was over with you long ago. Even your
acquaintance with her was at an end, I thought.'

'In a measure it is at an end. But let me tell you that what you
call a fancy has been anything but a fancy with me, to be over

like a spring shower. To speak plainly, Neigh, I consider myself
badly used by that woman; damn badly used.'

'Badly used?' said Neigh mechanically, and wondering all the
time if Ladywell had been informed that Ethelberta was to be
one of the party today.

'Well, I ought not to talk like that,' said Ladywell, adopting a
lighter tone. 'All is fair in courtship, I suppose, now as ever.
Indeed, I mean to put a good face upon it: if I am beaten, I am.
But it is very provoking, after supposing matters to be going on
smoothly, to find out that you are quite mistaken.'

'I told you you were quite mistaken in supposing she cared
for you.'

'That is just the point I was not mistaken in,' said Ladywell
warmly. 'She did care for me, and I stood as well with her as
any man could stand until this fellow came, whoever he is. I
sometimes feel so disturbed about it that I have a good mind to
call upon her and ask his name. Wouldn't you, Neigh? Will you
accompany me?'

'I would in a moment, but, but – I strongly advise you not to
go,' said Neigh earnestly. 'It would be rash, you know, and
rather unmannerly; and would only hurt your feelings.'

'Well, I am always ready to yield to a friend's arguments . . .
A sneaking scamp, that's what he is. Why does he not show
himself?'

'Don't you really know who he is?' said Neigh, in a pronounced and exceptional tone, on purpose to give Ladywell a
chance of suspecting, for the position was getting awkward. But
Ladywell was blind as Bartimeus* in that direction, so well had
indifference to Ethelberta's charms been feigned by Neigh until
he thought seriously of marrying her. Yet, unfortunately for the
interests of calmness, Ladywell was less blind with his outward
eye. In his reflections his glance had lingered again upon the
pocket-book which Neigh still held in his hand, and upon the
two or three rose-leaves on the floor, until he said idly, super-
imposing humorousness upon misery, as men in love can:

'Rose-leaves, Neigh? I thought you did not care for flowers.
What makes you amuse yourself with such sentimental objects
as those, only fit for women, or painters like me? If I had not
observed you with my own eyes I should have said that you
were about the last man in the world to care for things of that

sort. Whatever makes you keep rose-leaves in your pocket-book?'

'The best reason on earth,' said Neigh. 'A woman gave them to me.'

'That proves nothing unless she is a great deal to you,' said Ladywell, with the experienced air of a man who, whatever his inferiority in years to Neigh, was far beyond him in knowledge of that sort, by virtue of his recent trials.

'She is a great deal to me.'

'If I did not know you to be such a confirmed misogynist I should say that this is a serious matter.'

'It is serious,' said Neigh quietly. 'The probability is that I shall marry the woman who gave me these. Anyhow I have asked her the question, and she has not altogether said no.'

'I am glad to hear it, Neigh,' said Ladywell heartily. 'I am glad to hear that your star is higher than mine.'

Before Neigh could make further reply Ladywell was attracted by the glow of green sunlight reflected through the south door by the grass of the churchyard, now in all its spring freshness and luxuriance. He bent his steps thither, followed anxiously by Neigh.

'I had no idea there was such a lovely green spot in the city,' Ladywell continued, passing out. 'Trees, too, planted in the manner of an orchard. What a charming place!'

The place was truly charming just at that date. The untainted leaves of the lime and plane trees and the newly-sprung grass had in the sun a brilliancy of beauty that was brought into extraordinary prominence by the sable soil showing here and there, and the charcoaled stems and trunks out of which the leaves budded: they seemed an importation, not a produce, and their delicacy such as would perish in a day.

'What is this round tower?' Ladywell said again, walking towards the iron-grey bastion, partly covered with ivy and Virginia creeper, which stood obtruding into the enclosure.

'O, didn't you know that was here? That's a piece of the old city wall,' said Neigh, looking furtively around at the same time. Behind the bastion the churchyard ran into a long narrow strip, grassed like the other part, but completely hidden from it by the cylinder of ragged masonry. On rounding this projection, Lady-well beheld within a few feet of him a lady whom he knew too well.

'Mrs Petherwin here!' exclaimed he, proving how ignorant he had been of the composition of the party he was to meet, and accounting at the same time for his laxity in attending it.

'I forgot to tell you,' said Neigh awkwardly, behind him, 'that Mrs Petherwin was to come with us.'

Ethelberta's look was somewhat blushful and agitated, as if from some late transaction: she appeared to have been secluding herself there till she should have recovered her equanimity. However, she came up to him and said, 'I did not see you before this moment: we had been thinking you would not come.'

While these words were being prettily spoken, Ladywell's face became pale as death. On Ethelberta's bosom were the stem and green calyx of a rose, almost all its flower having disappeared. It had been a Harlequin rose, for two or three of its striped leaves remained to tell the tale.

She could not help noticing his fixed gaze, and she said quickly, 'Yes, I have lost my pretty rose: this may as well go now,' and she plucked the stem from its fastening in her dress and flung it away.

Poor Ladywell turned round to meet Mr and Mrs Belmaine, whose voices were beginning to be heard just within the church door, leaving Neigh and Ethelberta together. It was a graceful act of young Ladywell's that, in the midst of his own pain at the strange tale the rose-leaves suggested – Neigh's rivalry, Ethelberta's mutability, his own defeat – he was not regardless of the intense embarrassment which might have been caused had he remained.

The two were silent at first, and it was evident that Ethelberta's mood was one of anger at something that had gone before. She turned aside from him to follow the others, when Neigh spoke in a tone somewhat bitter and somewhat stern.

'What – going like that! After being compromised together, why don't you close with me? Ladywell knows all: I had already told him that the rose-leaves were given me by my intended wife. We seem to him to be practising deceptions all of a piece, and what folly it is to play off so! As to what I did, that I ask your forgiveness for.'

Ethelberta looked upon the ground and maintained a compressed lip. Neigh resumed: 'If I showed more feeling than you care for, I insist that it was not more than was natural under the circumstances, if not quite proper. Opinions may differ, but my experience goes to prove that conventional squeamishness at such times as these is more talked and written about than practised. Plain behaviour must be expected when marriage is the question. Nevertheless, I do say – and I cannot say more – that I am sincerely sorry to have offended you by exceeding my privileges. I will never do so again.'

'Don't say privileges. You have none.'

'I am sorry that I thought otherwise, and that others will think so too. Ladywell is, at any rate, bent on thinking so . . . It might have been made known to him in a gentle way – but God disposes.'

'There is nothing to make known – I don't understand,' said Ethelberta, going from him.

By this time Ladywell had walked round the gravel walks with the two other ladies and Mr Belmaine, and they were all turning to come back again. The young painter had deputed his voice to reply to their remarks, but his understanding continued poring upon other things. When he came up to Ethelberta, his agitation had left him: she too was free from constraint; while Neigh was some distance off, carefully examining nothing in particular in an old fragment of wall.

The little party was now united again as to its persons; though in spirit far otherwise. They went through the church in general talk, Ladywell sad but serene, and Ethelberta keeping far-removed both from him and from Neigh. She had at this juncture entered upon that Sphinx-like* stage of existence in which, contrary to her earlier manner, she signified to no one of her ways, plans, or sensations, and spoke little on any subject at all. There were occasional smiles now which came only from the face, and speeches from the lips merely.

The journey home was performed as they had come, Ladywell not accepting the seat in Neigh's cab which was phlegmatically offered him. Mrs Doncastle's acquaintance with Ethelberta had been slight until this day; but the afternoon's proceeding had much impressed the matron with her younger friend. Before they parted she said, with the sort of affability which is meant to signify the beginning of permanent friendship: 'A friend of my husband's, Lord Mountclere, has been anxious for some time to meet you. He is a great admirer of the poems, and more still of the story-telling invention, and your power in it. He has been present many times at the Mayfair Hall to hear you. When will you dine with us to meet him? I know you will like him. Will Thursday be convenient?'

Ethelberta stood for a moment reflecting, and reflecting hoped that Mrs Doncastle had not noticed her momentary perplexity. Crises were becoming as common with her as blackberries;* and she had foreseen this one a long time. It was not that she was to meet Lord Mountclere, for he was only a name and a distant profile to her: it was that her father would necessarily be present at the meeting, in the most anomalous position that human nature could endure.

However, having often proved in her disjointed experience that the shortest way out of a difficulty lies straight through it, Ethelberta decided to dine at the Doncastles', and, as she murmured that she should have great pleasure in meeting any friend of theirs, set about contriving how the encounter with her dearest relative might be made safe and unsuspected. She bade them adieu blithely; but the thoughts engendered by the invitation stood before her as sorrowful and rayless ghosts which could not be laid. Often at such conjunctures as these, when the futility of her great undertaking was more than usually manifest, did Ethelberta long like a tired child for the conclusion of the whole matter; when her work should be over, and the evening come; when she might draw her boat upon the shore, and in some thymy nook await eternal night with a placid mind.*

Ethelberta's
Mr Chickerel's Room

28

The question of Neigh or no Neigh had reached pitch of insistence which no longer permitted of dallying, even by a popular beauty. His character was becoming defined to Ethelberta as something very differently composed from that of her first imagining. She had set him down to be a man whose external inexcitability owed nothing to self-repression, but stood as the natural surface of the mass within. Neigh's urban torpor, she said, might have been in the first instance produced by art, but, were it thus, it had gone so far as to permeate him. This had been disproved, first surprisingly, by his reported statement; wondrously, in the second place, by his call upon her and sudden proposal; thirdly, to a degree simply astounding, by what had occurred in the city that day. For Neigh, before the fervour had subsided which was produced in him by her look and general power while reading 'Paradise Lost', found himself alone with her in a nook outside the church, and there had almost demanded her promise to be his wife. She had replied by asking for time, and idly offering him the petals of her rose, that had shed themselves in her hand. Neigh, in taking them, pressed her fingers more warmly than she thought she had given him warrant for, which offended her. It was certainly a very momentary affair, and when it was over seemed to surprise himself almost as much as it had vexed her; but it had reminded her of one truth which she was in danger of forgetting. The town gentleman was not half so far removed from Sol and Dan, and the hard-handed order* in general, in his passions as in his philosophy. He still continued to be the male of his species, and when the heart was hot with a dream Pall Mall had much the same aspect as Wessex.

Well, she had not accepted him yet; indeed, for the moment they were in a pet* with one another. Yet that might soon be cleared off, and then recurred the perpetual question, would the advantage that might accrue to her people by her marriage be worth the sacrifice? One palliative feature must be remembered when we survey the matrimonial ponderings of the poetess and romancer. What she contemplated was not meanly to ensnare a husband just to provide incomes for her and her family, but to find some man she might respect, who would maintain her in such a stage of comfort as should, by setting her mind free from temporal anxiety, enable her to further organize her talent, and provide incomes for them herself. Plenty of saleable originality was left in her as yet, but it was getting crushed under the rubbish of her necessities.

She was not sure that Neigh would stand the test of her revelations. It would be possible to lead him to marry her without revealing anything – the events of the last few days had shown her that – yet Ethelberta's honesty shrank from the safe course of holding her tongue. It might be pleasant to many a modern gentleman to find himself allied with a lady, none of whose ancestors had ever pandered to a court, lost an army, taken a bribe, oppressed a community, or broken a bank; but the added disclosure that, in avoiding these stains, her kindred had worked and continued to work with their hands for bread, might lead such an one to consider that the novelty was dearly purchased.

Ethelberta was, upon the whole, dissatisfied with her progress thus far. She had planned many things and fulfilled few. Had her father been by this time provided for and made independent of the world, as she had thought he might be, not only would her course with regard to Neigh be quite clear, but the impending awkwardness of dining with her father behind her chair could not have occurred. True, that was a small matter beside her regret for his own sake that he was still in harness; and a mere change of occupation would be but a tribute to a fastidiousness which he did not himself share. She had frequently tried to think of a vocation for him that would have a more dignified sound, and be less dangerously close to her own path: the post of caretaker at some provincial library, country stationer, registrar of births and deaths, and many others had been discussed and dismissed in face of the unmanageable fact that her father was serenely happy and comfortable as a butler, looking with dread at any hint of change short of perfect retirement. Since, then, she could not offer him this retirement, what right had she to interfere with his mode of life at all? In no other social groove on earth would he thrive as he throve in his present one, to which he had been accustomed from boyhood, and where the remuneration was actually greater than in professions ten times as stately in name.

For the rest, too, Ethelberta had indulged in hopes, the high education of the younger ones being the chief of these darling wishes. Picotee wanted looking to badly enough. Sol and Dan required no material help; they had quickly obtained good places of work under a Pimlico builder; for though the brothers scarcely showed as yet the light-fingered deftness of London artizans, the want was in a measure compensated by their painstaking, and employers are far from despising country hands who bring with them strength, industry, and a desire to please. But their sister had other lines laid down for them than those of level progress; to start them some day as masters instead of men was a long-cherished wish of Ethelberta's.

Thus she had quite enough machinery in her hands to keep

decently going, even were she to marry a man who would take a kindly view of her peculiar situation, and afford her opportunities of strengthening her powers for her kindred's good. But what would be the result if, eighteen months hence – the date at which her occupation of the house in Exonbury Crescent came to an end – she were still a widow, with no accumulated capital, her platform talents grown homely and stunted through narrow living and her tender vein of poesy completely dispersed by it? To calmly relinquish the struggle at that point would have been the act of a stoic, but not of a woman, particularly when she considered the children, the hopes of her mother for them, and her own condition – though this was least – under the ironical cheers which would greet a slip back into the mire.

It here becomes necessary to turn for a moment to Master Joey Chickerel, Ethelberta's troublesome page and brother. The face of this juvenile was that of a Græco-Roman satyr to the furthest degree of completeness. Viewed in front, the outer line of his upper lip rose in a double arch nearly to his little round nostrils, giving an expression of a jollity so delicious to himself as to compel a perpetual drawing in of his breath. During half-laughs his lips parted in the middle, and remained closed at the corners, which were small round pits like his nostrils, the same form being repeated as dimples a little further back upon his cheek. The opening for each eye formed a sparkling crescent, both upper and under lid having the convexity upwards.

But during some few days preceding the dinner-party at the Doncastles' all this changed. The luxuriant curves departed, a compressed lineality was to be observed everywhere, the pupils of his eyes seemed flattened, and the carriage of his head was limp and sideways. This was a feature so remarkable and new in him that Picotee noticed it, and was lifted from the melancholy current of her own affairs in contemplating his.

'Well, what's the matter?' said Picotee.

'O – nothing,' said Joey.

'Nothing? How can you say so?'

'The world's a holler mockery – that's what I say.'

'Yes, so it is, to some; but not to you,' said Picotee, sighing.

'Don't talk argument, Picotee. I only hope you'll never feel what I feel now. If it wasn't for my juties here I know what I'd do; I'd 'list,* that's what I'd do. But having my position to fill here as the only responsible man-servant in the house, I can't leave.'

'Has anybody been beating you?'

'Beating! Do I look like a person who gets beatings? No, it is a madness,' said Joey, putting his hand upon his chest. 'The case is, I am in love.'

'O Joey, a boy no bigger than you are!' said Picotee reprovingly. Her personal interest in the passion, however, provoked her to inquire, in the next breath, 'Who is it? Do tell, Joey.'

'No bigger than I! What hev bigness to do with it? That's just like your old-fashioned notions. Bigness is no more wanted in courting nowadays than in soldiering or smoking or any other duty of man. Husbands is rare;* and a promising courter who means business will fetch his price in these times, big or small, I assure 'ee. I might have been engaged a dozen times over as far as the bigness goes. You should see what a miserable little fellow my rival is afore you talk like that. Now you know I've got a rival, perhaps you'll own there must be something in it.'

'Yes, that seems like the real thing. But who is the young woman?'

'Well, I don't mind telling you, Picotee. It is Mrs Doncastle's new maid. I called to see father last night, and had supper there; and you should have seen how lovely she were – eating sparrowgrass* sideways, as if she were born to it. But, of course, there's a rival – there always is – I might have known that, and I will crush him!'

'But Mry Doncastle's new maid – if that was she I caught a glimpse of the other day – is ever so much older than you – a dozen years.'

'What's that to a man in love? Pooh – I wish you would leave me, Picotee; I wants to be alone.'

A short time after this Picotee was in the company of Ethelberta, and she took occasion to mention Joey's attachment. Ethelberta grew exceedingly angry directly she heard of it.

'What a fearful nuisance that boy is becoming,' she said. 'Does father know anything of this?'

'I think not,' said Picotee. 'O no, he cannot; he would not allow any such thing to go on; she is so much older than Joey.'

'I should think he wouldn't allow it! The fact is I must be more strict about this growing friendliness between you all and the Doncastle servants. There shall be absolutely no intimacy or visiting of any sort. When father wants to see any of you he must come here, unless there is a most serious reason for your calling upon him. Some disclosure or reference to me otherwise than as your mistress, will certainly be made else, and then I am ruined. I will speak to father myself about Joey's absurd nonsense this evening. I am going to see him on another matter.' And Ethelberta sighed. 'I am to dine there on Thursday,' she added.

'To dine there, Berta? Well, that is a strange thing! Why, father will be close to you!'

'Yes,' said Ethelberta quietly.

'How I should like to see you sitting at a grand dinner-table, among lordly dishes and shining people, and father about the room unnoticed! Berta, I have never seen a dinner-party in my life, and father said that I should some day; he promised me long ago.'

'How will he be able to carry out that, my dear child?' said Ethelberta, drawing her sister gently to her side.

'Father says that for an hour and a half the guests are quite fixed in the dining-room, and as unlikely to move as if they were trees planted round the table. Do let me go and see you, Berta,' Picotee added coaxingly. 'I would give anything to see how you look in the midst of elegant people talking and laughing, and you my own sister all the time, and me looking on like puss-in-the-corner.'*

Ethelberta could hardly resist the entreaty, in spite of her recent resolution.

'We will leave that to be considered when I come home tonight,' she said. 'I must hear what father says.'

After dark the same evening a woman, dressed in plain black and wearing a hood, went to the servants' entrance of Mr Doncastle's house, and inquired for Mr Chickerel. Ethelberta found him in a room by himself, and on entering she closed the door behind her, and unwrapped her face.

'Can you sit with me a few minutes, father?' she said.

'Yes, for a quarter of an hour or so, said the butler. 'Has anything happened? I thought it might be Picotee.'

'No. All's well yet. But I thought it best to see you upon one or two matters which are harassing me a little just now. The first is, that stupid boy Joey has got entangled in some way with the lady's-maid at this house; a ridiculous affair it must be by all account, but it is too serious for me to treat lightly. She will worm everything out of him, and a pretty business it will be then.'

'God bless my soul! why, the woman is old enough to be his mother! I have never heard a sound of it till now. What do you propose to do?'

'I have hardly thought: I cannot tell at all. But we will consider that after I have done. The next thing is, I am to dine here Thursday – that is, tomorrow.'

'You going to dine here, are you?' said her father in surprise. 'Dear me, that's news. We have a dinner-party tomorrow, but I was not aware that you knew my people.'

'I have accepted the invitation,' said Ethelberta. 'But if you think I had better stay away, I will get out of it by some means. Heavens! what does that mean – will anybody come in?' she added, rapidly pulling up her hood and jumping from the seat as the loud tones of a bell clanged forth in startling proximity.

'O no – it is all safe,' said her father. 'It is the area door – nothing to do with me. About the dinner: I don't see why you may not come. Of course you will take no notice of me, nor shall I of you. It is to be rather a large party. Lord What's-his-name is coming, and several good people.'

'Yes; he is coming to meet me, it appears. But, father,' she said more softly and slowly, 'how wrong it will be for me to come so close to you, and never recognize you! I don't like it. I wish you could have given up service by this time; it would have been so much less painful for us all round. I thought we might have been able to manage it somehow.'

'Nonsense, nonsense,' said Mr Chickerel crossly. 'There is not the least reason why I should give up. I want to save a little money first. If you don't like me as I am, you must keep away from me. Don't be uneasy about my comfort; I am right enough, thank God. I can mind myself for many a year yet.'

Ethelberta looked at him with tears in her eyes, but she did not speak. She never could help crying when she met her father here.

'I have been in service now for more than seven and-thirty years,' her father went on. 'It is an honourable calling; and why should you maintain me because you can earn a few pounds by your gifts, and an old woman left you her house and a few sticks of furniture? If she had left you any money it would have been a different thing, but as you have to work for every penny you get, I cannot think of it. Suppose I should agree to come and live with you, and then you should be ill, or such like, and I no longer able to help myself? O no, I'll stick where I am, for here I am safe as to food and shelter at any rate. Surely, Ethelberta, it is only right that I, who ought to keep you all, should at least keep your mother and myself? As to our position, that we cannot help; and I don't mind that you are unable to own me.'

'I wish I could own you – all of you.'

'Well, you chose your course, my dear; and you must abide by it. Having put your hand to the plough, it will be foolish to turn back.'

'It would, I suppose. Yet I wish I could get a living by some simple humble occupation, and drop the name of Petherwin, and be Berta Chickerel again, and live in a green cottage as we used to do when I was small. I am miserable to a pitiable degree sometimes, and sink into regrets that I ever fell into such a groove as this. I don't like covert deeds, such as coming here tonight, and many are necessary with me from time to time. There is something without which splendid energies are a drug; and that is a cold heart. There is another thing necessary to energy, too – the power of distinguishing your visions from your reasonable forecasts when looking into the future, so as to allow your energy to lay hold of the forecasts only. I begin to have a fear that mother is right when she implies that I undertook to carry out visions and all. But ten of us are so many to cope with. If God Almighty had only killed off three-quarters of us when we were little, a body might have done something for the rest; but as we are it is hopeless!'

'There is no use in your going into high doctrine like that,' said Chickerel. 'As I said before, you chose your course. You have begun to fly high, and you had better keep there.'

'And to do that there is only one way – that is, to do it surely, so that I have some groundwork to enable me to keep up to the mark in my profession. That way is marriage.'

'Marriage? Who are you going to marry?'

'God knows. Perhaps Lord Mountclere. Stranger things have happened.'

'Yes, so they have; though not many wretcheder things. I would sooner see you in your grave, Ethelberta, than Lord

Mountclere's wife, or the wife of anybody like him, great as the honour would be.'

'Of course that was only something to say; I don't know the man even.'

'I know his valet. However, marry who you may, I hope you'll be happy, my dear girl. You would be still more divided from us in that event; but when your mother and I are dead, it will make little difference.'

Ethelberta placed her hand upon his shoulder, and smiled cheerfully. 'Now, father, don't despond. All will be well, and we shall see no such misfortune as that for many a year. Leave all to me. I am a rare hand at contrivances.'

'You are indeed, Berta. It seems to me quite wonderful that we should be living so near together and nobody suspect the relationship, because of the precautions you have taken.'

'Yet the precautions were rather Lady Petherwin's than mine, as you know. Consider how she kept me abroad. My marriage being so secret made it easy to cut off all traces, unless anybody had made it a special business to search for them. That people should suspect as yet would be by far the more wonderful thing of the two. But we must, for one thing, have no visiting between our girls and the servants here, or they soon will suspect.'

Ethelberta then laid down a few laws on the subject, and, explaining the other details of her visit, told her father soon that she must leave him.

He took her along the passage and into the area. They were standing at the bottom of the steps, saying a few parting words about Picotee's visit to see the dinner, when a female figure appeared by the railing above, slipped in at the gate, and flew down the steps past the father and daughter. At the moment of passing she whispered breathlessly to him, 'Is that you, Mr Chickerel?'

'Yes,' said the butler.

She tossed into his arms a quantity of wearing apparel, and adding, 'Please take them upstairs for me – I am late,' rushed into the house.

'Good heavens, what does that mean?' said Ethelberta, holding her father's arm in her uneasiness.

'That's the new lady's-maid, just come in from an evening walk – that young scamp's sweetheart, if what you tell me is true. I don't yet know what her character is, but she runs neck and neck with time closer than any woman I ever met. She stays out at night like this till the last moment, and often throws off her dashing courting-clothes in this way, as she runs down the steps, to save a journey to the top of the house to her room before going to Mrs Doncastle's, who is in fact at this minute waiting for her. Only look here.' Chickerel gathered up a hat decked with feathers and flowers, a parasol, and a light muslin train-skirt, out of the pocket of the latter tumbling some long golden tresses of hair.

'What an extraordinary woman,' said Ethelberta. 'A perfect Cinderella. The idea of Joey getting desperate about a woman like that; no doubt she has just come in from meeting him.'

'No doubt – a blockhead. That's his taste, is it! I'll soon see if I can't cure his taste if it inclines towards Mrs Menlove.'

'Mrs what?'

'Menlove; that's her name. She came about a fortnight ago.'

'And is that Menlove – what shall we do!' exclaimed Ethelberta. 'The idea of the boy singling out her – why it is ruin to him, to me, and to us all!'

She hastily explained to her father that Menlove had been Lady Petherwin's maid and her own at some time before the death of her mother-in-law, that she had only stayed with them through a three months' tour because of her flightiness, and hence had learnt nothing of Ethelberta's history, and probably had never thought at all about it. But nevertheless they were as well acquainted as a lady and her maid well could be in the time. 'Like all such doubtful characters,' continued Ethelberta, 'she was one of the cleverest and lightest-handed women we ever had about us. When she first came, my hair was getting quite weak; but by brushing it every day in a peculiar manner, and treating it as only she knew how, she brought it into splendid condition.'

'Well, this is the devil to pay, upon my life!' said Mr Chickerel, with a miserable gaze at the bundle of clothes and the general situation at the same time. 'Unfortunately for her friendship, I have snubbed her two or three times already, for I don't care about her manner. You know she has a way of trading on a man's sense of honour till it puts him into an awkward position. She is perfectly well aware that, whatever scrape I find her out in, I shall not have the conscience to report her, because I am a man, and she is a defenceless woman; and so she takes advantage of one's feeling by making me, or either of the men-servants, her bottle-holder,* as you see she has done now.'

'This is all simply dreadful,' said Ethelberta. 'Joey is shrewd and trustworthy; but in the hands of such a woman as that! I suppose she did not recognize me.'

'There was no chance of that in the dark.'

'Well, I cannot do anything in it,' said she. 'I cannot manage Joey at all.'

'I will see if I can,' said Mr Chickerel. 'Courting at his age, indeed – what shall we hear next!'

Chickerel then accompanied his daughter along the street till an empty cab passed them, and putting her into it he returned to the house again.

Ethelberta's Dressing-room
Mr Doncastle's House

29

The dressing of Ethelberta for the dinner-party was an undertaking into which Picotee threw her whole skill as tirewoman. Her energies were brisker that day than they had been at any time since the Julians first made preparations for departure from town; for a letter had come to her from Faith, telling of their arrival at the old cathedral city, which was found to suit their inclinations and habits infinitely better than London; and that she would like Picotee to visit them there some day. Picotee felt, and so probably felt the writer of the letter, that such a visit would not be very practicable just now; but it was a pleasant idea, and for fastening dreams upon was better than nothing.

Such musings were encouraged also by Ethelberta's remarks as the dressing went on.

'We will have a change soon,' she said; 'we will go out of town for a few days. It will do good in many ways. I am getting so alarmed about the health of the children; their faces are becoming so white and thin and pinched that an old acquaintance would hardly know them; and they were so plump when they came. You are looking as pale as a ghost, and I daresay I am too. A week or two at Knollsea will see us right.'

'O, how charming!' said Picotee gladly.

Knollsea was a village on the coast, not very far from Melchester, the new home of Christopher; not very far, that is to say, in the eye of a sweetheart; but seeing that there was, as the crow flies, a stretch of thirty-five miles between the two places, and that more than one-third the distance was without a railway, an elderly gentleman might have considered their situations somewhat remote from each other.

'Why have you chosen Knollsea?' inquired Picotee.

'Because of aunt's letter from Rouen – have you seen it?'

'I did not read it through.'

'She wants us to get a copy of the register of her baptism; and she is not absolutely certain which of the parishes in and about Knollsea they were living in when she was born. Mother, being a year younger, cannot tell of course. First I thought of writing to the clergyman of each parish, but that would be troublesome, and might reveal the secret of my birth; but if we go down there for a few days, and take some lodgings, we shall be able to find out all about it at leisure. Gwendoline and Joey can attend to mother and the people downstairs, especially as father will look in every evening until he goes out of town, to see if they are getting on properly. It will be such a weight off my soul to slip away from acquaintances here.'

'Will it?'

'Yes. At the same time I ought not to speak so, for they have been very kind. I wish we could go to Rouen afterwards; aunt repeats her invitation as usual. However, there is time enough to think of that.'

Ethelberta was dressed at last, and, beholding the lonely look of poor Picotee when about to leave the room, she could not help having a sympathetic feeling that it was rather hard for her sister to be denied so small an enjoyment as a menial peep at a feast when she herself was to sit down to it as guest.

'If you still want to go and see the procession downstairs you may do so,' she said reluctantly; 'provided that you take care of your tongue when you come in contact with Menlove, and adhere to father's instructions as to how long you may stay. It may be in the highest degree unwise; but never mind, go.'

Then Ethelberta departed for the scene of action, just at the hour of the sun's lowest decline, when it was fading away, yellow and mild as candle-light, and when upper windows facing north-west reflected to persons in the street dissolving views of tawny cloud with brazen edges, the original picture of the same being hidden from sight by soiled walls and slaty slopes.

Before entering the presence of host and hostess, Ethelberta contrived to exchange a few words with her father.

'In excellent time,' he whispered, full of paternal pride at the superb audacity of her situation here in relation to his. 'About half of them are come.'

'Mr Neigh?'

'Not yet; he's coming.'

'Lord Mountclere?'

'Yes. He came absurdly early; ten minutes before anybody else, so that Mrs D. could hardly get on her bracelets and things soon enough to scramble downstairs and receive him; and he's as nervous as a boy. Keep up your spirits, dear, and don't mind me.'

'I will, father. And let Picotee see me at dinner if you can. She is very anxious to look at me. She will be here directly.'

And Ethelberta, having been announced, joined the chamberful of assembled guests, among whom for the present we lose sight of her.

Meanwhile the evening outside the house was deepening in tone, and the lamps began to blink up. Her sister having departed, Picotee hastily arrayed herself in a little black jacket and chip hat,* and tripped across the park to the same point. Chickerel had directed a maid-servant known as Jane to receive his humbler daughter and make her comfortable; and that friendly person, who spoke as if she had known Picotee five-and-twenty years, took her to the housekeeper's room, where the visitor deposited her jacket and hat, and rested awhile.

A quick-eyed, light-haired, slight-built woman came in when Jane had gone. 'Are you Miss Chickerel?' she said to Picotee.

'Yes,' said Picotee, guessing that this was Menlove, and fearing her a little.

'Jane tells me that you have come to visit your father, and would like to look at the company going to dinner. Well, they are not much to see, you know; but such as they are you are welcome to the sight of. Come along with me.'

'I think I would rather wait for father, if you will excuse me, please.'

'Your father is busy now; it is no use for you to think of saying anything to him.'

Picotee followed her guide up a back staircase to the height of several flights, and then, crossing a landing, they descended to the upper part of the front stairs.

'Now look over the balustrade, and you will see them all in a minute,' said Mrs Menlove. 'O, you need not be timid; you can look out as far as you like. We are all independent here; no slavery for us: it is not as it is in the country, where servants are considered to be of different blood and bone from their employers, and to have no eyes for anything but their work. Here they are coming.'

Picotee then had the pleasure of looking down upon a series of human crowns – some black, some white, some strangely built upon, some smooth and shining – descending the staircase in disordered column and great discomfort, their owners trying to talk, but breaking off in the midst of syllables to look to their footing. The young girl's eyes had not drooped over the handrail more than a few moments when she softly exclaimed, 'There she is, there she is! How lovely she looks, does she not?'

'Who?' said Mrs Menlove.

Picotee recollected herself, and hastily drew in her impulses. 'My dear mistress,' she said blandly. 'That is she on Mr Doncastle's arm. And look, who is that funny old man the elderly lady is helping downstairs?'

'He is our honoured guest, Lord Mountclere. Mrs Doncastle will have him all through the dinner, and after that he wil devote himself to Mrs Petherwin, your "dear mistress". He keeps looking towards her now, and no doubt thinks it a nuisance that she is not with him. Well, it is useless to stay here. Come a little further – we'll follow them.' Menlove began to lead the way downstairs, but Picotee held back.

'Won't they see us?' she said.

'No. And if they do, it doesn't matter. Mrs Doncastle would not object in the least to the daughter of her respected head man being accidentally seen in the hall.'

They descended to the bottom and stood in the hall. 'O, there's father!' whispered Picotee, with childlike gladness, as Chickerel became visible to her by the door. The butler nodded to his daughter, and became again engrossed in his duties.

'I wish I could see her – my mistress – again,' said Picotee.

'You seem mightily concerned about your mistress,' said Menlove. 'Do you want to see if you have dressed her properly?'

'Yes, partly; and I like her, too. She is very kind to me.'

'You will have a chance of seeing her soon. When the door is nicely open you can look in for a moment. I must leave you now for a few minutes, but I will come again.'

Menlove departed, and Picotee stood waiting. She wondered how Ethelberta was getting on, and whether she enjoyed herself as much as it seemed her duty to do in such a superbly hospitable place. Picotee then turned her attention to the hall, every article of furniture therein appearing worthy of scrutiny to her unaccustomed eyes. Here she walked and looked about for a long time till an excellent opportunity offered itself of seeing how affairs progressed in the dining-room.

Through the partly-opened door there became visible a sideboard which first attracted her attention by its richness. It was, indeed, a noticeable example of modern art-workmanship,* in being exceptionally large, with curious ebony mouldings at different stages; and, while the heavy cupboard doors at the bottom were enriched with inlays of paler wood, other panels were decorated with tiles, as if the massive composition had been erected on the spot as part of the solid building. However, it was on a space higher up that Picotee's eyes and thoughts were fixed. In the great mirror above the middle ledge she could see reflected the upper part of the dining-room, and this suggested to her that she might see Ethelberta and the other guests reflected in the same way by standing on a chair, which, quick as thought, she did.

To Picotee's dazed young vision her beautiful sister appeared as the chief figure of a glorious pleasure-parliament of both sexes, surrounded by whole regiments of candles grouped here and there about the room. She and her companions were seated before a large flower-bed, or small hanging garden, fixed at about the level of the elbow, the attention of all being concentrated rather upon the uninteresting margin of the bed, and upon each other, than on the beautiful natural objects growing in the middle, as it seemed to Picotee. In the ripple of conversation Ethelberta's clear voice could occasionally be heard, and her young sister could see that her eyes were bright, and her face beaming, as if divers social wants and looming penuriousness had never been within her experience. Mr Doncastle was quite absorbed in what she was saying. So was the queer old man whom Menlove had called Lord Mountclere.

'The dashing widow looks very well, does she not?' said a person at Picotee's elbow.

It was her conductor Menlove, now returned again, whom Picotee had quite forgotten.

'She will do some damage here tonight you will find,' continued Menlove. 'How long have you been with her?'

'O, a long time – I mean rather a short time,' stammered Picotee.

'I know her well enough. I was her maid once, or rather her mother-in-law's, but that was long before you knew her. I did not by any means find her so lovable as you seem to think her when I had to do with her at close quarters. An awful flirt – awful. Don't you find her so?'

'I don't know.'

'If you don't yet you will know. But come down from your perch – the dining-room door will not be open again for some time – and I will show you about the rooms upstairs. This is a larger house than Mrs Petherwin's, as you see. Just come and look at the drawing-rooms.'

Wishing much to get rid of Menlove, yet fearing to offend her, Picotee followed upstairs. Dinner was almost over by this time, and when they entered the front drawing-room a young man-servant and maid were there rekindling the lights.

'Now let's have a game of cat-and-mice,' said the maid-servant cheerily. 'There's plenty of time before they come up.'

'Agreed,' said Menlove promptly. 'You will play, will you not, Miss Chickerel?'

'No, indeed,' said Picotee, aghast.

'Never mind, then; you look on.'

Away then ran the housemaid and Menlove, and the young footman started at their heels. Round the room, over the furniture, under the furniture, through the furniture, out of one window, along the balcony, in at another window, again round the room – so they glided with the swiftness of swallows and the noiselessness of ghosts.

Then the housemaid drew a jew's-harp* from her pocket, and struck up a lively waltz *sotto voce*.* The footman seized Menlove, who appeared nothing loth, and began spinning gently round the room with her, to the time of the fascinating measure

Which fashion hails, from countesses to queens,
And maids and valets dance behind the scenes.*

Picotee, who had been accustomed to unceiled* country
cottages all her life, wherein the scamper of a mouse is heard
distinctly from floor to floor, exclaimed in a terrified whisper, at
viewing all this, 'They'll hear you underneath, they'll hear you,
and we shall all be ruined!'

'Not at all,' came from the cautious dancers. 'These are some
of the best built houses in London – double floors, filled in with
material that will deaden any row you like to make, and we
make none. But come and have a turn yourself, Miss Chickerel.'

The young man relinquished Menlove, and on the spur of the
moment seized Picotee. Picotee flounced away from him in
indignation, backing into a corner with ruffled feathers, like a
pullet trying to appear a hen.

'How dare you touch me!' she said, with rounded eyes. 'I'll
tell somebody downstairs of you, who'll soon see about it!'

'What a baby; she'll tell her father.'

'No I shan't; somebody you are all afraid of, that's who I'll
tell.'

'Nonsense,' said Menlove; 'he meant no harm.'

Playtime was now getting short, and further antics being
dangerous on that account, the performers retired again downstairs, Picotee of necessity following. Her nerves were screwed
up to the highest pitch of uneasiness by the grotesque habits of
these men and maids, who were quite unlike the country
servants she had known, and resembled nothing so much as
pixies, elves, or gnomes, peeping up upon human beings from
their shady haunts underground, sometimes for good, sometimes
for ill – sometimes doing heavy work, sometimes none; teasing
and worrying with impish laughter half suppressed, and vanishing directly mortal eyes were bent on them. Separate and distinct
from overt existence under the sun, this life could hardly be
without its distinctive pleasures, all of them being more or less
pervaded by thrills and titillations from games of hazard, and
the perpetual risk of sensational surprises.

Long before this time Picotee had begun to be anxious to get
home again, but Menlove seemed particularly to desire her
company, and pressed her to sit awhile, telling her young friend,
by way of entertainment, of various extraordinary love

adventures in which she had figured as heroine when travelling on the Continent. These stories had one and all a remarkable likeness in a certain point – Menlove was always unwilling to love the adorer, and the adorer was always unwilling to live afterwards on account of it.

'Ha – ha – ha!' in men's voices was heard from the distant dining-room as the two women went on talking.

'And then,' continued Menlove, 'there was that duel I was the cause of between the courier and the French valet. Dear me, what a trouble that was; yet I could do nothing to prevent it. This courier was a very handsome man – they are handsome sometimes.'

'Yes, they are. My aunt married one.'

'Did she? Where do they live?'

'They keep an hotel at Rouen,' murmured Picotee, in doubt whether this should have been told or not.

'Well, he used to follow me to the English Church every Sunday regularly, and I was so determined not to give my hand where my heart could never be, that I slipped out at the other door while he stood expecting me by the one I entered. Here I met M. Pierre, when, as ill luck would have it, the other came round the corner, and seeing me talking to the valet, he challenged him at once.'

'Ha – ha – ha!' was heard again afar.

'Did they fight?' said Picotee.

'Yes, I believe they did. We left Nice the next day; but I heard some time after of a duel not many miles off, and although I could not get hold of the names, I make no doubt it was between those two gentlemen. I never knew which of them fell; poor fellow, whichever it was.'

'Ha – ha – ha – ha – ha – ha!' came from the dining-room.

'Whatever are those boozy men laughing at, I wonder?' said Menlove. 'They are always so noisy when the ladies have gone upstairs. Upon my soul, I'll run up and find out.'

'No, no, don't,' entreated Picotee, putting her hand on her entertainer's arm. 'It seems wrong; it is no concern of ours.'

'Wrong be hanged – anything on an impulse,' said Mrs Menlove, skipping across the room and out of the door, which stood open, as did others in the house, the evening being sultry and oppressive.

Picotee waited in her seat until it occurred to her that she could escape the lady's-maid by going off into her father's pantry in her absence. But before this had been put into effect Menlove appeared again.

'Such fun as they are having up there,' she said. 'Somebody asked Mr Neigh to tell a story which he had told at some previous time, but he was very reluctant to do so, and pretended he could not recollect it. Well, then, the other man – I could not distinguish him by his voice – began telling it, to prompt Mr Neigh's memory; and, as far as I could understand, it was about some lady who thought Mr Neigh was in love with her, and, to find whether he was worth accepting or not, she went with her maid at night to see his estate, and wandered about and got lost, and was frightened, and I don't know what besides. Then Mr Neigh laughed too, and said he liked such common sense in a woman. No names were mentioned, but I fancy, from the awkwardness of Mr Neigh at being compelled to tell it, that the lady is one of those in the drawing-room. I should like to know which it was.'

'I know – have heard something about it,' said Picotee, blushing with anger. 'It was nothing at all like that. I wonder Mr Neigh had the audacity ever to talk of the matter, and to misrepresent it so greatly!'

'Tell all about it, do,' said Menlove.

'O no,' said Picotee. 'I promised not to say a word.'

'It is your mistress, I expect.'

'You may think what you like; but the lady is anything but a mistress of mine.'

The flighty Menlove pressed her to tell the whole story, but finding this useless the subject was changed. Presently her father came in, and, taking no notice of Menlove, told his daughter that she had been called for. Picotee very readily put on her things, and on going outside found Joey awaiting her. Mr Chickerel followed closely, with sharp glances from the corner of his eye, and it was plain from Joey's nervous manner of lingering in the shadows of the area doorway instead of entering the house, that the butler had in some way set himself to prevent all communion between the fair lady's-maid and his son for that evening at least.

He watched Picotee and her brother off the premises, and the pair went on their way towards Exonbury Crescent, very few words passing between them. Picotee's thoughts had turned to the proposed visit to Knollsea, and Joey was sulky under disappointment, and the blank of thwarted purposes.

On the Housetop

30

'Picotee, are you asleep?' Ethelberta whispered softly at dawn the next morning, by the half-opened door of her sister's bedroom.

'No, I keep waking, it is so warm.'

'So do I. Suppose we get up and see the sun rise. The east is filling with flame.'

'Yes, I should like it,' said Picotee.

The restlessness which had brought Ethelberta hither in slippers and dressing-gown at such an early hour owed its origin to another cause than the warmth of the weather; but of that she did not speak as yet. Picotee's room was an attic, with windows in the roof – a chamber dismal enough at all times, and very shadowy now. While Picotee was wrapping up, Ethelberta placed a chair under the window, and mounting upon this they stepped outside, and seated themselves within the parapet.

The air was as clear and fresh as on a mountain side; sparrows chattered, and birds of a species unsuspected at later hours could be heard singing in the park hard by, while here and there on ridges and flats a cat might be seen going calmly home from the devilries of the night to resume the amiabilities of the day.

'I am so sorry I was asleep when you reached home,' said Picotee. 'I was so anxious to tell you something I heard of, and to know what you did; but my eyes would shut, try as I might, and then I tried no longer. Did you see me at all, Berta?'

'Never once. I had an impression that you were there. I fancied you were from father's carefully vacuous look whenever I glanced at his face. But were you careful about what you said, and did you see Menlove? I felt all the time that I had done wrong in letting you come; the gratification to you was not worth the risk to me.'

'I saw her, and talked to her. But I am certain she suspected nothing. I enjoyed myself very much, and there was no risk at all.'

'I am glad it is no worse news. However, you must not go there again: upon that point I am determined.'

'It was a good thing I did go, all the same. I'll tell you why when you have told me what happened to you.'

'Nothing of importance happened to me.'

'I expect you got to know the lord you were to meet?'

'O yes – Lord Mountclere.'

'And it's dreadful how fond he is of you – quite ridiculously taken up with you – I saw that well enough. Such an old man, too; I wouldn't have him for the world!'

'Don't jump at conclusions so absurdly, Picotee. Why wouldn't you have him for the world?'

'Because he is old enough to be my grandfather, and yours too.'

'Indeed he is not; he is only middle-aged.'

'Berta! Sixty-five at least.'

'He may or may not be that; and if he is, it is not old. He is so entertaining that one forgets all about age in connection with him.'

'He laughs like this – "Hee-hee-hee!"' Picotee introduced as much antiquity into her face as she could by screwing it up and suiting the action to the word.

'This very odd thing occurred,' said Ethelberta, to get Picotee off the track of Lord Mountclere's peculiarities, as it seemed. 'I was saying to Mr Neigh that we were going to Knollsea for a time, feeling that he would not be likely to know anything about such an out-of-the-way place, when Lord Mountclere, who was near, said, "I shall be at Enckworth Court in a few days, probably at the time you are at Knollsea. The Imperial Archæological Association holds its meetings in that part of Wessex this season, and Corvsgate Castle, near Knollsea, is one of the places on our list." Then he hoped I should be able to attend. Did you ever hear anything so strange? Now, I should like to attend very much, not on Lord Mountclere's account, but because such gatherings are interesting, and I have never been to one; yet there is this to be considered, would it be right for me to go without a friend to such a place? Another point is, that we shall live in menagerie style at Knollsea for the sake of the children, and we must do it economically in case we accept

Aunt Charlotte's invitation to Rouen; hence, if he or his friends find us out there it will be awkward for me. So the alternative is Knollsea or some other place for us.'

'Let it be Knollsea, now we have once settled it,' said Picotee anxiously. 'I have mentioned to Faith Julian that we shall be there.'

'Mentioned it already! You must have written instantly.'

'I had a few minutes to spare, and I thought I might as well write.'

'Very well; we will stick to Knollsea,' said Ethelberta, half in doubt. 'Yes – otherwise it will be difficult to see about aunt's baptismal certificate. We will hope nobody will take the trouble to pry into our household . . . And now, Picotee, I want to ask you something – something very serious. How would you like me to marry Mr Neigh?'

Ethelberta could not help laughing with a faint shyness as she asked the question under the searching east ray. 'He has asked me to marry him,' she continued, 'and I want to know what you would say to such an arrangement. I don't mean to imply that the event is certain to take place; but, as a mere supposition, what do you say to it, Picotee?' Ethelberta was far from putting this matter before Picotee for advice or opinion; but, like all people who have an innate dislike to hole-and-corner policy, she felt compelled to speak of it to some one.

'I should not like him for you at all,' said Picotee vehemently. 'I would rather you had Mr Ladywell.'

'O, don't name him!'

'I wouldn't have Mr Neigh at any price, nevertheless. It is about him that I was going to tell you.' Picotee proceeded to relate Menlove's account of the story of Ethelberta's escapade, which had been dragged from Neigh the previous evening by the friend to whom he had related it before he was so enamoured of Ethelberta as to regard that performance as a positive virtue in her. 'Nobody was told, or even suspected, who the lady of the anecdote was,' Picotee concluded; 'but I knew instantly, of course, and I think it very unfortunate that we ever went to that dreadful ghostly estate of his, Berta.'

Ethelberta's face heated with mortification. She had no fear that Neigh had told names or other particulars which might lead to her identification by any friend of his, and she could make allowance for bursts of confidence; but there remained the awkward fact that he himself knew her to be the heroine of the episode. What annoyed her most was that Neigh could ever have looked upon her indiscretion as a humorous incident, which he certainly must have done at some time or other to account for his telling it. Had he been angry with her, or sneered at her for going, she could have forgiven him; but to see her manœuvre in the light of a joke, to use it as illustrating his grim theory of womankind, and neither to like nor to dislike her the more for it from first to last, this was to treat her with a cynicism which was intolerable. That Neigh's use of the incident as a stock anecdote ceased long before he had decided to ask her to marry him she had no doubt, but it showed that his love for her was of that sort in which passion makes war upon judgment, and prevails in spite of will. Moreover, he might have been speaking ironically when he alluded to the act as a virtue in a woman, which seemed the more likely when she remembered his cool bearing towards her in the drawing-room. Possibly it was an antipathetic reaction, induced by the renewed recollection of her proceeding.

'I will never marry Mr Neigh!' she said, with decision. 'That shall settle it. You need not think over any such contingency, Picotee. He is one of those horrid men who love with their eyes, the remainder part of him objecting all the time to the feeling; and even if his objections prove the weaker, and the man marries, his general nature conquers again by the time the wedding trip is over, so that the woman is miserable at last, and had better not have had him at all.'

'That applies still more to Lord Mountclere, to my thinking. I never saw anything like the look of his eyes upon you.'

'O no, no – you understand nothing if you say that. But one thing be sure of, there is no marriage likely to take place between myself and Mr Neigh. I have longed for a sound reason for disliking him, and now I have got it. Well, we will talk no more of this – let us think of the nice little pleasure we have in store – our stay at Knollsea. There we will be as free as the wind. And when we are down there, I can drive across to Corvsgate Castle if I wish to attend the Imperial Association meeting, and nobody will know where I came from. Knollsea is not more than five miles from the Castle, I think.'

Picotee was by this time beginning to yawn, and Ethelberta did not feel nearly so wakeful as she had felt half an hour earlier.

Tall and swarthy columns of smoke were now soaring up from the kitchen chimneys around, spreading horizontally when at a great height, and forming a roof of haze which was turning the sun to a copper colour, and by degrees spoiling the sweetness of the new atmosphere that had rolled in from the country during the night, giving it the usual city smell. The resolve to make this rising the beginning of a long and busy day, which should set them beforehand with the rest of the world, weakened with their growing weariness, and an impulse to lie down just for a quarter of an hour before dressing, ended in a sound sleep that did not relinquish its hold upon them till late in the forenoon.

Knollsea
A Lofty Down
A Ruined Castle

31

Knollsea was a seaside village lying snug within two headlands as between a finger and thumb. Everybody in the parish who was not a boatman was a quarrier, unless he were the gentleman who owned half the property and had been a quarryman, or the other gentleman who owned the other half, and had been to sea.

The knowledge of the inhabitants was of the same special sort as their pursuits. The quarrymen in white fustian understood practical geology, the laws and accidents of dips, faults, and cleavage, far better than the ways of the world and mammon; the seafaring men in Guernsey frocks* had a clearer notion of Alexandria, Constantinople, the Cape, and the Indies than of any inland town in their own country. This, for them, consisted of a busy portion, the Channel, where they lived and laboured, and a dull portion, the vague unexplored miles of interior at the back of the ports' which they seldom thought of.

Some wives of the village, it is true, had learned to let lodgings, and others to keep shops. The doors of these latter places were formed of an upper hatch, usually kept open, and a lower hatch, with a bell attached, usually kept shut. Whenever a stranger went in, he would hear a whispering of astonishment from a back room, after which a woman came forward, looking suspiciously at him as an intruder, and advancing slowly enough to allow her mouth to get clear of the meal she was partaking of. Meanwhile the people in the back room would stop their knives and forks in absorbed curiosity as to the reason of the stranger's entry, who by this time feels ashamed of his unwarrantable intrusion into this hermit's cell, and thinks he must take his hat off. The woman is quite alarmed at seeing that he is not one of the fifteen native women and children who patronize her, and nervously puts her hand to the side of her face, which she carries slanting. The visitor finds himself saying what he wants in an apologetic tone, when the woman tells him that they did keep that article once, but do not now; that nobody does, and probably never will again; and as he turns away she looks relieved that the dilemma of having to provide for a stranger has passed off with no worse mishap than disappointing him.

A cottage which stood on a high slope above this townlet and its bay resounded one morning with the notes of a merry company. Ethelberta had managed to find room for herself and her young relations in the house of one of the boatmen, whose wife attended upon them all. Captain Flower, the husband, assisted her in the dinner preparations, when he slipped about the house as lightly as a girl and spoke of himself as cook's mate. The house was so small that the sailor's rich voice, developed by shouting in high winds during a twenty years' experience in the coasting trade, could be heard coming from the kitchen between the chirpings of the children in the parlour. The furniture of this apartment consisted mostly of the painting of a full-rigged ship, done by a man whom the captain had especially selected for the purpose because he had been seven-and-twenty years at sea before touching a brush, and thereby offered a sufficient guarantee that he understood how to paint a vessel properly.

Before this picture sat Ethelberta in a light linen dress, and with tightly-knotted hair – now again Berta Chickerel as of old – serving out breakfast to the rest of the party, and sometimes lifting her eyes to the outlook from the window, which presented a happy combination of grange scenery with marine. Upon the irregular slope between the house and the quay was an orchard of aged trees wherein every apple ripening on the boughs presented its rubicund side towards the cottage, because that building chanced to lie upwards in the same direction as the sun. Under the trees were a few Cape sheep, and over them the stone chimneys of the village below: outside these lay the tanned sails of a ketch or smack, and the violet waters of the bay, seamed and creased by breezes insufficient to raise waves; beyond all a curved wall of cliff, terminating in a promontory, which was flanked by tall and shining obelisks of chalk rising sheer from the trembling blue race beneath.

By anyone sitting in the room that commanded this prospect a white butterfly among the apple-trees might be mistaken for the sails of a yacht far away on the sea; and in the evening when the light was dim, what seemed like a fly crawling upon the window-pane would turn out to be a boat in the bay.

When breakfast was over Ethelberta sat leaning on the window-sill considering her movements for the day. It was the time fixed for the meeting of the Imperial Association at Corvsgate Castle, the celebrated ruin five miles off, and the meeting had some fascinations for her. For one thing, she had never been present at a gathering of the kind, although what was left in any shape from the past was her constant interest, because it recalled her to herself and fortified her mind. Persons waging a harassing social fight are apt in the interest of the combat to forget the smallness of the end in view; and the hints that perishing historical remnants afforded her of the attenuating effects of time even upon great struggles corrected the apparent scale of her own. She was reminded that in a strife for such a ludicrously small object as the entry of drawing-rooms, winning, equally with losing, is below the zero of the true philosopher's concern.

There could never be a more excellent reason than this for going to view the meagre stumps remaining from flourishing bygone centuries, and it had weight with Ethelberta this very day; but it would be difficult to state the whole composition of her motive. The approaching meeting had been one of the great themes at Mr Doncastle's dinner-party, and Lord Mountclere, on learning that she was to be at Knollsea, had recommended her attendance at some, if not all of the meetings, as a desirable and exhilarating change after her laborious season's work in town. It was pleasant to have won her way so far in high places that her health of body and mind should be thus considered –

pleasant, less as personal gratification, than that it casually reflected a proof of her good judgment in a course which everybody among her kindred had condemned by calling a foolhardy undertaking.

And she might go without the restraint of ceremony. Unconventionality – almost eccentricity – was *de rigueur** for one who had been first heard of as a poetess; from whose red lips magic romance had since trilled for weeks to crowds of listeners, as from a perennial spring.

So Ethelberta went, after a considerable pondering how to get there without the needless sacrifice either of dignity or cash. It would be inconsiderate to the children to spend a pound on a brougham when as much as she could spare was wanted for their holiday. It was almost too far to walk. She had, however, decided to walk, when she met a boy with a donkey, who offered to lend it to her for three shillings. The animal was rather sad-looking, but Ethelberta found she could sit upon the pad without discomfort. Considering that she might pull up some distance short of the castle, and leave the ass at a cottage before joining her four-wheeled friends, she struck the bargain and rode on her way.

This was, first by a path on the shore where the tide dragged huskily up and down the shingle without disturbing it, and thence up the steep crest of land opposite, where in she lingered awhile to let the ass breathe. On one of the spires of chalk into which the hill here had been split was perched a cormorant, silent and motionless, with wings spread out to dry in the sun after his morning's fishing, their white surface shining like mail. Retiring without disturbing him and turning to the left along the lofty ridge which ran inland, the country on each side lay beneath her like a map, domains behind domains' parishes by the score, harbours, fir-woods, and little inland seas mixing curiously together. Thence she ambled along through a huge cemetery of barrows, containing human dust from prehistoric times.

Standing on the top of a giant's grave in this antique land, Ethelberta lifted her eyes to behold two sorts of weather pervading Nature at the same time. Far below on the right hand it was a fine day, and the silver sunbeams lighted up a many-armed inland sea which stretched round an island with fir-trees and gorse, and amid brilliant crimson heaths wherein white paths and roads occasionally met the eye in dashes and zig-zags like flashes of lightning. Outside, where the broad Channel appeared, a beryl-line and opalized variegation of ripples, currents, deeps, and shallows, lay as fair under the sun as a New Jerusalem,* the shores being of gleaming sand. Upon the radiant heather bees and butterflies were busy, she knew, and the birds on that side were just beginning their autumn songs.

On the left, quite up to her position, was dark and cloudy weather, shading a valley of heavy greens and browns, which at its further side rose to meet the sea in tall cliffs, suggesting even here at their back how terrible were their aspects seaward in a growling south-west gale. Here grassed hills rose like knuckles gloved in dark olive, and little plantations between them formed a still deeper and sadder monochrome. A zinc sky met a leaden sea on this hand, the low wind groaned and whined, and not a bird sang.

The ridge along which Ethelberta rode – Nine-Barrow Down by name – divided these two climates like a wall; it soon became apparent that they were wrestling for mastery immediately in her pathway. The issue long remained doubtful, and this being an imaginative hour with her, she watched as typical of her own fortunes how the front of battle swayed – now to the west, flooding her with sun, now to the east, covering her with shade: then the wind moved round to the north, a blue hole appeared in the overhanging cloud, at about the place of the north star; and the sunlight spread on both sides of her.

The towers of the notable ruin to be visited rose out of the furthermost shoulder of the upland as she advanced, its site being the slope and crest of a smoothly nibbled mount at the toe of the ridge she had followed. When observing the previous uncertainty of the weather on this side Ethelberta had been led to doubt if the meeting would be held here today, and she was now strengthened in her opinion that it would not by the total absence of human figures amid the ruins, though the time of appointment was past. This disposed of another question which had perplexed her: where to find a stable for the ass during the meeting, for she had scarcely liked the idea of facing the whole body of lords and gentlemen upon the animal's back. She now decided to retain her seat, ride round the ruin, and go home again, without troubling further about the movements of the Association or acquaintance with the members composing it.

Accordingly Ethelberta crossed the bridge over the moat, and rode under the first archway into the outer ward. As she had expected, not a soul was here. The arrow-slits, portcullis-grooves, and staircases met her eye as familiar friends, for in her childhood she had once paid a visit to the spot. Ascending the green incline and through another arch into the second ward, she still pressed on, till at last the ass was unable to clamber an inch further. Here she dismounted, and tying him to a stone which projected like a fang from a raw edge of wall, performed the remainder of the ascent on foot. Once among the towers above, she became so interested in the windy corridors, mildewed dungeons, and the tribe of daws peering invidiously upon her from overhead, that she forgot the flight of time.

Nearly three-quarters of an hour passed before she came out from the immense walls, and looked from an opening to the front over the wide expanse of the outer ward, by which she had ascended.

Ethelberta was taken aback to see there a file of shining carriages, which had arrived during her seclusion in the keep. From these began to burst a miscellany of many-coloured draperies, blue, buff, pied, and black; they united into one, and crept up the incline like a cloud, which then parted into fragments, dived into old doorways, and lost substance behind projecting piles. Recognizing in this the ladies and gentlemen of the meeting, her first thought was how to escape, for she was suddenly overcome with dread to meet them all single-handed as she stood. She drew back and hurried round to the side, as the laughter and voices of the assembly began to be audible; and, more than ever vexed that she could not have fallen in with them in some unobtrusive way, Ethelberta found that they were immediately beneath her.

Venturing to peep forward again, what was her mortification at finding them gathered in a ring, round no object of interest belonging to the ruin, but round her faithful beast, who had loosened himself in some way from the stone, and stood in the middle of a plat of grass, placidly regarding them.

Being now in the teeth of the Association, there was nothing to do but to go on, since, if she did not, the next few steps of their advance would disclose her. She made the best of it, and began to descend in the broad view of the assembly, from the midst of which proceeded a laugh – 'Hee-hee-hee!' Ethelberta knew that Lord Mountclere was there.

'The poor thing has strayed from its owner,' said one lady, as they all stood eyeing the apparition of the ass.

'It may belong to some of the villagers,' said the President in a historical voice: 'and it may be appropriate to mention that many were kept here in olden times: they were largely used as beasts of burden in victualling the castle previous to the last siege,* in the year sixteen hundred and forty-five.'

'It is very weary, and has come a long way, I think,' said a lady; adding, in an imaginative tone, 'the humble creature looks so aged and is so quaintly saddled that we may suppose it to be only an animated relic, of the same date as the other remains.'

By this time Lord Mountclere had noticed Ethelberta's presence, and straightening himself to ten years younger he lifted his hat in answer to her smile, and came up jauntily. It was a good time now to see what the viscount was really like. He appeared to be about sixty-five, and the dignified aspect which he wore to a gazer at a distance became depreciated to jocund slyness upon nearer view, when the small type could be read between the leading lines. Then it could be seen that his upper lip dropped to a point in the middle, as if impressing silence upon his too demonstrative lower one. His right and left profiles were different, one corner of his mouth being more compressed than the other, producing a deep line thence downwards to the side of his chin. Each eyebrow rose obliquely outwards and upwards, and was thus far above the little eye, shining with the clearness of a pond that has just been able to weather the heats of summer. Below this was a preternaturally fat jowl, which, by thrusting against cheeks and chin, caused the arch old mouth to be almost buried at the corners.

A few words of greeting passed, and Ethelberta told him how she was fearing to meet them all, united and primed with their morning's knowledge as they appeared to be.

'Well, we have not done much yet,' said Lord Mountclere. 'As for myself, I have given no thought at all to our day's work. I had not forgotten your promise to attend, if you could possibly drive across, and – hee-hee-hee! – I have frequently looked towards the hill where the road descends ... Will you now permit me to introduce some of my party – as many of them as you care to know by name? I think they would all like to speak to you.'

Ethelberta then found herself nominally made known to ten or a dozen ladies and gentlemen who had wished for special acquaintance with her. She stood there, as all women stand who have made themselves remarkable by their originality, or devotion to any singular cause, as a person freed of her hampering and inconvenient sex, and, by virtue of her popularity, unfettered from the conventionalities of manner prescribed by custom for household womankind. The charter to move abroad unchaperoned, which society for good reasons grants only to women of three sorts – the famous, the ministering, and the improper – Ethelberta was in a fair way to make splendid use of: instead of walking in protected lanes she experienced that luxury of isolation which normally is enjoyed by men alone, in conjunction with the attention naturally bestowed on a woman young and fair. Among the presentations were Mr and Mrs Tynn, member and member's mainspring for North Wessex; Sir Cyril and Lady Blandsbury; Lady Jane Joy; and the Honourable Edgar Mountclere, the viscount's brother. There also hovered near her the learned Doctor Yore; Mr Small, a profound writer, who never printed his works; the Reverend Mr Brook, rector; the Very Reverend Dr Taylor, dean; and the moderately Reverend Mr Tinkleton, Nonconformist, who had slipped into the fold by chance.

These and others looked with interest at Ethelberta; the old county fathers hard, as at a questionable town phenomenon, the county sons tenderly, as at a pretty creature, and the county daughters with great admiration, as at a lady reported by their mammas to be no better than she should be. It will be seen that Ethelberta was the sort of woman that well-rooted local people might like to look at on such a free and friendly occasion as an archæological meeting, where, to gratify a pleasant whim, the picturesque form of acquaintance is for the nonce preferred to the useful, the spirits being so brisk as to swerve from strict attention to the select and sequent gifts of heaven, blood and acres, to consider for an idle moment the subversive Mephistophelian* endowment, brains.

'Our progress in the survey of the castle has not been far as yet,' Lord Mountclere resumed; 'indeed we have only just arrived, the weather this morning being so unsettled. When you came up we were engaged in a preliminary study of the poor animal you see there: how it could have got up here we cannot understand.'

He pointed as he spoke to the donkey which had brought Ethelberta thither, whereupon she was silent, and gazed at her untoward beast as if she had never before beheld him.

The ass looked at Ethelberta as though he would say, 'Why don't you own me, after safely bringing you over those weary hills?' But the pride and emulation which had made her what she was would not permit her, as the most lovely woman there, to take upon her own shoulders the ridicule that had already been cast upon the ass. Had he been young and gaily caparisoned, she might have done it; but his age, the clumsy trappings of rustic make, and his needy woeful look of hard servitude, were too much to endure.

'Many come and picnic here,' she said serenely, 'and the animal may have been left till they return from some walk.'

'True,' said Lord Mountclere, without the slightest suspicion of the truth. The humble ass hung his head in his usual manner, and it demanded little fancy from Ethelberta to imagine that he despised her. And then her mind flew back to her history and extraction, to her father – perhaps at that moment inventing a private plate-powder* in an underground pantry – and with a groan at her inconsistency in being ashamed of the ass, she said in her heart, 'My God, what a thing am I!'

They then all moved on to another part of the castle, the viscount busying himself round and round her person like the head scraper at a pig-killing; and as they went indiscriminately mingled, jesting lightly or talking in earnest, she beheld ahead of her the form of Neigh among the rest.

Now, there could only be one reason on earth for Neigh's presence – her remark that she might attend – for Neigh took no more interest in antiquities than in the back of the moon. Ethelberta was a little flurried; perhaps he had come to scold her, or to treat her badly in that indefinable way of his by which he could make a woman feel as nothing without any direct act at all. She was afraid of him, and, determining to shun him, was thankful that Lord Mountclere was near, to take off the edge of Neigh's manner towards her if he approached.

'Do you know in what part of the ruins the lecture is to be given?' she said to the viscount.

'Wherever you like,' he replied gallantly. 'Do you propose a place, and I will get Dr Yore to adopt it. Say, shall it be here, or where they are standing?'

How could Ethelberta refrain from exercising a little power when it was put into her hands in this way?

'Let it be here,' she said, 'if it makes no difference to the meeting.'

'It shall be,' said Lord Mountclere.

And then the lively old nobleman skipped like a roe to the President and to Dr Yore, who was to read the paper on the castle, and they soon appeared coming back to where the viscount's party and Ethelberta were beginning to seat themselves. The bulk of the company followed, and Dr Yore began.

He must have had a countenance of leather – as, indeed, from his colour he appeared to have – to stand unmoved in his position, and read, and look up to give explanations, without a change of muscle, under the dozens of bright eyes that were there converged upon him, like the sticks of a fan, from the ladies who sat round him in a semicircle upon the grass. However, he went on calmly, and the women sheltered themselves from the heat with their umbrellas and sunshades, their ears lulled by the hum of insects, and by the drone of the doctor's voice. The reader buzzed on with the history of the castle* tracing its development from a mound with a few earthworks to its condition in Norman times; he related monkish marvels connected with the spot; its resistance under Matilda to Stephen, its probable shape while a residence of King John, and the sad story of the Damsel of Brittany, sister of his victim Arthur, who was confined here in company with the two daughters of Alexander, king of Scotland. He went on to recount the confinement of Edward II herein, previous to his murder at Berkeley, the gay doings in the reign of Elizabeth, and so downward through time to the final overthrow of the stern old pile. As he proceeded, the lecturer pointed with his finger at the various features appertaining to the date of his story, which he told with splendid vigour when he had warmed to his work, till his narrative, particularly in the conjectural and romantic parts, where it became coloured rather by the speaker's imagination than by the pigments of history, gathered together the wandering thoughts of all. It was easy for him then to meet those fair concentred eyes, when the sunshades were thrown back, and

complexions forgotten, in the interest of the history. The doctor's face was then no longer criticized as a rugged boulder, a
dried fig, an oak carving, or a walnut shell, but became blotted
out like a mountain top in a shining haze by the nebulous
pictures conjured by his tale.

Then the lecture ended, and questions were asked, and
individuals of the company wandered at will, the light dresses
of the ladies sweeping over the hot grass and brushing up
thistledown which had hitherto lain quiescent, so that it rose in
a flight from the skirts of each like a comet's tail.

Some of Lord Mountclere's party, including himself and
Ethelberta, wandered now into a cool dungeon, partly open to
the air overhead, where long arms of ivy hung between their
eyes and the white sky. While they were here, Lady Jane Joy and
some other friends of the viscount told Ethelberta that they were
probably coming on to Knollsea.

She instantly perceived that getting into close quarters in that
way might be very inconvenient, considering the youngsters she
had under her charge, and straightway decided upon a point
that she had debated for several days – a visit to her aunt in
Normandy. In London it had been a mere thought, but the
Channel had looked so tempting from its brink that the journey
was virtually fixed as soon as she reached Knollsea, and found
that a little pleasure steamer crossed to Cherbourg once a week
during the summer, so that she would not have to enter the
crowded routes at all.

'I am afraid I shall not see you in Knollsea,' she said. 'I am
about to go to Cherbourg and then to Rouen.'

'How sorry I am. When do you leave?'

'At the beginning of next week,' said Ethelberta, settling the
time there and then.

'Did I hear you say that you were going to Cherbourg and
Rouen?' Lord Mountclere inquired.

'I think to do so,' said Ethelberta.

'I am going to Normandy myself,' said a voice behind her,
and without turning she knew that Neigh was standing there.

They next went outside, and Lord Mountclere offered Ethelberta his arm on the ground of assisting her down the burnished
grass slope. Ethelberta, having pity upon him, took it; but the
assistance was all on her side; she stood like a statue amid his
slips and totterings, some of which taxed her strength heavily,

and her ingenuity more, to appear as the supported and not the supporter. The incident brought Neigh still further from his retirement, and she learnt that he was one of a yachting party which had put in at Knollsea that morning; she was greatly relieved to find that he was just now on his way to London, whence he would probably proceed on his journey abroad.

Ethelberta adhered as well as she could to her resolve that Neigh should not speak with her alone, but by dint of perseverance he did manage to address her without being overheard.

'Will you give me an answer?' said Neigh. 'I have come on purpose.'

'I cannot just now. I have been led to doubt you.'

'Doubt me? What new wrong have I done?'

'Spoken jestingly of my visit to Farnfield.'

'Good ——! I did not speak or think of you. When I told that incident I had no idea who the lady was – I did not know it was you till two days later, and I at once held my tongue. I vow to you upon my soul and life that what I say is true. How shall I prove my truth better than by my errand here?'

'Don't speak of this now. I am so occupied with other things. I am going to Rouen, and will think of it on my way.'

'I am going there too. When do you go?'

'I shall be in Rouen next Wednesday, I hope.'

'May I ask where?'

'Hôtel Beau Séjour.'

'Will you give me an answer there? I can easily call upon you. It is now a month and more since you first led me to hope—'

'I did not lead you to hope – at any rate clearly.'

'Indirectly you did. And although I am willing to be as considerate as any man ought to be in giving you time to think over the question, there is a limit to my patience. Any necessary delay I will put up with, but I won't be trifled with. I hate all nonsense, and can't stand it.'

'Indeed. Good morning.'

'But Mrs Petherwin – just one word.'

'I have nothing to say.'

'I will meet you at Rouen for an answer. I would meet you in Hades* for the matter of that. Remember this: next Wednesday, if I live, I shall call upon you at Rouen.'

She did not say nay.

'May I?' he added.

'If you will.'

'But say it shall be an appointment?'

'Very well.'

Lord Mountclere was by this time toddling towards them to ask if they would come on to his house, Enckworth Court, not very far distant, to lunch with the rest of the party. Neigh, having already arranged to go on to town that afternoon, was obliged to decline, and Ethelberta thought fit to do the same, idly asking Lord Mountclere if Enckworth Court lay in the direction of a gorge that was visible where they stood.

'No; considerably to the right,' he said. 'The opening you are looking at would reveal the sea if it were not for the trees that block the way. Ah, those trees have a history; they are half-a-dozen elms which I planted myself when I was a boy. How time flies!'

'It is unfortunate they stand just so as to cover the blue bit of sea. That addition would double the value of the view from here.'

'You would prefer the blue sea to the trees?'

'In that particular spot I should; they might have looked just as well, and yet have hidden nothing worth seeing. The narrow slit would have been invaluable there.'

'They shall fall before the sun sets, in deference to your opinion,' said Lord Mountclere.

'That would be rash indeed,' said Ethelberta, laughing, 'when my opinion on such a point may be worth nothing whatever.'

'Where no other is acted upon, it is practically the universal one,' he replied gaily.

And then Ethelberta's elderly admirer bade her adieu, and away the whole party drove in a long train over the hills towards the valley wherein stood Enckworth Court. Ethelberta's carriage was supposed by her friends to have been left at the village inn, as were many others, and her retiring from view on foot attracted no notice.

She watched them out of sight, and she also saw the rest depart – those who, their interest in archeology having begun and ended with this spot, had, like herself, declined the hospitable viscount's invitation, and started to drive or walk at once home again. Thereupon the castle was quite deserted except by Ethelberta, the ass, and the jackdaws, now floundering at ease again in and about the ivy of the keep.

Not wishing to enter Knollsea till the evening shades were falling, she still walked amid the ruins, examining more leisurely some points which the stress of keeping herself companionable would not allow her to attend to while the assemblage was present. At the end of the survey, being somewhat weary with her clambering, she sat down on the slope commanding the gorge where the trees grew, to make a pencil sketch of the landscape as it was revealed between the ragged walls. Thus engaged she weighed the circumstances of Lord Mountclere's invitation, and could not be certain if it were prudishness or simple propriety in herself which had instigated her to refuse. She would have liked the visit for many reasons, and if Lord Mountclere had been anybody but a remarkably attentive old widower, she would have gone. As it was, it had occurred to her that there was something in his tone which should lead her to hesitate. Were any among the elderly or married ladies who had appeared upon the ground in a detached form as she had done – and many had appeared thus – invited to Enckworth; and if not, why were they not? That Lord Mountclere admired her there was no doubt, and for this reason it behoved her to be careful. His disappointment at parting from her was, in one aspect, simply laughable, from its odd resemblance to the unfeigned sorrow of a boy of fifteen at a first parting from his first love; in another aspect it caused reflection; and she thought again of his curiosity about her doings for the remainder of the summer.

While she sketched and thought thus, the shadows grew longer, and the sun low. And then she perceived a movement in the gorge. One of the trees forming the curtain across it began to wave strangely: it went further to one side, and fell. Where the tree had stood was now a rent in the foliage, and through the narrow rent could be seen the distant sea.

Ethelberta uttered a soft exclamation. It was not caused by the surprise she had felt, nor by the intrinsic interest of the sight, nor by want of comprehension. It was a sudden realization of vague things hitherto dreamed of from a distance only – a sense of novel power put into her hands without request or expectation. A landscape was to be altered to suit her whim. She had in her life-time moved essentially larger mountains,* but they had seemed of far less splendid material than this; for it was the nature of the gratification rather than its magnitude which enchanted the fancy of a woman whose poetry, in spite of her necessities, was hardly yet extinguished. But there was something more, with which poetry had little to do. Whether the opinion of any pretty woman in England was of more weight with Lord Mountclere than memories of his boyhood, or whether that distinction was reserved for her alone; this was a point that she would have liked to know.

The enjoyment of power in a new element, an enjoyment somewhat resembling in kind that which is given by a first ride or swim, held Ethelberta to the spot, and she waited, but sketched no more. Another tree-top swayed and vanished as before, and the slit of sea was larger still. Her mind and eye were so occupied with this matter that, sitting in her nook, she did not observe a thin young man, his boots white with the dust of a long journey on foot, who arrived at the castle by the valley-road from Knollsea. He looked awhile at the ruin, and, skirting its flank instead of entering by the great gateway, climbed up the scarp and walked in through a breach. After standing for a moment among the walls, now silent and apparently empty, with a disappointed look he descended the slope, and proceeded along on his way.

Ethelberta, who was in quite another part of the castle, saw the black spot diminishing to the size of a fly as he receded along the dusty road, and soon after she descended on the other side, where she remounted the ass, and ambled homeward as she had come, in no bright mood. What, seeing the precariousness of her state, was the day's triumph worth after all, unless, before her beauty abated, she could ensure her position against the attacks of chance?

> To be thus is nothing;
> But to be safely thus.*

– she said it more than once on her journey that day.

On entering the sitting-room of their cot up the hill she found it empty, and from a change perceptible in the position of small articles of furniture, something unusual seemed to have taken place in her absence. The dwelling being of that sort in which whatever goes on in one room is audible through all the rest, Picotee, who was upstairs, heard the arrival and came down. Picotee's face was rosed over with the brilliance of some excitement. 'What do you think I have to tell you, Berta?' she said.

'I have no idea,' said her sister. 'Surely,' she added, her face intensifying to a wan sadness, 'Mr Julian has not been here?'

'Yes,' said Picotee. 'And we went down to the sands – he, and Myrtle, and Georgina, and Emmeline, and I – and Cornelia came down when she had put away the dinner. And then we dug wriggles* out of the sand with Myrtle's spade: we got such a lot, and had such fun; they are in a dish in the kitchen. Mr Julian came to see you; but at last he could wait no longer, and when I told him you were at the meeting in the castle ruins he said he would try to find you there on his way home, if he could get there before the meeting broke up.'

'Then it was he I saw far away on the road – yes, it must have been.' She remained in gloomy reverie a few moments, and then said, 'Very well – let it be. Picotee, get me some tea: I do not want dinner.'

But the news of Christopher's visit seemed to have taken away her appetite for tea also, and after sitting a little while she flung herself down upon the couch, and told Picotee that she had settled to go and see their aunt Charlotte.

'I am going to write to Sol and Dan to ask them to meet me there,' she added. 'I want them, if possible, to see Paris. It will improve them greatly in their trades, I am thinking, if they can see the kinds of joinery and decoration practised in France. They agreed to go, if I should wish it, before we left London. You, of course, will go as my maid.'

Picotee gazed upon the sea with a crestfallen look, as if she would rather not cross it in any capacity just then.

'It would scarcely be worth going to the expense of taking me, would it?' she said.

The cause of Picotee's sudden sense of economy was so plain that her sister smiled; but young love, however foolish, is to a thinking person far too tragic a power for ridicule; and Ethelberta forbore, going on as if Picotee had not spoken: 'I must have you with me. I may be seen there: so many are passing through Rouen at this time of the year. Cornelia can take excellent care of the children while we are gone. I want to get out of England, and I will get out of England. There is nothing but vanity and vexation* here.'

'I am sorry you were away when he called,' said Picotee gently.

'O, I don't mean that. I wish there were no different ranks in the world, and that contrivance were not a necessary faculty to have at all. Well, we are going to cross by the little steamer that puts in here, and we are going on Monday.' She added in another minute, 'What had Mr Julian to tell us that he came here? How did he find us out?'

'I mentioned that we were coming here in my letter to Faith. Mr Julian says that perhaps he and his sister may also come for a few days before the season is over. I should like to see Miss Julian again. She is such a nice girl.'

'Yes.' Ethelberta played with her hair, and looked at the ceiling as she reclined. 'I have decided after all,' she said, 'that it will be better to take Cornelia as my maid, and leave you here with the children. Cornelia is stronger as a companion than you, and she will be delighted to go. Do you think you are competent to keep Myrtle and Georgina out of harm's way?'

'O yes – I will be exceedingly careful,' said Picotee, with great vivacity. 'And if there is time I can go on teaching them a little.' Then Picotee caught Ethelberta's eye, and colouring red, sank down beside her sister, whispering, 'I know why it is! But if you would rather have me with you I will go, and not once wish to stay.'

Ethelberta looked as if she knew all about that, and said, 'Of course there will be no necessity to tell the Julians about my departure until they have fixed the time for coming, and cannot alter their minds.'

The sound of the children with Cornelia, and their appearance outside the window, pushing between the fuchsia bushes which overhung the path, put an end to this dialogue; they entered armed with buckets and spades, a very moist and sandy aspect pervading them as far up as the high-water mark of their clothing, and began to tell Ethelberta of the wonders of the deep.*

A Room in Enckworth Court

32

'Are you sure the report is true?'

'I am sure that what I say is true, my lord; but it is hardly to be called a report. It is a secret, known at present to nobody but myself and Mrs Doncastle's maid.'

The speaker was Lord Mountclere's trusty valet, and the conversation was between him and the viscount in a dressing-room at Enckworth Court, on the evening after the meeting of archæologists at Corvsgate Castle.

'H'm-h'm; the daughter of a butler. Does Mrs Doncastle know of this yet, or Mr Neigh, or any of their friends?'

'No, my lord.'

'You are quite positive?'

'Quite positive. I was, by accident, the first that Mrs Menlove named the matter to, and I told her it might be much to her advantage if she took particular care it should go no further.'

'Mrs Menlove! Who's she?'

'The lady's-maid at Mrs Doncastle's, my lord.'

'O, ah – of course. You may leave me now, Tipman.' Lord Mountclere remained in thought for a moment. 'A clever little puss, to hoodwink us all like this – hee-hee!' – he murmured. 'Her education – how finished; and her beauty – so seldom that I meet with such a woman. Cut down my elms to please a butler's daughter – what a joke – certainly a good joke! To interest me in her on the right side instead of the wrong was strange. But it can be made to change sides – hee-hee! – it can be made to change sides! Tipman!'

Tipman came forward from the doorway.

'Will you take care that that piece of gossip you mentioned to me is not repeated in this house? I strongly disapprove of talebearing of any sort, and wish to hear no more of this. Such stories are never true. Answer me – do you hear? Such stories are never true.'

'I beg pardon, but I think your lordship will find this one true,' said the valet quietly.

'Then where did she get her manners and education? Do you know?'

'I do not, my lord. I suppose she picked 'em up by her wits.'

'Never mind what you suppose,' said the old man impatiently. 'Whenever I ask a question of you tell me what you know, and no more.'

'Quite so, my lord. I beg your lordship's pardon for supposing.'

'H'm-h'm. Have the fashion-books and plates arrived yet?'

'*Le Follet** has, my lord; but not the others.'

'Let me have it at once. Always bring it to me at once. Are there any handsome ones this time?'

'They are much the same class of female as usual, I think, my lord,' said Tipman, fetching the paper and laying it before him.

'Yes, they are,' said the viscount, leaning back and scrutinizing the faces of the women one by one, and talking softly to himself in a way that had grown upon him as his age increased. 'Yet they are very well: that one with her shoulder turned is pure and charming – the brown-haired one will pass. All very harmless and innocent, but without character; no soul, or inspiration, or eloquence of eye. What an eye was hers! There is not a girl among them so beautiful . . . Tipman! Come and take it away. I don't think I will subscribe to these papers any longer – how long have I subscribed? Never mind – I take no interest in these things, and I suppose I must give them up. What white article is that I see on the floor yonder?'

'I can see nothing, my lord.'

'Yes, yes, you can. At the other end of the room. It is a white handkerchief. Bring it to me.'

'I beg pardon, my lord, but I cannot see any white handkerchief. Whereabouts does your lordship mean?'

'There in the corner. If it is not a handkerchief, what is it? Walk along till you come to it – that is it; now a little further – now your foot is against it.'

'O that – it is not anything. It is the light reflected against the skirting, so that it looks like a white patch of something – that is all.'

'H'm-h'm. My eyes – how weak they are! I am getting old, that's what it is: I am an old man.'

'O no, my lord.'

'Yes, an old man.'

'Well, we shall all be old some day, and so will your lordship, I suppose; but as yet—'

'I tell you I am an old man!'

'Yes, my lord – I did not mean to contradict. An old man in one sense – old in a young man's sense, but not in a house-of-parliament or historical sense. A little oldish – I meant that, my lord.'

'I may be an old man in one sense or in another sense in your mind; but let me tell you there are men older than I.'

'Yes, so there are, my lord.'

'People may call me what they please, and you may be impertinent enough to repeat to me what they say, but let me tell you I am not a very old man after all. I am not an old man.'

'Old in knowledge of the world I meant, my lord, not in years.'

'Well, yes. Experience of course I cannot be without. And I like what is beautiful. Tipman, you must go to Knollsea; don't send, but go yourself, as I wish nobody else to be concerned in this. Go to Knollsea, and find out when the steamboat for Cherbourg starts; and when you have done that, I shall want you to send Taylor to me. I wish Captain Strong to bring the *Fawn* round into Knollsea Bay. Next week I may want you to go to Cherbourg in the yacht with me – if the Channel is pretty calm – and then perhaps to Rouen and Paris. But I will speak of that tomorrow.'

'Very good, my lord.'

'Meanwhile I recommend that you and Mrs Menlove repeat nothing you may have heard concerning the lady you just now spoke of. Here is a slight present for Mrs Menlove; and accept this for yourself.' He handed money.

'Your lordship may be sure we will not,' the valet replied.

The English Channel
Normandy

33

On Monday morning the little steamer *Speedwell* made her appearance round the promontory by Knollsea Bay, to take in passengers for the transit to Cherbourg. Breezes the freshest that could blow without verging on keenness flew over the quivering deeps and shallows; and the sunbeams pierced every detail of barrow, path, and rabbit-run upon the lofty convexity of down and waste which shut in Knollsea from the world to the west.

They left the pier at eight o'clock, faking at first a short easterly course to avoid a sinister ledge of lime-stones jutting from the water like crocodile's teeth, which first obtained notoriety in English history through being the spot whereon a formidable Danish fleet* went to pieces a thousand years ago. At the moment that the *Speedwell* turned to enter upon the direct course, a schooner-yacht, whose sheets gleamed like bridal satin, loosed from a remoter part of the bay; continuing to bear off, she cut across the steamer's wake, and took a course almost due southerly, which was precisely that of the *Speedwell.* The wind was very favourable for the yacht, blowing a few points from north in a steady pressure on her quarter, and, having been built with every modern appliance that shipwrights could offer, the schooner found no difficulty in getting abreast, and even ahead, of the steamer, as soon as she had escaped the shelter of the hills.

The more or less parallel courses of the vessels continued for some time without causing any remark among the people on board the *Speedwell.* At length one noticed the fact, and another; and then it became the general topic of conversation in the group upon the bridge, where Ethelberta, her hair getting frizzed and her cheeks carnationed by the wind, sat upon a camp-stool looking towards the prow.

'She is bound for Guernsey,' said one. 'In half-an-hour she will put about for a more westerly course, you'll see.'

'She is not for Guernsey or anywhere that way,' said an acquaintance, looking through his glass. 'If she is out for anything more than a morning cruise, she is bound for our port. I should not wonder if she is crossing to get stocked, as most of them do, to save the duty on her wine and provisions.'

'Do you know whose yacht it is?'

'I do not.'

Ethelberta looked at the light leaning figure of the pretty schooner, which seemed to skate along upon her bilge and make white shavings of all the sea that touched her. She at first imagined that this might be the yacht Neigh had arrived in at the end of the previous week, for she knew that he came as one of a yachting party, and she had noticed no other boat of that sort in the bay since his arrival. But as all his party had gone ashore and not yet returned, she was surprised to see the supposed vessel here. To add to her perplexity, she could not be positive, now that it came to a real nautical query, whether the craft of Neigh's friends had one mast or two, for she had caught but a fragmentary view of the topsail over the apple-trees.

'Is that the yacht which has been lying at Knollsea for the last few days?' she inquired of the master of the *Speedwell*, as soon as she had an opportunity.

The master warmed beneath his copper-coloured rind. 'O no, miss; that one you saw was a cutter – a smaller boat altogether,' he replied. 'Built on the sliding-keel principle, you understand, miss – and red below her water-line, if you noticed. This is Lord Mountclere's yacht – the *Fawn*. You might have seen her re'ching* in round Old-Harry Rock this morning afore we started.'

'Lord Mountclere's?'

'Yes – a nobleman of this neighbourhood. But he don't do so much at yachting as he used to in his younger days. I believe he's aboard this morning, however.'

Ethelberta now became more absorbed than ever in their ocean comrade, and watched its motions continually. The schooner was considerably in advance of them by this time, and seemed to be getting by degrees out of their course. She wondered if Lord Mountclere could be really going to Cherbourg: if so, why had he said nothing about the trip to her when she spoke of her own approaching voyage thither? The yacht changed its character in her eyes; losing the indefinite interest of the unknown, it acquired the charm of a riddle on motives, of which the alternatives were, had Lord Mountclere's journey anything to do with her own, or had it not? Common probability pointed to the latter supposition; but the time of starting, the course of the yacht, and recollections of Lord Mountclere's homage, suggested the more extraordinary possibility.

She went across to Cornelia. 'The man who handed us on board – didn't I see him speaking to you this morning?' she said.

'O yes,' said Cornelia. 'He asked if my mistress was the popular Mrs Petherwin?'

'And you told him, I suppose?'

'Yes.'

'What made you do that, Cornelia?'

'I thought I might: I couldn't help it. When I went through

the toll-gate, such a gentlemanly-looking man asked me if he should help me to carry the things to the end of the pier; and as we went on together he said he supposed me to be Mrs Petherwin's maid. I said, "Yes." The two men met afterwards, so there would ha' been no good in my denying it to one of 'em.'

'Who was this gentlemanly person?'

'I asked the other man that, and he told me one of Lord Mountclere's upper servants. I knew then there was no harm in having been civil to him. He is well-mannered, and talks splendid language.'

'That yacht you see on our right hand is Lord Mountclere's property. If I do not mistake, we shall have her closer by-and-by, and you may meet your gentlemanly friend again. Be careful how you talk to him.'

Ethelberta sat down, thought of the meeting at Corvsgate Castle, of the dinner-party at Mr Doncastle's, of the strange position she had there been in, and then of her father. She suddenly reproached herself for thoughtlessness; for in her pocket lay a letter from him, which she had taken from the postman that morning at the moment of coming from the door, and in the hurry of embarking had forgotten ever since. Opening it quickly, she read: –

MY DEAR ETHELBERTA, – Your letter reached me yesterday, and I called round at Exonbury Crescent in the afternoon, as you wished. Everything is going on right there, and you have no occasion to be anxious about them. I do not leave town for another week or two, and by the time I am gone Sol and Dan will have returned from Paris, if your mother and Gwendoline want any help: so that you need not hurry back on their account.

I have something else to tell you, which is not quite so satisfactory, and it is this that makes me write at once; but do not be alarmed. It began in this way. A few nights after the dinner-party here I was determined to find out if there was any truth in what you had been told about that boy, and having seen Menlove go out as usual after dark, I followed her. Sure enough, when she had got into the park, up came master Joe, smoking a cigar. As soon as they had met I went towards them, and Menlove, seeing somebody draw nigh, began to edge off, when the blockhead said, 'Never mind, my love, it is only the old man.' Being very provoked with both of them, though she was really the most to blame, I

gave him some smart cuts across the shoulders with my cane, and
told him to go home, which he did with a flea in his ear, the
rascal. I believe I have cured his courting tricks for some little
time.

Well, Menlove then walked by me, quite cool, as if she were
merely a lady passing by chance at the time, which provoked me
still more, knowing the whole truth of it, and I could not help
turning upon her and saying, 'You, madam, ought to be served
the same way.' She replied in very haughty words, and I walked
away, saying that I had something better to do than argue with a
woman of her character at that hour of the evening. This so set
her up that she followed me home, marched into my pantry, and
told me that if I had been more careful about my manners in
calling her a bad character, it might have been better both for me
and my stuck-up daughter – a daw in eagle's plumes* – and so on.
Now it seems that she must have coaxed something out of Joey
about you – for what lad in the world could be a match for a
woman of her experience and arts! I hope she will do you no
serious damage; but I tell you the whole state of affairs exactly as
they are, that you may form your own opinions. After all, there is
no real disgrace, for none of us have ever done wrong, but have
worked honestly for a living. However, I will let you know if
anything serious really happens.

This was all that her father said on the matter, the letter
concluding with messages to the children and directions from
their mother with regard to their clothes.

Ethelberta felt very distinctly that she was in a strait; the old
impression that, unless her position were secured soon, it never
would be secured, returned with great force. A doubt whether it
was worth securing would have been very strong ere this, had
not others besides herself been concerned in her fortunes. She
looked up from her letter, and beheld the pertinacious yacht; it
led her up to a conviction that therein lay a means and an
opportunity.

Nothing further of importance occurred in crossing. Ethelberta's head ached after a while, and Cornelia's healthy cheeks of
red were found to have diminished their colour to the size of a
wafer and the quality of a stain. The *Speedwell* entered the
breakwater at Cherbourg to find the schooner already in
the roadstead; and by the time the steamer was brought up

Ethelberta could see the men on board the yacht clewing up*
and making things snug in a way from which she inferred that
they were not going to leave the harbour again that day. With
the aspect of a fair galleon that could easily out-manœuvre her
persevering buccaneer, Ethelberta passed alongside. Could it be
possible that Lord Mountclere had on her account fixed this day
for his visit across the Channel?

'Well, I would rather be haunted by him than by Mr Neigh,'
she said; and began laying her plans so as to guard against
inconvenient surprises.

The next morning Ethelberta was at the railway station,
taking tickets for herself and Cornelia, when she saw an old yet
sly and somewhat merry-faced Englishman a little way off. He
was attended by a younger man, who appeared to be his valet.

'I will exchange one of these tickets,' she said to the clerk, and
having done so she went to Cornelia to inform her that it would
after all be advisable for them to travel separate, adding, 'Lord
Mountclere is in the station, and I think he is going on by our
train. Remember, you are my maid again now. Is not that the
gentlemanly man who assisted you yesterday?' She signified the
valet as she spoke.

'It is,' said Cornelia.

When the passengers were taking their seats, and Ethelberta
was thinking whether she might not after all enter a second-
class with Cornelia instead of sitting solitary in a first because
of an old man's proximity, she heard a shuffling at her elbow,
and the next moment found that he was overtly observing her
as if he had not done so in secret at all. She at once gave him an
unsurprised gesture of recognition. 'I saw you some time ago;
what a singular coincidence,' she said.

'A charming one,' said Lord Mountclere, smiling a half-
minute smile, and making as if he would take his hat off and
would not quite. 'Perhaps we must not call it coincidence
entirely,' he continued; 'my journey, which I have contemplated
for some time, was not fixed this week altogether without a
thought of your presence on the road – hee-hee! Do you go far
today?'

'As far as Caen,' said Ethelberta.

'Ah! That's the end of my day's journey, too,' said Lord
Mountclere. They parted and took their respective places, Lord
Mountclere choosing a compartment next to the one Ethelberta

was entering, and not, as she had expected, attempting to join her.

Now she had instantly fancied when the viscount was speaking that there were signs of some departure from his former respectful manner towards her; and an enigma lay in that. At their earlier meetings he had never ventured upon a distinct coupling of himself and herself as he had done in his broad compliment today – if compliment it could be called. She was not sure that he did not exceed his license in telling her deliberately that he had meant to hover near her in a private journey which she was taking without reference to him. She did not object to the act, but to the avowal of the act; and, being as sensitive as a barometer on signs affecting her social condition, it darted upon Ethelberta for one little moment that he might possibly have heard a word or two about her being nothing more nor less than one of a tribe of thralls; hence his freedom of manner. Certainly a plain remark of that sort was exactly what a susceptible peer might be supposed to say to a pretty woman of far inferior degree. A rapid redness filled her face at the thought that he might have smiled upon her as upon a domestic whom he was disposed to chuck under the chin. 'But no,' she said. 'He would never have taken the trouble to follow and meet with me had he learnt to think me other than a lady. It is extremity of devotion – that's all.'

It was not Ethelberta's inexperience, but that her conception of self precluded such an association of ideas, which led her to dismiss the surmise that his attendance could be inspired by a motive beyond that of paying her legitimate attentions as a co-ordinate with him and his in the social field. Even if he only meant flirtation, she read it as of that sort from which courtship with an eye to matrimony differs only in degree. Hence, she thought, his interest in her was not likely, under the ordinary influences of caste feeling, to continue longer than while he was kept in ignorance of her consanguinity with a stock proscribed. She sighed at the anticipated close of her full-feathered towering when her ties and bonds should be uncovered. She might have seen matters in a different light, and sighed more. But in the stir of the moment it escaped her thought that ignorance of her position, and a consequent regard for her as a woman of good standing, would have prevented his indulgence in any course which was open to the construction of being disrespectful.

Valognes, Carentan, Isigny, Bayeux, were passed, and the train drew up at Caen. Ethelberta's intention had been to stay here for one night, but having learnt from Lord Mountclere, as previously described, that this was his destination, she decided to go on. On turning towards the carriage after a few minutes of promenading at the Caen station, she was surprised to perceive that Lord Mountclere, who had alighted as if to leave, was still there.

They spoke again to each other. 'I find I have to go further,' he suddenly said, when she had chatted with him a little time. And beckoning to the man who was attending to his baggage, he directed the things to be again placed in the train.

Time passed, and they changed at the next junction. When Ethelberta entered a carriage on the branch line to take her seat for the remainder of the journey, there sat the viscount in the same division. He explained that he was going to Rouen.

Ethelberta came to a quick resolution. Her audacity, like that of a child getting nearer and nearer a parent's side, became wonderfully vigorous as she approached her destination; and though there were three good hours of travel to Rouen as yet, the heavier part of the journey was past. At her aunt's would be a safe refuge, play what pranks she might, and there she would tomorrow meet those bravest of defenders Sol and Dan, to whom she had sent as much money as she could conveniently spare towards their expenses, with directions that they were to come by the most economical route, and meet her at the house of her aunt, Madame Moulin, previous to their educational trip to Paris, their own contribution being the value of the week's work they would have to lose. Thus backed up by Sol and Dan, her aunt, and Cornelia, Ethelberta felt quite the reverse of a lonely female persecuted by a wicked lord in a foreign country. 'He shall pay for his weaknesses, whatever they mean,' she thought; 'and what they mean I will find out at once.'

'I am going to Paris,' she said.

'You cannot tonight, I think.'

'Tomorrow, I mean.'

'I should like to go on tomorrow. Perhaps I may. So that there is a chance of our meeting again.'

'Yes; but I do not leave Rouen till the afternoon. I first shall go to the cathedral, and drive round the city.'

Lord Mountclere smiled pleasantly. There seemed a sort of

encouragement in her words. Ethelberta's thoughts, however, had flown at that moment to the approaching situation at her aunt's hotel: it would be extremely embarrassing if he should go there.

'Where do you stay, Lord Mountclere?' she said.

Thus directly asked, he could not but commit himself to the name of the hotel he had been accustomed to patronize, which was one in the upper part of the city.

'Mine is not that one,' said Ethelberta frigidly.

No further remark was made under this head, and they conversed for the remainder of the daylight on scenery and other topics, Lord Mountclere's air of festivity lending him all the qualities of an agreeable companion. But notwithstanding her resolve, Ethelberta failed, for that day at least, to make her mind clear upon Lord Mountclere's intentions. To that end she would have liked first to know what were the exact limits set by society to conduct under present conditions, if society had ever set any at all, which was open to question: since experience had long ago taught her that much more freedom actually prevails in the communion of the sexes than is put on paper as etiquette, or admitted in so many words as correct behaviour. In short, everything turned upon whether he had learnt of her position when off the platform at Mayfair Hall.

Wearied with these surmises, and the day's travel, she closed her eyes. And then her enamoured companion more widely opened his, and traced the beautiful features opposite him. The arch of the brows – like a slur in music* – the droop of the lashes, the meeting of the lips, and the sweet rotundity of the chin – one by one, and all together, they were adored, till his heart was like a retort full of spirits of wine.

It was a warm evening, and when they arrived at their journey's end distant thunder rolled behind heavy and opaque clouds. Ethelberta bade adieu to her attentive satellite, called to Cornelia, and entered a cab; but before they reached the inn the thunder had increased. Then a cloud cracked into flame behind the iron spire of the cathedral, showing in relief its black ribs and stanchions, as if they were the bars of a blazing cresset* held on high.

'Ah, we will clamber up there tomorrow,' said Ethelberta.

A wondrous stillness pervaded the streets of the city after this, though it was not late; and their arrival at M. Moulin's door was quite an event for the quay. No rain came, as they had expected, and by the time they halted the western sky had cleared, so that the newly-lit lamps on the quay, and the evening glow shining over the river, inwove their harmonious rays as the warp and woof of one lustrous tissue. Before they had alighted there appeared from the archway Madame Moulin in person, followed by the servants of the hotel in a manner signifying that they did not receive a visitor once a fortnight, though at that moment the clatter of sixty knives, forks, and tongues was audible through an open window from the adjoining dining-room, to the great interest of a group of idlers outside. Ethelberta had not seen her aunt since she last passed through the town with Lady Petherwin, who then told her that this landlady was the only respectable relative she seemed to have in the world.

Aunt Charlotte's face was an English outline filled in with French shades under the eyes, on the brows, and round the mouth, by the natural effect of years; she resembled the British hostess as little as well could be, no point in her causing the slightest suggestion of drops taken for the stomach's sake.* Telling the two young women she would gladly have met them at the station had she known the hour of their arrival, she kissed them both without much apparent notice of a difference in their conditions; indeed, seeming rather to incline to Cornelia, whose country face and homely style of clothing may have been more to her mind than Ethelberta's finished travelling-dress, a class of article to which she appeared to be well accustomed. Her husband was at this time at the head of the table-d'hôte,* and mentioning the fact as an excuse for his non-appearance, she accompanied them upstairs.

After the strain of keeping up smiles with Lord Mountclere, the rattle and shaking, and the general excitements of the chase across the water and along the rail, a face in which she saw a dim reflex of her mother's was soothing in the extreme, and Ethelberta went up to the staircase with a feeling of expansive thankfulness. Cornelia paused to admire the clean court and the small caged birds sleeping on their perches, the boxes of veronica in bloom, of oleander, and of tamarisk, which freshened the air of the court and lent a romance to the lamplight, the cooks in their paper caps and white blouses appearing at odd moments from an Avernus* behind; while the prompt 'v'la!'* of teetotums* in mob caps, spinning down the staircase in answer to the periodic clang of bells, filled her with wonder, and pricked her conscience with thoughts of how seldom such transcendent nimbleness was attempted by herself in a part so nearly similar.

The Hôtel Beau Séjour and Spots Near It

34

The next day, much to Ethelberta's surprise, there was a letter for her in her mother's up-hill hand. She neglected all the rest of its contents for the following engrossing sentences: –

Menlove has wormed everything out of poor Joey, we find, and your father is much upset about it. She had another quarrel with him, and then declared she would expose you and us to Mrs Doncastle and all your friends. I think that Menlove is the kind of woman who will stick to her word, and the question for you to consider is, how can you best face out any report of the truth which she will spread, and contradict the lies that she will add to it? It appears to me to be a dreadful thing, and so it will probably appear to you. The worst part will be that your sisters and brothers are your servants, and that your father is actually engaged in the house where you dine. I am dreadful afraid that this will be considered a fine joke for gossips, and will cause no end of laughs in society at your expense. At any rate, should Menlove spread the report, it would absolutely prevent people from attending your lectures next season, for they would feel like dupes, and be angry with theirselves, and you, and all of us.

The only way out of the muddle that I can see for you is to put some scheme of marrying into effect as soon as possible, and before these things are known. Surely by this time, with all your opportunities, you have been able to strike up an acquaintance with some gentleman or other, so as to make a suitable match. You see, my dear Berta, marriage is a thing which, once carried out, fixes you more firm in a position than any personal brains can do; for as you stand at present, every loose tooth, and every combed-out hair, and every new wrinkle, and every sleepless night, is so much took away from your chance for the future, depending as it do upon your skill in charming. I know that you have had some good offers, so do listen to me, and warm up the best man of them again a bit, and get him to repeat his words before your roundness shrinks away, and 'tis too late.

Mr Ladywell has called here to see you; it was just after I had heard that this Menlove might do harm, so I thought I could do no better than send down word to him that you would much like to see him, and were wondering sadly why he had not called lately. I gave him your address at Rouen, that he might find you, if he chose, at once, and be got to propose, since he is better than nobody. I believe he said, directly Joey gave him the address, that he was going abroad, and my opinion is that he will come to you, because of the encouragement I gave him. If so, you must thank me for my foresight and care for you.

I heave a sigh of relief sometimes at the thought that I, at any rate, found a husband before the present man-famine* began. Don't refuse him this time, there's a dear, or, mark my words, you'll have cause to rue it – unless you have beforehand got engaged to somebody better than he. You will not if you have not already, for the exposure is sure to come soon.

'O, this false position! – it is ruining your nature, my too thoughtful mother! But I will not accept any of them – I'll brazen it out!' said Ethelberta, throwing the letter wherever it chose to fly, and picking it up to read again. She stood and thought it all over. 'I must decide to do something!' was her sigh again; and, feeling an irresistible need of motion, she put on her things and went out to see what resolve the morning would bring.

No rain had fallen during the night, and the air was now quiet in a warm heavy fog, through which old cider-smells, reminding her of Wessex, occasionally came from narrow streets in the background. Ethelberta passed up the Rue Grand-Pont into the little dusky Rue Saint-Romain, behind the cathedral,* being driven mechanically along by the fever and fret of her thoughts. She was about to enter the building by the transept door, when she saw Lord Mountclere coming towards her.

Ethelberta felt equal to him, or a dozen such, this morning. The looming spectres raised by her mother's information, the wearing sense of being over-weighted in the race, were driving

her to a Hamlet-like fantasticism and defiance of augury*;
moreover, she was abroad.

'I am about to ascend to the parapets of the cathedral,' said
she, in answer to a half inquiry.

'I should be delighted to accompany you,' he rejoined, in a
manner as capable of explanation by his knowledge of her secret
as was Ethelberta's manner by her sense of nearing the end of
her maying. But whether this frequent glide into her company
was meant as ephemeral flirtation, to fill the half-hours of his
journey, or whether it meant a serious love-suit – which were
the only alternatives that had occurred to her on the subject –
did not trouble her now. 'I am bound to be civil to so great a
lord,' she lightly thought, and expressing no objection to his
presence, she passed with him through the outbuildings, containing Gothic lumber from the shadowy pile above, and ascended
the stone staircase. Emerging from its windings, they duly came
to the long wooden ladder suspended in mid-air that led to the
parapet of the tower. This being wide enough for two abreast,
she could hardly do otherwise than wait a moment for the
viscount, who up to this point had never faltered, and who
amused her as they went by scraps of his experience in various
countries, which, to do him justice, he told with vivacity and
humour. Thus they reached the end of the flight, and entered
behind a balustrade.

'The prospect will be very lovely from this point when the fog
has blown off,' said Lord Mountclere faintly, for climbing and
chattering at the same time had fairly taken away his breath. He
leant against the masonary to rest himself. 'The air is clearing
already; I fancy I saw a sunbeam or two.'

'It will be lovelier above,' said Ethelberta. 'Let us go to the
platform at the base of the *flèche*,* and wait for a view there.'

'With all my heart,' said her attentive companion.

They passed in at a door and up some more stone steps, which
landed them finally in the upper chamber of the tower. Lord
Mountclere sank on a beam, and asked smilingly if her ambition
was not satisfied with this goal. 'I recollect going to the top
some years ago,' he added, 'and it did not occur to me as being
a thing worth doing a second time. And there was no fog then,
either.'

'O,' said Ethelberta, 'it is one of the most splendid things a
person can do! The fog is going fast, and everybody with the

least artistic feeling in the direction of bird's-eye views makes the ascent every time of coming here.'

'Of course, of course,' said Lord Mountclere. 'And I am only too happy to go to any height with you.'

'Since you so kindly offer, we will go to the very top of the spire – up through the fog and into the sunshine,' said Ethelberta.

Lord Mountclere covered a grim misgiving by a gay smile, and away they went up a ladder admitting to the base of the huge iron framework above; then they entered upon the regular ascent of the cage, towards the hoped-for celestial blue, and among breezes which never descended so low as the town. The journey was enlivened with more breathless witticisms from Lord Mountclere, till she stepped ahead of him again; when he asked how many more steps there were.

She inquired of the man in the blue blouse who accompanied them. 'Fifty-five,' she returned to Lord Mountclere a moment later.

They went round, and round, and yet around.

'How many are there now?' Lord Mountclere demanded this time of the man.

'A hundred and ninety, Monsieur,' he said.

'But there were only fifty-five ever so long ago!'

'Two hundred and five, then,' said the man. 'Perhaps the mist prevented Mademoiselle hearing me distinctly?'

'Never mind: I would follow were there five thousand more, did Mademoiselle bid me!' said the exhausted nobleman gallantly, in English.

'Hush!' said Ethelberta, with displeasure.

'He doesn't understand a word,' said Lord Mountclere.

They paced the remainder of their spiral pathway in silence, and having at last reached the summit, Lord Mountclere sank down on one of the steps, panting out, 'Dear me, dear me!'

Ethelberta leaned and looked around, and said, 'How extraordinary this is. It is sky above, below, everywhere.'

He dragged himself together and stepped to her side. They formed as it were a little world to themselves, being completely ensphered by the fog, which here was dense as a sea of milk. Below was neither town, country, nor cathedral – simply whiteness, into which the iron legs of their gigantic perch faded to nothing.

'We have lost our labour; there is no prospect for you, after all, Lord Mountclere,' said Ethelberta, turning her eyes upon him. He looked at her face as if there were, and she continued, 'Listen; I hear sounds from the town: people's voices, and carts, and dogs, and the noise of a railway-train. Shall we now descend, and own ourselves disappointed?'

'Whenever you choose.'

Before they had put their intention in practice there appeared to be reasons for waiting awhile. Out of the plain of fog beneath a stone tooth seemed to be upheaving itself: then another showed forth. These were the summits of the St Romain and the Butter Towers – at the western end of the building. As the fog stratum collapsed other summits manifested their presence further off – among them the two spires and lantern* of St Ouen's; when to the left the dome of St Madeleine's caught a first ray from the peering sun, under which its scaly surface glittered like a fish. Then the mist rolled off in earnest, and revealed far beneath them a whole city, its red, blue, and grey roofs forming a variegated pattern, small and subdued as that of a pavement in mosaic. Eastward in the spacious outlook lay the hill of St Catherine, breaking intrusively into the large level valley of the Seine; south was the river which had been the parent of the mist, and the Ile Lacroix, gorgeous in scarlet, purple, and green. On the western horizon could be dimly discerned melancholy forests, and further to the right stood the hill and rich groves of Boisguillaume.

Ethelberta having now done looking around, the descent was begun and continued without intermission till they came to the passage behind the parapet.

Ethelberta was about to step airily forward, when there reached her ear the voices of persons below. She recognized as one of them the slow unaccented tones of Neigh.

'Please wait a minute!' she said in a peremptory manner of confusion sufficient to attract Lord Mountclere's attention.

A recollection had sprung to her mind in a moment. She had half made an appointment with Neigh at her aunt's hotel for this very week, and here was he in Rouen to keep it. To meet him while indulging in this vagary with Lord Mountclere – which, now that the mood it had been engendered by was passing off, she somewhat regretted – would be the height of imprudence.

'I should like to go round to the other side of the parapet for a few moments,' she said, with decisive quickness. 'Come with me, Lord Mountclere.'

They went round to the other side. Here she kept the viscount and their *suisse** until she deemed it probable that Neigh had passed by, when she returned with her companions and descended to the bottom. They emerged into the Rue Saint-Romain, whereupon a woman called from the opposite side of the way to their guide, stating that she had told the other English gentleman that the English lady had gone into the *flèche*.

Ethelberta turned and looked up. She could just discern Neigh's form upon the steps of the *flèche* above, ascending toilsomely in search of her.

'What English gentleman could that have been?' said Lord Mountclere, after paying the man. He spoke in a way which showed he had not overlooked her confusion. 'It seems that he must have been searching for us, or rather for you?'

'Only Mr Neigh,' said Ethelberta. 'He told me he was coming here. I believe he is waiting for an interview with me.'

'H'm,' said Lord Mountclere.

'Business – only business,' said she.

'Shall I leave you? Perhaps the business is important – most important.'

'Unfortunately it is.'

'You must forgive me this once: I cannot help – will you give me permission to make a difficult remark?' said Lord Mountclere, in an impatient voice.

'With pleasure.'

'Well, then, the business I meant was – an engagement to be married.'

Had it been possible for a woman to be perpetually on the alert she might now have supposed that Lord Mountclere knew all about her; a mechanical deference must have restrained such an allusion had he seen her in any other light than that of a distracting slave. But she answered quietly, 'So did I.'

'But how does he know – dear me, dear me! I beg pardon,' said the viscount.

She looked at him curiously, as if to imply that he was seriously out of his reckoning in respect of her if he supposed that he would be allowed to continue this little play at love-making as long as he chose, when she was offered the position of wife by a man so good as Neigh.

They stood in silence side by side till, much to her ease, Cornelia appeared at the corner waiting. At the last moment he said, in somewhat agitated tones, and with what appeared to be a renewal of the respect which had been imperceptibly dropped since they crossed the Channel, 'I was not aware of your engagement to Mr Neigh. I fear I have been acting mistakenly on that account.'

'There is no engagement as yet,' said she.

Lord Mountclere brightened like a child. 'Then may I have a few words in private—'

'Not now – not today,' said Ethelberta, with a certain irritation at she knew not what. 'Believe me, Lord Mountclere, you are mistaken in many things. I mean, you think more of me than you ought. A time will come when you will despise me for this day's work, and it is madness in you to go further.'

Lord Mountclere, knowing what he did know, may have imagined what she referred to; but Ethelberta was without the least proof that he had the key to her humour. 'Well, well, I'll be responsible for the madness,' he said. 'I know you to be – a famous woman, at all events; and that's enough. I would say more, but I cannot here. May I call upon you?'

'Not now.'

'When shall I?'

'If you must, let it be a month hence at my house in town,' she said indifferently, the Hamlet mood being still upon her. 'Yes, call upon us then, and I will tell you everything that may remain to be told, if you should be inclined to listen. A rumour is afloat which will undeceive you in much, and depress me to death. And now I will walk back: pray excuse me.' She entered the street, and joined Cornelia.

Lord Mountclere paced irregularly along, turned the corner, and went towards his inn, nearing which his tread grew lighter, till he scarcely seemed to touch the ground. He became gleeful, and said to himself, nervously palming his hip with his left hand, as if previous to plunging it into hot water for some prize: 'Upon my life I've a good mind! Upon my life I have! . . . I must make a straightforward thing of it, and at once; or he will have her. But he shall not, and I will – hee-hee!'

The fascinated man, screaming inwardly with the excitement,

glee, and agony of his position, entered the hotel, wrote a hasty note to Ethelberta and despatched it by hand, looked to his dress and appearance, ordered a carriage, and in a quarter of an hour was being driven towards the Hôtel Beau Séjour, whither his note had preceded him.

The Hôtel (continued) and the Quay in Front

35

Ethelberta, having arrived there some time earlier, had gone straight to her aunt, whom she found sitting behind a large ledger in the office, making up the accounts with her husband, a well-framed reflective man with a grey beard. M. Moulin bustled, waited for her remarks and replies, and made much of her in a general way, when Ethelberta said, what she had wanted to say instantly, 'Has a gentleman called Mr Neigh been here?'

'O yes – I think it is Neigh – there's a card upstairs,' replied her aunt. 'I told him you were alone at the cathedral, and I believe he walked that way. Besides that one, another has come for you – a Mr Ladywell, and he is waiting.'

'Not for me?'

'Yes, indeed. I thought he seemed so anxious, under a sort of assumed calmness, that I recommended him to remain till you came in.'

'Goodness, aunt; why did you?' Ethelberta said, and thought how much her mother's sister resembled her mother in doings of that sort.

'I thought he had some good reason for seeing you. Are these men intruders, then?'

'O no – a woman who attempts a public career must expect to be treated as public property: what would be an intrusion on a domiciled gentlewoman is a tribute to me. You cannot have celebrity and sex-privilege both.' Thus Ethelberta laughed off the awkward conjuncture, inwardly deploring the unconscionable maternal meddling which had led to this, though not resentfully, for she had too much staunchness of heart to decry a parent's misdirected zeal. Had the clanship feeling been universally as strong as in the Chickerel family, the fable of the well-bonded fagot* might have remained unwritten.

Ladywell had sent her a letter about getting his picture of herself engraved for an illustrated paper, and she had not replied, considering that she had nothing to do with the matter, her form and feature having been given in the painting as no portrait at all, but as those of an ideal. To see him now would be vexatious; and yet it was chilly and formal to an ungenerous degree to keep aloof from him, sitting lonely in the same house. 'A few weeks hence,' she thought, 'when Menlove's disclosures make me ridiculous, he may slight me as a lackey's girl, an upstart, an adventuress, and hardly return my bow in the street. Then I may wish I had given him no personal cause for additional bitterness.' So, putting off the fine lady, Ethelberta thought she would see Ladywell at once.

Ladywell was unaffectedly glad to meet her; so glad, that Ethelberta wished heartily, for his sake, there could be warm friendship between herself and him, as well as all her lovers, without that insistent courtship-and-marriage question, which sent them all scattering like leaves in a pestilent blast, at enmity with one another. She was less pleased when she found that Ladywell, after saying all there was to say about his painting, gently signified that he had been misinformed, as he believed, concerning her future intensions, which had led to his absenting himself entirely from her; the remark being, of course, a natural product of her mother's injudicious message to him.

She cut him short with terse candour. 'Yes,' she said, 'a false report is in circulation. I am not yet engaged to be married to any one, if that is your meaning.'

Ladywell looked cheerful at this frank answer, and said tentatively, 'Am I forgotten?'

'No; you are exactly as you always were in my mind.'

'Then I have been cruelly deceived. I was guided too much by appearances, and they were very delusive. I am beyond measure glad I came here today. I called at your house and learnt that you were here; and as I was going out of town, in any indefinite direction, I settled then to come this way. What a happy idea it was! To think of you now – and I may be permitted to —'

'Assuredly you may not. How many times I have told you that!'

'But I do not wish for any formal engagement,' said Ladywell quickly, fearing she might commit herself to some expression of positive denial, which he could never surmount. 'I'll wait – I'll wait any length of time. Remember, you have never absolutely forbidden my – friendship. Will you delay your answer till some time hence, when you have thoroughly considered; since I fear it may be a hasty one now?'

'Yes, indeed; it may be hasty.'

'You will delay it?'

'Yes.'

'When shall it be?'

'Say a month hence. I suggest that, because by that time you will have found an answer in your own mind: strange things may happen before then. "She shall follow after her lovers, but she shall not overtake them; and she shall seek them, but shall not find them; then shall she say, I will go and return to my first" * – however, that's no matter.'

'What – did you – ?' Ladywell began, altogether bewildered by this.

'It is a passage in Hosea which came to my mind, as possibly applicable to myself some day,' she answered. 'It was mere impulse.'

'Ha-ha! – a jest – one of your romances broken loose. There is no law for impulse: that is why I am here.'

Thus fancifully they conversed till the interview concluded. Getting her to promise that she would see him again, Ladywell retired to a sitting-room on the same landing, in which he had been writing letters before she came up. Immediately upon this her aunt, who began to suspect that something peculiar was in the wind, came to tell her that Mr Neigh had been inquiring for her again.

'Send him in,' said Ethelberta.

Neigh's footsteps approached, and the well-known figure entered. Ethelberta received him smilingly, for she was getting so used to awkward juxtapositions that she treated them quite as a natural situation. She merely hoped that Ladywell would not hear them talking through the partition.

Neigh scarcely said anything as a beginning: she knew his errand perfectly; and unaccountable as it was to her, the strange and unceremonious relationship between them, that had origi- nated in the peculiar conditions of their first close meeting, was continued now as usual.

'Have you been able to bestow a thought on the question between us? I hope so,' said Neigh.

'It is no use,' said Ethelberta. 'Wait a month, and you will not require an answer. You will not mind speaking low, because of a person in the next room?'

'Not at all. – Why will that be?'

'I might say; but let us speak of something else.'

'I don't see how we can,' said Neigh brusquely. 'I had no other reason on earth for calling here. I wished to get the matter settled, and I could not be satisfied without seeing you. I hate writing on matters of this sort. In fact I can't do it, and that's why I am here.'

He was still speaking when an attendant entered with a note.

'Will you excuse me one moment?' said Ethelberta, stepping to the window and opening the missive. It contained these words only, in a scrawl so full of deformities that she could hardly piece its meaning together: –

> I must see you again today unless you absolutely deny yourself to me, which I shall take as a refusal to meet me any more. I will arrive, punctually, five minutes after you receive this note. Do pray be alone if you can, and eternally gratify, – Yours,
>
> MOUNTCLERE

'If anything has happened I shall be pleased to wait,' said Neigh, seeing her concern when she had closed the note.

'O no, it is nothing,' said Ethelberta precipitately. 'Yet I think I will ask you to wait,' she added, not liking to dismiss Neigh in a hurry; for she was not insensible to his perseverance in seeking her over all these miles of sea and land; and secondly, she feared that if he were to leave on the instant he might run into the arms of Lord Mountclere and Ladywell.

'I shall be only too happy to stay till you are at leisure,' said Neigh, in the unimpassioned delivery he used whether his meaning were a trite compliment or the expression of his most earnest feeling.

'I may be rather a long time,' said Ethelberta dubiously.

'My time is yours.'

Ethelberta left the room and hurried to her aunt, exclaiming, 'O, Aunt Charlotte, I hope you have rooms enough to spare for my visitors, for they are like the fox, the goose, and the corn, in the riddle; I cannot leave them together, and I can only be with one at a time. I want the nicest drawing-room you have for an interview of a bare two minutes with an old gentleman. I am so sorry this has happened, but it is not altogether my fault! I only arranged to see one of them; but the other was sent to me by mother, in a mistake, and the third met with me on my journey: that's the explanation. There's the oldest of them just come.'

She looked through the glass partition, and under the arch of the court-gate, as the wheels of the viscount's carriage were heard outside. Ethelberta ascended to a room on the first floor, Lord Mountclere was shown up, and the door closed upon them.

At this time Neigh was very comfortably lounging in an arm-chair in Ethelberta's room on the second floor. This was a pleasant enough way of passing the minutes with such a tender interview in prospect; and as he leant he looked with languid and luxurious interest through the open casement at the spars and rigging of some luggers* on the Seine, the pillars of the suspension bridge, and the scenery of the Faubourg St Sever on the other side of the river. How languid his interest might ultimately have become there is no knowing; but there soon arose upon his ear the accents of Ethelberta in low distinctness from somewhere outside the room.

'Yes; the scene is pleasant today,' she said. 'I like a view over a river.'

'I should think the steamboats are objectionable when they stop here,' said another person.

Neigh's face closed in to an aspect of perplexity. 'Surely that cannot be Lord Mountclere?' he muttered.

Had he been certain that Ethelberta was only talking to a stranger, Neigh would probably have felt their conversation to be no business of his, much as he might have been surprised to find her giving audience to another man at such a place. But his impression that the voice was that of his acquaintance, Lord Mountclere, coupled with doubts as to its possibility, was enough to lead him to rise from the chair and put his head out of the window.

Upon a balcony beneath him were the speakers, as he had suspected – Ethelberta and the viscount.

Looking right and left, he saw projecting from the next window the head of his friend Ladywell, gazing right and left likewise, apparently just drawn out by the same voice which had attracted himself.

'What – you, Neigh! – how strange,' came from Ladywell's lips before he had time to recollect that great coolness existed between himself and Neigh on Ethelberta's account, which had led to the reduction of their intimacy to the most attenuated of nods and good-mornings ever since the Harlequin-rose incident at Cripplegate.

'Yes; it is rather strange,' said Neigh, with saturnine evenness. 'Still a fellow must be somewhere.'

Each then looked over his window-sill downwards, upon the speakers who had attracted them thither.

Lord Mountclere uttered something in a low tone which did not reach the young men; to which Ethelberta replied, 'As I have said, Lord Mountclere, I cannot give you an answer now. I must consider what to do with Mr Neigh and Mr Ladywell. It is too sudden for me to decide at once. I could not do so until I have got home to England, when I will write you a letter, stating frankly my affairs and those of my relatives. I shall not consider that you have addressed me on the subject of marriage until, having received my letter, you —'

'Repeat my proposal,' said Lord Mountclere.

'Yes.'

'My dear Mrs Petherwin, it is as good as repeated! But I have no right to assume anything you don't wish me to assume, and I will wait. How long is it that I am to suffer in this uncertainty?'

'A month. By that time I shall have grown weary of my other two suitors perhaps.'

'A month! Really inflexible?'

Ethelberta had returned inside the window, and her answer was inaudible. Ladywell and Neigh looked up, and their eyes met. Both had been reluctant to remain where they stood, but they were too fascinated to retire instantly. Neigh moved now, and Ladywell did the same. Each saw that the face of his companion was flushed.

'Come in and see me,' said Ladywell quickly, before quite withdrawing his head. 'I am staying in this room.'

'I will,' said Neigh; and taking his hat he left Ethelberta's apartment forthwith.

On entering the quarters of his friend he found him seated at a table whereon writing materials were strewn. They shook hands in silence, but the meaning in their looks was enough.

'Just let me write a note, Ladywell, and I'm your man,' said Neigh then, with the freedom of an old acquaintance.

'I was going to do the same thing,' said Ladywell.

Neigh then sat down, and for a minute or two nothing was to be heard but the scratching of a pair of pens, ending on the one side with a more boisterous scratch, as the writer shaped 'Eustace Ladywell', and on the other, with slow firmness in the characters, 'Alfred Neigh'.

'There's for you, my fair one,' said Neigh, closing and directing his letter.

'Yours is for Mrs Petherwin? So is mine,' said Ladywell, grasping the bell-pull. 'Shall I direct it to be put on her table with this one?'

'Thanks.' And the two letters went off to Ethelberta's sitting-room, which she had vacated to receive Lord Mountclere in an empty one beneath. Neigh's letter was simply a pleading of a sudden call away which prevented his waiting till she should return; Ladywell's, though stating the same reason for leaving, was more of an upbraiding nature, and might almost have told its reader, were she to take the trouble to guess, that he knew of the business of Lord Mountclere with her today.

'Now, let us get out of this place,' said Neigh. He proceeded at once down the stairs, followed by Ladywell, who – settling his account at the bureau without calling for a bill, and directing his portmanteau to be sent to the Right-bank railway station – went with Neigh into the street.

They had not walked fifty yards up the quay when two British workmen, in holiday costume, who had just turned the corner of the Rue Jeanne d'Arc, approached them. Seeing him to be an Englishman, one of the two addressed Neigh, saying, 'Can you tell us the way, sir, to the Hotel Bold Soldier?'

Neigh pointed out the place he had just come from to the tall young men, and continued his walk with Ladywell.

Ladywell was the first to break silence. 'I have been consider-ably misled, Neigh,' he said; 'and I imagine from what has just happened that you have been misled too.'

'Just a little,' said Neigh, bringing abstracted lines of medita-tion into his face. 'But it was my own fault: for I ought to have known that these stage and platform women have what they are pleased to call Bohemianism* so thoroughly engrained with their natures that they are no more constant to usage in their sentiments than they are in their way of living. Good Lord, to think she has caught old Mountclere! She is sure to have him if she does not dally with him so long that he gets cool again.'

'A beautiful creature like her to think of marrying such an infatuated idiot as he!'

'He can give her a title as well as younger men. It will not be the first time that such matches have been made.'

'I can't believe it,' said Ladywell vehemently. 'She has too much poetry in her – too much good sense; her nature is the essence of all that's romantic. I can't help saying it, though she has treated me cruelly.'

'She has good looks, certainly. I'll own to that. As for her romance and good-feeling, that I leave to you. I think she has treated you no more cruelly, as you call it, than she has me, come to that.'

'She told me she would give me an answer in a month,' said Ladywell emotionally.

'So she told me,' said Neigh.

'And so she told him,' said Ladywell.

'And I have no doubt she will keep her word to him in her usual precise manner.'

'But see what she implied to me! I distinctly understood from her that the answer would be favourable.'

'So did I.'

'So does he.'

'And he is sure to be the one who gets it, since only one of us can. Well, I wouldn't marry her for love, money, nor—'

'Offspring.'

'Exactly: I would not. "I'll give you an answer in a month" – to all three of us! For God's sake let's sit down here and have something to drink.'

They drew up a couple of chairs to one of the tables of a wine-shop close by, and shouted to the waiter with the vigour of persons going to the dogs. Here, behind the horizontal-headed trees that dotted this part of the quay, they sat over their bottles denouncing womankind till the sun got low down upon the river, and the houses on the further side began to be toned by a blue mist. At last they rose from their seats and departed,

Neigh to dine and consider his route, and Ladywell to take the train for Dieppe.

While these incidents had been in progress the two workmen had found their way into the hotel where Ethelberta was staying. Passing through the entrance, they stood at gaze in the court, much perplexed as to the door to be made for; the difficulty was solved by the appearance of Cornelia, who in expectation of them had been for the last half-hour leaning over the sill of her bed-room window, which looked into the interior, amusing herself by watching the movements to and fro in the court beneath.

After conversing awhile in undertones as if they had no real right there at all, Cornelia told them she would call their sister, if an old gentleman who had been to see her were gone again. Cornelia then ran away, and Sol and Dan stood aloof, till they had seen the old gentleman alluded to go to the door and drive off, shortly after which Ethelberta ran down to meet them.

'Whatever have you got as your luggage?' she said, after hearing a few words about their journey, and looking at a curious object like a huge extended accordion with bellows of gorgeous-patterned carpeting.

'Well, I thought to myself,' said Sol, ''tis a terrible bother about carrying our things. So what did I do but turn to and make a carpet-bag that would hold all mine and Dan's too. This, you see, Berta, is a deal top and bottom out of three-quarter stuff, stained and varnished. Well, then you see I've got carpet sides tacked on with these brass nails, which make it look very handsome; and so when my bag is empty 'twill shut up and be only a couple of boards under yer arm, and when 'tis open it will hold a'most anything you like to put in it. That portmantle* didn't cost more than three half-crowns altogether, and ten pound wouldn't ha' got anything so strong from a portmantle maker, would it, Dan?'

'Well, no.'

'And then you see, Berta,' Sol continued in the same earnest tone, and further exhibiting the article; 'I've made this trap-door in the top with hinges and padlock complete, so that—'

'I am afraid it is tiring you after your journey to explain all this to me,' said Ethelberta gently, noticing that a few Gallic smilers were gathering round. 'Aunt has found a nice room for you at the top of the staircase in that corner – "Escalier D" you'll see painted at the bottom – and when you have been up come across to me at number thirty-four on this side, and we'll talk about everything.'

'Look here, Sol,' said Dan, who had left his brother and gone on to the stairs. 'What a rum staircase – the treads all in little blocks, and painted chocolate, as I am alive!'

'I am afraid I shall not be able to go on to Paris with you, after all,' Ethelberta continued to Sol. 'Something has just happened which makes it desirable for me to return at once to England. But I will write a list of all you are to see, and where you are to go, so that it will make little difference I hope.'

Ten minutes before this time Ethelberta had been frankly and earnestly asked by Lord Mountclere to become his bride; not only so, but he pressed her to consent to have the ceremony performed before they returned to England. Ethelberta had unquestionably been much surprised; and, barring the fact that the viscount was somewhat ancient in comparison with herself, the temptation to close with his offer was strong, and would have been felt as such by any woman in the position of Ethelberta, now a little reckless by stress of circumstances, and tinged with a bitterness of spirit against herself and the world generally. But she was experienced enough to know what heaviness might result from a hasty marriage, entered into with a mind full of concealments and suppressions which, if told, were likely to stop the marriage altogether; and after trying to bring herself to speak of her family and situation to Lord Mountclere as he stood, a certain caution triumphed, and she concluded that it would be better to postpone her reply till she could consider which of two courses it would be advisable to adopt; to write and explain to him, or to explain nothing and refuse him. The third course, to explain nothing and hasten the wedding, she rejected without hesitation. With a pervading sense of her own obligations in forming this compact it did not occur to her to ask if Lord Mountclere might not have duties of explanation equally with herself, though bearing rather on the moral than the social aspects of the case.

Her resolution not to go on to Paris was formed simply because Lord Mountclere himself was proceeding in that direction, which might lead to other unseemly rencounters* with him had she, too, persevered in her journey. She accordingly gave Sol and Dan directions for their guidance to Paris and back, starting herself with Cornelia the next day to return again to Knollsea, and to decide finally and for ever what to do in the vexed question at present agitating her.

Never before in her life had she treated marriage in such a terribly cool and cynical spirit as she had done that day; she was almost frightened at herself in thinking of it. How far any known system of ethics might excuse her on the score of those curious pressures which had been brought to bear upon her life, or whether it could excuse her at all, she had no spirit to inquire. English society appeared a gloomy concretion enough to abide in as she contemplated it on this journey home; yet, since its gloominess was less an essential quality than an accident of her point of view, that point of view she had determined to change.

There lay open to her two directions in which to move. She might annex herself to the easy-going high by wedding an old nobleman, or she might join for good and all the easy-going low, by plunging back to the level of her family, giving up all her ambitions for them, settling as the wife of a provincial music-master named Julian, with a little shop of fiddles and flutes, a couple of old pianos, a few sheets of stale music pinned to a string, and a narrow back parlour, wherein she would wait for the phenomenon of a customer. And each of these divergent grooves had its fascinations, till she reflected with regard to the first that, even though she were a legal and indisputable Lady Mountclere, she might be despised by my lord's circle, and left lone and lore. The intermediate path of accepting Neigh or Ladywell had no more attractions for her taste than the fact of disappointing them had qualms for her conscience; and how few these were may be inferred from her opinion, true or false, that two words about the spigot on her escutcheon* would sweep her lovers' affections to the antipodes. She had now and then imagined that her previous intermarriage with the Petherwin family might efface much besides her surname, but experience proved that the having been wife for a few weeks to a minor who died in his father's lifetime, did not weave such a tissue of glory about her course as would resist a speedy undoing by startling confessions on her station before her marriage, and her environments now.

The House in Town

36

Returning by way of Knollsea, where she remained a week or two, Ethelberta appeared one evening at the end of September before her house in Exonbury Crescent, accompanied by a pair of cabs with the children and luggage; but Picotee was left at Knollsea, for reasons which Ethelberta explained when the family assembled in conclave. Her father was there, and began telling her of a surprising change in Menlove – an unasked-for concession to their cause, and a vow of secrecy which he could not account for, unless any friend of Ethelberta's had bribed her.

'O no – that cannot be,' said she. Any influence of Lord Mountclere to that effect was the last thing that could enter her thoughts. 'However, what Menlove does makes little difference to me now.' And she proceeded to state that she had almost come to a decision which would entirely alter their way of living.

'I hope it will not be of the sort your last decision was,' said her mother.

'No; quite the reverse. I shall not live here in state any longer. We will let the house throughout as lodgings, while it is ours; and you and the girls must manage it. I will retire from the scene altogether, and stay for the winter at Knollsea with Picotee. I want to consider my plans for next year, and I would rather be away from town. Picotee is left there, and I return in two days with the books and papers I require.'

'What are your plans to be?'

'I am going to be a schoolmistress – I think I am.'

'A schoolmistress?'

'Yes. And Picotee returns to the same occupation, which she ought never to have forsaken. We are going to study arithmetic and geography until Christmas; then I shall send her adrift to finish her term as pupil-teacher, while I go into a training-school. By the time I have to give up this house I shall just have got a little country school.'

'But,' said her mother, aghast, 'why not write more poems and sell 'em?'

'Why not be a governess as you were?' said her father.

'Why not go on with your tales at Mayfair Hall?' said Gwendoline.

'I'll answer as well as I can. I have decided to give up romancing because I cannot think of any more that pleases me. I have been trying at Knollsea for a fortnight, and it is no use. I will never be a governess again: I would rather be a servant. If I am a schoolmistress I shall be entirely free from all contact with the great, which is what I desire, for I hate them, and am getting almost as revolutionary as Sol. Father, I cannot endure this kind of existence any longer. I sleep at night as if I had committed a murder: I start up and see processions of people, audiences, battalions of lovers obtained under false pretences – all denouncing me with the finger of ridicule. Mother's suggestion about my marrying I followed out as far as dogged resolution would carry me, but during my journey here I have broken down; for I don't want to marry a second time among people who would regard me as an upstart or intruder. I am sick of ambition. My only longing now is to fly from society altogether, and go to any hovel on earth where I could be at peace.'

'What – has anybody been insulting you?' said Mrs Chickerel.

'Yes; or rather I sometimes think he may have: that is, if a proposal of marriage is only removed from being a proposal of a very different kind by an accident.'

'A proposal of marriage can never be an insult,' her mother returned.

'I think otherwise,' said Ethelberta.

'So do I,' said her father.

'Unless the man was beneath you, and I don't suppose he was that,' added Mrs Chickerel.

'You are quite right; he was not that. But we will not talk of this branch of the subject. By far the most serious concern with me is that I ought to do some good by marriage, or by heroic performance of some kind; while going back to give the rudiments of education to remote hamleteers will do none of you any good whatever.'

'Never you mind us,' said her father; 'mind yourself.'

'I shall hardly be minding myself either, in your opinion, by doing that,' said Ethelberta dryly. 'But it will be more tolerable than what I am doing now. Georgina, and Myrtle, and Emmeline, and Joey will not get the education I intended for them; but that must go, I suppose.'

'How full of vagaries you are,' said her mother. 'Why won't it do to continue as you are? No sooner have I learnt up your schemes, and got enough used to 'em to see something in 'em, than you must needs bewilder me again by starting some fresh one, so that my mind gets no rest at all.'

Ethelberta too keenly felt the justice of this remark, querulous as it was, to care to defend herself. It was hopeless to attempt to explain to her mother that the oscillations of her mind might arise as naturally from the perfection of its balance, like those of a logan-stone,* as from inherent lightness; and such an explanation, however comforting to its subject, was little better than none to simple hearts who only could look to tangible outcrops.

'Really, Ethelberta,' remonstrated her mother, 'this is very odd. Making yourself miserable in trying to get a position on our account is one thing, and not necessary; but I think it ridiculous to rush into the other extreme, and go wilfully down in the scale. You may just as well exercise your wits in trying to swim as in trying to sink.'

'Yes; that's what I think,' said her father. 'But of course Berta knows best.'

'I think so too,' said Gwendoline.

'And so do I,' said Cornelia. 'If I had once moved about in large circles like Ethelberta, I wouldn't go down and be a schoolmistress – not I.'

'I own it is foolish – suppose it is,' said Ethelberta wearily, and with a readiness of misgiving that showed how recent and hasty was the scheme. 'Perhaps you are right, mother; anything rather than retreat. I wonder if you are right! Well, I will think again of it tonight. Do not let us speak more about it now.'

She did think of it that night, very long and painfully. The arguments of her relatives seemed ponderous as opposed to her own inconsequent longing for escape from galling trammels. If she had stood alone, the sentiment that she had begun to build but was not able to finish, by whomsoever it might have been entertained, would have had few terrors; but that the opinion should be held by her nearest of kin, to cause them pain for life, was a grievous thing. The more she thought of it, the less easy seemed the justification of her desire for obscurity. From regarding it as a high instinct she passed into a humour that gave that desire the appearance of a whim. But could she really set in train events, which, if not abortive, would take her to the altar with Viscount Mountclere?

In one determination she never faltered; to commit her sin thoroughly if she committed it at all. Her relatives believed her choice to lie between Neigh and Ladywell alone. But once having decided to pass over Christopher, whom she had loved, there could be no pausing for Ladywell because she liked him, or for Neigh in that she was influenced by him. They were both too near her level to be trusted to bear the shock of receiving her from her father's hands. But it was possible that though her genesis might tinge with vulgarity a commoner's household, susceptible of such depreciation, it might show as a picturesque contrast in the family circle of a peer. Hence it was just as well to go to the end of her logic, where reasons for tergiversation would be most pronounced. This thought of the viscount, however, was a secret for her own breast alone.

Nearly the whole of that night she sat weighing – first, the question itself of marrying Lord Mountclere; and, at other times, whether, for safety, she might marry him without previously revealing family particulars hitherto held necessary to be revealed – a piece of conduct she had once felt to be indefensible. The ingenious Ethelberta, much more prone than the majority of women to theorize on conduct, felt the need of some soothing defence of the actions involved in any ambiguous course before finally committing herself to it.

She took down a well-known treatise on Utilitarianism* which she had perused once before, and to which she had given her adherence ere any instance had arisen wherein she might wish to take it as a guide. Here she desultorily searched for argument, and found it; but the application of her author's philosophy to the marriage question was an operation of her own, as unjustifiable as it was likely in the circumstances.

'The ultimate end,' she read, 'with reference to and for the sake of which all other things are desirable (whether we are considering our own good or that of other people) is an existence exempt as far as possible from pain, and as rich as possible in enjoyments, both in point of quantity and quality. . . . This being, according to the utilitarian opinion, the end of human action, is necessarily also the standard of morality.'

It was an open question, so far, whether her own happiness should or should not be preferred to that of others. But that her personal interests were not to be considered as paramount appeared further on: –

'The happiness which forms the standard of what is right in conduct is not the agent's own happiness but that of all concerned. As between his own happiness and that of others, utilitarianism requires him to be as strictly impartial as a disinterested and benevolent spectator.

As to whose happiness was meant by that of 'other people', 'all concerned', and so on, her luminous moralist soon enlightened her: –

The occasions on which any person (except one in a thousand) has it in his power to do this on an extended scale – in other words, to be a public benefactor – are but exceptional; and on these occasions alone is he called on to consider public utility; in every other case private utility, the interest or happiness of some few persons, is all he has to attend to.'

And that these few persons should be those endeared to her by every domestic tie no argument was needed to prove. That their happiness would be in proportion to her own well-doing, and power to remove their risks of indigence, required no proving either to her now.

By a sorry but unconscious misapplication of sound and wide reasoning did the active mind of Ethelberta thus find itself a solace. At about the midnight hour she felt more fortified on the expediency of marriage with Lord Mountclere than she had done at all since musing on it. In respect of the second query, whether or not, in that event, to conceal from Lord Mountclere the circumstances of her position till it should be too late for him to object to them, she found her conscience inconveniently in the way of her theory, and the oracle before her afforded no hint. 'Ah – it is a point for a casuist!' she said.

An old treatise on Casuistry* lay on the top shelf. She opened it – more from curiosity than for guidance this time, it must be observed – at a chapter, bearing on her own problem, 'The *disciplina arcani*,* or, the doctrine of reserve'.

Here she read that there were plenty of apparent instances of this in Scripture, and that it was formed into a recognized system in the early Church. With reference to direct acts of deception, it was argued that since there were confessedly cases where killing is no murder, might there not be cases where lying is no sin? It could not be right – or, indeed, anything but most absurd – to say in effect that no doubt circumstances would occur where every sound man would tell a lie, and would be a brute or a fool if he did not, and to say at the same time that it is quite indefensible in principle. Duty was the key to conduct then, and if in such cases duties appeared to clash they would be found not to do so on examination. The lesser duty would yield to the greater, and therefore ceased to be a duty.

This author she found to be not so tolerable; he distracted her. She put him aside and gave over reading, having decided on this second point, that she would, at any hazard, represent the truth to Lord Mountclere before listening to another word from him. 'Well, at last I have done,' she said, 'and am ready for my *rôle*.'

In looking back upon her past as she retired to rest, Ethelberta could almost doubt herself to be the identical woman with her who had entered on a romantic career a few short years ago. For that doubt she had good reason. She had begun as a poet of the Satanic school* in a sweetened form; she was ending as a *pseudo*-utilitarian. Was there ever such a transmutation effected before by the action of a hard environment? It was not without a qualm of regret that she discerned how the last infirmity of a noble mind* had at length nearly departed from her. She wondered if her early notes had had the genuine ring in them, or whether a poet who could be thrust by realities to a distance beyond recognition as such was a true poet at all. Yet Ethelberta's gradient had been regular: emotional poetry, light verse, romance as an object, romance as a means, thoughts of marriage as an aid to her pursuits, a vow to marry for the good of her family; in other words, from soft and playful Romanticism to distorted Benthamism.* Was the moral incline upward or down?

Her energies collected and fermented anew by the results of the vigil, Ethelberta left town for Knollsea, where she joined Picotee the same evening. Picotee produced a letter, which had been addressed to her sister at their London residence, but was not received by her there, Mrs Chickerel having forwarded it to Knollsea the day before Ethelberta arrived in town.

The crinkled writing, in character like the coastline of Tierra del Fuego,* was becoming familiar by this time. While reading the note she informed Picotee, between a quick breath and a rustle of frills, that it was from Lord Mountclere, who wrote on the subject of calling to see her, suggesting a day in the following week. 'Now, Picotee,' she continued, 'we shall have to receive him, and make the most of him, for I have altered my plans since I was last in Knollsea.'

'Altered them again? What are you going to be now – not a poor person after all?'

'Indeed not. And so I turn and turn. Can you imagine what Lord Mountclere is coming for? But don't say what you think. Before I reply to this letter we must go into new lodgings, to give them as our address. The first business tomorrow morning will be to look for the gayest house we can find; and Captain Flower and this little cabin of his must be things we have never known.'

The next day after breakfast they accordingly sallied forth.

Knollsea had recently begun to attract notice in the world. It had this year undergone visitation from a score of professional gentlemen and their wives, a minor canon* three marine painters, seven young ladies with books in their hands, and nine-and-thirty babies. Hence a few lodging-houses, of a dash and pretentiousness far beyond the mark of the old cottages which formed the original substance of the village, had been erected to meet the wants of such as these. To a building of this class Ethelberta now bent her steps, and the crush of the season having departed in the persons of three-quarters of the above-named visitors, who went away by a coach, a van, and a couple of wagonettes one morning, she found no difficulty in arranging for a red and yellow streaked villa, which was so bright and glowing that the sun seemed to be shining upon it even on a cloudy day, and the ruddiest native looked pale when standing by its walls. It was not without regret that she renounced the sailor's pretty cottage for this porticoed and balconied dwelling; but her lines were laid down clearly at last, and thither she removed forthwith.

From this brand-new house did Ethelberta pen the letter fixing the time at which she would be pleased to see Lord Mountclere.

When the hour drew nigh enormous force of will was required to keep her perturbation down. She had not distinctly told Picotee of the object of the viscount's visit, but Picotee guessed nearly enough. Ethelberta was upon the whole better pleased that the initiative had again come from him than if the first step in the new campaign had been her sending the explanatory letter, as intended and promised. She had thought almost directly after the interview at Rouen that to enlighten him by writing a confession in cold blood, according to her first intention, would be little less awkward for her in the method of telling than in the facts to be told.

So the last hair was arranged and the last fold adjusted, and she sat down to await a new page of her history. Picotee sat with her, under orders to go into the next room when Lord Mountclere should call; and Ethelberta determined to waste no time, directly he began to make advances, in clearing up the phenomena of her existence to him; to the end that no fact which, in the event of his taking her to wife, could be used against her as an example of concealment, might remain unrelated. The collapse of his attachment under the test might, however, form the grand climax of such a play as this.

The day was rather cold for the season, and Ethelberta sat by a fire; but the windows were open, and Picotee was amusing herself on the balcony outside. The hour struck: Ethelberta fancied she could hear the wheels of a carriage creeping up the steep ascent which led to the drive before the door.

'Is it he?' she said quickly.

'No,' said Picotee, whose indifference contrasted strangely with the restlessness of her who was usually the coolest. 'It is a man shaking down apples in the garden over the wall.'

They lingered on till some three or four minutes had gone by. 'Surely that's a carriage?' said Ethelberta, then.

'I think it is,' said Picotee outside, stretching her neck forward as far as she could. 'No, it is the men on the beach dragging up their boats; they expect wind tonight.'

'How wearisome! Picotee, you may as well come inside; if he means to call he will; but he ought to be here by this time.'

It was only once more, and that some time later that she again said 'Listen!'

'That's not the noise of a carriage; it is the fizz of a rocket. The coastguardsmen are practising the life-apparatus today, to be ready for the autumn wrecks.'

'Ah!' said Ethelberta, her face clearing up. Hers had not been a sweetheart's impatience, but her mood had intensified during these minutes of suspense to a harassing mistrust of her man-compelling power, which was, if that were possible, more gloomy than disappointed love. 'I know now where he is. That operation with the cradle-apparatus is very interesting, and he is stopping to see it . . . But I shall not wait indoors much longer, whatever he may be stopping to see. It is very unaccountable, and vexing, after moving into this new house too. We were much more comfortable in the old one. In keeping any previous appointment in which I have been concerned he has been ridiculously early.'

'Shall I run round?' said Picotee, 'and if he is not watching them we will go out.'

'Very well,' said her sister.

The time of Picotee's absence seemed an age. Ethelberta heard the roar of another rocket, and still Picotee did not return. 'What can the girl be thinking of?' she mused . . . 'What a half-and-half policy mine has been! Thinking of marrying for position, and yet not making it my rigid plan to secure the man the first moment that he made his offer. So I lose the comfort of having a soul above worldliness, and my compensation for not having it likewise!' A minute or two more and in came Picotee.

'What has kept you so long – and how excited you look,' said Ethelberta.

'I thought I would stay a little while, as I had never seen a rocket-apparatus,' said Picotee, faintly and strangely.

'But is he there?' asked her sister impatiently.

'Yes – he was. He's gone now!'

'Lord Mountclere?'

'No. There is no old man there at all. Mr Julian was there.'

A little 'Ah!' came from Ethelberta, like a note from a storm-bird at night. She turned round and went into the back room. 'Is Mr Julian going to call here?' she inquired, coming forward again.

'No – he's gone by the steamboat. He was only passing through on his way to Sandbourne, where he is gone to settle a small business relating to his father's affairs. He was not in Knollsea ten minutes, owing to something which detained him on the way.'

'Did he inquire for me?'

'No. And only think, Ethelberta – such a remarkable thing has happened, though I nearly forgot to tell you. He says that coming along the road he was overtaken by a carriage, and when it had just passed him one of the horses shied, pushed the other down a slope, and overturned the carriage. One wheel came off and trundled to the bottom of the hill by itself. Christopher of course ran up, and helped out of the carriage an old gentleman – now do you know what's likely?'

'It was Lord Mountclere. I am glad that's the cause,' said Ethelberta involuntarily.

'I imagined you would suppose it to be Lord Mountclere. But Mr Julian did not know the gentleman, and said nothing about who he might be.'

'Did he describe him?'

'Not much – just a little.'

'Well?'

'He said he was a sly old dog apparently, to hear how he swore in whispers. This affair is what made Mr Julian so late that he had no time to call here. Lord Mountclere's ankle – if it was Lord Mountclere – was badly sprained. But the servants were not injured, beyond a scratch on the coachman's face. Then they got another carriage and drove at once back again. It must be he, or else why is he not come? It is a pity, too, that Mr Julian was hindered by this, so that there was no opportunity for him to bide a bit in Knollsea.'

Ethelberta was not disposed to believe that Christopher would have called, had time favoured him to the utmost. Between himself and her there was that kind of division which is more insurmountable than enmity; for estrangements produced by good judgment will last when those of feeling break down in smiles. Not the lovers who part in passion, but the lovers who part in friendship, are those who most frequently part for ever.

'Did you tell Mr Julian that the injured gentleman was possibly Lord Mountclere, and that he was coming here?' said Ethelberta.

'I made no remark at all – I did not think of him till afterwards.'

The inquiry was hardly necessary, for Picotee's words would dry away like a brook in the sands when she held conversation with Christopher.

As they had anticipated, the sufferer was no other than their intending visitor. Next morning there was a note explaining the accident, and expressing its writer's suffering from the cruel delay as greater than that from the swollen ankle, which was progressing favourably.

Nothing further was heard of Lord Mountclere for more than a week, when she received another letter, which put an end to her season of relaxation, and once more braced her to the contest. This epistle was very courteously written, and in point of correctness, propriety, and gravity, might have come from the quill of a bishop. Herein the old nobleman gave a further description of the accident, but the main business of the communication was to ask her if, since he was not as yet very active, she would come to Enckworth Court and delight himself and a small group of friends who were visiting there.

She pondered over the letter as she walked by the shore that day, and after some hesitation decided to go.

Enckworth Court

38

It was on a dull, stagnant, noiseless afternoon of autumn that Ethelberta first crossed the threshold of Enckworth Court. The daylight was so lowered by the impervious roof of cloud overhead that it scarcely reached further into Lord Mountclere's entrance-hall than to the splays of the windows, even but an hour or two after midday; and indoors the glitter of the fire reflected itself from the very panes, so inconsiderable were the opposing rays.

Enckworth Court, in its main part, had not been standing more than a hundred years. At that date the weakened portions of the original mediæval structure were pulled down and cleared away, old jambs* being carried off for rick-staddles,* and the foliated* timbers of the hall roof making themselves useful as fancy chairs in the summer-houses of rising inns. A new block of masonry was built up from the ground of such height and lordliness that the remnant of the old pile left standing became as a mere cup-bearer and culinary menial beside it. The rooms in this old fragment, which had in times past been considered sufficiently dignified for dining-hall, withdrawing-room, and so on, were now reckoned barely high enough for sculleries, servants' hall, and laundries, the whole of which were arranged therein.

The modern portion had been planned with such a total disregard of association, that the very rudeness of the contrast gave an interest to the mass which it might have wanted had perfect harmony been attempted between the old nucleus and its adjuncts, a probable result if the enlargement had taken place later on in time. The issue was that the hooded windows,* simple string-courses,* and random masonry of the Gothic workman, stood elbow to elbow with the equal-spaced ashlar,* architraves,* and fasciæ* of the Classic addition, each telling its distinct tale as to stage of thought and domestic habit without any of those artifices of blending or restoration by which the seeker for history in stones will be utterly hoodwinked in time to come.

To the left of thie door and vestibule which Ethelberta passed through rose the principal staircase, constructed of a freestone* so milk-white and delicately moulded as to be easily conceived in the lamplight as of biscuit-ware. Who, unacquainted with the secrets of geometrical construction, could imagine that, hanging so airily there, to all appearance supported on nothing, were twenty or more tons dead weight of stone, that would have made a prison for an elephant if so arranged? The art which produced this illusion was questionable, but its success was undoubted. 'How lovely!' said Ethelberta, as she looked at the fairy ascent. 'His staircase alone is worth my hand!'

Passing along by the colonnade, which partly fenced the

staircase from the visitor, the saloon was reached, an apartment forming a double cube.* About the left-hand end of this were grouped the drawing-rooms and library; while on the right was the dining hall, with billiard, smoking, and gun rooms in mysterious remoteness beyond.

Without attempting to trace an analogy between a man and his mansion, it may be stated that everything here, though so dignified and magnificent, was not conceived in quite the true and eternal spirit of art. It was a house in which Pugin* would have torn his hair. Those massive blocks of red-veined marble lining the hall – emulating in their surface-glitter the Escalier de Marbre at Versailles* were cunning imitations in paint and plaster by workmen brought from afar for the purpose, at a prodigious expense, by the present viscount's father, and recently repaired and re-varnished. The dark green columns and pilasters corresponding were brick at the core. Nay, the external walls, apparently of massive and solid freestone, were only veneered with that material, being, like the pillars, of brick within.

To a stone mask worn by a brick face a story naturally appertained – one which has since done service in other quarters. When the vast addition had just been completed King George* visited Enckworth. Its owner pointed out the features of his grand architectural attempt, and waited for commendation.

'Brick, brick, brick,' said the king.

The Georgian Lord Mountclere blushed faintly, albeit to his very poll,* and said nothing more about his house that day. When the king was gone he sent frantically for the craftsmen recently dismissed, and soon the green lawns became again the colour of a Nine-Elms* cement wharf. Thin freestone slabs were affixed to the whole series of fronts by copper cramps and dowels,* each one of substance sufficient to have furnished a poor boy's pocket with pennies for a month, till not a speck of the original surface remained, and the edifice shone in all the grandeur of massive masonry that was not massive at all. But who remembered this save the builder and his crew? and as long as nobody knew the truth, pretence looked just as well.

What was honest in Enckworth Court was that portion of the original edifice which still remained, now degraded to subservient uses. Where the untitled Mountclere of the White Rose faction* had spread his knees over the brands,* when the place was a castle and not a court, the still-room maid now simmered her preserves; and where Elizabethan mothers and daughters of that sturdy line had tapestried the love-scenes of Isaac and Jacob,* boots and shoes were now cleaned and coals stowed away.

Lord Mountclere had so far recovered from the sprain as to be nominally quite well, under pressure of a wish to receive guests. The sprain had in one sense served him excellently. He had now a reason, apart from that of years, for walking with his stick, and took care to let the reason be frequently known. Today he entertained a larger number of persons than had been assembled within his walls for a great length of time.

Until after dinner Ethelberta felt as if she were staying at an hotel. Few of the people whom she had met at the meeting of the Imperial Association greeted her here. The viscount's brother was not present, but Sir Cyril Blandsbury and his wife were there, a lively pair of persons, entertaining as actors, and friendly as dogs. Beyond these all the faces and figures were new to her, though they were handsome and dashing enough to satisfy a court chronicler. Ethelberta, in a dress sloped about as high over the shoulder as would have drawn approval from Reynolds,* and expostulation from Lely* thawed and thawed each friend who came near her, and sent him or her away smiling; yet she felt a little surprise. She had seldom visited at a country-house, and knew little of the ordinary composition of a group of visitors within its walls; but the present assemblage seemed to want much of that old-fashioned stability and quaint monumental dignity she had expected to find under this historical roof. Nobody of her entertainer's own rank appeared. Not a single clergyman was there. A tendency to talk Walpolean scandal* about foreign courts was particularly manifest. And although tropical travellers, Indian officers and their wives, courteous exiles, and descendants of Irish kings, were infinitely more pleasant than Lord Mountclere's landed neighbours would probably have been, to such a cosmopolite as Ethelberta a calm Tory or old Whig company would have given a greater treat. They would have struck as gratefully upon her senses as sylvan scenery after crags and cliffs, or silence after the roar of a cataract.

It was evening, and all these personages at Enckworth Court were merry, snug, and warm within its walls. Dinner-time had passed, and everything had gone on well, when Mrs Tara O'Fanagan, who had a gold-clamped tooth, which shone every now and then, asked Ethelberta if she would amuse them by telling a story, since nobody present, except Lord Mountclere, had ever heard one from her lips.

Seeing that Ethelberta had been working at that art as a profession, it can hardly be said that the question was conceived with tact, though it was put with grace. Lord Mountclere evidently thought it objectionable, for he looked unhappy. To only one person in the brilliant room did the request appear as a timely accident, and that was to Ethelberta herself. Her honesty was always making war upon her manœuvres, and shattering their delicate meshes, to her great inconvenience and delay. Thus there arose those devious impulses and tangential flights which spoil the works of every would-be schemer who instead of being wholly machine is half heart. One of these now was to show herself as she really was, not only to Lord Mountclere, but to his friends assembled, whom, in her ignorance, she respected more than they deserved, and so get rid of that self-reproach which had by this time reached a morbid pitch, through her over-sensitiveness to a situation in which a large majority of women and men would have seen no falseness.

Full of this curious intention, she quietly assented to the request, and laughingly bade them put themselves in listening order.

'An old story will suit us,' said the lady who had importuned her. 'We have never heard one.'

'No; it shall be quite new,' she replied. 'One not yet made public; though it soon will be.'

The narrative began by introducing to their notice a girl of the poorest and meanest parentage, the daughter of a serving-man, and the fifth of ten children. She graphically recounted, as if they were her own, the strange dreams and ambitious longings of this child when young, her attempts to acquire education, partial failures, partial successes, and constant struggles; instancing how, on one of these occasions, the girl concealed herself under a bookcase of the library belonging to the mansion in which her father served as footman, and having taken with her there, like a young Fawkes,* matches and a halfpenny candle, was going to sit up all night reading when the family had retired, until her father discovered and prevented her scheme. Then followed her experiences as nursery-governess, her evening lessons under self-selected masters, and her ultimate rise to a higher grade among the teaching sisterhood. Next came another epoch. To the mansion in which she was engaged returned a truant son, between whom and the heroine an attachment sprang up. The master of the house was an ambitious gentleman just knighted, who, perceiving the state of their hearts, harshly dismissed the homeless governess, and rated the son, the consequence being that the youthful pair resolved to marry secretly, and carried their resolution into effect. The runaway journey came next, and then a moving description of the death of the young husband, and the terror of the bride.

The guests began to look perplexed, and one or two exchanged whispers. This was not at all the kind of story that they had expected; it was quite different from her usual utterances, the nature of which they knew by report. Ethelberta kept her eye upon Lord Mountclere. Soon, to her amazement, there was that in his face which told her that he knew the story and its heroine quite well. When she delivered the sentence ending with the professedly fictitious words: 'I thus was reduced to great distress, and vainly cast about me for directions what to do,' Lord Mountclere's manner became so excited and anxious that it acted reciprocally upon Ethelberta; her voice trembled, she moved her lips but uttered nothing. To bring the story up to the date of that very evening had been her intent, but it was beyond her power. The spell was broken; she blushed with distress and turned away, for the folly of a disclosure here was but too apparent.

Though every one saw that she had broken down, none of them appeared to know the reason why, or to have the clue to her performance. Fortunately Lord Mountclere came to her aid.

'Let the first part end here,' he said, rising and approaching her. 'We have been well entertained so far. I could scarcely believe that the story I was listening to was utterly an invention, so vividly does Mrs Petherwin bring the scenes before our eyes. She must now be exhausted; we will have the remainder tomorrow.'

They all agreed that this was well, and soon after fell into groups, and dispersed about the rooms. When everybody's attention was thus occupied Lord Mountclere whispered to Ethelberta tremulously, 'Don't tell more: you think too much of them: they are no better than you! Will you meet me in the little winter garden two minutes hence? Pass through that door, and along the glass passage.' He himself left the room by an opposite door.

She had not set three steps in the warm snug octagon of glass and plants when he appeared on the other side.

'You knew it all before!' she said, looking keenly at him. 'Who told you, and how long have you known it?'

'Before yesterday or last week,' said Lord Mountclere. 'Even before we met in France. Why are you so surprised?'

Ethelberta had been surprised, and very greatly, to find him, as it were, secreted in the very rear of her position. That nothing she could tell was new to him was a good deal to think of, but it was little beside the recollection that he had actually made his first declaration in the face of that knowledge of her which she had supposed so fatal to all her matrimonial ambitions.

'And now only one point remains to be settled,' he said, taking her hand. 'You promised at Rouen that at our next interview you would honour me with a decisive reply – one to make me happy for ever.'

'But my father and friends?' said she.

'Are nothing to be concerned about. Modern developments have shaken up the classes like peas in a hopper. An annuity, and a comfortable cottage—'

'My brothers are workmen.'

'Manufacture is the single vocation in which a man's prospects may be said to be illimitable. Hee-hee! – they may buy me up before they die! And now what stands in the way? It would take fifty alliances with fifty families so little disreputable as yours, darling, to drag mine down.'

Ethelberta had anticipated the scene, and settled her course; what had to be said and done here was mere formality; yet she had been unable to go straight to the assent required. However, after these words of self-depreciation, which were let fall as much for her own future ease of conscience as for his present warning, she made no more ado.

'I shall think it a great honour to be your wife,' she said simply.

The year was now moving on apace, but Ethelberta and Picotee chose to remain at Knollsea, in the brilliant variegated brick and stone villa to which they had removed in order to be in keeping with their ascending fortunes. Autumn had begun to make itself felt and seen in bolder and less subtle ways than at first. In the morning now, on coming downstairs, in place of a yellowish-green leaf or two lying in a corner of the lowest step, which had been the only previous symptoms around the house, she saw dozens of them playing at corkscrews in the wind, directly the door was opened. Beyond, towards the sea, the slopes and scarps that had been muffled with a thick robe of cliff herbage, were showing their chill grey substance through the withered verdure, like the background of velvet whence the pile has been fretted away. Unexpected breezes broomed and rasped the smooth bay in evanescent patches of stippled shade, and, besides the small boats, the ponderous lighters used in shipping stone were hauled up the beach in anticipation of the equinoctial attack.

A few days after Ethelberta's reception at Enkworth, an improved stanhope,* driven by Lord Mountclere himself, climbed up the hill until it was opposite her door. A few notes from a piano softly played reached his ear as he descended from his place: on being shown in to his betrothed, he could perceive that she had just left the instrument. Moreover, a tear was visible in her eye when she came near him.

They discoursed for several minutes in the manner natural between a defenceless young widow and an old widower in Lord Mountclere's position to whom she was plighted – a great deal of formal considerateness making itself visible on her part, and of extreme tenderness on his. While thus occupied, he turned to the piano, and casually glanced at a piece of music lying open upon it. Some words of writing at the top expressed that it was the composer's original copy, presented by him, Christopher Julian, to the author of the song. Seeing that he noticed the sheet somewhat lengthily, Ethelberta remarked that it had been an

offering made to her a long time ago – a melody written to one
of her own poems.

'In the writing of the composer,' observed Lord Mountclere,
with interest. 'An offering from the musician himself – very
gratifying and touching. Mr Christopher Julian is the name I see
upon it, I believe? I knew his father, Dr Julian, a Sandbourne
man, if I recollect.'

'Yes,' said Ethelberta placidly. But it was really with an effort.
The song was the identical one which Christopher sent up to her
from Sandbourne when the fire of her hope burnt high for less
material ends; and the discovery of the sheet among her music
that day had started eddies of emotion for some time checked.

'I am sorry you have been grieved,' said Lord Mountclere,
with gloomy restlessness.

'Grieved?' said Ethelberta.

'Did I not see a tear there? or did my eyes deceive me?'

'You might have seen one.'

'Ah! a tear, and a song. I think—'

'You naturally think that a woman who cries over a man's
gift must be in love with the giver?' Ethelberta looked him
serenely in the face.

Lord Mountclere's jealous suspicions were considerably
shaken.

'Not at all,' he said hastily, as if ashamed. 'One who cries
over a song is much affected by its sentiment.'

'Do you expect authors to cry over their own words?' she
inquired, merging defence in attack. 'I am afraid they don't
often do that.'

'You would make me uneasy.'

'On the contrary, I would reassure you. Are you not still
doubting?' she asked, with a pleasant smile.

'I cannot doubt you!'

'Swear, like a faithful knight.'

'I swear, my fairy, my flower!'

After this the old man appeared to be pondering; indeed, his
thoughts could hardly be said to be present when he uttered the
words. For though the tabernacle* was getting shaky by reason
of years and merry living, so that what was going on inside
might often be guessed without by the movement of the hangings, as in a puppet-show with worn canvas, he could be quiet
enough when scheming any plot of particular neatness, which

had less emotion than impishness in it. Such an innocent amusement he was pondering now.

Before leaving her, he asked if she would accompany him to a morning instrumental concert at Melchester, which was to take place in the course of that week for the benefit of some local institution.

'Melchester,' she repeated faintly, and observed him as searchingly as it was possible to do without exposing herself to a raking fire in return. Could he know that Christopher was living there, and was this said in prolongation of his recent suspicion? But Lord Mountclere's face gave no sign.

'You forget one fatal objection,' said she; 'the secrecy in which it is imperative that the engagement between us should be kept.'

'I am not known in Melchester without my carriage; nor are you.'

'We may be known by somebody on the road.'

'Then let it be arranged in this way. I will not call here to take you up, but will meet you at the station at Anglebury; and we can go on together by train without notice. Surely there can be no objection to that? It would be mere prudishness to object, since we are to become one so shortly.' He spoke a little impatiently. It was plain that he particularly wanted her to go to Melchester.

'I merely meant that there was a chance of discovery in our going out together. And discovery means no marriage.' She was pale now, and sick at heart, for it seemed that the viscount must be aware that Christopher dwelt at that place, and was about to test her concerning him.

'Why does it mean no marriage?' said he.

'My father might, and almost certainly would, object to it. Although he cannot control me, he might entreat me.'

'Why would he object?' said Lord Mountclere uneasily, and somewhat haughtily.

'I don't know.'

'But you will be my wife – say again that you will.'

'I will.'

He breathed. 'He will not object – hee-hee!' he said. 'O no – I think you will be mine now.'

'I have said so. But look to me all the same.'

'You malign yourself, dear one. But you will meet me at Anglebury, as I wish, and go on to Melchester with me?'

'I shall be pleased to – if my sister may accompany me.'

'Ah – your sister. Yes, of course.'

They settled the time of the journey, and when the visit had been stretched out as long as it reasonably could be with propriety, Lord Mountclere took his leave.

When he was again seated on the driving-phaeton* which he had brought that day, Lord Mountclere looked gleeful, and shrewd enough in his own opinion to outwit Mephistopheles. As soon as they were ascending a hill, and he could find time to free his hand, he pulled off his glove, and drawing from his pocket a programme of the Melchester concert referred to, contemplated therein the name of one of the intended performers. The name was that of Mr C. Julian. Replacing it again, he looked ahead, and some time after murmured with wily mirth, 'An excellent test – a lucky thought!'

Nothing of importance occurred during the intervening days. At two o'clock on the appointed afternoon Ethelberta stepped from the train at Melchester with the viscount, who had met her as proposed; she was followed behind by Picotee.

The concert was to be held at the Town-hall half-an-hour later. They entered a fly* in waiting, and secure from recognition, were driven leisurely in that direction, Picotee silent and absorbed with her own thoughts.

'There's the Cathedral,' said Lord Mountclere humorously, as they caught a view of one of its towers through a street leading into the Close.

'Yes.'

'It boasts of a very fine organ.'

'Ah.'

'And the organist is a clever young man.'

'Oh.'

Lord Mountclere paused a moment or two. 'By the way, you may remember that he is the Mr Julian who set your song to music!'

'I recollect it quite well.' Her heart was horrified, and she thought Lord Mountclere must be developing into an inquisitor, which perhaps he was. But none of this reached her face.

They turned in the direction of the Hall, were set down, and entered.

The large assembly-room set apart for the concert was upstairs, and it was possible to enter it in two ways: by the large doorway in front of the landing, or by turning down a side passage leading to council-rooms and subsidiary apartments of small size, which were allotted to performers in any exhibition; who could thus enter from one of these directly upon the platform, without passing through the audience.

'Will you seat yourselves here?' said Lord Mountclere, who, instead of entering by the direct door, had brought the young women round into this green-room, as it may be called. 'You see we have come in privately enough; when the musicians arrive we can pass through behind them, and step down to our seats from the front.'

The players could soon be heard tuning in the next room. Then one came through the passage-room where the three waited, and went in, then another, then another. Last of all came Julian.

Ethelberta sat facing the door, but Christopher, never in the least expecting her there, did not recognize her till he was quite inside. When he had really perceived her to be the one who had troubled his soul so many times and long, the blood in his face – never very much – passed off and left it, like the shade of a cloud. Between them stood a table covered with green baize, which, reflecting upwards a band of sunlight shining across the chamber, flung upon his already white features the virescent hues of death. The poor musician, whose person, much to his own inconvenience, constituted a complete breviary of the gentle emotions, looked as if he were going to fall down in a faint.

Ethelberta flung at Lord Mountclere a look which clipped him like pincers: he never forgot it as long as he lived.

'This is your pretty jealous scheme – I see it!' she hissed to him, and without being able to control herself went across to Julian.

But a slight gasp came from behind the door where Picotee had been sitting. Ethelberta and Lord Mountclere looked that way: and behold, Picotee had nearly swooned.

Ethelberta's show of passion went as quickly as it had come, for she felt that a splendid triumph had been put into her hands. 'Now do you see the truth?' she whispered to Lord Mountclere without a drachm of feeling; pointing to Christopher and then to Picotee – as like as two snowdrops now.

'I do, I do,' murmured the viscount hastily.

They both went forward to help Christopher in restoring the

fragile Picotee: he had set himself to that task as suddenly as he possibly could to cover his own near approach to the same condition. Not much help was required, the little girl's indisposition being quite momentary, and she sat up in the chair again.

'Are you better?' said Ethelberta to Christopher.

'Quite well – quite,' he said, smiling faintly. 'I am glad to see you. I must, I think, go into the next room now.' He bowed and walked out awkwardly.

'Are you better, too?' she said to Picotee.

'Quite well,' said Picotee.

'You are quite sure you know between whom the love lies now – eh?' Ethelberta asked in a sarcastic whisper of Lord Mountclere.

'I am – beyond a doubt,' murmured the anxious nobleman; he feared that look of hers, which was not less dominant than irresistible.

Some additional moments given to thought on the circumstances rendered Ethelberta still more indignant and intractable. She went out at the door by which they had entered, along the passage, and down the stairs. A shuffling footstep followed, but she did not turn her head. When they reached the bottom of the stairs the carriage had gone, their exit not being expected till two hours later. Ethelberta, nothing daunted, swept along the pavement and down the street in a turbulent prance, Lord Mountclere trotting behind with a jowl reduced to a mere nothing by his concern at the discourtesy into which he had been lured by jealous whisperings.

'My dearest – forgive me; I confess I doubted you – but I was beside myself,' came to her ears from over her shoulder. But Ethelberta walked on as before.

Lord Mountclere sighed like a poet over a ledger. 'An old man – who is not very old – naturally torments himself with fears of losing – no, no – it was an innocent jest of mine – you will forgive a joke – hee-hee?' he said again, on getting no reply.

'You had no right to mistrust me!'

'I do not – you did not blench. You should have told me before that it was your sister and not yourself who was entangled with him.'

'You brought me to Melchester on purpose to confront him!'

'Yes, I did.'

'Are you not ashamed?'

'I am satisfied. It is better to know the truth by any means than to die of suspense; better for us both – surely you see that?'

They had by this time got to the end of a long street, and into a deserted side road by which the station could be indirectly reached. Picotee appeared in the distance as a mere distracted speck of girlhood, following them because not knowing what else to do in her sickness of body and mind. Once out of sight here, Ethelberta began to cry.

'Ethelberta,' said Lord Mountclere, in an agony of trouble, 'don't be vexed! It was an inconsiderate trick – I own it. Do what you will, but do not desert me now! I could not bear it – you would kill me if you were to leave me. Anything, but be mine.'

Ethelberta continued her way, and drying her eyes entered the station, where, on searching the time-tables, she found there would be no train for Anglebury for the next two hours. Then more slowly she turned towards the town again, meeting Picotee and keeping in her company.

Lord Mountclere gave up the chase, but as he wished to get into the town again, he followed in the same direction. When Ethelberta had proceeded as far as the Red Lion Hotel, she turned towards it with her companion, and being shown to a room, the two sisters shut themselves in. Lord Mountclere paused and entered the White Hart, the rival hotel to the Red Lion, which stood in an adjoining street.

Having secluded himself in an apartment here, walked from window to window awhile, and made himself generally uncomfortable, he sat down to the writing materials on the table, and concocted a note:

WHITE HART HOTEL

MY DEAR MRS PETHERWIN, – You do not mean to be so cruel as to break your plighted word to me? Remember, there is no love without much jealousy, and lovers are ever full of sighs and misgiving. I have owned to as much contrition as can reasonably be expected. I could not endure the suspicion that you loved another. – Yours always,

MOUNTCLERE.

This he sent, watching from the window its progress along the street. He waited anxiously for an answer, and waited long. It was nearly twenty minutes before he could hear a messenger approaching the door. Yes – she had actually sent a reply, he prized it as if it had been the first encouragement he had ever in his life received from woman: –

MY LORD (wrote Ethelberta), – I am not prepared at present to enter into the question of marriage at all. The incident which has occurred affords me every excuse for withdrawing my promise, since it was given under misapprehensions on a point that materially affects my happiness.

E. PETHERWIN.

'Ho-ho-ho – Miss Hoity-toity!' said Lord Mountclere, trotting up and down. But, remembering it was her June against his November, this did not last long, and he frantically replied: –

MY DARLING, – I cannot release you – I must do anything to keep my treasure. Will you not see me for a few minutes, and let bygones go to the winds?

Was ever a thrush so safe in a cherry net* before!

The messenger came back with the information that Mrs Petherwin had taken a walk to the Close, her companion alone remaining at the hotel. There being nothing else left for the viscount to do, he put on his hat, and went out on foot in the same direction. He had not walked far when he saw Ethelberta moving slowly along the High Street before him.

Ethelberta was at this hour wandering without any fixed intention beyond that of consuming time. She was very wretched, and very indifferent: the former when thinking of her past, the latter when thinking of the days to come. While she walked thus unconscious of the streets, and their groups of other wayfarers, she saw Christopher emerge from a door not many paces in advance, and close it behind him: he stood for a moment on the step before descending into the road.

She could not, even had she wished it, easily check her progress without rendering the chance of his perceiving her still more certain. But she did not wish any such thing, and it made little difference, for he had already seen her in taking his survey round, and came down from the door to her side. It was impossible for anything formal to pass between them now.

'You are not at the concert, Mr Julian?' she said. 'I am glad to have a better opportunity of speaking to you, and of asking for your sister. Unfortunately there is not time for us to call upon her today.'

'Thank you, but it makes no difference,' said Julian, with somewhat sad reserve. 'I will tell her I have met you; she is away from home just at present.' And finding that Ethelberta did not rejoin immediately he observed, 'The chief organist, old Dr Breeve, has taken my place at the concert, as it was arranged he should do after the opening part. I am now going to the Cathedral for the afternoon service. You are going there too?'

'I thought of looking at the interior for a moment.'

So they went on side by side, saying little; for it was a situation in which scarcely any appropriate thing could be spoken. Ethelberta was the less reluctant to walk in his company because of the provocation to skittishness that Lord Mountclere had given, a provocation which she still resented. But she was far from wishing to increase his jealousy; and yet this was what she was doing, Lord Mountclere being a perturbed witness from behind of all that was passing now.

They turned the corner of the short street of connection which led under an archway to the Cathedral Close, the old peer dogging them still. Christopher seemed to warm up a little, and repeated the invitation. 'You will come with your sister to see us before you leave?' he said. 'We have tea at six.'

'We shall have left Melchester before that time. I am now only waiting for the train.'

'You two have not come all the way from Knollsea alone?'

'Part of the way,' said Ethelberta evasively.

'And going back alone?'

'No. Only for the last five miles. At least that was the arrangement – I am not quite sure if it holds good.'

'You don't wish me to see you safely in the train?'

'It is not necessary: thank you very much. We are well used to getting about the world alone, and from Melchester to Knollsea is no serious journey, late or early . . . Yet I think I ought, in honesty, to tell you that we are not entirely by ourselves in Melchester today.'

'I remember I saw your friend – relative – in the room at the Town-hall. It did not occur to my mind for the moment that he was any other than a stranger standing there.'

'He is not a relative,' she said, with perplexity. 'I hardly know, Christopher, how to explain to you my position here today, because of some difficulties that have arisen since we have been in the town, which may alter it entirely. On that account I will be less frank with you than I should like to be, considering how long we have known each other. It would be wrong, however, if I were not to tell you that there has been a possibility of my marriage with him.'

'The elderly gentleman?'

'Yes. And I came here in his company, intending to return with him. But you shall know all soon. Picotee shall write to Faith.'

'I always think the Cathedral looks better from this point than from the point usually chosen by artists,' he said, with nervous quickness, directing her glance upwards to the silent structure, now misty and unrelieved by either high light or deep shade. 'We get the grouping of the chapels and choir-aisles more clearly shown – and the whole culminates to a more perfect pyramid from this spot – do you think so?'

'Yes. I do.'

A little further, and Christopher stopped to enter, when Ethelberta bade him farewell. 'I thought at one time that our futures might have been different from what they are apparently becoming,' he said then, regarding her as a stall-reader regards the brilliant book he cannot afford to buy. 'But one gets weary of repining about that. I wish Picotee and yourself could see us oftener; I am as confirmed a bachelor now as Faith is an old maid. I wonder if – should the event you contemplate occur – you and he will ever visit us, or we shall ever visit you!'

Christopher was evidently imagining the elderly gentleman to be some retired farmer, or professional man already so inter-mixed with the metamorphic classes of society as not to be surprised or inconvenienced by her beginnings; one who wished to secure Ethelberta as an ornament to his parlour fire in a quiet spirit, and in no intoxicated mood regardless of issues. She could scarcely reply to his supposition; and the parting was what might have been predicted from a conversation so carefully controlled.

Ethelberta, as she had intended, now went on further, and entering the nave began to inspect the sallow monuments which lined the grizzled pile. She did not perceive amid the shadows an old gentleman who had crept into the mouldy place as stealthily as a worm into a skull, and was keeping himself carefully beyond her observation. She continued to regard feature after feature till the choristers had filed in from the south side, and peals broke forth from the organ on the black oaken mass at the junction of nave and choir, shaking every cobweb in the dusky vaults, and Ethelberta's heart no less. She knew the fingers that were pressing out those rolling sounds, and knowing them, became absorbed in tracing their progress. To go towards the organ-loft was an act of unconsciousness, and she did not pause till she stood almost beneath it.

Ethelberta was awakened from vague imaginings by the close approach of the old gentleman alluded to, who spoke with a great deal of agitation.

'I have been trying to meet with you,' said Lord Mountclere. 'Come, let us be friends again! – Ethelberta, I *must* not lose you! You cannot mean that the engagement shall be broken off?' He was far too desirous to possess her at any price now to run a second risk of exasperating her, and forbore to make any allusion to the recent pantomime between herself and Christopher that he had beheld, though it might reasonably have filled him with dread and petulance.

'I do not mean anything beyond this,' said she, 'that I entirely withdraw from it on the faintest sign that you have not abandoned such miserable jealous proceedings as those you adopted today.'

'I have quite abandoned them. Will you come a little further this way, and walk in the aisle? You do still agree to be mine?'

'If it gives you any pleasure, I do.'

'Yes, yes. I implore that the marriage may be soon – very soon.' The viscount spoke hastily, for the notes of the organ which were plunging into their ears ever and anon from the hands of his young rival seemed inconveniently and solemnly in the way of his suit.

'Well, Lord Mountclere?'

'Say in a few days? – it is the only thing that will satisfy me.'

'I am absolutely indifferent as to the day. If it pleases you to have it early I am willing.'

'Dare I ask that it may be this week?' said the delighted old man.

'I could not say that.'

'But you can name the earliest day?'

'I cannot now. We had better be going from here, I think.'

The Cathedral was filling with shadows, and cold breathings came round the piers, for it was November, when night very soon succeeds noon in spots where noon is sobered to the pallor of eve. But the service was not yet over, and before quite leaving the building Ethelberta cast one other glance towards the organ and thought of him behind it. At this moment her attention was arrested by the form of her sister Picotee, who came in at the north door, closed the lobby-wicket softly, and went lightly forward to the choir. When within a few yards of it she paused by a pillar, and lingered there looking up at the organ as Ethelberta had done. No sound was coming from the ponderous mass of tubes just then; but in a short space a whole crowd of tones spread from the instrument to accompany the words of a response. Picotee started at the burst of music as if taken in a dishonest action, and moved on in a manner intended to efface the lover's loiter of the preceding moments from her own consciousness no less than from other people's eyes.

'Do you see that?' said Ethelberta. 'That little figure is my dearest sister. Could you but ensure a marriage between her and him she listens to, I would do anything you wish!'

'That is indeed a gracious promise,' said Lord Mountclere. 'And would you agree to what I asked just now?'

'Yes.'

'When?' A gleeful spark accompanied this.

'As you requested.'

'This week? The day after tomorrow?'

'If you will. But remember what lies on your side of the contract. I fancy I have given you a task beyond your powers.'

'Well, darling, we are at one at last,' said Lord Mountclere, rubbing his hand against his side. 'And if my task is heavy and I cannot guarantee the result, I can make it very probable. Marry me on Friday – the day after tomorrow – and I will do all that money and influence can effect to bring about their union.'

'You solemnly promise? You will never cease to give me all the aid in your power until the thing is done?'

'I do solemnly promise – on the conditions named.'

'Very good. You will have ensured my fulfilment of my promise before I can ensure yours; but I take your word.'

'You will marry me on Friday! Give me your hand upon it.'

She gave him her hand.

'Is it a covenant?' he asked.

'It is,' said she.

Lord Mountclere warmed from surface to centre as if he had drunk of hippocras,* and, after holding her hand for some moments, raised it gently to his lips.

'Two days and you are mine,' he said.

'That I believe I never shall be.'

'Never shall be? Why, darling?'

'I don't know. Some catastrophe will prevent it. I shall be dead perhaps.'

'You distress me. Ah, – you meant me – you meant that I should be dead, because you think I am old! But that is a mistake – I am not very old!'

'I thought only of myself – nothing of you.'

'Yes, I know. Dearest, it is dismal and chilling here – let us go.'

Ethelberta mechanically moved with him, and felt there was no retreating now. In the meantime the young ladykin whom the solemn vowing concerned had lingered round the choir screen, as if fearing to enter, yet loth to go away. The service terminated, the heavy books were closed, doors were opened, and the feet of the few persons who had attended evensong began pattering down the paved alleys. Not wishing Picotee to know that the object of her secret excursion had been discovered, Ethelberta now stepped out of the west doorway with the viscount before Picotee had emerged from the other; and they walked along the path together until she overtook them.

'I fear it becomes necessary for me to stay in Melchester tolnight,' said Lord Mountclere. 'I have a few matters to attend to here, as the result of our arrangements. But I will first accompany you as far as Anglebury, and see you safely into a carriage there that shall take you home. Tomorrow I will drive to Knollsea, when we will make the final preparations.'

Ethelberta would not have him go so far and back again, merely to attend upon her; hence they parted at the railway, with due and correct tenderness; and when the train had gone, Lord Mountclere returned into the town on the special business he had mentioned, for which there remained only the present evening and the following morning, if he were to call upon her in the afternoon of the next day – the day before the wedding – now so recklessly hastened on his part, and so coolly assented to on hers.

By the time that the two young people had started it was nearly dark. Some portions of the railway stretched through little copses and plantations where, the leaf-shedding season being now at its height, red and golden patches of fallen foliage lay on either side of the rails; and as the travellers passed, all these death-stricken bodies boiled up in the whirlwind created by the velocity, and were sent flying right and left of them in myriads, a clean-fanned track being left behind.

Picotee was called from the observation of these phenomena by a remark from her sister: 'Picotee, the marriage is to be very early indeed. It is to be the day after tomorrow – if it can. Nevertheless I don't believe in the fact – I cannot.'

'Did you arrange it so? Nobody can make you marry so soon.'

'I agreed to the day,' murmured Ethelberta languidly.

'How can it be? The gay dresses and the preparations and the people – how can they be collected in the time, Berta? And so much more of that will be required for a lord of the land than for a common man. O, I can't think it possible for a sister of mine to marry a lord!'

'And yet it has been possible any time this last month or two, strange as it seems to you . . . It is to be not only a plain and simple wedding, without any lofty appliances, but a secret one – as secret as if I were some under-age heiress to an Indian fortune,* and he a young man of nothing a year.'

'Has Lord Mountclere said it must be so private? I suppose it is on account of his family.'

'No. I say so; and it is on account of my family. Father might object to the wedding, I imagine, from what he once said, or he might be much disturbed about it; so I think it better that he and the rest should know nothing till all is over. You must dress again as my sister tomorrow, dear. Lord Mountclere is going to pay us an early visit to conclude necessary arrangements.'

'O, the life as a lady at Enckworth Court! The flowers, the woods, the rooms, the pictures, the plate, and the jewels! Horses and carriages rattling and prancing, seneschals* and pages, footmen hopping up and hopping down. It will be glory then!'

'We might hire our father as one of my retainers to increase it,' said Ethelberta drily.

Picotee's countenance fell. 'How shall we manage all about that? 'Tis terrible, really!'

'The marriage granted, those things will right themselves by time and weight of circumstances. You take a wrong view in thinking of glories of that sort. My only hope is that my life will be quite private and simple, as will best become my inferiority and Lord Mountclere's staidness. Such a splendid library as there is at Enckworth, Picotee – quartos, folios, history, verse, Elzevirs, Caxtons* all that has been done in literature from Moses down to Scott* – with such companions I can do without all other sorts of happiness.'

'And you will not go to town from Easter to Lammastide,* as other noble ladies do?' asked the younger girl, rather disappointed at this aspect of a viscountess's life.

'I don't know.'

'But you will give dinners, and travel, and go to see his friends, and have them to see you?'

'I don't know.'

'Will you not be, then, as any other peeress; and shall not I be as any other peeress's sister?'

'That, too, I do not know. All is mystery. Nor do I even know that the marriage will take place. I feel that it may not; and perhaps so much the better, since the man is a stranger to me, I know nothing whatever of his nature, and he knows nothing of mine.'

Melchester (*continued*)

40

The commotion wrought in Julian's mind by the abrupt incursion of Ethelberta into his quiet sphere was thorough and protracted. The witchery of her presence he had grown strong enough to withstand in part; but her composed announcement that she had intended to marry another, and, as far as he could understand, was intending it still, added a new chill to the old shade of disappointment which custom was day by day enabling him to endure. During the whole interval in which he had produced those diapason blasts,* heard with such inharmonious feelings by the three auditors outside the screen, his thoughts had wandered wider than his notes in conjectures on the character and position of the gentleman seen in Ethelberta's company. Owing to his assumption that Lord Mountclere was but a stranger who had accidentally come in at the side door, Christopher had barely cast a glance upon him, and the wide difference between the years of the viscount and those of his betrothed was not so particularly observed as to raise that point to an item in his objections now. Lord Mountclere was dressed with all the cunning that could be drawn from the metropolis by money and reiterated dissatisfaction; he prided himself on his upright carriage; his stick was so thin that the most malevolent could not insinuate that it was of any possible use in walking; his teeth had put on all the vigour and freshness of a second spring. Hence his look was the slowest of possible clocks in respect of his age, and his manner was equally as much in the rear of his appearance.

Christopher was now over seven-and-twenty. He was getting so well accustomed to the spectacle of a world passing him by and splashing him with its wheels that he wondered why he had ever minded it. His habit of dreaming instead of doing had led him up to a curious discovery. It is no new thing for a man to fathom profundities by indulging humours: the active, the rapid, the people of splendid momentum, have been surprised to behold what results attend the lives of those whose usual plan for discharging their active labours has been to postpone them indefinitely. Certainly, the immediate result in the present case was, to all but himself, small and invisible; but it was of the nature of highest things. What he had learnt was that a woman who has once made a permanent impression upon a man cannot altogether deny him her image by denying him her company, and that by sedulously cultivating the acquaintance of this Creature of Contemplation she becomes to him almost a living soul. Hence a sublimated Ethelberta accompanied him everywhere – one who never teased him, eluded him, or disappointed him: when he smiled she smiled, when he was sad she sorrowed. He may be said to have become the literal duplicate of that whimsical unknown rhapsodist who wrote of his own similar situation –

> By absence this good means I gain,
>> That I can catch her,
>> Where none can watch her,
> In some close corner of my brain:

There I embrace and kiss her;
And so I both enjoy and miss her.*

This frame of mind naturally induced an amazing abstraction in the organist, never very vigilant at the best of times. He would stand and look fixedly at a frog in a shady pool, and never once think of batrachians,* or pause by a green bank to split some tall blade of grass into filaments without removing it from its stalk, passing on ignorant that he had made a cat-o'-nine-tails of a graceful slip of vegetation. He would hear the cathedral clock strike one, and go the next minute to see what time it was. 'I never seed such a man as Mr Julian is,' said the head blower.* 'He'll meet me anywhere out-of-doors, and never wink or nod. You'd hardly expect it. I don't find fault, but you'd hardly expect it, seeing how I play the same instrument as he do himself, and have done it for so many years longer than he. How I have indulged that man, too! If 'tis Pedals for two martel hours of practice I never complain; and he has plenty of vagaries. When 'tis hot summer weather there's nothing will do for him but Choir, Great, and Swell* altogether, till yer face is in a vapour; and on a frosty winter night he'll keep me there while he tweedles upon the Dulcianner* till my arms be scrammed* for want of motion. And never speak a word out-of-doors.' Somebody suggested that perhaps Christopher did not notice his coadjutor's presence in the street; and time proved to the organ-blower that the remark was just.

Whenever Christopher caught himself at these vacuous tricks he would be struck with admiration of Ethelberta's wisdom, foresight, and self-command in refusing to wed such an incapable man: he felt that he ought to be thankful that a bright memory of her was not also denied to him, and resolved to be content with it as a possession, since it was as much of her as he could decently maintain.

Wrapped thus in a humorous sadness he passed the afternoon under notice, and in the evening went home to Faith, who still lived with him, and showed no sign of ever being likely to do otherwise. Their present place and mode of life suited her well. She revived at Melchester like an exotic sent home again. The leafy Close, the climbing buttresses, the pondering ecclesiastics, the great doors, the singular keys, the whispered talk, echoes of lonely footsteps, the sunset shadow of the tall steeple, reaching further into the town than the good bishop's teaching, and the general complexion of a spot where morning had the stillness of evening and spring some of the tones of autumn, formed a proper background to a person constituted as Faith, who, like Miss Hepzibah Pyncheon's chicken,* possessed in miniature all the antiquity of her progenitors.

After tea Christopher went into the streets, as was frequently his custom, less to see how the world crept on there than to walk up and down for nothing at all. It had been market-day, and remnants of the rural population that had visited the town still lingered at corners, their toes hanging over the edge of the pavement, and their eyes wandering about the street.

The angle which formed the turning-point of Christopher's promenade was occupied by a jeweller's shop, of a standing which completely outshone every other shop in that or any trade throughout the town. Indeed, it was a staple subject of discussion in Melchester how a shop of such pretensions could find patronage sufficient to support its existence in a place which, though well populated, was not fashionable. It had not long been established there, and was the enterprise of an incoming man whose whole course of procedure seemed to be dictated by an intention to astonish the native citizens very considerably before he had done. Nearly everything was glass in the frontage of this fairy mart, and its contents glittered like the hammochrysos stone.* The panes being of plate-glass, and the shop having two fronts, a diagonal view could be had through it from one to the other of the streets to which it formed a corner.

This evening, as on all evenings, a flood of radiance spread from the window-lamps into the thick autumn air, so that from a distance that corner appeared as the glistening nucleus of all the light in the town. Towards it idle men and women unconsciously bent their steps, and closed in upon the panes like night-birds upon the lantern of a lighthouse.

When Christopher reached the spot there stood close to the pavement a plain close carriage, apparently waiting for some person who was purchasing inside. Christopher would hardly have noticed this had he not also perceived, pressed against the glass of the shop window, an unusual number of local noses belonging to overgrown working lads, tosspots, an idiot, the ham-smoker's assistant with his sleeves rolled up, a scot-and-lot freeholder,* three or four seamstresses, the young woman who brought home the washing, and so on. The interest of these gazers in some proceedings within, which by reason of the gaslight were as public as if carried on in the open air, was very great.

'Yes, that's what he's a buying o' – haw, haw!' said one of the young men, as the shopman removed from the window a gorgeous blue velvet tray of wedding-rings, and laid it on the counter.

''Tis what you may come to yerself, sooner or later, God have mercy upon ye; and as such no scoffing matter,' said an older man, 'Faith, I'd as lief cry as laugh to see a man in that corner.'

'He's a gent getting up in years too. He must hev been through it a few times afore, seemingly, to sit down and buy the tools so cool as that.'

'Well, no. See what the shyest will do at such times. You bain't yerself then; no man living is hisself then.'

'True,' said the ham-smoker's man. ''Tis a thought to look at that a chap will take all this trouble to get a woman into his house, and a twelvemonth after would as soon hear it thunder as hear her sing!'

The policeman standing near was a humane man, through having a young family he could hardly keep; and he hesitated about telling them to move on. Christopher had before this time perceived that the articles were laid down before an old gentleman who was seated in the shop, and that the gentleman was none other than he who had been with Ethelberta in the concert-room. The discovery was so startling that, constitutionally indisposed as he was to stand and watch, he became as glued to the spot as the other idlers. Finding himself now for the first time directly confronting the preliminaries of Ethelberta's marriage to a stranger, he was left with far less equanimity than he could have supposed possible to the situation.

'So near the time!' he said, and looked hard at Lord Mountclere.

Christopher had now a far better opportunity than before for observing Ethelberta's betrothed. Apart from any bias of jealousy, disappointment, or mortification, he was led to judge that this was not quite the man to make Ethelberta happy. He had fancied her companion to be a man under fifty; he was now visibly sixty or more. And it was not the sort of sexagenarianism beside which a young woman's happiness can sometimes contrive to keep itself alive in a quiet sleepy way. Suddenly it occurred to him that this was the man whom he had helped in the carriage accident on the way to Knollsea. He looked again.

By no means undignified, the face presented that combination of slyness and jocundity which we are accustomed to imagine of the canonical jolly-dogs in mediæval tales. The gamesome Curate of Meudon* might have supplied some parts of the countenance; cunning Friar Tuck* the remainder. Nothing but the viscount's constant habit of going to church every Sunday morning when at his country residence kept unholiness out of his features, for though he lived theologically enough on the Sabbath, as it became a man in his position to do, he was strikingly mundane all the rest of the week, always preferring the devil to God in his oaths. And nothing but antecedent good-humour prevented the short fits of crossness incident to his passing infirmities from becoming established. His look was exceptionally jovial now, and the corners of his mouth twitched as the telegraph-needles of a hundred little erotic messages from his heart to his brain. Anybody could see that he was a merry man still, who loved good company, warming drinks, nymph-like shapes, and pretty words, in spite of the disagreeable suggestions he received from the pupils of his eyes, and the joints of his lively limbs, that imps of mischief were busy sapping and mining in those regions, with the view of tumbling him into a certain cool cellar under the church aisle.

In general, if a lover can find any ground at all for serenity in the tide of an elderly rival's success, he finds it in the fact itself of that ancientness. The other side seems less a rival than a makeshift. But Christopher no longer felt this, and the significant signs before his eyes of the imminence of Ethelberta's union with this old hero filled him with restless dread. True, the gentleman, as he appeared illuminated by the jeweller's gas-jets, seemed more likely to injure Ethelberta by indulgence than by severity, while her beauty lasted; but there was a nameless something in him less tolerable than this.

The purchaser having completed his dealings with the gold-smith, was conducted to the door by the master of the shop, and into the carriage, which was at once driven off up the street.

Christopher now much desired to know the name of the man whom a nice chain of circumstantial evidence taught him to regard as the happy winner where scores had lost. He was grieved that Ethelberta's confessed reserve should have extended so far as to limit her to mere indefinite hints of marriage when they were talking almost on the brink of the wedding-day. That the ceremony was to be a private one – which it probably would be because of the disparity of ages – did not in his opinion justify her secrecy. He had shown himself capable of a transmutation as valuable as it is rare in men, the change from pestering lover to staunch friend, and this was all he had got for it. But even an old lover sunk to an indifferentist might have been tempted to spend an unoccupied half-hour in discovering particulars now, and Christopher had not lapsed nearly so far as to absolute unconcern.

That evening, however, nothing came in his way to enlighten him. But the next day, when skirting the Close on his ordinary duties, he saw the same carriage standing at a distance, and paused to behold the same old gentleman come from a well-known office and re-enter the vehicle – Lord Mountclere, in fact, in earnest pursuit of the business of yesternight, having just pocketed a document in which romance, rashness, law, and gospel are so happily made to work together that it may safely be regarded as the neatest compromise which has ever been invented since Adam sinned.

This time Julian perceived that the brougham was one belonging to the White Hart Hotel, which Lord Mountclere was using partly from the necessities of these hasty proceedings, and also because, by so doing, he escaped the notice that might have been bestowed upon his own equipage, or men-servants, the Mountclere hammer-cloths* being known in Melchester. Christopher now walked towards the hotel, leisurely, yet with anxiety. He inquired of a porter what people were staying there that day, and was informed that they had only one person in the house, Lord Mountclere, whom sudden and unexpected business had detained in Melchester since the previous day.

Christopher lingered to hear no more. He retraced the street much more quickly than he had come; and he only said, 'Lord Mountclere – it must never be!'

As soon as he entered the house, Faith perceived that he was greatly agitated. He at once told her of his discovery, and she exclaimed, 'What a brilliant match!'

'O Faith,' said Christopher, 'you don't know! You are far

from knowing. It is as gloomy as midnight. Good God, can it be possible?'

Faith blinked in alarm, without speaking.

'Did you never hear anything of Lord Mountclere when we lived at Sandbourne?'

'I knew the name – no more.'

'No, no – of course you did not. Well, though I never saw his face, to my knowledge, till a short time ago, I know enough to say that, if earnest representations can prevent it, this marriage shall not be. Father knew him, or about him, very well; and he once told me – what I cannot tell you. Fancy, I have seen him three times – yesterday, last night, and this morning – besides helping him on the road some weeks ago, and never once considered that he might be Lord Mountclere. He is here almost in disguise, one may say; neither man nor horse is with him; and his object accounts for his privacy. I see how it is – she is doing this to benefit her brothers and sisters, if possible; but she ought to know that if she is miserable they will never be happy. That's the nature of women – they take the form for the essence, and that's what she is doing now. I should think her guardian angel must have quitted her when she agreed to a marriage which may tear her heart out like a claw.'

'You are too warm about it, Kit – it cannot be so bad as that. It is not the thing, but the sensitiveness to the thing, which is the true measure of its pain. Perhaps what seems so bad to you falls lightly on her mind. A campaigner in a heavy rain is not more uncomfortable than we are in a slight draught; and Ethelberta, fortified by her sapphires and gold cups and wax candles, will not mind facts which look like spectres to us outside. A title will turn troubles into romances, and she will shine as an interesting viscountess in spite of them.'

The discussion with Faith was not continued, Christopher stopping the argument by saying that he had a good mind to go off at once to Knollsea, and show her her danger. But till the next morning Ethelberta was certainly safe; no marriage was possible anywhere before then. He passed the afternoon in a state of great indecision, constantly reiterating, 'I will go!'

Workshops
An Inn
The Street

41

On an extensive plot of ground, lying somewhere between the Thames and the Kensington squares, stood the premises of Messrs Nockett & Perch, builders and contractors. The yard with its workshops formed part of one of those frontier lines between mangy business and garnished domesticity that occur in what are called improving neighbourhoods. We are accustomed to regard increase as the chief feature in a great city's progress, its well-known signs greeting our eyes on every outskirt. Slush-ponds may be seen turning into basement-kitchens; a broad causeway of shattered earthenware smothers plots of budding gooseberry-bushes and vegetable trenches, foundations following so closely upon gardens that the householder may be expected to find cadaverous sprouts from overlooked potatoes rising through the chinks of his cellar floor. But the other great process, that of internal transmutation, is not less curious than this encroachment of grey upon green. Its first erections are often only the milk-teeth of a suburb, and as the district rises in dignity they are dislodged by those which are to endure. Slightness becomes supplanted by comparative solidity, commonness by novelty, lowness and irregularity by symmetry and height.

An observer of the precinct which has been named as an instance in point might have stood under a lamp-post and heard simultaneously the peal of the visitor's bell from the new terrace on the right hand, and the stroke of tools from the musty workshops on the left. Waggons laden with deals* came up on this side, and landaus* came down on the other – the former to lumber heavily through the old-established contractors' gates, the latter to sweep fashionably into the square.

About twelve o'clock on the day following Lord Mountclere's exhibition of himself to Christopher in the jeweller's shop at Melchester, and almost at the identical time when the viscount was seen to come from the office for marriage-licences in the same place, a carriage drove nearly up to the gates of Messrs

Nockett & Co.'s yard. A gentleman stepped out and looked around. He was a man whose years would have been pronounced as five-and-forty by the friendly, fifty by the candid, fifty-two or three by the grim. He was as handsome a study in grey as could be seen in town, there being far more of the raven's plumage than of the gull's in the mixture as yet; and he had a glance of that practised sort which can measure people, weigh them, repress them, encourage them to sprout and blossom as a March sun encourages crocuses, ask them questions, give them answers – in short, a glance that could do as many things as an American cooking-stove or a multum-in-parvo* pocket-knife. But, as with most men of the world, this was mere mechanism; his actual emotions were kept so far within his person that they were rarely heard or seen near his features.

On reading the builders' names over the gateway he entered the yard, and asked at the office if Solomon Chickerel was engaged on the premises. The clerk was going to be very attentive, but finding the visitor had come only to speak to a workman, his tense attitude slackened a little, and he merely signified the foot of a Flemish ladder* on the other side of the yard, saying, 'You will find him, sir, up there in the joiner's shop.'

When the man in the black coat reached the top he found himself at the end of a long apartment as large as a chapel and as low as a malt-room, across which ran parallel carpenters' benches to the number of twenty or more, a gangway being left at the side for access throughout. Behind every bench there stood a man or two, planing, fitting or chiselling, as the case might be. The visitor paused for a moment, as if waiting for some cessation of their violent motions and uproar till he could make his errand known. He waited ten seconds, he waited twenty; but, beyond that a quick look had been thrown upon him by every pair of eyes, the muscular performances were in no way interrupted: every one seemed oblivious of his presence, and absolutely regardless of his wish. In truth, the texture of that salmon-coloured skin could be seen to be aristocratic without a microscope, and the exceptious* artizan has an off-hand way when contrasts are made painfully strong by an idler of this kind coming, gloved and brushed, into the very den where he is sweating and muddling in his shirt-sleeves.

The gentleman from the carriage then proceeded down the workshop, wading up to his knees in a sea of shavings, and bruising his ankles against corners of board and sawn-off blocks, that lay hidden like reefs beneath. At the ninth bench he made another venture.

'Sol Chickerel?' said the man addressed, as he touched his plane-iron upon the oilstone. 'He's one of them just behind.'

'Damn it all, can't one of you show me?' the visitor angrily observed, for he had been used to more attention than this. 'Here, point him out.' He handed the man a shilling.

'No trouble to do that,' said the workman; and he turned and signified Sol by a nod without moving from his place.

The stranger entered Sol's division, and, nailing him with his eye, said at once: 'I want to speak a few words with you in private. Is not a Mrs Petherwin your sister?'

Sol started suspiciously. 'Has anything happened to her?' he at length said hurriedly.

'O no. It is on a business matter that I have called. You need not mind owning the relationship to me – the secret will be kept. I am the brother of one whom you may have heard of from her – Lord Mountclere.'

'I have not. But if you will wait a minute, sir—' He went to a little glazed box at the end of the shop, where the foreman was sitting, and, after speaking a few words to this person, Sol led Mountclere to the door, and down the ladder.

'I suppose we cannot very well talk here, after all?' said the gentleman, when they reached the yard, and found several men moving about therein.

'Perhaps we had better go to some room – the nearest inn will answer the purpose, won't it?'

'Excellently.'

'There's the "Green Bushes" over the way. They have a very nice private room upstairs.'

'Yes, that will do.' And passing out of the yard, the man with the glance entered the inn with Sol, where they were shown to the parlour as requested.

While the waiter was gone for some wine, which Mountclere ordered, the more ingenuous of the two resumed the conversation by saying, awkwardly: 'Yes, Mrs Petherwin is my sister, as you supposed, sir; but on her account I do not let it be known.'

'Indeed,' said Mountclere. 'Well, I came to see you in order to speak of a matter which I thought you might know more about than I do, for it has taken me quite by surprise. My brother, Lord Mountclere, is, it seems, to be privately married to Mrs Petherwin tomorrow.'

'Is that really the fact?' said Sol, becoming quite shaken. 'I had no thought that such a thing could be possible!'

'It is imminent.'

'Father has told me that she has lately got to know some nobleman; but I never supposed there could be any meaning in that.'

'You were altogether wrong,' said Mountclere, leaning back in his chair and looking at Sol steadily. 'Do you feel it to be a matter upon which you will congratulate her?'

'A very different thing!' said Sol vehemently. 'Though he is your brother, sir, I must say this, that I would rather she married the poorest man I know.'

'Why?'

'From what my father has told me of him, he is not – a more desirable brother-in-law to me than I shall be in all likelihood to him. What business has a man of that character to marry Berta, I should like to ask?'

'That's what I say,' returned Mountclere, revealing his satisfaction at Sol's estimate of his noble brother: it showed that he had calculated well in coming here. 'My brother is getting old, and he has lived strangely: your sister is a highly respectable young lady.'

'And he is not respectable, you mean? I know he is not. I worked near Enckworth once.'

'I cannot say that,' returned Mountclere. Possibly a certain fraternal feeling repressed a direct assent: and yet this was the only representation which could be expected to prejudice the young man against the wedding, if he were such an one as the visitor supposed Sol to be – a man vulgar in sentiment and ambition, but pure in his anxiety for his sister's happiness. 'At any rate, we are agreed in thinking that this would be an unfortunate marriage for both,' added Mountclere.

'About both I don't know. It may be a good thing for him. When do you say it is to be, sir – tomorrow?'

'Yes.'

'I don't know what to do!' said Sol, walking up and down. 'If half what I have heard is true, I would lose a winter's work to prevent her marrying him. What does she want to go mixing in with people who despise her for? Now look here, Mr Mountclere, since you have been and called me out to talk this over, it is only fair that you should tell me the exact truth about your brother. Is it a lie, or is it true, that he is not fit to be the husband of a decent woman?'

'That is a curious inquiry,' said Mountclere, whose manner and aspect, neutral as a winter landscape, had little in common with Sol's warm and unrestrained bearing. 'There are reasons why I think your sister will not be happy with him.'

'Then it is true what they say,' said Sol, bringing down his fist upon the table. 'I know your meaning well enough. What's to be done? If I could only see her this minute, she might be kept out of it.'

'You think your presence would influence your sister – if you could see her before the wedding?'

'I think it would. But who's to get at her?'

'I am going, so you had better come on with me – unless it would be best for your father to come.'

'Perhaps it might,' said the bewildered Sol. 'But he will not be able to get away; and it's no use for Dan to go. If anybody goes I must! If she has made up her mind nothing can be done by writing to her.'

'I leave at once to see Lord Mountclere,' the other continued. 'I feel that as my brother is evidently ignorant of the position of Mrs Petherwin's family and connections, it is only fair in me, as his nearest relative, to make them clear to him before it is too late.'

'You mean that if he knew her friends were working-people he would not think of her as a wife? 'Tis a reasonable thought. But make your mind easy: she has told him. I make a great mistake if she has for a moment thought of concealing that from him.'

'She may not have deliberately done so. But – and I say this with no ill-feeling – it is a matter known to few, and she may have taken no steps to undeceive him. I hope to bring him to see the matter clearly. Unfortunately the thing has been so secret and hurried that there is barely time. I knew nothing until this morning – never dreamt of such a preposterous occurrence.'

'Preposterous! If it should come to pass, she would play her part as his lady as well as any other woman, and better. I wish there was no more reason for fear on my side than there is on yours! Things have come to a sore head when she is not considered lady enough for such as he. But perhaps your meaning is, that if your brother were to have a son, you would lose your heir-presumptive title to the cor'net of Mountclere? Well, 'twould be rather hard for 'ee, now I come to think o't – upon my life, 'twould.'

'The suggestion is as delicate as the —— atmosphere of this vile room. But let your ignorance be your excuse, my man. It is hardly worth while for us to quarrel when we both have the same object in view: do you think so?'

'That's true – that's true. When do you start, sir?'

'We must leave almost at once,' said Mountclere, looking at his watch. 'If we cannot catch the two o'clock train, there is no getting there tonight – and tomorrow we could not possibly arrive before one.'

'I wish there was time for me to go and tidy myself a bit,' said Sol, anxiously looking down at his working clothes. 'I suppose you would not like me to go with you like this?

'Confound the clothes! If you cannot start in five minutes, we shall not be able to go at all.'

'Very well, then – wait while I run across to the shop, then I am ready. How do we get to the station?'

'My carriage is at the corner waiting. When you come out I will meet you at the gates.'

Sol then hurried downstairs, and a minute or two later Mr Mountclere followed, looking like a man bent on policy at any price. The carriage was brought round by the time that Sol reappeared from the yard. He entered and sat down beside Mountclere, not without a sense that he was spoiling good upholstery; the coachman then allowed the lash of his whip to alight with the force of a small fly upon the horses, which set them up in an angry trot. Sol rolled on beside his new acquaintance with the shamefaced look of a man going to prison in a van, for pedestrians occasionally gazed at him, full of what seemed to himself to be ironical surprise.

'I am afraid I ought to have changed my clothes after all,' he said, writhing under a perception of the contrast between them. 'Not knowing anything about this, I ain't a bit prepared. If I had got even my second-best hat, it wouldn't be so bad.'

'It makes no difference,' said Mountclere inanimately.

'Or I might have brought my portmantle, with some things.'

'It really is not important.'

On reaching the station they found there were yet a few minutes to spare, which Sol made use of in writing a note to his father, to explain what had occurred.

The Doncastles' Residence and Outside the Same

42

Mrs Doncastle's dressing-bell had rung, but Menlove, the lady's-maid, having at the same time received a letter by the evening post, paused to read it before replying to the summons: –

ENCKWORTH COURT, *Wednesday*

DARLING LOUISA, – I can assure you that I am no more likely than yourself to form another attachment, as you will perceive by what follows. Before we left town I thought that to be able to see you occasionally was sufficient for happiness, but down in this lonely place the case is different. In short, my dear, I ask you to consent to a union with me as soon as you possibly can. Your prettiness has won my eyes and lips completely, sweet, and I lie awake at night to think of the golden curls you allowed to escape from their confinement on those nice times of private clothes, when we walked in the park and slipped the bonds of service, which you were never born to any more than I . . .

Had not my own feelings been so strong, I should have told you at the first dash of my pen that what I expected is coming to pass at last – the old dog is going to be privately married to Mrs P. Yes, indeed, and the wedding is coming off tomorrow, secret as the grave. All her friends will doubtless leave service on account of it. What he does now makes little difference to me, of course, as I had already given warning, but I shall stick to him like a Briton in spite of it. He has today made me a present, and a further five pounds for yourself, expecting you to hold your tongue on every matter connected with Mrs P.'s friends, and to say nothing to any of them about this marriage until it is over. His lordship impressed this upon me very strong, and familiar as a brother, and of course we obey his instructions to the letter; for I need hardly say that unless he keeps his promise to help me in setting up the shop, our nuptials cannot be consumed.* His help depends upon our obedience, as you are aware . . .

This, and much more, was from her very last lover, Lord Mountclere's valet, who had been taken in hand directly she had convinced herself of Joey's hopeless youthfulness. The missive sent Mrs Menlove's spirits soaring like spring larks; she flew upstairs in answer to the bell with a joyful, triumphant look, which the illuminated figure of Mrs Doncastle in her dressing-room could not quite repress. One could almost forgive Menlove her arts when so modest a result brought such vast content.

Mrs Doncastle seemed inclined to make no remark during the dressing, and at last Menlove could repress herself no longer.

'I should like to name something to you, m'm.'

'Yes.'

'I shall be wishing to leave soon, if it is convenient.'

'Very well, Menlove,' answered Mrs Doncastle, as she serenely surveyed her right eyebrow in the glass. 'Am I to take this as a formal notice?'

'If you please; but I could stay a week or two beyond the month if suitable. I am going to be married – that's what it is, m'm.'

'O! I am glad to hear it, though I am sorry to lose you.'

'It is Lord Mountclere's valet – Mr Tipman – m'm.'

'Indeed.'

Menlove went on building up Mrs Doncastle's hair awhile in silence.

'I suppose you heard the other news that arrived in town to-day, m'm?' she said again. 'Lord Mountclere is going to be married tomorrow.'

'Tomorrow? Are you quite sure?'

'O yes, m'm. Mr Tipman has just told me so in his letter. He is going to be married to Mrs Petherwin. It is to be quite a private wedding.'

Mrs Doncastle made no remark, and she remained in the same still position as before; but a countenance expressing transcendent surprise was reflected to Menlove by the glass.

At this sight Menlove's tongue so burned to go further, and unfold the lady's relations with the butler downstairs, that she would have lost a month's wages to be at liberty to do it. The disclosure was almost too magnificent to be repressed. To deny herself so exquisite an indulgence required an effort which nothing on earth could have sustained save the one thing that did sustain it – the knowledge that upon her silence hung the most enormous desideratum in the world, her own marriage. She said no more, and Mrs Doncastle went away.

It was an ordinary family dinner that day, but their nephew Neigh happened to be present. Just as they were sitting down Mrs Doncastle said to her husband: 'Why have you not told me of the wedding tomorrow? – or don't you know anything about it?'

'Wedding?' said Mr Doncastle.

'Lord Mountclere is to be married to Mrs Petherwin quite privately.'

'Good God!' said some person.

Mr Doncastle did not speak the words; they were not spoken by Neigh: they seemed to float over the room and round the walls, as if originating in some spiritualistic source. Yet Mrs Doncastle, remembering the symptoms of attachment between Ethelberta and her nephew which had appeared during the summer, looked towards Neigh instantly, as if she thought the words must have come from him after all; but Neigh's face was perfectly calm; he, together with her husband, was sitting with his eyes fixed in the direction of the sideboard; and turning to the same spot she beheld Chickerel standing pale as death, his lips being parted as if he did not know where he was.

'Did you speak?' said Mrs Doncastle, looking with astonishment at the butler.

'Chickerel, what's the matter – are you ill?' said Mr Doncastle simultaneously. 'Was it you who said that?'

'I did, sir,' said Chickerel in a husky voice, scarcely above a whisper. 'I could not help it.'

'Why?'

'She is my daughter, and it shall be known at once!'

'Who is your daughter?'

He paused a few moments nervously. 'Mrs Petherwin,' he said.

Upon this announcement Neigh looked at poor Chickerel as if he saw through him into the wall. Mrs Doncastle uttered a faint exclamation and leant back in her chair: the bare possibility of the truth of Chickerel's claims to such paternity shook her to pieces when she viewed her intimacies with Ethelberta during the past season – the court she had paid her, the arrangements she had entered into to please her; above all, the dinner-party which she had contrived and carried out solely to gratify Lord Mountclere and bring him into personal communication with the general favourite; thus making herself probably the chief though unconscious instrument in promoting a match by which her butler was to become father-in-law to a peer she delighted to honour. The crowd of perceptions almost took away her life; she closed her eyes in a white shiver.

'Do you mean to say that the lady who sat here at dinner at the same time that Lord Mountclere was present, is your daughter?' asked Doncastle.

'Yes, sir,' said Chickerel respectfully.

'How did she come to be your daughter?'

'I— Well, she is my daughter, sir.'

'Did you educate her?'

'Not altogether, sir. She was a very clever child. Lady Petherwin took a deal of trouble about her education. They were both left widows about the same time: the son died, then the father. My daughter was only eighteen then. But though she's older now, her marriage with Lord Mountclere means misery. He ought to marry another woman.'

'It is very extraordinary,' Mr Doncastle murmured. 'If you are ill you had better go and rest yourself, Chickerel. Send in Thomas.'

Chickerel, who seemed to be much disturbed, then very gladly left the room, and dinner proceeded. But such was the peculiarity of the case, that, though there was in it neither murder, robbery, illness, accident, fire, or any other of the tragic and legitimate shakers of human nerves, two of the three who were gathered there sat through the meal without the least consciousness of what viands had composed it. Impressiveness depends as much upon propinquity as upon magnitude; and to have honoured unawares the daughter of the vilest Antipodean miscreant and murderer* would have been less discomfiting to Mrs Doncastle than it was to make the same blunder with the daughter of a respectable servant who happened to live in her own house. To Neigh the announcement was as the catastrophe of a story already begun, rather than as an isolated wonder. Ethelberta's words had prepared him for something, though the nature of that thing was unknown.

'Chickerel ought not to have kept us in ignorance of this – of course he ought not!' said Mrs Doncastle as soon as they were left alone.

'I don't see why not,' replied Mr Doncastle, who took the matter very coolly, as was his custom.

'Then she herself should have let it be known.'

'Nor does that follow. You didn't tell Mrs Petherwin that your grandfather narrowly escaped hanging for shooting his rival in a duel.'

'Of course not. There was no reason why I should give extraneous information.'

'Nor was there any reason why she should. As for Chickerel, he doubtless felt how unbecoming it would be to make personal remarks upon one of your guests – Ha-ha-ha! Well, well – Ha-ha-ha-ha!'

'I know this,' said Mrs Doncastle, in great anger, 'that if my father had been in the room, I should not have let the fact pass unnoticed, and treated him like a stranger!'

'Would you have had her introduce Chickerel to us all round? My dear Margaret, it was a complicated position for a woman.'

'Then she ought not to have come!'

'There may be something in that, though she was dining out at other houses as good as ours. Well, I should have done just as she did, for the joke of the thing. Ha-ha-ha! – it is very good – very. It was a case in which the appetite for a jest would overpower the sting of conscience in any well-constituted being – that, my dear, I must maintain.'

'I say she should not have come!' answered Mrs Doncastle firmly. 'Of course I shall dismiss Chickerel.'

'Of course you will do no such thing. I have never had a butler in the house before who suited me so well. It is a great credit to the man to have such a daughter, and I am not sure that we do not derive some lustre of a humble kind from his presence in the house. But, seriously, I wonder at your shortsightedness, when you know the troubles we have had through getting new men from nobody knows where.'

Neigh, perceiving that the breeze in the atmosphere might ultimately intensify to a palpable white squall, seemed to think it would be well to take leave of his uncle and aunt as soon as he conveniently could; nevertheless, he was much less discomposed by the situation than by the active cause which had led to it. When Mrs Doncastle arose, her husband said he was going to speak to Chickerel for a minute or two, and Neigh followed his aunt upstairs.

Presently Doncastle joined them. 'I have been talking to Chickerel,' he said. 'It is a very curious affair – this marriage of his daughter and Lord Mountclere. The whole situation is the most astounding I have ever met with. The man is quite ill about the news. He has shown me a letter which has just reached him from his son on the same subject. Lord Mountclere's brother and this young man have actually gone off together to try to prevent the wedding, and Chickerel has asked to be allowed to go himself, if he can get soon enough to the station to catch the night mail. Of course he may go if he wishes.'

'What a funny thing!' said the lady, with a wretchedly factitious smile. 'The times have taken a strange turn when the angry parent of the comedy, who goes post-haste to prevent the undutiful daughter's rash marriage, is a gentleman from below stairs, and the unworthy lover a peer of the realm!'

Neigh spoke for almost the first time. 'I don't blame Chickerel in objecting to Lord Mountclere. I should object to him myself if I had a daughter. I never liked him.'

'Why?' said Mrs Doncastle, lifting her eyelids as if the act were a heavy task.

'For reasons which don't generally appear.'

'Yes,' said Mr Doncastle, in a low tone. 'Still we must not believe all we hear.'

'Is Chickerel going?' said Neigh.

'He leaves in five or ten minutes,' said Doncastle.

After a few further words Neigh mentioned that he was unable to stay longer that evening, and left them. When he had reached the outside of the door he walked a little way up the pavement and back again, as if reluctant to lose sight of the street, finally standing under a lamp-post whence he could command a view of Mr Doncastle's front. Presently a man came out in a great-coat and with a small bag in his hand; Neigh, at once recognizing the person as Chickerel, went up to him.

'Mr Doncastle tells me you are going on a sudden journey. At what time does your train leave?' Neigh asked.

'I go by the ten o'clock, sir: I hope it is a third-class,' said Chickerel; 'though I am afraid it may not be.'

'It is as much as you will do to get to the station,' said Neigh, turning the face of his watch to the light.

'Here, come into my cab – I am driving that way.'

'Thank you, sir,' said Chickerel.

Neigh called a cab at the first opportunity, and they entered and drove along together. Neither spoke during the journey. When they were driving up to the station entrance Neigh looked again to see the hour.

'You have not a minute to lose,' he said, in repressed anxiety. 'And your journey will be expensive: instead of walking from Anglebury to Knollsea, you had better drive – above all, don't lose time. Never mind what class the train is. Take this from me, since the emergency is great.' He handed something to Chickerel folded up small.

The butler took it without inquiry, and stepped out hastily.

'I sincerely hope she – Well, good night, Chickerel,' continued Neigh, ending his words abruptly. The cab containing him drove again towards the station-gates, leaving Chickerel standing on the kerb.

He passed through the booking-office, and looked at the paper Neigh had put into his hand. It was a five-pound note.

Chickerel mused on the circumstance as he took his ticket and got into the train.

The Railway
The Sea
The Shore Beyond

43

By this time Sol and the Honourable Edgar Mountclere had gone far on their journey into Wessex. Enckworth Court, Mountclere's destination, though several miles from Knollsea, was most easily accessible by the same route as that to the village, the latter being the place for which Sol was bound.

From the few words that passed between them on the way, Mountclere became more stubborn than ever in a belief that this was a carefully laid trap of the fair Ethelberta's to ensnare his brother without revealing to him her family ties, which it therefore behoved him to make clear, with the utmost force of representation, before the fatal union had been contracted. Being himself the viscount's only remaining brother and near relative, the disinterestedness of his motives may be left to imagination; that there was much real excuse for his conduct must, however, be borne in mind. Whether his attempt would prevent the union was another question: he believed that, conjoined with his personal influence over the viscount, and the importation of Sol as a fire-brand to throw between the betrothed pair, it might do so.

About half-an-hour before sunset the two individuals, linked by their differences, reached the point of railway at which the branch to Sandbourne left the main line. They had taken tickets for Sandbourne, intending to go thence to Knollsea by the steamer that plied between the two places during the summer months – making this a short and direct route. But it occurred to Mountclere on the way that, summer being over, the steamer might possibly have left off running, the wind might be too high for a small boat, and no large one might be at hand for hire: therefore it would be safer to go by train to Anglebury, and the remaining sixteen miles by driving over the hills, even at a great loss of time.

Accident, however, determined otherwise. They were in the station at the junction, inquiring of an official if the *Speedwell* had ceased to sail, when a countryman who had just come up

from Sandbourne stated that, though the *Speedwell* had left off
for the year, there was that day another steamer at Sandbourne.
This, the *Spruce*, would of necessity return to Knollsea that
evening, partly because several people from that place had been
on board, and also because the Knollsea folk were waiting for
groceries and draperies from London: there was not an ounce of
tea or a hundredweight of coal in the village, owing to the recent
winds, which had detained the provision parcels at Sandbourne,
and kept the colliers up-channel until the change of weather this
day. To introduce necessaries by a roundabout land journey was
not easy when they had been ordered by the other and habitual
route. The boat returned at six o'clock.

So on they went to Sandbourne, driving off to the pier directly
they reached that place, for it was getting towards night. The
steamer was there, as the man had told them, much to the relief
of Sol, who, being extremely anxious to enter Knollsea before a
late hour, had known that this was the only way in which it
could be done.

Some unforeseen incident delayed the boat, and they walked
up and down the pier to wait. The prospect was gloomy enough.
The wind was north-east; the sea along shore was a chalky-
green, though comparatively calm, this part of the coast forming
a shelter from wind in its present quarter. The clouds had
different velocities, and some of them shone with a coppery
glare, produced by rays from the west which did not enter the
inferior atmosphere at all. It was reflected on the distant waves
in patches, with an effect as if the waters were at those particular
spots stained with blood. This departed, and what daylight was
left to the earth came from strange and unusual quarters of the
heavens. The zenith would be bright, as if that were the place of
the sun; then all overhead would close, and a whiteness in the
east would give the appearance of morning; while a bank as
thick as a wall barricaded the west, which looked as if it had no
acquaintance with sunsets, and would blush red no more.

'Any other passengers?' shouted the master of the steamboat.
'We must be off: it may be a dirty night.'

Sol and Mountclere went on board, and the pier receded in
the dusk.

'Shall we have any difficulty in getting into Knollsea Bay?'
said Mountclere.

'Not if the wind keeps where it is for another hour or two.'

'I fancy it is shifting to the east'ard,' said Sol.

The captain looked as if he had thought the same thing.

'I hope I shall be able to get home tonight,' said a Knollsea woman. 'My little children be left alone. Your mis'ess is in a bad way, too – isn't she, skipper?'

'Yes.'

'And you've got the doctor from Sandbourne aboard, to tend her?'

'Yes.'

'Then you'll be sure to put into Knollsea, if you can?'

'Yes. Don't be alarmed, ma'am. We'll do what we can. But no one must boast.'

The skipper's remark was the result of an observation that the wind had at last flown to the east, the single point of the compass whence it could affect Knollsea Bay. The result of this change was soon perceptible. About midway in their transit the land elbowed out to a bold chalk promontory; beyond this stretched a vertical wall of the same cliff, in a line parallel with their course. In fair weather it was possible and customary to steer close along under this hoary façade for the distance of a mile, there being six fathoms of water within a few boats' lengths of the precipice. But it was an ugly spot at the best of times, landward no less than seaward, the cliff rounding off at the top in vegetation, like a forehead with low-grown hair, no defined edge being provided as a warning to unwary pedestrians on the downs above.

As the wind sprung up stronger, white clots could be discerned at the water level of the cliff, rising and falling against the black band of shaggy weed that formed a sort of skirting to the base of the wall. They were the first-fruits of the new east blast, which shaved the face of the cliff like a razor – gatherings of foam in the shape of heads, shoulders, and arms of snowy whiteness, apparently struggling to rise from the deeps, and ever sinking back to their old levels again. They reminded an observer of a drowning scene in a picture of the Deluge.* At some points the face of rock was hollowed into gaping caverns, and the water began to thunder into these with a leap that was only topped by the rebound seaward again. The vessel's head was kept a little further to sea, but beyond that everything went on as usual.

The precipice was still in view, and before it several huge

columns of rock appeared, detached from the mass behind. Two of these were particularly noticeable in the grey air – one vertical, stout and square; the other slender and tapering. They were individualized as husband and wife by the coast men. The waves leapt up their sides like a pack of hounds; this, however, though fearful in its boisterousness, was nothing to the terrible games that sometimes went on round the knees of those giants in stone. Yet it was sufficient to cause the course of the frail steamboat to be altered yet a little more – from south-west-by-south to south-by-west – to give the breakers a still wider berth.

'I wish we had gone by land, sir; 'twould have been surer play,' said Sol to Mountclere, a cat-and-dog friendship having arisen between them.

'Yes,' said Mountclere. 'Knollsea is an abominable place to get into with an east wind blowing, they say.'

Another circumstance conspired to make their landing more difficult, which Mountclere knew nothing of. With the wind easterly, the highest sea prevailed in Knollsea Bay from the slackening of flood-tide to the first hour of ebb. At that time the water outside stood without a current, and ridges and hollows chased each other towards the beach unchecked. When the tide was setting strong up or down Channel its flow across the mouth of the bay thrust aside, to some extent, the landward plunge of the waves.

We glance for a moment at the state of affairs on the land they were nearing.

This was the time of year to know the truth about the inner nature and character of Knollsea; for to see Knollsea smiling to the summer sun was to see a courtier before a king; Knollsea was not to be known by such simple means. The half-dozen detached villas used as lodging-houses in the summer, standing aloof from the cots of the permanent race, rose in the dusk of this gusty evening, empty, silent, damp, and dark as tombs. The gravel walks leading to them were invaded by leaves and tufts of grass. As the darkness thickened the wind increased, and each blast raked the iron railings before the houses till they hummed as if in a song of derision. Certainly it seemed absurd at this time of year that human beings should expect comfort in a spot capable of such moods as these.

However, one of the houses looked cheerful, and that was the dwelling to which Ethelberta had gone. Its gay external colours might as well have been black for anything that could be seen of them now, but an unblinded window revealed inside it a room bright and warm. It was illuminated by firelight only. Within, Ethelberta appeared against the curtains, close to the glass. She was watching through a binocular a faint light which had become visible in the direction of the bluff far away over the bay.

'Here is the *Spruce* at last, I think,' she said to her sister, who was by the fire. 'I hope they will be able to land the things I have ordered. They are on board I know.'

The wind continued to rise till at length something from the lungs of the gale alighted like a feather upon the pane, and remained there sticking. Seeing the substance, Ethelberta opened the window to secure it. The fire roared and the pictures kicked the walls; she closed the sash, and brought to the light a crisp fragment of foam.

'How suddenly the sea must have risen,' said Picotee.

The servant entered the room. 'Please, mis'ess says she is afraid you won't have your things tonight, m'm. They say the steamer can't land, and mis'ess wants to know if she can do anything?'

'It is of no consequence,' said Ethelberta. 'They will come some time, unless they go to the bottom.'

The girl left the room. 'Shall we go down to the shore and see what the night is like?' said Ethelberta. 'This is the last opportunity I shall have.'

'Is it right for us to go, considering you are to be married tomorrow?' said Picotee, who had small affection for nature in this mood.

Her sister laughed. 'Let us put on our cloaks – nobody will know us. I am sorry to leave this grim and primitive place, even for Enckworth Court.'

They wrapped themselves up, and descended the hill.

On drawing near the battling line of breakers which marked the meeting of sea and land they could perceive within the nearly invisible horizon an equilateral triangle of lights. It was formed of three stars, a red on the one side, a green on the other, and a white on the summit. This, composed of mast-head and side lamps, was all that was visible of the *Spruce*, which now faced end-on about half-a-mile distant, and was still nearing the pier. The girls went further, and stood on the foreshore, listening to the din. Seaward appeared nothing distinct save a black horizontal band embodying itself out of the grey water, strengthening its blackness, and enlarging till it looked like a nearing wall. It was the concave face of a coming wave. On its summit a white edging arose with the aspect of a lace frill; it broadened, and fell over the front with a terrible concussion. Then all before them was a sheet of whiteness, which spread with amazing rapidity, till they found themselves standing in the midst of it, as in a field of snow. Both felt an insidious chill encircling their ankles, and they rapidly ran up the beach.

'You girls, come away there, or you'll be washed off: what need have ye for going so near?'

Ethelberta recognized the stentorian voice as that of Captain Flower, who, with a party of boatmen, was discovered to be standing near, under the shelter of a wall. He did not know them in the gloom, and they took care that he should not. They retreated further up the beach, when the hissing fleece of froth slid again down the shingle, dragging the pebbles under it with a rattle as of a beast gnawing bones.

The spot whereon the men stood was called 'Down-under-wall'; it was a nook commanding a full view of the bay, and hither the nautical portion of the village unconsciously gravitated on windy afternoons and nights, to discuss past disasters in the reticent spirit induced by a sense that they might at any moment be repeated. The stranger who should walk the shore on roaring and sobbing November eves when there was not light sufficient to guide his footsteps, and muse on the absoluteness of the solitude, would be surprised by a smart 'Good night' being returned from this corner in company with the echo of his tread. In summer the six or eight perennial figures stood on the breezy side of the wall – in winter and in rain to leeward; but no weather was known to dislodge them.

'I had no sooner come ashore than the wind began to fly round,' said the previous speaker; 'and it must have been about the time they were off Old-Harry Point. "She'll put back for certain," I said; and I had no more thought o' seeing her than John's set-net,* that was carried round the point o' Monday.'

'Poor feller: his wife being in such a state makes him anxious to land if 'a can: that's what 'tis, plain enough.'

'Why that?' said Flower.

'The doctor's aboard, 'a believe: "I'll have the most under-standing man in Sandbourne, cost me little or much," he said.'

''Tis all over and she's better,' said the other. 'I called half-an-hour afore dark.'

Flower, being an experienced man, knew how the judgment of a ship's master was liable to be warped by family anxieties, many instances of the same having occurred in the history of navigation. He felt uneasy, for he knew the deceit and guile of this bay far better than did the master of the *Spruce*, who, till within a few recent months, had been a stranger to the place. Indeed, it was the bay which had made Flower what he was, instead of a man in thriving retirement. The two great ventures of his life had been blown ashore and broken up within that very semicircle. The sturdy sailor now stood with his eyes fixed on the triangle of lights which showed that the steamer had not relinquished her intention of bringing up inside the pier if possible; his right hand was in his pocket, where it played with a large key which lay there. It was the key of the lifeboat shed, and Flower was coxswain. His musing was on the possibility of a use for it this night.

It appeared that the captain of the *Spruce* was aiming to pass in under the lee of the pier; but a strong current of four or five knots was running between the piles, drifting the steamer away at every attempt as soon as she slowed. To come in on the other side was dangerous, the hull of the vessel being likely to crash against and overthrow the fragile erection, with damage to herself also. Flower, who had disappeared for a few minutes, now came back.

'It is just possible I can make 'em hear with the trumpet, now they be to leeward,' he said, and proceeded with two or three others to grope his way out upon the pier, which consisted simply of a row of rotten piles covered with rotten planking, no balustrade of any kind existing to keep the unwary from tumbling off. At the water level the piles were eaten away by the action of the sea to about the size of a man's wrist, and at every fresh influx the whole structure trembled like a spider's web. In this lay the danger of making fast, for a strong pull from a headfast rope* might drag the erection completely over. Flower arrived at the end, where a lantern hung.

'*Spruce* ahoy!' he blared through the speaking-trumpet two or three times.

There seemed to be a reply of some sort from the steamer.

'Tuesday's gale hev loosened the pier, Cap'n Ounce; the bollards be too weak to make fast to: must land in boats if ye will land, but dangerous; yer wife is out of danger, and 'tis a boy-y-y-y!'

Ethelberta and Picotee were at this time standing on the beach a hundred and fifty yards off. Whether or not the master of the steamer received the information volunteered by Flower, the two girls saw the triangle of lamps get narrow at its base, reduce themselves to two in a vertical line, then to one, then to darkness. The *Spruce* had turned her head from Knollsea.

'They have gone back, and I shall not have my wedding things after all!' said Ethelberta. 'Well, I must do without them.'

'You see, 'twas best to play sure,' said Flower to his comrades, in a tone of complacency. 'They might have been able to do it, but 'twas risky. The shop-folk be out of stock, I hear, and the visiting lady up the hill is terribly in want of clothes, so 'tis said. But what's that? Ounce ought to have put back afore.'

Then the lantern which hung at the end of the jetty was taken down, and the darkness enfolded all around from view. The bay became nothing but a voice, the foam an occasional touch upon the face, the *Spruce* an imagination, the pier a memory. Everything lessened upon the senses but one; that was the wind. It mauled their persons like a hand, and caused every scrap of their raiment to tug westward. To stand with the face to sea brought semi-suffocation, from the intense pressure of air.

The boatmen retired to their position under the wall, to lounge again in silence. Conversation was not considered necessary: their sense of each other's presence formed a kind of conversation. Meanwhile Picotee and Ethelberta went up the hill.

'If your wedding were going to be a public one, what a misfortune this delay of the packages would be,' said Picotee.

'Yes,' replied the elder.

'I think the bracelet the prettiest of all the presents he brought today – do you?'

'It is the most valuable.'

'Lord Mountclere is very kind, is he not? I like him a great deal better than I did – do you, Berta?'

'Yes, very much better,' said Ethelberta, warming a little. 'If he were not so suspicious at odd moments I should like him exceedingly. But I must cure him of that by a regular course of treatment, and then he'll be very nice.'

'For an old man. He likes you better than any young man would take the trouble to do. I wish somebody else were old too.'

'He will be some day.'

'Yes, but—'

'Never mind: time will straighten many crooked things.'

'Do you think Lord Mountclere has reached home by this time?'

'I should think so: though I believe he had to call at the parsonage before leaving Knollsea.'

'Had he? What for?'

'Why, of course somebody must—'

'O yes. Do you think anybody in Knollsea knows it is going to be except us and the parson?'

'I suppose the clerk knows.'

'I wonder if a lord has ever been married so privately before.'

'Frequently: when he marries far beneath him, as in this case. But even if I could have had it, I should not have liked a showy wedding. I have had no experience as a bride except in the private form of the ceremony.'

'Berta, I am sometimes uneasy about you even now, and I want to ask you one thing, if I may. Are you doing this for my sake? Would you have married Mr Julian if it had not been for me?'

'It is difficult to say exactly. It is possible that if I had had no relations at all, I might have married him. And I might not.'

'I don't intend to marry.'

'In that case you will live with me at Enckworth. However, we will leave such details till the groundwork is confirmed. When we get indoors will you see if the boxes have been properly corded, and are quite ready to be sent for? Then come in and sit by the fire, and I'll sing some songs to you.'

'Sad ones, you mean.'

'No, they shall not be sad.'

'Perhaps they may be the last you will ever sing to me.'

'They may be. Such a thing has occurred.'

'But we will not think so. We'll suppose you are to sing many to me yet.'

'Yes. There's good sense in that, Picotee. In a world where the blind only are cheerful we should all do well to put out our eyes. There, I did not mean to get into this state: forgive me, Picotee. It is because I have had a thought – why I cannot tell – that as much as this man brings to me in rank and gifts he may take out of me in tears.'

'Berta!'

'But there's no reason in it – not any; for not in a single matter does what has been supply us with any certain ground for knowing what will be in the world. I have seen marriages where happiness might have been said to be ensured, and they have been all sadness afterwards; and I have seen those in which the prospect was black as night, and they have led on to a time of sweetness and comfort. And I have seen marriages neither joyful nor sorry, that have become either as accident forced them to become, the persons having no voice in it at all. Well, then, why should I be afraid to make a plunge when chance is as trustworthy as calculation?'

'If you don't like him well enough, don't have him, Berta. There's time enough to put it off even now.'

'O no. I would not upset a well-considered course on the haste of an impulse. Our will should withstand our misgivings. Now let us see if all has been packed, and then we'll sing.'

That evening, while the wind was wheeling round and round the dwelling, and the calm eye of the light-house afar was the single speck perceptible of the outside world from the door of Ethelberta's temporary home, the music of songs mingled with the stroke of the wind across the iron railings, and was swept on in the general tide of the gale, and the noise of the rolling sea, till not the echo of a tone remained.

An hour before this singing, an old gentleman might have been seen to alight from a little one-horse brougham, and enter the door of Knollsea parsonage. He was bent upon obtaining an entrance to the vicar's study without giving his name.

But it happened that the vicar's wife was sitting in the front room, making a pillow-case for the children's bed out of an old surplice which had been excommunicated the previous Easter; she heard the newcomer's voice through the partition, started, and went quickly to her husband, who was, where he ought to have been, in his study. At her entry he looked up with an abstracted gaze, having been lost in meditation over a little schooner which he was attempting to rig for their youngest boy.

At a word from his wife on the suspected name of the visitor, he resumed his earlier occupation of inserting a few strong sentences, full of the observation of maturer life, between the lines of a sermon written during his first years of ordination, in order to make it available for the coming Sunday. His wife then vanished with the little ship in her hand, and the visitor appeared. A talk went on in low tones.

After a ten minutes' stay he departed as secretly as he had come. His errand was the cause of much whispered discussion between the vicar and his wife during the evening, but nothing was said concerning it to the outside world.

Sandbourne
A Lonely Heath
The 'Red Lion'
The Highway

44

It was half-past eleven before the *Spruce*, with Mountclere and Sol Chickerel on board, had steamed back again to Sandbourne. The direction and increase of the wind had made it necessary to keep the vessel still further to sea on their return than in going, that they might clear without risk the windy, sousing, thwacking, basting, scourging Jack Ketch* of a corner called Old-Harry Point, which lay about halfway along their track, and stood, with its detached posts and stumps of white rock, like a skeleton's lower jaw, grinning at British navigation. Here strong currents and cross currents were beginning to interweave their scrolls and meshes, the water rising behind them in tumultuous heaps, and slamming against the fronts and angles of cliff, whence it flew into the air like clouds of flour. Who could now believe that this roaring abode of chaos smiled in the sun as gently as an infant during the summer days not long gone by, every pinnacle, crag, and cave returning a doubled image across the glassy sea?

They were now again at Sandbourne, a point in their journey reached more than four hours ago. It became necessary to consider anew how to accomplish the difficult remainder. The wind was not blowing much beyond what seamen call half a gale, but there had been enough unpleasantness afloat to make landsmen glad to get ashore, and this dissipated in a slight measure their vexation at having failed in their purpose. Still, Mountclere loudly cursed their confidence in that treacherously short route, and Sol abused the unknown Sandbourne man who had brought the news of the steamer's arrival to them at the Junction. The only course left open to them now, short of giving up the undertaking, was to go by the road along the shore, which, curving round the various little creeks and inland seas between their present position and Knollsea, was of little less length than thirty miles. There was no train back to the Junction till the next morning, and Sol's proposition that they should drive thither in hope of meeting the mail-train, was overruled by Mountclere.

'We will have nothing more to do with chance,' he said. 'We may miss the train, and then we shall have gone out of the way for nothing. More than that, the down mail does not stop till it gets several miles beyond the nearest station for Knollsea; so it is hopeless.'

'If there had only been a telegraph to the confounded place!'

'Telegraph – we might as well telegraph to the devil as to an old booby and a damned scheming young widow. I very much question if we shall do anything in the matter, even if we get there. But I suppose we had better go on now?'

'You can do as you like. I shall go on, if I have to walk every step o't.'

'That's not necessary. I think the best posting-house at this end of the town is Tempett's – we must knock them up at once. Which will you do – attempt supper here, or break the back of our journey first, and get on to Anglebury? We may rest an hour or two there, unless you feel really in want of a meal.'

'No. I'll leave eating to merrier men, who have no sister in the hands of a cursed old Vandal.'*

'Very well,' said Mountclere. 'We'll go on at once.'

An additional half-hour elapsed before they were fairly started, the lateness and abruptness of their arrival causing delay in getting a conveyance ready: the tempestuous night had apparently driven the whole town, gentle and simple, early to their beds. And when at length the travellers were on their way the aspect of the weather grew yet more forbidding. The rain came down unmercifully, the booming wind caught it, bore it across the plain, whizzed it against the carriage like a sower sowing his seed. It was precisely such weather, and almost at the same season, as when Picotee traversed the same moor, stricken with her great disappointment at not meeting Christopher Julian.

Further on for several miles the drive lay through an open heath, dotted occasionally with fir plantations, the trees of which told the tale of their species without help from outline or colour; they spoke in those melancholy moans and sobs which give to their sound a solemn sadness surpassing even that of the sea. From each carriage-lamp the long rays stretched like feelers into the air, and somewhat cheered the way, until the insidious damp that pervaded all things above, around, and underneath, overpowered one of them, and rendered every attempt to rekindle it ineffectual. Even had the two men's dislike to each other's society been less, the general din of the night would have prevented much talking; as it was, they sat in a rigid reticence that was almost a third personality. The roads were laid hereabouts with a light sandy gravel, which, though not clogging, was soft and friable. It speedily became saturated, and the wheels ground heavily and deeply into its substance.

At length, after crossing from ten to twelve miles of these eternal heaths under the eternally drumming storm, they could discern eyelets of light winking to them in the distance from under a nebulous brow of pale haze. They were looking on the little town of Havenpool. Soon after this cross-roads were reached, one of which, at right angles to their present direction, led down on the left to that place. Here the man stopped, and informed them that the horses would be able to go but a mile or two further.

'Very well, we must have others that can,' said Mountclere. 'Does our way lie through the town?'

'No, sir – unless we go there to change horses, which I thought to do. The direct road is straight on. Havenpool lies about three miles down there on the left. But the water is over the road, and we had better go round. We shall come to no place for two or three miles, and then only to Flychett.'

'What's Flychett like?'

'A trumpery small bit of a village.'

'Still, I think we had better push on,' said Sol. 'I am against running the risk of finding the way flooded about Havenpool.'

'So am I,' returned Mountclere.

'I know a wheelwright in Flychett,' continued Sol, 'and he keeps a beer-house, and owns two horses. We could hire them, and have a bit of sommat in the shape of victuals, and then get on to Anglebury. Perhaps the rain may hold up by that time. Anything's better than going out of our way.'

'Yes. And the horses can last out to that place,' said Mountclere. 'Up and on again, my man.'

On they went towards Flychett. Still the everlasting heath, the black hills bulging against the sky, the barrows upon their round summits like warts on a swarthy skin. The storm blew huskily over bushes of heather and furze that it was unable materially to disturb, and the travellers proceeded as before. But the horses were now far from fresh, and the time spent in reaching the next village was quite half as long as that taken up by the previous heavy portion of the drive. When they entered Flychett it was about three.

'Now, where's the inn?' said Mountclere, yawning.

'Just on the knap,'* Sol answered. ''Tis a little small place, and we must do as well as we can.'

They pulled up before a cottage, upon the whitewashed front of which could be seen a square board representing the sign. After an infinite labour of rapping and shouting, a casement opened overhead, and a woman's voice inquired what was the matter. Sol explained, when she told them that the horses were away from home.

'Now we must wait till these are rested,' growled Mountclere. 'A pretty muddle!'

'It cannot be helped,' answered Sol; and he asked the woman to open the door. She replied that her husband was away with the horses and van, and that they could not come in.

Sol was known to her, and he mentioned his name; but the woman only began to abuse him.

'Come, publican, you'd better let us in, or we'll have the law for't,'* rejoined Sol, with more spirit. 'You don't dare to keep nobility waiting like this.'

'Nobility!'

'My mate bears the title of Honourable, whether or no; so let's have none of your slack,' said Sol.

'Don't be a fool, young chopstick,' exclaimed Mountclere. 'Get the door opened.'

'I will – in my own way,' said Sol testily. 'You mustn't mind my trading upon your quality, as 'tis a case of necessity. This is a woman nothing will bring to reason but an appeal to the higher powers. If every man of title was as useful as you are tonight, sir, I'd never call them lumber again as long as I live.'

'How singular!'

'There's never a bit of rubbish that won't come in use if you keep it seven years.'

'If my utility depends upon keeping you company, may I go to h—— for lacking every atom of the virtue.'

'Hear, hear! But it hardly is becoming in me to answer up to a man so much older than I, or I could say more. Suppose we draw a line here for the present, sir, and get indoors?'

'Do what you will, in Heaven's name.'

A few more words to the woman resulted in her agreeing to admit them if they would attend to themselves afterwards. This Sol promised, and the key of the door was let down to them from the bedroom window by a string. When they had entered, Sol, who knew the house well, busied himself in lighting a fire, the driver going off with a lantern to the stable, where he found standing-room for the two horses. Mountclere walked up and down the kitchen, mumbling words of disgust at the situation, the few of this kind that he let out being just enough to show what a fearfully large number he kept in.

'A-calling up people at this time of morning!' the woman occasionally exclaimed down the stairs. 'But folks show no mercy upon their flesh and blood – not one bit or mite.'

'Now never be stomachy,* my good soul,' cried Sol from the fireplace, where he stood blowing the fire with his breath. 'Only tell me where the victuals bide, and I'll do all the cooking. We'll pay like princes – especially my mate.'

'There's but little in house,' said the sleepy woman from her bedroom. 'There's pig's fry, a side of bacon, a conger eel, and pickled onions.'

'Conger eel?' said Sol to Mountclere.

'No, thank you.'

'Pig's fry?'

'No, thank you.'

'Well, then, tell me where the bacon is,' shouted Sol to the woman.

'You must find it,' came again down the stairs. ''Tis somewhere up in chimley, but in which part I can't mind. Really I don't know whether I be upon my head or my heels, and my brain is all in a spin, wi' being rafted up* in such a larry!'*

'Bide where you be, there's a dear,' said Sol. 'We'll do it all. Just tell us where the tea-caddy is, and the gridiron, and then you can go to sleep again.'

The woman appeared to take his advice, for she gave the information, and silence soon reigned upstairs.

When one piece of bacon had been with difficulty cooked over the newly-lit fire, Sol said to Mountclere, with the rasher on his fork: 'Now look here, sir, I think while I am making the tea, you ought to go on griddling some more of these, as you haven't done nothing at all?'

'I do the paying . . . Well, give me the bacon.'

'And when you have done yours, I'll cook the man's, as the poor feller's hungry, I make no doubt.'

Mountclere, fork in hand, then began with his rasher, tossing it about the gridiron in masterly style, Sol attending to the tea. He was attracted from this occupation by a brilliant flame up the chimney, Mountclere exclaiming, 'Now the cursed thing is on fire!'

'Blow it out – hard – that's it! Well now, sir, do you come and begin upon mine, as you must be hungry. I'll finish the griddling. Ought we to mind the man sitting down in our company, as there's no other roam for him? I hear him coming in.'

'O no – not at all. Put him over at that table.'

'And I'll join him. You can sit here by yourself sir.'

The meal was despatched, and the coachman again retired, promising to have the horses ready in about an hour and a half. Sol and Mountclere made themselves comfortable upon either side of the fireplace, since there was no remedy for the delay: after sitting in silence awhile, they nodded and slept.

How long they would have remained thus, in consequence of their fatigues, there is no telling, had not the mistress of the cottage descended the stairs about two hours later, after peeping down upon them at intervals of five minutes during their sleep, lest they should leave without her knowledge. It was six o'clock, and Sol went out for the man, whom he found snoring in the hay-loft. There was now real necessity for haste, and in ten minutes they were again on their way.

Day dawned upon the 'Red Lion' inn at Anglebury with a timid and watery eye. From the shadowy archway came a shining lantern, which was seen to be dangling from the hand of a little bow-legged old man – the hostler, John. Having reached the front, he looked around to measure the daylight, opened the lantern, and extinguished it by a pinch of his fingers. He paused for a moment to have the customary word or two with his neighbour the milkman, who usually appeared at this point at this time.

'It sounds like the whistle of the morning train,' the milkman said as he drew near, a scream from the further end of the town reaching their ears. 'Well, I hope, now the wind's in that quarter, we shall ha'e a little more fine weather – hey, hostler?'

'What be ye a talking o'?'

'Can hear the whistle plain, I say.'

'O ay. I suppose you do. But faith, 'tis a poor fist* I can make at hearing anything. There, I could have told all the same that the wind was in the east, even if I had not seed poor Thomas Tribble's smoke blowing across the little orchard. Joints be a true weathercock enough when past three-score. These easterly rains, when they do come, which is not often, come wi' might enough to squail* a man into his grave.'

'Well, we must look for it, hostler ... Why, what mighty ekkypage* is this, come to town at such a purblinking* time of day?'

''Tis what time only can tell – though 'twill not be long first,' the hostler replied, as the driver of the pair of horses and carriage containing Sol and Mountclere slackened pace, and drew rein before the inn.

Fresh horses were immediately called for, and while they were being put in the two travellers walked up and down.

'It is now a quarter to seven o'clock,' said Mountclere; 'and the question arises, shall I go on to Knollsea, or branch off at Corvsgate Castle for Enckworth? I think the best plan will be to drive first to Enckworth, set me down, and then get him to take you on at once to Knollsea. What do you say?'

'When shall I reach Knollsea by that arrangement?'

'By half-past eight o'clock. We shall be at Enckworth before eight, which is excellent time.'

'Very well, sir, I agree to that,' said Sol, feeling that as soon as one of the two birds had been caught, the other could not mate without their knowledge.

The carriage and horses being again ready, away they drove at once, both having by this time grown too restless to spend in Anglebury a minute more than was necessary.

The hostler and his lad had taken the jaded Sandbourne horses to the stable, rubbed them down, and fed them, when another noise was heard outside the yard; the omnibus had returned from meeting the train. Relinquishing the horses to the small stable-lad, the old hostler again looked out from the arch.

A young man had stepped from the omnibus, and he came forward. 'I want a conveyance of some sort to take me to Knollsea, at once. Can you get a horse harnessed in five minutes?'

'I'll make shift to do what I can master, not promising about the minutes. The truest man can say no more. Won't ye step into the bar, sir, and give your order? I'll let ye know as soon as 'tis ready.'

Christopher turned into a room smelling strongly of the night before, and stood by the newly-kindled fire to wait. He had just come in haste from Melchester. The upshot of his excitement about the wedding, which, as the possible hour of its solemnization drew near, had increased till it bore him on like a wind, was this unpremeditated journey. Lying awake the previous night, the hangings of his bed pulsing to every beat of his heart, he decided that there was one last and great service which it behoved him, as an honest man and friend, to say nothing of lover, to render to Ethelberta at this juncture. It was to ask her by some means whether or not she had engaged with open eyes to marry Lord Mountclere; and if not, to give her a word or two of enlightenment. That done, she might be left to take care of herself.

His plan was to obtain an interview with Picotee, and learn from her accurately the state of things. Should he, by any possibility, be mistaken in his belief as to the contracting parties, a knowledge of the mistake would be cheaply purchased by the journey. Should he not, he would send up to Ethelberta the strong note of expostulation which was already written, and waiting in his pocket. To intrude upon her at such a time was unseemly; and to despatch a letter by a messenger before evidence of its necessity had been received was most undesirable. The whole proceeding at best was clumsy; yet earnestness is mostly clumsy; and how could he let the event pass without a protest? Before daylight on that autumn morning he had risen, told Faith of his intention, and started off.

As soon as the vehicle was ready, Christopher hastened to the door and stepped up. The little stable-boy led the horse a few paces on the way before relinquishing his hold; at the same moment a respectably dressed man on foot, with a small black bag in his hand, came up from the opposite direction, along the street leading from the railway. He was a thin, elderly man, with grey hair; that a great anxiety pervaded him was as plainly visible as were his features. Without entering the inn, he came up at once to old John.

'Have you anything going to Knollsea this morning that I can get a lift in?' said the pedestrian – no other than Ethelberta's father.

'Nothing empty, that I know of.'

'Or carrier?'

'No.'

'A matter of fifteen shillings, then, I suppose?'

'Yes – no doubt. But yond there's a young man just now starting; he might not take it ill if ye were to ask him for a seat, and go halves in the hire of the trap. Shall I call out?'

'Ah, do.'

The hostler bawled to the stable-boy, who put the question to Christopher. There was room for two in the dogcart,* and Julian had no objection to save the shillings of a fellow-traveller who was evidently not rich. When Chickerel mounted to his seat, Christopher paused to look at him as we pause in some enactment that seems to have been already before us in a dream long ago. Ethelberta's face was there, as the landscape is in the map, the romance the history, the aim in the deed: denuded, rayless, and sorry, but discernible.

For the moment, however, this did not occur to Julian. He took the whip, the boy loosed his hold upon the horse, and they proceeded on their way.

'What slap-dash jinks* may there be going on at Knollsea, then, my sonny?' said the hostler to the lad, as the dogcart and the backs of the two men diminished on the road. 'You be a Knollsea boy: have anything reached your young ears about what's in the wind there, David Straw?'

'No, nothing: except that 'tis going to be Christmas day in five weeks, and then a hide-bound* bull is going to be killed if he don't die afore the time, and gi'ed away by my lord in three-pound junks,* as a reward to good people who never curse and sing bad songs, except when they be drunk; mother says perhaps she will have some, and 'tis excellent if well stewed, mother says.'

'A very fair chronicle for a boy to give, but not what I asked for. When you try to answer a old man's question, always bear in mind what it was that old man asked. A hide-bound bull is good when well stewed, I make no doubt – for they who like it; but that's not it. What I said was, do you know why three folk, a rich man, a middling man, and a poor man, should want horses for Knollsea afore seven o'clock in the morning on a blinking* day in Fall, when everything is as wet as a dishclout, whereas that's more than often happens in fine summer weather?'

'No – I don't know, hostler.'

'Then go home and tell your mother that ye be no wide-awake boy, and that old John, who went to school with her father afore she was born or thought o', says so . . . Chok' it all, why should I think there's sommat going on at Knollsea? Honest travelling have been so rascally abused since I was a boy in pinners,* by tribes of nobodies* tearing from one end of the country to t'other, to see the sun go down in salt water, or the moon play jack-lantern* behind some rotten tower or other, that, upon my song, when life and death's in the wind there's no telling the difference!'

'I like their sixpences ever so much.'

'Young sonny, don't you answer up to me when you bain't in the story – stopping my words in that fashion. I won't have it, David. Now up in the tallet* with 'ee, there's a good boy, and down with another lock or two of hay – as fast as you can do it for me.'

The boy vanished under the archway, and the hostler followed at his heels. Meanwhile the carriage bearing Mr Mountclere and Sol was speeding on its way to Enckworth. When they reached the spot at which the road forked into two, they left the Knollsea route, and keeping thence between the hills for the distance of five or six miles, drove into Lord Mountclere's park. In ten minutes the house was before them, framed in by dripping trees.

Mountclere jumped out, and entered without ceremony. Sol, being anxious to know if Lord Mountclere was there, ordered the coachman to wait a few moments. It was now nearly eight o'clock, and the smoke which ascended from the newly-lit fires of the Court painted soft blue tints upon the brown and golden leaves of lofty boughs adjoining.

'O, Ethelberta!' said Sol, as he regarded the fair prospect.

The gravel of the drive had been washed clean and smooth by the night's rain, but there were fresh wheel-marks other than their own upon the track. Yet the mansion seemed scarcely awake, and stillness reigned everywhere around.

Not more than three or four minutes had passed when the door was opened for Mountclere, and he came hastily from the doorsteps.

'I must go on with you,' he said, getting into the vehicle. 'He's gone.'

'Where – to Knollsea?' said Sol.

'Yes,' said Mountclere. 'Now, go ahead to Knollsea!' he shouted to the man. 'To think I should be fooled like this! I had no idea that he would be leaving so soon! We might perhaps have been here an hour earlier by hard striving. But who was to dream that he would arrange to leave it at such an unearthly time of the morning at this dark season of the year? Drive – drive!' he called again out of the window, and the pace was increased.

'I have come two or three miles out of my way on account of you,' said Sol sullenly. 'And all this time lost. I don't see why you wanted to come here at all. I knew it would be a waste of time.'

'Damn it all, man,' said Mountclere; 'it is no use for you to be angry with me!'

'I think it is, for 'tis you have brought me into this muddle,' said Sol, in no sweeter tone. 'Ha, ha! Upon my life I should be inclined to laugh, if I were not so much inclined to do the other thing, at Berta's trick of trying to make close family allies of such a cantankerous pair as you and I! So much of one mind as we be, so alike in our ways of living, so close connected in our callings and principles, so matched in manners and customs! 'twould be a thousand pities to part us – hey, Mr Mountclere!'

Mountclere faintly laughed with the same hideous merriment at the same idea, and then both remained in a withering silence, meant to express the utter contempt of each for the other, both in family and in person. They passed the Lodge, and again swept into the high-road.

'Drive on!' said Mountclere, putting his head again out of the window, and shouting to the man. 'Drive like the devil!' he roared again a few minutes afterwards, in fuming dissatisfaction with their rate of progress.

'Bain't I doing of it?' said the driver, turning angrily round. 'I ain't going to ruin my governor's horses for strangers who won't pay double for 'em – not I. I am driving as fast as I can. If other folks get in the way with their traps I suppose I must drive round 'em, sir?'

There was a slight crash.

'There!' continued the coachman. 'That's what comes of my turning round!'

Sol looked out on the other side, and found that the forewheel of their carriage had become locked in the wheel of a dogcart they had overtaken, the road here being very narrow. Their coachman, who knew he was to blame for this mishap, felt the advantage of taking time by the forelock in a case of accusation, and began swearing at his victim as if he were the sinner. Sol jumped out, and looking up at the occupants of the other conveyance, saw against the sky the back elevation of his father and Christopher Julian, sitting upon a little seat which they overhung, like two big puddings upon a small dish.

'Father – what, you going?' said Sol. 'Is it about Berta that you've come?'

'Yes, I got your letter,' said Chickerel, 'and I felt I should like to come – that I ought to come, to save her from what she'll regret. Luckily, this gentleman, a stranger to me, has given me a lift from Anglebury, or I must have hired.' He pointed to Christopher.

'But he's Mr Julian!' said Sol.

'You are Mrs Petherwin's father. – I have travelled in your company without knowing it!' exclaimed Christopher, feeling and looking both astonished and puzzled. At first, it had appeared to him that, in direct antagonism to his own purpose, her friends were favouring Ethelberta's wedding; but it was evidently otherwise.

'Yes, that's father,' said Sol. 'Father, this is Mr Julian. Mr Julian, this gentleman here is Lord Mountclere's brother – and, to cut the story short, we all wish to stop the wedding.'

'Then let us get on, in Heaven's name!' said Mountclere. 'You are the lady's father?'

'I am,' said Chickerel.

'Then you had better come into this carriage. We shall go faster than the dogcart. Now, driver, are the wheels right again?'

Chickerel hastily entered with Mountclere, Sol joined them, and they sped on. Christopher drove close in their rear, not quite certain whether he did well in going further, now that there were plenty of people to attend to the business, but anxious to see the end. The other three sat in silence, with their eyes upon their knees, though the clouds were dispersing, and the morning grew bright. In about twenty minutes the square unembattled tower of Knollsea Church appeared below them in the vale, its summit just touching the distant line of sea upon sky. The element by which they had been victimized on the previous evening now smiled falsely to the low morning sun.

They descended the road to the village at a little more mannerly pace than that of the earlier journey, and saw the rays glance upon the hands of the church clock, which marked five-and-twenty minutes to nine.

Knollsea
The Road Thence
Enckworth

45

All eyes were directed to the church-gate, as the travellers descended the hill. No wedding carriages were there, no favours, no slatternly group of women brimming with interest, no aged pauper on two sticks, who comes because he has nothing else to do till dying time, no nameless female passing by on the other side with a laugh of indifference, no ringers taking off their coats as they vanish up a turret, no hobbledehoys on tiptoe outside the chancel windows – in short, none whatever of the customary accessories of a country wedding was anywhere visible.

'Thank God!' said Chickerel.

'Wait till you know he deserves it,' said Mountclere.

'Nothing's done yet between them.'

'It is not likely that anything is done at this time of day. But I have decided to go to the church first. You will probably go to your relative's house at once?'

Sol looked to his father for a reply.

'No, I too shall go to the church first, just to assure myself,' said Chickerel. 'I shall then go on to Mrs Petherwin's.'

The carriage was stopped at the corner of a steep incline leading down to the edifice. Mountclere and Chickerel alighted and walked on towards the gates, Sol remaining in his place. Christopher was some way off, descending the hill on foot, having halted to leave his horse and trap at a small inn at the entrance to the village.

When Chickerel and Mountclere reached the churchyard gate they found it slightly open. The church-door beyond it was also open, but nobody was near the spot.

'We have arrived not a minute too soon, however,' said Mountclere. 'Preparations have apparently begun. It was to be an early wedding, no doubt.'

Entering the building, they looked around; it was quite empty. Chickerel turned towards the chancel, his eye being attracted by a red kneeling-cushion, placed at about the middle of the altar-railing, as if for early use. Mountclere strode to the vestry, somewhat at a loss how to proceed in his difficult task of unearthing his brother, obtaining a private interview with him, and then, by the introduction of Sol and Chickerel, causing a general convulsion.

'Ha! here's somebody,' he said, observing a man in the vestry. He advanced with the intention of asking where Lord Mountclere was to be found. Chickerel came forward in the same direction.

'Are you the parish clerk?' said Mountclere to the man, who was dressed up in his best clothes.

'I have the honour of that calling,' the man replied.

Two large books were lying before him on the vestry table,

one of them being open. As the clerk spoke he looked slantingly on the page, as a person might do to discover if some writing were dry. Mountclere and Chickerel gazed on the same page. The book was the marriage-register.

'Too late!' said Chickerel.

There plainly enough stood the signatures of Lord Mountclere and Ethelberta. The viscount's was very black, and had not yet dried. Her strokes were firm, and comparatively thick for a woman's, though paled by juxtaposition with her husband's muddled characters. In the space for witnesses' names appeared in trembling lines as fine as silk the autograph of Picotee, the second name being that of a stranger, probably the clerk.

'Yes, yes – we are too late, it seems,' said Mountclere coolly. 'Who could have thought they'd marry at eight!'

Chickerel stood like a man baked hard and dry. Further than his first two words he could say nothing.

'They must have set about it early, upon my soul,' Mountclere continued. 'When did the wedding take place?' he asked of the clerk sharply.

'It was over about five minutes before you came in,' replied that luminary pleasantly, as he played at an invisible game of pitch-and-toss* with some half-sovereigns in his pocket. 'I received orders to have the church ready at five minutes to eight this morning, though I knew nothing about such a thing till bedtime last night. It was very private and plain, not that I should mind another such a one, sir'; and he secretly pitched and tossed again.

Meanwhile Sol had found himself too restless to sit waiting in the carriage for more than a minute after the other two had left it. He stepped out at the same instant that Christopher came past, and together they too went on to the church.

'Father, ought we not to go on at once to Ethelberta's, instead of waiting?' said Sol, on reaching the vestry, still in ignorance. ''Twas no use in coming here.'

'No use at all,' said Chickerel, as if he had straw in his throat. 'Look at this. I would almost sooner have had it that in leaving this church I came from her grave – well, no, perhaps not that, but I fear it is a bad thing.'

Sol then saw the names in the register, Christopher saw them, and the man closed the book. Christopher could not well command himself, and he retired.

'I knew it. I always said that pride would lead Berta to marry an unworthy man, and so it has!' said Sol bitterly. 'What shall we do now? I'll see her.'

'Do no such thing, young man,' said Mountclere. 'The best course is to leave matters alone. They are married. If you are wise, you will try to think the match a good one, and be content to let her keep her position without inconveniencing her by your intrusions or complaints. It is possible that the satisfaction of her ambition will help her to endure any few surprises to her propriety that may occur. She is a clever young woman, and has played her cards adroitly. I only hope she may never repent of the game! A-hem. Good morning.' Saying this, Mountclere slightly bowed to his relations, and marched out of the church with dignity; but it was told afterwards by the coachman, who had no love for Mountclere, that when he stepped into the fly, and was as he believed unobserved, he was quite overcome with fatuous rage, his lips frothing like a mug of hot ale.

'What an impertinent gentleman 'tis,' said Chickerel. 'As if we had tried for her to marry his brother!'

'He knows better than that,' said Sol. 'But he'll never believe that Berta didn't lay a trap for the old fellow. He thinks at this moment that Lord Mountclere has never been told of us and our belongings.'

'I wonder if she has deceived him in anything,' murmured Chickerel. 'I can hardly suppose it. But she is altogether beyond me. However, if she has misled him on any point she will suffer for it.'

'You need not fear that, father. It isn't her way of working. Why couldn't she have known that when a title is to be had for the asking, the owner must be a shocking one indeed?'

'The title is well enough. Any poor scrubs in our place must be fools not to think the match a very rare and astonishing honour, as far as the position goes. But that my brave girl will be miserable is a part of the honour I can't stomach so well. If he had been any other lord in the kingdom, we might have been merry indeed. I believe he will ruin her happiness – yes, I do – not by any personal snubbing or rough conduct, but by other things, causing her to be despised; and that is a thing she can't endure.'

'She's not to be despised without a deal of trouble – we must remember that. And if he insults her by introducing new favourites, as they say he did his first wife, I'll call upon him and ask his meaning, and take her away.'

'Nonsense – we shall never know what he does, or how she feels; she will never let out a word. However unhappy she may be, she will always deny it – that's the unfortunate part of such marriages.'

'An old chap like that ought to leave young women alone, damn him!'

The clerk came nearer. 'I am afraid I cannot allow bad words to be spoke in this sacred pile,' he said. 'As far as my personal self goes, I should have no objection to your cussing as much as you like, but as a official of the church my conscience won't allow it to be done.'

'Your conscience has allowed something to be done that cussing and swearing are godly worship to.'

'The prettiest maid is left out of harness, however,' said the clerk. 'The little witness was the chicken to my taste – Lord forgive me for saying it, and a man with a wife and family!'

Sol and his father turned to withdraw, and soon forgot the remark, but it was frequently recalled by Christopher.

'Do you think of trying to see Ethelberta before you leave?' said Sol.

'Certainly not,' said Chickerel. 'Mr Mountclere's advice was good in that. The more we keep out of the way the more good we are doing her. I shall go back to Anglebury by the carrier, and get on at once to London. You will go with me, I suppose?'

'The carrier does not leave yet for an hour or two.'

'I shall walk on, and let him overtake me. If possible, I will get one glimpse of Enckworth Court, Berta's new home; there may be time, if I start at once.'

'I will walk with you,' said Sol.

'There is room for one with me,' said Christopher, 'I shall drive back early in the afternoon.'

'Thank you,' said Sol. 'I will endeavour to meet you at Corvsgate.'

Thus it was arranged. Chickerel could have wished to search for Picotee, and learn from her the details of this mysterious matter. But it was particularly painful to him to make himself busy after the event; and to appear suddenly and uselessly where he was plainly not wanted to appear would be an awkwardness which the pleasure of seeing either daughter could scarcely counter-balance. Hence he had resolved to return at once to town, and there await the news, together with the detailed directions as to his own future movements, carefully considered and laid down, which were sure to be given by the far-seeing Ethelberta.

Sol and his father walked on together, Chickerel to meet the carrier just beyond Enckworth, Sol to wait for Christopher at Corvsgate. His wish to see, in company with his father, the outline of the seat to which Ethelberta had been advanced that day, was the triumph of youthful curiosity and interest over dogged objection. His father's wish was based on calmer reasons.

Christopher, lone and out of place, remained in the church yet a little longer. He desultorily walked round. Reaching the organ chamber, he looked at the instrument, and was surprised to find behind it a young man. Julian first thought him to be the organist; on second inspection, however, he proved to be a person Christopher had met before, under far different circumstances; it was our young friend Ladywell, looking as sick and sorry as a lily with a slug in its stalk.

The occasion, the place, and their own condition, made them kin. Christopher had despised Ladywell, Ladywell had disliked Christopher; but a third item neutralized the other two – it was their common lot.

Christopher just nodded, for they had only met on Ethelberta's stairs. Ladywell nodded more, and spoke. 'The church appears to be interesting,' he said.

'Yes. Such a tower is rare in England,' said Christopher.

They then dwelt on other features of the building, thence enlarging to the village, and then to the rocks and marine scenery – both avoiding the malady they suffered from – the marriage of Ethelberta.

'The village streets are very picturesque, and the cliff scenery is good of its kind,' rejoined Ladywell. 'The rocks represent the feminine side of grandeur. Here they are white, with delicate tops. On the west coast they are higher, black, and with angular summits. Those represent grandeur in its masculine aspect. It is merely my own idea, and not very bright, perhaps.'

'It is very ingenious,' said Christopher, 'and perfectly true.'

Ladywell was pleased. 'I am here at present making sketches

for my next subject – a winter sea. Otherwise I should not have – happened to be in the church.'

'You are acquainted with Mrs Petherwin – I think you are Mr Ladywell, who painted her portrait last season?'

'Yes,' said Ladywell, colouring.

'You may have heard her speak of Mr Julian?'

'O yes,' said Ladywell, offering his hand. Then by degrees their tongues wound more closely round the subject of their sadness, each tacitly owning to what he would not tell.

'I saw it,' said Ladywell heavily.

'Did she look troubled?'

'Not in the least – bright and fresh as a May morning. She has played me many a bitter trick, and poor Neigh too, a friend of mine. But I cannot help forgiving her . . . I saw a carriage at the door, and strolled in. The ceremony was just proceeding, so I sat down here. Well, I have done with Knollsea. The place has no further interest for me now. I may own to you as a friend, that if she had not been living here I should have studied at some other coast – of course that's in confidence.'

'I understand, quite.'

'I arrived in the neighbourhood only two days ago, and did not set eyes upon her till this morning, she has kept so entirely indoors.'

Then the young men parted, and half an hour later the ingenuous Ladywell came from the visitors' inn by the shore, a man walking behind him with a quantity of artists' materials and appliances. He went on board the steamer, which this morning had performed the passage in safety. Ethelberta single having been the loadstone in the cliffs that had attracted Ladywell hither, Ethelberta married was the negative pole of the same, sending him away. And thus did a woman put an end to the only opportunity of distinction, on Art-exhibition walls, that ever offered itself to the tortuous ways, quaint alleys, and marbled bluffs of Knollsea, as accessories in the picture of a winter sea.

Christopher's interest in the village was of the same evaporating nature. He looked upon the sea, and the great swell, and the waves sending up a sound like the huzzas of multitudes; but all the wild scene was irksome now. The ocean-bound steamers far away on the horizon inspired him with no curiosity as to their destination; the house Ethelberta had occupied was positively hateful; and he turned away to wait impatiently for the hour at which he had promised to drive on to meet Sol at Corvsgate.

Sol and Chickerel plodded along the road, in order to skirt Enckworth before the carrier came up. Reaching the top of a hill on their way, they paused to look down on a peaceful scene. It was a park and wood, glowing in all the matchless colours of late autumn, parapets and pediments peering out from a central position afar. At the bottom of the descent before them was a lodge, to which they now descended. The gate stood invitingly open. Exclusiveness was no part of the owner's instincts: one could see that at a glance. No appearance of a well-rolled garden-path attached to the park-drive, as is the case with many, betokening by the perfection of their surfaces their proprietor's deficiency in hospitality. The approach was like a turnpike road full of great ruts, clumsy mendings; bordered by trampled edges and incursions upon the grass at pleasure. Butchers and bakers drove as freely herein as peers and peeresses. Christening parties, wedding companies, and funeral trains passed along by the doors of the mansion without check or question. A wild untidiness in this particular has its recommendations; for guarded grounds ever convey a suspicion that their owner is young to landed possessions, as religious earnestness implies newness of conversion, and conjugal tenderness recent marriage.

Half-an-hour being wanting as yet to Chickerel's time with the carrier, Sol and himself, like the rest of the world when at leisure, walked into the extensive stretch of grass and grove. It formed a park so large that not one of its owners had ever wished it larger, not one of its owner's rivals had ever failed to wish it smaller, and not one of its owner's satellites had ever seen it without praise. They somewhat avoided the roadway, passing under the huge, misshapen, ragged trees, and through fern brakes, ruddy and crisp in their decay. On reaching a suitable eminence, the father and son stood still to look upon the many-chimneyed building, or rather conglomeration of buildings, to which these groves and glades formed a setting.

'We will just give a glance,' said Chickerel, 'and then go away. It don't seem well to me that Ethelberta should have this; it is too much. The sudden change will do her no good. I never believe in anything that comes in the shape of wonderful luck. As it comes, so it goes. Had she been brought home today to one of those tenant-farms instead of these woods and walls, I could have called it good fortune. What she should have done was glorify herself by glorifying her own line of life, not by forsaking that line for another. Better have been admired as a governess than shunned as a peeress, which is what she will be. But it is just the same everywhere in these days. Young men will rather wear a black coat and starve than wear fustian and do well.'

'One man to want such a monstrous house as that! Well, 'tis a fine place. See, there's the carpenters' shops, the timber-yard, and everything, as if it were a little town. Perhaps Berta may hire me for a job now and then.'

'I always knew she would cut herself off from us. She marked for it from childhood, and she has finished the business thoroughly.'

'Well, it is no matter, father, for why should we want to trouble her? She may write, and I shall answer; but if she calls to see me, I shall not return the visit; and if she meets me with her husband or any of her new society about her, I shall behave as a stranger.'

'It will be best,' said Chickerel. 'Well, now I must move.'

However, by the sorcery of accident, before they had very far retraced their steps an open carriage became visible round a bend in the drive. Chickerel, with a servant's instinct, was for beating a retreat.

'No,' said Sol. 'Let us stand our ground. We have already been seen, and we do no harm.'

So they stood still on the edge of the drive, and the carriage drew near. It was a landau, and the sun shone in upon Lord Mountclere, with Lady Mountclere sitting beside him, like Abishag beside King David.*

Very blithe looked the viscount, for he rode upon a cherub* today. She appeared fresh, rosy, and strong, but dubious; though if mien was anything, she was a viscountess twice over. Her dress was of a dove-coloured material, with a bonnet to match, a little tufted white feather resting on the top, like a truce-flag between the blood of noble and vassal. Upon the cool grey of her shoulders hung a few locks of hair, toned warm as fire by the sunshiny addition to its natural hue.

Chickerel instinctively took off his hat; Sol did the same.

For only a moment did Ethelberta seem uncertain how to act.

But a solution to her difficulty was given by the face of her brother. There she saw plainly at one glance more than a dozen speeches would have told – for Sol's features thoroughly expressed his intention that to him she was to be a stranger. Her eyes flew to Chickerel, and he slightly shook his head. She understood them now. With a tear in her eye for her father, and a sigh in her bosom for Sol, she bowed in answer to their salute; her husband moved his hat and nodded, and the carriage rolled on. Lord Mountclere might possibly be making use of the fine morning in showing her the park and premises. Chickerel, with a moist eye, now went on with his son towards the high-road. When they reached the lodge, the lodge-keeper was walking in the sun, smoking his pipe. 'Good morning,' he said to Chickerel.

'Any rejoicings at the Court today?' the butler inquired.

'Quite the reverse. Not a soul there. 'Tisn't knowed anywhere at all. I had no idea of such a thing till he brought my lady here. Not going off, neither. They've come home like the commonest couple in the land, and not even the bells allowed to ring.'

They walked along the public road, and the carrier came in view.

'Father,' said Sol, 'I don't think I'll go further with you. She's gone into the house; and suppose she should run back without him to try to find us? It would be cruel to disappoint her. I'll bide about here for a quarter of an hour, in case she should. Mr Julian won't have passed Corvsgate till I get there.'

'Well, one or two of her old ways may be left in her still, and it is not a bad thought. Then you will walk the rest of the distance if you don't meet Mr Julian? I must be in London by the evening.'

'Any time tonight will do for me. I shall not begin work until tomorrow, so that the four o'clock train will answer my purpose.'

Thus they parted, and Sol strolled leisurely back. The road was quite deserted, and he lingered by the park fence.

'Sol!' said a bird-like voice; 'how did you come here?'

He looked up, and saw a figure peering down upon him from the top of the park wall, the ground on the inside being higher than the road. The speaker was to the expected Ethelberta what the moon is to the sun, a star to the moon. It was Picotee.

'Hullo, Picotee!' said Sol.

'There's a little gate a quarter of a mile further on,' said

Picotee. 'We can meet there without your passing through the
big lodge. I'll be there as soon as you.'

Sol ascended the hill, passed through the second gate, and
turned back again, when he met Picotee coming forward under
the trees. They walked together in this secluded spot.

'Berta says she wants to see you and father,' said Picotee
breathlessly. 'You must come in and make yourselves comfortable. She had no idea you were here so secretly, and she didn't
know what to do.'

'Father's gone,' said Sol.

'How vexed she will be! She thinks there is something the
matter – that you are angry with her for not telling you earlier.
But you will come in, Sol?'

'No, I can't come in,' said her brother.

'Why not? It is such a big house, you can't think. You need
not come near the front apartments, if you think we shall be
ashamed of you in your working clothes. How came you not to
dress up a bit, Sol? Still, Berta won't mind it much. She says
Lord Mountclere must take her as she is, or he is kindly welcome
to leave her.'

'Ah, well! I might have had a word or two to say about that,
but the time has gone by for it, worse luck. Perhaps it is best
that I have said nothing, and she has had her way. No, I shan't
come in, Picotee. Father is gone, and I am going too.'

'O Sol!'

'We are rather put out at her acting like this – father and I
and all of us. She might have let us know about it beforehand,
even if she is a lady and we what we always was. It wouldn't
have let her down so terrible much to write a line. She might
have learnt something that would have led her to take a different
step.'

'But you will see poor Berta? She has done no harm. She was
going to write long letters to all of you today, explaining her
wedding, and how she is going to help us all on in the world.'

Sol paused irresolutely. 'No, I won't come in,' he said. 'It
would disgrace her, for one thing, dressed as I be; more than
that, I don't want to come in. But I should like to see her, if she
would like to see me; and I'll go up there to that little fir
plantation, and walk up and down behind it for exactly half-an-
hour. She can come out to me there.' Sol had pointed as he

spoke to a knot of young trees that hooded a knoll a little way off.

'I'll go and tell her,' said Picotee.

'I suppose they will be off somewhere, and she is busy getting ready?'

'O no. They are not going to travel till next year. Ethelberta does not want to go anywhere; and Lord Mountclere cannot endure this changeable weather in any place but his own house.'

'Poor fellow!'

'Then you will wait for her by the firs? I'll tell her at once.'

Picotee left him, and Sol went across the glade.

Enckworth (*continued*)
The Anglebury Highway

46

He had not paced behind the firs more than ten minutes when Ethelberta appeared from the opposite side. At great inconvenience to herself she had complied with his request.

Ethelberta was trembling. She took her brother's hand, and said, 'Is father, then, gone?'

'Yes,' said Sol. 'I should have been gone likewise, but I thought you wanted to see me.'

'Of course I did, and him too. Why did you come so mysteriously, and, I must say, unbecomingly? I am afraid I did wrong in not informing you of my intention.'

'To yourself you may have. Father would have liked a word with you before – you did it.'

'You both looked so forbidding that I did not like to stop the carriage when we passed you. I want to see him on an important matter – his leaving Mrs Doncastle's service at once. I am going to write and beg her to dispense with a notice, which I have no doubt she will do.'

'He's very much upset about you.'

'My secrecy was perhaps an error of judgment,' she said sadly. 'But I had reasons. Why did you and my father come here at all if you did not want to see me?'

'We did want to see you up to a certain time.'

'You did not come to prevent my marriage?'

'We wished to see you before the marriage – I can't say more.'

'I thought you might not approve of what I had done,' said Ethelberta mournfully. 'But a time may come when you will approve.'

'Never.'

'Don't be harsh, Sol. A coronet covers a multitude of sins.'*

'A coronet: good Lord – and you my sister! Look at my hand.' Sol extended his hand. 'Look how my thumb stands out at the root, as if it were out of joint, and that hard place inside there. Did you ever see anything so ugly as that hand – a misshaped monster, isn't he? That comes from the jack-plane,* and my pushing against it day after day and year after year. If I were found drowned or buried, dressed or undressed, in fustian or in broadcloth, folk would look at my hand and say, "That man's a carpenter." Well now, how can a man, branded with work as I be, be brother to a viscountess without something being wrong? Of course there's something wrong in it, or he wouldn't have married you – something which won't be righted without terrible suffering.'

'No, no,' said she. 'You are mistaken. There is no such wonderful quality in a title in these days. What I really am is second wife to a quiet old country nobleman, who has given up society. What more commonplace? My life will be as simple, even more simple, than it was before.'

'Berta, you have worked to false lines. A creeping up among the useless lumber of our nation that'll be the first to burn if there comes a flare. I never see such a deserter of your own lot as you be! But you were always like it, Berta, and I am ashamed of 'ee. More than that, a good woman never marries twice.'

'You are too hard, Sol,' said the poor viscountess, almost crying. 'I've done it all for you! Even if I have made a mistake, and given my ambition an ignoble turn, don't tell me so now, or you may do more harm in a minute than you will cure in a lifetime. It is absurd to let republican passions so blind you to fact. A family which can be honourably traced through history for five hundred years does affect the heart of a person not entirely hardened against romance. Whether you like the peerage or no, they appeal to our historical sense and love of old associations.'

'I don't care for history. Prophecy is the only thing can do poor men any good. When you were a girl, you wouldn't drop a curtsey to 'em, historical or otherwise, and there you were right. But, instead of sticking to such principles, you must needs push up, so as to get girls such as you were once to curtsey to you, not even thinking marriage with a bad man too great a price to pay for't.'

'A bad man? What do you mean by that? Lord Mountclere is rather old, but he's worthy. What did you mean, Sol?'

'Nothing – a mere sommat to say.'

At that moment Picotee emerged from behind a tree, and told her sister that Lord Mountclere was looking for her.

'Well, Sol, I cannot explain all to you now,' she said. 'I will send for you in London.' She wished him good-bye, and they separated, Picotee accompanying Sol a little on his way.

Ethelberta was greatly perturbed by this meeting. After retracing her steps a short distance, she still felt so distressed and unpresentable that she resolved not to allow Lord Mountclere to see her till the clouds had somewhat passed off; it was but a bare act of justice to him to hide from his sight such a bridal mood as this. It was better to keep him waiting than to make him positively unhappy. She turned aside, and went up the valley, where the park merged in miles of wood and copse.

She opened an iron gate and entered the wood, casually interested in the vast variety of colours that the half-fallen leaves of the season wore: more, much more, occupied with personal thought. The path she pursued became gradually involved in bushes as well as trees, giving to the spot the character rather of a coppice than a wood. Perceiving that she had gone far enough, Ethelberta turned back by a path which at this point intersected that by which she had approached, and promised a more direct return towards the Court. She had not gone many steps among the hazels, which here formed a perfect thicket, when she observed a belt of holly-bushes in their midst; towards the outskirts of these an opening on her left hand directly led, thence winding round into a clear space of greensward, which they completely enclosed. On this isolated and mewed-up bit of lawn stood a timber-built cottage, having ornamental barge-boards,* balconettes,* and porch. It was an erection interesting enough as an experiment, and grand as a toy, but as a building contemptible.

A blue gauze of smoke floated over the chimney, as if

somebody was living there; round towards the side some empty
hen-coops were piled away; while under the hollies were divers
frameworks of wire netting and sticks, showing that birds were
kept here at some seasons of the year.

Being lady of all she surveyed, Ethelberta crossed the leafy
sward, and knocked at the door. She was interested in knowing
the purpose of the peculiar little edifice.

The door was opened by a woman wearing a clean apron
upon a not very clean gown. Ethelberta asked who lived in so
pretty a place.

'Miss Gruchette,' the servant replied. 'But she is not here
now.'

'Does she live here alone?'

'Yes – excepting myself and a fellow-servant.'

'Oh.'

'She lives here to attend to the pheasants and poultry, because
she is so clever in managing them. They are brought here from
the keeper's over the hill. Her father was a fancier.'

'Miss Gruchette attends to the birds, and two servants attend
to Miss Gruchette?'

'Well, to tell the truth, m'm, the servants do almost all of it.
Still, that's what Miss Gruchette is here for. Would you like to
see the house? It is pretty.' The woman spoke with hesitation,
as if in doubt between the desire of earning a shilling and the
fear that Ethelberta was not a stranger. That Ethelberta was
Lady Mountclere she plainly did not dream.

'I fear I can scarcely stay long enough; yet I will just look in,'
said Ethelberta. And as soon as they had crossed the threshold
she was glad of having done so.

The cottage internally may be described as a sort of boudoir
extracted from the bulk of a mansion and deposited in a wood.
The front room was filled with nicknacks, curious work-tables,
filigree baskets, twisted brackets supporting statuettes, in which
the grotesque in every case – ruled the design; love-birds, in gilt
cages; French bronzes, wonderful boxes, needlework of strange
patterns, and other attractive objects. The apartment was one of
those which seem to laugh in a visitor's face and on closer
examination express frivolity more distinctly than by words.

'Miss Gruchette is here to keep the fowls?' said Ethelberta, in
a puzzled tone, after a survey.

'Yes. But they don't keep her.'

Ethelberta did not attempt to understand, and ceased to occupy her mind with the matter. They came from the cottage to the door, where she gave the woman a trifling sum, and turned to leave. But footsteps were at that moment to be heard beating among the leaves on the other side of the hollies, and Ethelberta waited till the walkers should have passed. The voices of two men reached herself and the woman as they stood. They were close to the house, yet screened from it by the holly-bushes, when one could be heard to say distinctly, as if with his face turned to the cottage –

'Lady Mountclere gone for good?'

'I suppose so. Ha-ha! So come, so go.'

The speakers passed on, their backs becoming visible through the opening. They appeared to be woodmen.

'What Lady Mountclere do they mean?' said Ethelberta.

The woman blushed. 'They meant Miss Gruchette.'

'Oh – a nickname.'

'Yes.'

'Why?'

The woman whispered why in a story of about two minutes' length. Ethelberta turned pale.

'Is she going to return?' she inquired, in a thin hard voice.

'Yes; next week. You know her, m'm?'

'No. I am a stranger.'

'So much the better. I may tell you, then, that an old tale is flying about the neighbourhood – that Lord Mountclere was privately married to another woman, at Knollsea, this morning early. Can it be true?'

'I believe it to be true.'

'And that she is of no family?'

'Of no family.'

'Indeed. Then the Lord only knows what will become of the poor thing! There will be murder between 'em.'

'Between whom?'

'Her and the lady who lives here. She won't budge an inch – not she!'

Ethelberta moved aside. A shade seemed to overspread the world, the sky, the trees, and the objects in the foreground. She kept her face away from the woman, and, whispering a reply to her Good morning, passed through the hollies into the leaf-strewn path. As soon as she came to a large trunk she placed her hands against it and rested her face upon them. She drew herself lower down, lower, lower, till she crouched upon the leaves. 'Ay – 'tis what father and Sol meant! O Heaven!' she whispered.

She soon arose, and went on her way to the house. Her fair features were firmly set, and she scarcely heeded the path in the concentration which had followed her paroxysm. When she reached the park proper she became aware of an excitement that was in progress there.

Ethelberta's absence had become unaccountable to Lord Mountclere, who could hardly permit her retirement from his sight for a minute. But at first he had made due allowance for her eccentricity as a woman of genius, and would not take notice of the half-hour's desertion, unpardonable as it might have been in other classes of wives. Then he had inquired, searched, been alarmed: he had finally sent men-servants in all directions about the park to look for her. He feared she had fallen out of a window, down a well, or into the lake. The next stage of search was to have been drags and grapnels: but Ethelberta entered the house.

Lord Mountclere rushed forward to meet her, and such was her contrivance that he noticed no change. The searchers were called in, Ethelberta explaining that she had merely obeyed the wish of her brother in going out to meet him. Picotee, who had returned from her walk with Sol, was upstairs in one of the rooms which had been allotted to her. Ethelberta managed to run in there on her way upstairs to her own chamber.

'Picotee, put your things on again,' she said. 'You are the only friend I have in this house, and I want one badly. Go to Sol, and deliver this message to him – that I want to see him at once. You must overtake him, if you walk all the way to Anglebury. But the train does not leave till four, so that there is plenty of time.'

'What is the matter?' said Picotee. 'I cannot walk all the way.'

'I don't think you will have to do that – I hope not.'

'He is going to stop at Corvsgate to have a bit of lunch: I might overtake him there, if I must!'

'Yes. And tell him to come to the east passage door. It is that door next to the entrance to the stable-yard. There is a little yew-tree outside it. On second thoughts you, dear, must not come back. Wait at Corvsgate in the little inn parlour till Sol

comes to you again. You will probably then have to go home to
London alone; but do not mind it. The worst part for you will
be in going from the station to the Crescent; but nobody will
molest you in a four-wheel cab: you have done it before.
However, he will tell you if this is necessary when he gets back.
I can best fight my battles alone. You shall have a letter from
me the day after tomorrow, stating where I am. I shall not be
here.'

'But what is it so dreadful?'

'Nothing to frighten you.' But she spoke with a breathlessness
that completely nullified the assurance. 'It is merely that I find I
must come to an explanation with Lord Mountclere before I can
live here permanently, and I cannot stipulate with him while I
am here in his power. Till I write, good-bye. Your things are not
unpacked, so let them remain here for the present – they can be
sent for.'

Poor Picotee, more agitated than her sister, but never ques-
tioning her orders, went downstairs and out of the house. She
ran across the shrubberies, into the park, and to the gate whereat
Sol had emerged some half-hour earlier. She trotted along upon
the turnpike road like a lost doe, crying as she went at the new
trouble which had come upon Berta, whatever that trouble
might be. Behind her she heard wheels and the stepping of a
horse, but she was too concerned to turn her head. The pace of
the vehicle slackened, however, when it was abreast of Picotee,
and she looked up to see Christopher as the driver.

'Miss Chickerel!' he said, with surprise.

Picotee had quickly looked down again, and she murmured,
'Yes.'

Christopher asked what he could not help asking in the
circumstances, 'Would you like to ride?'

'I should be glad,' said she, overcoming her flurry. 'I am
anxious to overtake my brother Sol.'

'I have arranged to pick him up at Corvsgate,' said
Christopher.

He descended, and assisted her to mount beside him, and
drove on again, almost in silence. He was inclined to believe
that some supernatural legerdemain had to do with these
periodic impacts of Picotee on his path. She sat mute and
melancholy till they were within half a mile of Corvsgate.

'Thank you,' she said then, perceiving Sol upon the road, 'there is my brother; I will get down now.'

'He was going to ride on to Anglebury with me,' said Julian.

Picotee did not reply, and Sol turned round. Seeing her he instantly exclaimed, 'What's the matter, Picotee?'

She explained to him that he was to go back immediately, and meet her sister at the door by the yew, as Ethelberta had charged her. Christopher, knowing them so well, was too much an interested member of the group to be left out of confidence, and she included him in her audience.

'And what are you to do?' said Sol to her.

'I am to wait at Corvsgate till you come to me.'

'I can't understand it,' Sol muttered, with a gloomy face. 'There's something wrong; and it was only to be expected; that's what I say, Mr Julian.'

'If necessary I can take care of Miss Chickerel till you come,' said Christopher.

'Thank you,' said Sol. 'Then I will return to you as soon as I can, at the Castle Inn, just ahead. 'Tis very awkward for you to be so burdened by us, Mr Julian; but we are in a trouble that I don't yet see the bottom of.'

'I know,' said Christopher kindly. 'We will wait for you.'

He then drove on with Picotee to the inn, which was not far off, and Sol returned again to Enckworth. Feeling somewhat like a thief in the night, he zigzagged through the park, behind belts and knots of trees, until he saw the yew, dark and clear, as if drawn in ink upon the fair face of the mansion. The way up to it was in a little cutting between shrubs, the door being a private entrance, sunk below the surface of the lawn, and invisible from other parts of the same front. As soon as he reached it, Ethelberta opened it at once, as if she had listened for his footsteps.

She took him along a passage in the basement, up a flight of steps, and into a huge, solitary, chill apartment. It was the ballroom. Spacious mirrors in gilt frames formed panels in the lower part of the walls, the remainder being toned in sage-green. In each recess between the mirrors was a statue. The ceiling rose in a segmental curve, and bore sprawling upon its face gilt figures of wanton goddesses, cupids, satyrs with tambourines, drums, and trumpets, the whole ceiling seeming alive with them. But the room was very gloomy now, there being little light admitted from without, and the reflections from the mirrors gave a depressing coldness to the scene. It was a place intended to look joyous by night, and whatever it chose to look by day.

'We are safe here,' said she. 'But we must listen for footsteps. I have only five minutes: Lord Mountclere is waiting for me. I mean to leave this place, come what may.'

'Why?' said Sol, in astonishment.

'I cannot tell you – something has occurred, which makes it necessary that I should establish clearly that I am going to be mistress here, or I don't live with Lord Mountclere as his wife at all. Sol, listen, and do exactly what I say. Go to Anglebury, hire a brougham, bring it on as far as Little Enckworth: you will have to meet me with it at one of the park gates later in the evening – probably the west, at half-past seven. Leave it at the village, come on here on foot, and stay under the trees till just before six: it will then be quite dark, and you must stand under the projecting balustrade a little further on than the door you came in by. I will just step upon the balcony over it, and tell you more exactly than I can now the precise time that I shall be able to slip out, and where the carriage is to be waiting. But it may not be safe to speak on account of his closeness to me – I will hand down a note. I find it is impossible to leave the house by daylight – I am certain to be pursued – he already suspects something. Now I must be going, or he will be here, for he watches my movements because of some accidental words that escaped me.'

'Berta, I shan't have anything to do with this,' said Sol. 'It is not right!'

'I am only going to Rouen, to Aunt Charlotte!' she implored. 'I want to get to Southampton, to be in time for the midnight steamer. When I am at Rouen I can negotiate with Lord Mountclere the terms on which I will return to him. It is the only chance I have of rooting out a scandal and a disgrace which threatens the beginning of my life here! My letters to him, and his to me, can be forwarded through you or through father, and he will not know where I am. Any woman is justified in adopting such a course to bring her husband to a sense of her dignity. If I don't go away now, it will end in a permanent separation. If I leave at once, and stipulate that he gets rid of her, we may be reconciled.'

'I can't help you: you must stick to your husband. I don't like them, or any of their sort, barring about three or four, for the reason that they despise me and all my sort. But, Ethelberta, for all that I'll play fair with them. No half-and-half trimming business. You have joined 'em, and 'rayed yourself against us; and there you'd better bide. You have married your man, and your duty is towards him. I know what he is, and so does father; but if I were to help you to run away now, I should scorn myself more than I scorn him.'

'I don't care for that, or for any such politics! The Mountclere line is noble, and how was I to know that this member was not noble, too? As the representative of an illustrious family I was taken with him, but as a man – I must shun him till I've tackled him.'

'How can you shun him? You have married him!'

'Nevertheless, I won't stay! Neither law nor gospel demands it of me after what I have learnt. And if law and gospel did demand it, I would not stay. And if you will not help me to escape, I go alone.'

'You had better not try any such wild thing.'

The creaking of a door was heard. 'O Sol,' she said appealingly, 'don't go into the question whether I am right or wrong – only remember that I am very unhappy. Do help me – I have no other person in the world to ask! Be under the balcony at six o'clock. Say you will – I must go – say you will!'

'I'll think,' said Sol, very much disturbed. 'There, don't cry; I'll try to be under the balcony, at any rate. I cannot promise more, but I'll try to be there.'

She opened in the panelling one of the old-fashioned concealed modes of exit known as jib-doors,* which it was once the custom to construct without architraves in the walls of large apartments, so as not to interfere with the general design of the room. Sol found himself in a narrow passage, running down the whole length of the ball-room, and at the same time he heard Lord Mountclere's voice within, talking to Ethelberta. Sol's escape had been adroit: as it was the viscount might have seen her anxiety. He passed down some steps, along an area from which he could see into a row of servants' offices, among them a kitchen with a fireplace flaming like an altar of sacrifice. Nobody seemed to be concerned about him; there were workmen upon the premises, and he nearly matched them. At last he got again into the shrubberies and to the side of the park by which he had entered.

On reaching Corvsgate he found Picotee in the parlour of the little inn, as he had directed. Mr Julian, she said, had walked up to the ruins, and would be back again in a few minutes. Sol ordered the horse to be put in, and by the time it was ready Christopher came down from the hill. Room was made for Sol by opening the flap of the dogcart, and Christopher drove on.

He was anxious to know the trouble, and Sol was not reluctant to share the burden of it with one whom he believed to be a friend. He told, scrap by scrap, the strange request of Ethelberta. Christopher, though ignorant of Ethelberta's experience that morning, instantly assumed that the discovery of some concealed spectre had led to this precipitancy.

'When does she wish you to meet her with the carriage?'

'Probably at half-past seven, at the west lodge; but that is to be finally fixed by a note she will hand down to me from the balcony.'

'Which balcony?'

'The nearest to the yew-tree.'

'At what time will she hand the note?'

'As the Court clock strikes six, she says. And if I am not there to take her instructions of course she will give up the idea, which is just what I want her to do.'

Christopher begged Sol to go. Whether Ethelberta was right or wrong, he did not stop to inquire. She was in trouble; she was too clear-headed to be in trouble without good reason; and she wanted assistance out of it. But such was Sol's nature that the more he reflected the more determined was he in not giving way to her entreaty. By the time that they reached Anglebury he repented having given way so far as to withhold a direct refusal.

'It can do no good,' he said mournfully. 'It is better to nip her notion in its beginning. She says she wants to fly to Rouen, and from there arrange terms with him. But it can't be done – she should have thought of terms before.'

Christopher made no further reply. Leaving word at the 'Red Lion' that a man was to be sent to take the horse of him, he drove directly onwards to the station.

'Then you don't mean to help her?' said Julian, when Sol took the tickets – one for himself and one for Picotee.

'I serve her best by leaving her alone!' said Sol.

'I don't think so.'

'She has married him.'

'She is in distress.'

'She has married him.'

Sol and Picotee took their seats, Picotee upbraiding her brother. 'I can go by myself!' she said, in tears. 'Do go back for Berta, Sol. She said I was to go home alone, and I can do it!'

'You must not. It is not right for you to be hiring cabs and driving across London at midnight. Berta should have known better than propose it.'

She was flurried. 'Go, Sol!'

But her entreaty was fruitless.

'Have you got your ticket, Mr Julian?' said Sol. 'I suppose we shall go together till we get near Melchester?'

'I have not got my ticket yet – I'll be back in two minutes.'

The minutes went by, and Christopher did not reappear. The train moved off: Christopher was seen running up the platform, as if in a vain hope to catch it.

'He has missed the train,' said Sol. Picotee looked disappointed, and said nothing. They were soon out of sight.

'God forgive me for such a hollow pretence!' said Christopher to himself. 'But he would have been uneasy had he known I wished to stay behind. I cannot leave her in trouble like this!'

He went back to the 'Red Lion' with the manner and movement of a man who after a lifetime of desultoriness had at last found something to do. It was now getting late in the afternoon. Christopher ordered a one-horse brougham at the inn, and entering it was driven out of the town towards Enckworth as the evening shades were beginning to fall. They passed into the hamlet of Little Enckworth at half-past five, and drew up at a beer-house at the end. Jumping out here, Julian told the man to wait till he should return.

Thus far he had exactly obeyed her orders to Sol. He hoped to be able to obey them throughout, and supply her with the aid her brother refused. He also hoped that the change in the personality of her confederate would make no difference to her intention. That he was putting himself in a wrong position he allowed, but time and attention were requisite for such analysis: meanwhile Ethelberta was in trouble. On the one hand was she waiting hopefully for Sol; on the other was Sol many miles on his way to town; between them was himself.

He ran with all his might towards Enckworth Park, mounted the lofty stone stile by the lodge, saw the dark bronze figures on the piers through the twilight, and then proceeded to thread the trees. Among these he struck a light for a moment: it was ten minutes to six. In another five minutes he was panting beneath the walls of her house.

Enckworth Court was not unknown to Christopher, for he had frequently explored that spot in his Sandbourne days. He perceived now why she had selected that particular balcony for handing down directions; it was the only one round the house that was low enough to be reached from the outside, the basement here being a little way sunk in the ground.

He went close under, turned his face outwards, and waited. About a foot over his head was the stone floor of the balcony, forming a ceiling to his position. At his back, two or three feet behind, was a blank wall – the wall of the house. In front of him was the misty park, crowned by a sky sparkling with winter stars. This was abruptly cut off upward by the dark edge of the balcony which overhung him.

It was as if some person within the room above had been awaiting his approach. He had scarcely found time to observe his situation when a human hand and portion of a bare arm were thrust between the balusters,* descended a little way from the edge of the balcony, and remained hanging across the starlit sky. Something was between the fingers. Christopher lifted his hand, took the scrap, which was paper, and the arm was withdrawn. As it withdrew, a jewel on one of the fingers sparkled in the rays of a large planet that rode in the opposite sky.

Light steps retreated from the balcony, and a window closed. Christopher had almost held his breath lest Ethelberta should discover him at the critical moment to be other than Sol, and mar her deliverance by her alarm. The still silence was anything but silence to him; he felt as if he were listening to the clanging chorus of an oratorio. And then he could fancy he heard words between Ethelberta and the viscount within the room; they were evidently at very close quarters, and dexterity must have been required of her. He went on tiptoe across the gravel to the grass, and once on that he strode in the direction whence he had come. By the thick trunk of one of a group of aged trees he stopped to get a light, just as the Court clock struck six in loud long tones.

The transaction had been carried out, through her impatience possibly, four or five minutes before the time appointed.

The note contained, in a shaken hand, in which, however, the well-known characters were distinguishable, these words in pencil:

'At half-past seven o'clock. Just outside the north lodge; don't fail.'

This was the time she had suggested to Sol as that which would probably best suit her escape, if she could escape at all. She had changed the place from the west to the north lodge – nothing else. The latter was certainly more secluded, though a trifle more remote from the course of the proposed journey; there was just time enough and none to spare for fetching the brougham from Little Enckworth to the lodge, the village being two miles off. The few minutes gained by her readiness at the balcony were useful now. He started at once for the village, diverging somewhat to observe the spot appointed for the meeting. It was excellently chosen; the gate appeared to be little used, the lane outside it was covered with trees, and all around was silent as the grave. After this hasty survey by the wan starlight, he hastened on to Little Enckworth.

An hour and a quarter later a small brougham without lamps was creeping along by the park wall towards this spot. The leaves were so thick upon the unfrequented road that the wheels could not be heard, and the horse's pacing made scarcely more noise than a rabbit would have done in limping along. The vehicle progressed slowly, for they were in good time. About ten yards from the park entrance it stopped, and Christopher stepped out.

'We may have to wait here ten minutes,' he said to the driver. 'And then shall we be able to reach Anglebury in time for the up mail-train to Southampton?'

'Half-past seven, half-past eight, half-past nine – two hours. O yes, sir, easily. A young lady in the case perhaps, sir?'

'Yes.'

'Well, I hope she'll be done honestly by, even if she is of humble station. 'Tis best, and cheapest too, in the long run.' The coachman was apparently imagining the dove about to flit away to be one of the pretty maid-servants that abounded in Enckworth Court; such escapades as these were not unfrequent among them, a fair face having been deemed a sufficient recommendation to service in that house, without too close an inquiry into character, since the death of the first viscountess.

'Now then, silence; and listen for a footstep at the gate.'

Such calmness as there was in the musician's voice had been produced by considerable effort. For his heart had begun to beat fast and loud as he strained his attentive ear to catch the footfall of a woman who could only be his illegally.

The obscurity was as great as a starry sky would permit it to be. Beneath the trees where the carriage stood the darkness was total.

Enckworth and its Precincts
Melchester

47

To be wise after the event is often to act foolishly with regard to it; and to preserve the illusion which has led to the event would frequently be a course that omniscience itself could not find fault with. Reaction with Ethelberta was complete, and the more violent in that it threatened to be useless. Sol's bitter chiding had been the first thing to discompose her fortitude. It reduced her to a consciousness that she had allowed herself to be coerced in her instincts, and yet had not triumphed in her duty. She might have pleased her family better by pleasing her tastes, and have entirely avoided the grim irony of the situation disclosed later in the day.

After the second interview with Sol she was to some extent composed in mind by being able to nurse a definite intention. As momentum causes the narrowest wheel to stand upright, a scheme, fairly imbibed, will give the weakest some power to maintain a position stoically.

In the temporary absence of Lord Mountclere, about six o'clock, she slipped out upon the balcony and handed down a note. To her relief, a hand received it instantly.

The hour and a half wanting to half-past seven she passed with great effort. The main part of the time was occupied by dinner, during which she attempted to devise some scheme for leaving him without suspicion just before the appointed moment.

Happily, and as if by a Providence, there was no necessity for any such thing.

A little while before the half-hour, when she moved to rise from dinner, he also arose, tenderly begging her to excuse him for a few minutes, that he might go and write an important note to his lawyer, until that moment forgotten, though the postman was nearly due. She heard him retire along the corridor and shut himself into his study, his promised time of return being a quarter of an hour thence.

Five minutes after that memorable parting Ethelberta came from the little door by the bush of yew, well and thickly wrapped up from head to heels. She skimmed across the park and under the boughs like a shade, mounting then the stone steps for pedestrians which were fixed beside the park gates here as at all the lodges. Outside and below her she saw an oblong shape – it was a brougham, and it had been drawn forward close to the bottom of the steps that she might not have an inch further to go on foot than to this barrier. The whole precinct was thronged with trees; half their foliage being overhead, the other half under foot, for the gardeners had not yet begun to rake and collect the leaves; thus it was that her dress rustled as she descended the steps.

The carriage door was held open by the driver, and she entered instantly. He shut her in, and mounted to his seat. As they drove away she became conscious of another person inside.

'O! Sol – it is done!' she whispered, believing the man to be her brother. Her companion made no reply.

Ethelberta, familiar with Sol's moods of troubled silence, did not press for an answer. It was, indeed, certain that Sol's assistance would have been given under a sullen protest; even if unwilling to disappoint her, he might well have been taciturn and angry at her course.

They sat in silence, and in total darkness. The road ascended an incline, the horse's tramp being still deadened by the carpet of leaves. Then the large trees on either hand became interspersed by a low brushwood of varied sorts, from which a large bird occasionally flew, in its affright at their presence beating its wings recklessly against the hard stems with force enough to cripple the delicate quills. It showed how deserted was the spot after nightfall.

'Sol?' said Ethelberta again. 'Why not talk to me?'

She now noticed that her fellow-traveller kept his head and his whole person as snugly back in the corner, out of her way, as it was possible to do. She was not exactly frightened, but she could not understand the reason. The carriage gave a quick turn, and stopped.

'Where are we now?' she said. 'Shall we get to Anglebury by nine? What is the time, Sol?'

'I will see,' replied her companion. They were the first words he had uttered.

The voice was so different from her brother's that she was terrified; her limbs quivered. In another instant the speaker had struck a wax vesta, and holding it erect in his fingers he looked her in the face.

'Hee-hee-hee!' The laugher was her husband the viscount.

He laughed again, and his eyes gleamed like a couple of tarnished brass buttons in the light of the wax match.

Ethelberta might have fallen dead with the shock, so terrible and hideous was it. Yet she did not. She neither shrieked nor fainted; but no poor January fieldfare was ever colder, no icehouse more dank with perspiration, than she was then.

'A very pleasant joke, my dear – hee-hee! And no more than was to be expected on this merry, happy day of our lives. Nobody enjoys a good jest more than I do: I always enjoyed a jest – hee-hee! Now we are in the dark again; and we will alight and walk. The path is too narrow for the carriage, but it will not be far for you. Take your husband's arm.'

While he had been speaking a defiant pride had sprung up in her, instigating her to conceal every weakness. He had opened the carriage door and stepped out. She followed, taking the offered arm.

'Take the horse and carriage to the stables,' said the viscount to the coachman, who was his own servant, the vehicle and horse being also his. The coachman turned the horse's head and vanished down the woodland track by which they had ascended.

The viscount moved on, uttering private chuckles as numerous as a woodpecker's taps, and Ethelberta with him. She walked as by a miracle, but she would walk. She would have died rather than not have walked then.

She perceived now that they were somewhere in Enckworth wood. As they went, she noticed a faint shine upon the ground on the other side of the viscount, which showed her that they were walking beside a wet ditch. She remembered having seen it in the morning: it was a shallow ditch of mud. She might push him in, and run, and so escape before he could extricate himself. It would not hurt him. It was her last chance. She waited a moment for the opportunity.

'We are one to one, and I am the stronger!' she at last exclaimed triumphantly, and lifted her hand for a thrust.

'On the contrary, darling, we are one to half-a-dozen, and you considerably the weaker,' he tenderly replied, stepping back adroitly, and blowing a whistle. At once the bushes seemed to be animated in four or five places.

'John?' he said, in the direction of one of them.

'Yes, my lord,' replied a voice from the bush, and a keeper came forward.

'William?'

Another man advanced from another bush.

'Quite right. Remain where you are for the present. Is Tomkins there?'

'Yes, my lord,' said a man from another part of the thicket.

'You go and keep watch by the further lodge: there are poachers about. Where is Strongway?'

'Just below, my lord.'

'Tell him and his brother to go to the west gate, and walk up and down. Let them search round it, among the trees inside. Anybody there who cannot give a good account of himself to be brought before me tomorrow morning. I am living at the cottage at present. That's all I have to say to you.' And, turning round to Ethelberta: 'Now, dearest, we will walk a little further if you are able. I have provided that your friends shall be taken care of.' He tried to pull her hand towards him, gently, like a cat opening a door.

They walked a little onward, and Lord Mountclere spoke again, with imperturbable good-humour:

'I will tell you a story, to pass the time away. I have learnt the art from you – your mantle has fallen upon me, and all your inspiration with it. Listen, dearest. I saw a young man come to the house today. Afterwards I saw him cross a passage in your company. You entered the ball-room with him. That room is a treacherous place. It is panelled with wood, and between the panels and the walls is a passage for the servants, opening from the room by doors hidden in the woodwork. Lady Mountclere knew of one of these, and made use of it to let out her conspirator; Lord Mountclere knew of another, and made use of it to let in himself. His sight is not good, but his ears are unimpaired. A meeting was arranged to take place at the west gate at half-past seven, unless a note handed from the balcony mentioned another time and place. He heard it all – hee-hee!

'When Lady Mountclere's confederate came for the note, I was in waiting above, and handed one down a few minutes before the hour struck, confirming the time, but changing the place. When Lady Mountclere handed down her note, just as the clock was striking, her confederate had gone, and I was standing beneath the balcony to receive it. She dropped it into her husband's hands – ho-ho-ho-ho!

'Lord Mountclere ordered a brougham to be at the west lodge, as fixed by Lady Mountclere's note. Probably Lady Mountclere's friend ordered a brougham to be at the north gate, as fixed by my note, written in imitation of Lady Mountclere's hand. Lady Mountclere came to the spot she had mentioned, and like a good wife rushed into the arms of her husband – hoo-hoo-hoo-hoo-hoo!'

As if by an ungovernable impulse, Ethelberta broke into laughter also – laughter which had a wild unnatural sound; it was hysterical. She sank down upon the leaves, and there continued the fearful laugh just as before.

Lord Mountclere became greatly frightened. The spot they had reached was a green space within a girdle of hollies, and in front of them rose an ornamental cottage. This was the building which Ethelberta had visited earlier in the day: it was the Petit Trianon* of Enckworth Court.

The viscount left her side and hurried forward. The door of the building was opened by a woman.

'Have you prepared for us, as I directed?'

'Yes, my lord; tea and coffee are both ready.'

'Never mind that now. Lady Mountclere is ill; come and assist her indoors. Tell the other woman to bring wine and water at once.'

He returned to Ethelberta. She was better, and was sitting calmly on the bank. She rose without assistance.

'You may retire,' he said to the woman who had followed him, and she turned round. When Ethelberta saw the building, she drew back quickly.

'Where is the *other* Lady Mountclere?' she inquired.

'Gone!'

'She shall never return – never?'

'Never. It was not intended that she should.'

'That sounds well. Lord Mountclere, we may as well compromise matters.'

'I think so too. It becomes a lady to make a virtue of a necessity.'

'It was stratagem against stratagem. Mine was ingenious; yours was masterly! Accept my acknowledgment. We will enter upon an armed neutrality.'

'No. Let me be your adorer and slave again, as ever. Your beauty, dearest, covers everything! You are my mistress and queen! But here we are at the door. Tea is prepared for us here. I have a liking for life in this cottage mode, and live here on occasion. Women, attend to Lady Mountclere.'

The woman who had seen Ethelberta in the morning was alarmed at recognizing her, having since been informed officially of the marriage: she murmured entreaties for pardon. They assisted the viscountess to a chair, the door was closed, and the wind blew past as if nobody had ever stood there to interrupt its flight.

Full of misgivings, Christopher continued to wait at the north gate. Half-past seven had long since been past, and no Ethelberta had appeared. He did not for the moment suppose the delay to be hers, and this gave him patience; having taken up the position, he was induced by fidelity to abide by the consequences. It would be only a journey of two hours to reach Anglebury Station; he would ride outside with the driver, put her into the train, and bid her adieu for ever. She had cried for help, and he had heard her cry.

At last through the trees came the sound of the Court clock striking eight, and then, for the first time, a doubt arose in his mind whether she could have mistaken the gate. She had distinctly told Sol the west lodge; her note had expressed the north lodge. Could she by any accident have written one thing while meaning another? He entered the carriage, and drove round to the west gate. All was as silent there as at the other, the meeting between Ethelberta and Lord Mountclere being then long past; and he drove back again.

He left the carriage, and entered the park on foot, approaching the house slowly. All was silent; the windows were dark; moping sounds came from the trees and sky, as from Sorrow whispering to Night. By this time he felt assured that the scheme had miscarried. While he stood here a carriage without lights came up the drive; it turned in towards the stable-yard without going to the door. The carriage had plainly been empty.

Returning across the grass by the way he had come, he was startled by the voices of two men from the road hard by.

'Have ye zeed anybody?'

'Not a soul.'

'Shall we go across again?'

'What's the good? let's home to supper.'

'My lord must have heard somebody, or 'a wouldn't have said it.'

'Perhaps he's nervous now he's living in the cottage again. I thought that fancy was over. Well, I'm glad 'tis a young wife he's brought us. She'll have her routs and her rackets as well as the high-born ones, you'll see, as soon as she gets used to the place.'

'She must be a queer Christian to pick up with him.'

'Well, if she've charity 'tis enough for us poor men; her faith and hope may be as please God. Now I'm for on-along homeward.'

As soon as they had gone Christopher moved from his hiding, and, avoiding the gravel-walk, returned to his coachman, telling him to drive at once to Anglebury.

Julian was so impatient of the futility of his adventure that he wished to annihilate its existence. On reaching Anglebury he determined to get on at once to Melchester, that the event of the night might be summarily ended; to be still in the neighbourhood was to be still engaged in it. He reached home before midnight.

Walking into their house near the quiet Close, as dissatisfied with himself as a man well could be who still retained health and an occupation, he found Faith sitting up as usual. His news was simple: the marriage had taken place before he could get there, and he had seen nothing of either ceremony or viscountess. The remainder he reserved for a more convenient season.

Faith looked anxiously at him as he ate supper, smiling now and then.

'Well, I am tired of this life,' said Christopher.

'So am I,' said Faith. 'Ah, if we were only rich!'

'Ah, yes.'

'Or if we were not rich,' she said, turning her eyes to the fire. 'If we were only slightly provided for, it would be better than nothing. How much would you be content with, Kit?'

'As much as I could get.'

'Would you be content with a thousand a year for both of us?'

'I daresay I should,' he murmured, breaking his bread.

'Or five hundred for both?'

'Or five hundred.'

'Or even three hundred?'

'Bother three hundred. Less than double the sum would not satisfy me. We may as well imagine much as little.'

Faith's countenance had fallen. 'O Kit,' she said, 'you always disappoint me.'

'I do. How do I disappoint you this time?'

'By not caring for three hundred a year – a hundred and fifty each – when that is all I have to offer you.'

'Faith!' said he, looking up for the first time. 'Ah – of course! Lucy's will. I had forgotten.'

'It is true, and I had prepared such a pleasant surprise for you, and now you don't care! Our cousin Lucy did leave us something after all. I don't understand the exact total sum, but it comes to a hundred and fifty a year each – more than I expected, though not so much as you deserved. Here's the letter. I have been dwelling upon it all day, and thinking what a pleasure it would be; and it is not after all!'

'Good gracious, Faith, I was only supposing. The real thing is another matter altogether. Well, the idea of Lucy's will containing our names! I am sure I would have gone to the funeral had I known.'

'I wish it were a thousand.'

'O no – it doesn't matter at all. But, certainly, three hundred for two is a tantalizing sum: not enough to enable us to change our condition, and enough to make us dissatisfied with going on as we are.'

'We must forget we have it, and let it increase.'

'It isn't enough to increase much. We may as well use it. But how? Take a bigger house – what's the use? Give up the organ? – then I shall be rather worse off than I am at present. Positively, it is the most provoking amount anybody could have invented had they tried ever so long. Poor Lucy, to do that, and not even to come near us when father died . . . Ah, I know what we'll do. We'll go abroad – we'll live in Italy.'

Anglebury
Enckworth
Sandbourne

SEQUEL

Two years and a half after the marriage of Ethelberta, and the evening adventures which followed it, a man young in years, though considerably oldened in mood and expression, walked up to the 'Red Lion' Inn at Anglebury. The anachronism sat not unbecomingly upon him, and the voice was precisely that of the Christopher Julian of heretofore. His way of entering the inn and calling for a conveyance was more off-hand than formerly; he was much less afraid of the sound of his own voice now than when he had gone through the same performance on a certain chill evening the last time that he visited the spot. He wanted to be taken to Knollsea to meet the steamer there, and was not coming back by the same vehicle.

It was a very different day from that of his previous journey along the same road; different in season; different in weather; and the humour of the observer differed yet more widely from its condition then than did the landscape from its former hues. In due time they reached a commanding situation upon the road, from which were visible knots and plantations of trees on the Enckworth manor. Christopher broke the silence.

'Lord Mountclere is still alive and well, I am told?'

'O ay. He'll live to be a hundred. Never such a change as has come over the man of late years.'

'Indeed!'

'O, 'tis my lady. She's a one to put up with! Still, 'tis said here and there that marrying her was the best day's work that he ever did in his life, although she's got to be my lord and my lady both.'

'Is she happy with him?'

'She is very sharp with the poor man – about happy I don't know. He was a good-natured old man, for all his sins, and would sooner any day lay out money in new presents than pay it in old debts. But 'tis altered now. 'Tisn't the same place. Ah, in the old times I have seen the floor of the servants' hall over the vamp* of your boot in solid beer that we had poured outside the horns because we couldn't see straight enough to pour it in. See? No, we couldn't see a hole in a ladder! And now, even at Christmas or Whitsuntide, when a man, if ever he desires to be overcome with a drop, would naturally wish it to be, you can walk out of Enckworth as straight as you walked in. All her doings.'

'Then she holds the reins?'

'She do! There was a little tussle at first; but how could a old man hold his own against such a spry young body as that! She threatened to run away from him, and kicked up Bob's-a-dying,* and I don't know what all; and being the woman, of course she was sure to beat in the long run. Poor old nobleman, she marches him off to church every Sunday as regular as a clock, makes him read family prayers that haven't been read in Enckworth for the last thirty years to my certain knowledge, and keeps him down to three glasses of wine a day, strict, so that you never see him any the more generous for liquor or a bit elevated at all, as it used to be. There, 'tis true, it has done him good in one sense, for they say he'd have been dead in five years if he had gone on as he was going.'

'So that she's a good wife to him, after all.'

'Well, if she had been a little worse 'twould have been a little better for him in one sense, for he would have had his own way more. But he was a curious feller at one time, as we all know, and I suppose 'tis as much as he can expect; but 'tis a strange reverse for him. It is said that when he's asked out to dine, or to anything in the way of a jaunt, his eye flies across to hers afore he answers: and if her eye says yes, he says yes: and if her eye says no, he says no. 'Tis a sad condition for one who ruled womankind as he, that a woman should lead him in a string whether he will or no.'

'Sad indeed!'

'She's steward, and agent, and everything. She has got a room called "my lady's office" and great ledgers and cash-books you never see the like. In old times there were bailiffs to look after the workfolk, foremen to look after the tradesmen, a building-steward to look after the foremen, a land-steward to look after the building-steward, and a dashing grand agent to look after the land-steward: fine times they had then, I assure 'ee! My lady said they were eating out the property like a honeycomb, and then there was a terrible row. Half of 'em were sent flying; and now there's only the agent, and the viscountess, and a sort of surveyor man, and of the three she does most work, so 'tis said. She marks the trees to be felled, settles what horses are to be sold and bought, and is out in all winds and weathers. There, if somebody hadn't looked into things 'twould soon have been all up with his lordship, he was so very extravagant. In one sense 'twas lucky for him that she was born in humble life, because owing to it she knows the ins and outs of contriving, which he never did.'

'Then a man on the verge of bankruptcy will do better to marry a poor and sensible wife than a rich and stupid one. Well, here we are at the seventh milestone. I will walk the remainder of the distance to Knollsea, as there is ample time for meeting the last steamboat.'

When the man was gone Christopher proceeded slowly on foot down the hill, and reached that part of the highway at which he had stopped in the cold November breeze waiting for a woman who never came. He was older now, and he had ceased to wish that he had not been disappointed. There was the lodge, and around it were the trees, brilliant in the shining greens of June. Every twig sustained its bird, and every blossom its bee. The roadside was not muffled in a garment of dead leaves as it had been then, and the lodge-gate was not open as it always used to be. He paused to look through the bars. The drive was well kept and gravelled; the grass edgings, formerly marked by hoofs and ruts, and otherwise trodden away, were now green and luxuriant, bent sticks being placed at intervals as a protection.

While he looked through the gate a woman stepped from the lodge to open it. In her haste she nearly swung the gate into his face, and would have completely done so had he not jumped back.

'I beg pardon, sir,' she said, on perceiving him. 'I was going to open it for my lady, and I didn't see you.'

Christopher moved round the corner. The perpetual snubbing that he had received from Ethelberta ever since he had known her seemed about to be continued through the medium of her dependents.

A trotting, accompanied by the sound of light wheels, had become perceptible; and then a vehicle came through the gate, and turned up the road which he had come down. He saw the back of a basket carriage, drawn by a pair of piebald ponies. A lad in livery sat behind with folded arms; the driver was a lady. He saw her bonnet, her shoulders, her hair – but no more. She lessened in his gaze, and was soon out of sight.

He stood a long time thinking; but he did not wish her his.

In this wholesome frame of mind he proceeded on his way, thankful that he had escaped meeting her, though so narrowly. But perhaps at this remote season the embarrassment of a rencounter would not have been intense. At Knollsea he entered the steamer for Sandbourne.

Mr Chickerel and his family now lived at Firtop Villa in that place, a house which, like many others, had been built since Julian's last visit to the town. He was directed to the outskirts, and into a fir plantation where drives and intersecting roads had been laid out, and where new villas had sprung up like mushrooms. He entered by a swing gate, on which 'Firtop' was painted, and a maid-servant showed him into a neatly-furnished room, containing Mr Chickerel, Mrs Chickerel, and Picotee, the matron being reclined on a couch, which improved health had permitted her to substitute for a bed.

He had been expected, and all were glad to see again the sojourner in foreign lands, even down to the lady-like tabby, who was all purr and warmth towards him except when she was all claws and coldness. But had the prime sentiment of the meeting shown itself it would have been the unqualified surprise of Christopher at seeing how much Picotee's face had grown to resemble her sister's: it was less a resemblance in contours than in expression and tone.

They had an early tea, and then Mr Chickerel, sitting in a patriarchal chair, conversed pleasantly with his guest, being well acquainted with him through other members of the family. They talked of Julian's residence at different Italian towns with his sister; of Faith, who was at the present moment staying with some old friends in Melchester; and, as was inevitable, the discourse hovered over and settled upon Ethelberta, the prime ruler of the courses of them all, with little exception, through recent years.

'It was a hard struggle for her,' said Chickerel, looking reflectively out at the fir trees. 'I never thought the girl would have got through it. When she first entered the house everybody was against her. She had to fight a whole host of them single-handed. There was the viscount's brother, other relations, lawyers, ladies, servants, not one of them was her friend; and not one who wouldn't rather have seen her arrive there in evil relationship with him than as she did come. But she stood her ground. She was put upon her mettle; and one by one they got to feel there was somebody among them whose little finger, if they insulted her, was thicker than a Mountclere's loins.* She must have had a will of iron; it was a situation that would have broken the hearts of a dozen ordinary women, for everybody soon knew that we were of no family, and that's what made it so hard for her. But there she is as mistress now, and everybody respecting her. I sometimes fancy she is occasionally too severe with the servants, and I know what service is. But she says it is necessary, owing to her birth; and perhaps she is right.'

'I suppose she often comes to see you?'

'Four or five times a year,' said Picotee.

'She cannot come quite so often as she would,' said Mrs Chickerel, 'because of her lofty position, which has its juties. Well, as I always say, Berta doesn't take after me. I couldn't have married the man even though he did bring a coronet with him.'

'I shouldn't have cared to let him ask 'ee,' said Chickerel. 'However, that's neither here nor there – all ended better than I expected. He's fond of her.'

'And it is wonderful what can be done with an old man when you are his darling,' said Mrs Chickerel.

'If I were Berta I should go to London oftener,' said Picotee, to turn the conversation. 'But she lives mostly in the library. And, O, what do you think? She is writing an epic poem, and employs Emmeline as her reader.'

'Dear me. And how are Sol and Dan? You mentioned them once in your letters,' said Christopher.

'Berta has set them up as builders in London.'

'She bought a business for them,' said Chickerel. 'But Sol wouldn't accept her help for a long time, and now he has only agreed to it on condition of paying her back the money with interest, which he is doing. They have just signed a contract to build a hospital for twenty thousand pounds.'*

Picotee broke in – 'You knew that both Gwendoline and Cornelia married two years ago, and went to Queensland? They married two brothers, who were farmers, and left England the following week. Georgie and Myrtle are at school.'

'And Joey?'

'We are thinking of making Joseph a parson,' said Mrs Chickerel.

'Indeed! a parson.'

'Yes; 'tis a genteel living for the boy. And he's talents that way. Since he has been under masters he knows all the strange sounds the old Romans and Greeks used to make by way of talking, and the love stories of the ancient women as if they were his own. I assure you, Mr Julian, if you could hear how beautiful the boy tells about little Cupid with his bow and arrows, and the rows between that pagan apostle Jupiter and his wife because of another woman, and the handsome young gods who kissed Venus, you'd say he deserved to be made a bishop* at once!'

The evening advanced, and they walked in the garden. Here, by some means, Picotee and Christopher found themselves alone.

'Your letters to my sister have been charming,' said Christopher. 'And so regular, too. It was as good as a birthday every time one arrived.'

Picotee blushed and said nothing.

Christopher had full assurance that her heart was where it had always been. A suspicion of the fact had been the reason of his visit here today.

'Other letters were once written from England to Italy, and they acquired great celebrity. Do you know whose?'

'Walpole's?'* said Picotee timidly.

'Yes; but they never charmed me half as much as yours. You may rest assured that one person in the world thinks Walpole your second.'

'You should not have read them; they were not written to you. But I suppose you wished to hear of Ethelberta?'

'At first I did,' said Christopher. 'But, oddly enough, I got more interested in the writer than in her news. I don't know if ever before there has been an instance of loving by means of letters; if not, it is because there have never been such sweet ones written. At last I looked for them more anxiously than Faith.'

'You see, you knew me before.' Picotee would have withdrawn this remark if she could, fearing that it seemed like a suggestion of her love long ago.

'Then, on my return, I thought I would just call and see you, and go away and think what would be best for me to do with a view to the future. But since I have been here I have felt that I could not go away to think without first asking you what you think on one point – whether you could ever marry me?'

'I thought you would ask that when I first saw you.'

'Did you. Why?'

'You looked at me as if you would.'

'Well,' continued Christopher, 'the worst of it is I am as poor as Job.* Faith and I have three hundred a year between us, but only half is mine. So that before I get your promise I must let your father know how poor I am. Besides what I mention, I have only my earnings by music. But I am to be installed as chief organist at Melchester soon, instead of deputy, as I used to be; which is something.'

'I am to have five hundred pounds when I marry. That was Lord Mountclere's arrangement with Ethelberta. He is extremely anxious that I should marry well.'

'That's infortunate. A marriage with me will hardly be considered well.'

'O yes, it will,' said Picotee quickly, and then looked frightened.

Christopher drew her towards him, and imprinted a kiss upon her cheek, at which Picotee was not so wretched as she had been some years before when he mistook her for another in that performance.

'Berta will never let us come to want,' she said, with vivacity, when she had recovered. 'She always gives me what is necessary.'

'We will endeavour not to trouble her,' said Christopher, amused by Picotee's utter dependence now as ever upon her sister, as upon an eternal Providence. 'However, it is well to be kin to a coach though you never ride in it. Now, shall we go indoors to your father? You think he will not object?'

'I think he will be very glad,' replied Picotee. 'Berta will, I know.'

THE END

GENERAL PREFACE TO THE
WESSEX EDITION OF 1912

In accepting a proposal for a definite edition of these productions in prose and verse I have found an opportunity of classifying the novels under heads that show approximately the author's aim, if not his achievement, in each book of the series at the date of its composition. Sometimes the aim was lower than at other times; sometimes, where the intention was primarily high, force of circumstances (among which the chief were the necessities of magazine publication) compelled a modification, great or slight, of the original plan. Of a few, however, of the longer novels, and of many of the shorter tales, it may be assumed that they stand to-day much as they would have stood if no accidents had obstructed the channel between the writer and the public. That many of them, if any, stand as they would stand if written *now* is not to be supposed.

In the classification of these fictitious chronicles – for which the name of 'The Wessex Novels' was adopted, and is still retained – the first group is called 'Novels of Character and Environment', and contains those which approach most nearly to uninfluenced works; also one or two which, whatever their quality in some few of their episodes, may claim a verisimilitude in general treatment and detail.

The second group is distinguished as 'Romances and Fantasies', a sufficiently descriptive definition. The third class – 'Novels of Ingenuity' – show a not infrequent disregard of the probable in the chain of events, and depend for their interest mainly on the incidents themselves. They might also be characterized as 'Experiments', and were written for the nonce simply; though despite the artificiality of their fable some of their scenes are not without fidelity to life.*

---

* Novels of Character and Environment: *Under the Greenwood Tree, Far from the Madding Crowd, The Return of the Native, The Mayor of Caster-bridge, The Woodlanders, Wessex Tales, Tess of the d'Urbervilles, Life's Little*

It will not be supposed that these differences are distinctly perceptible in every page of every volume. It was inevitable that blendings and alternations should occur in all. Moreover, as it was not thought desirable in every instance to change the arrangement of the shorter stories to which readers have grown accustomed, certain of these may be found under headings to which an acute judgment might deny appropriateness.

It has sometimes been conceived of novels that evolve their action on a circumscribed scene – as do many (though not all) of these – that they cannot be so inclusive in their exhibition of human nature as novels wherein the scenes cover large extents of country, in which events figure amid towns and cities, even wander over the four quarters of the globe. I am not concerned to argue this point further than to suggest that the conception is an untrue one in respect of the elementary passions. But I would state that the geographical limits of the stage here trodden were not absolutely forced upon the writer by circumstances: he forced them upon himself from judgment. I considered that our magnificent heritage from the Greeks in dramatic literature found sufficient room for a large proportion of its action in an extent of their country not much larger than the half-dozen counties here reunited under the old name of Wessex, that the domestic emotions have throbbed in Wessex nooks with as much intensity as in the palaces of Europe, and that, anyhow, there was quite enough human nature in Wessex for one man's literary purpose. So far was I possessed by this idea that I kept within the frontiers when it would have been easier to overlap them and give more cosmopolitan features to the narrative.

Thus, though the people in most of the novels (and in much of the shorter verse) are dwellers in a province bounded on the north by the Thames, on the south by the English Channel, on the east by a line running from Hayling Island to Windsor Forest, and on the west by the Cornish coast, they were meant to be typically and essentially those of any and ever place where

Thought's the slave of life, and life time's fool

Ironies, Jude the Obscure.
    Romances and Fantasies: A Pair of Blue Eyes, The Trumpet-Major, Two on a Tower, A Group of Noble Dames, The Well-Beloved.
    Novels of Ingenuity: Desperate Remedies, The Hand of Ethelberta, A Laodicean. [Editor's note]

– beings in whose hearts and minds that which is apparently local should be really universal. But whatever the success of this intention, and the value of these novels as delineations of humanity, they have at least a humble supplementary quality of which I may be justified in reminding the reader, though it is one that was quite unintentional and unforeseen. At the dates represented in the various narrations things were like that in Wessex: the inhabitants lived in certain ways, engaged in certain occupations, kept alive certain customs, just as they are shown doing in these pages. And in particularizing such I have often been reminded of Boswell's remarks on the trouble to which he was put and the pilgrimages he was obliged to make to authenticate some details, though the labour was one which would bring him no praise. Unlike his achievement, however, on which an error would as he says have brought discredit, if these country customs and vocations, obsolete and obsolescent, had been detailed wrongly, nobody would have discovered such errors to the end of Time. Yet I have instituted inquiries to correct tricks of memory, and striven against temptations to exaggerate, in order to preserve for my own satisfaction a fairly true record of a vanishing life.

It is advisable also to state here, in response to inquiries from readers interested in landscape, prehistoric antiquities, and especially old English architecture, that the description of these backgrounds has been done from the real – that is to say, has something real for its basis, however illusively treated. Many features of the first two kinds have been given under their existing names; for instance, the Vale of Blackmoor or Blake-more, Hambledon Hill, Bulbarrow, Nettlecombe Tout, Dogbury Hill, High-Stoy, Bubb-Down Hill, The Devil's Kitchen, Cross-in-Hand, Long-Ash Lane, Benvill Lane, Giant's Hill, Crimmer-crock Lane, and Stonehenge. The rivers Froom, or Frome, and Stour, are, of course, well known as such. And the further idea was that large towns and points tending to mark the outline of Wessex – such as Bath, Plymouth, The Start, Portland Bill, Southampton, etc. – should be named clearly. The scheme was not greatly elaborated, but, whatever its value, the names remain still.

In respect of places described under fictitious or ancient names in the novels – for reasons that seemed good at the time of writing them – and kept up in the poems – discerning people have affirmed in print that they clearly recognize the originals: such as Shaftesbury in 'Shaston', Sturminster Newton in 'Stourcastle', Dorchester in 'Casterbridge', Salisbury Plain in 'The Great Plain', Cranborne Chase in 'The Chase', Beaminster in 'Emminster', Bere Regis in 'Kingsbere', Woodbury Hill in 'Greenhill', Wool Bridge in 'Wellbridge', Harfoot or Harput Lane in 'Stagfoot Lane', Hazlebury in 'Nuttlebury', Bridport in 'Port Bredy', Maiden Newton in 'Chalk Newton', a farm near Nettlecomb Tout in 'Flintcomb Ash', Sherborne in 'Sherton Abbas', Milton Abbey in 'Middleton Abbey', Cerne Abbas in 'Abbot's Cernel', Evershot in 'Evershed', Taunton in 'Toneborough', Bournemouth in 'Sandbourne', Winchester in 'Wintoncester', Oxford in 'Christminster', Reading in 'Aldbrickham', Newbury in 'Kennetbridge', Wantage in 'Alfredston', Basingstoke in 'Stoke Barehills', and so on. Subject to the qualifications above given, that no detail is guaranteed – that the portraiture of fictitiously named towns and villages was only suggested by certain real places, and wantonly wanders from inventorial descriptions of them – I do not contradict these keen hunters for the real; I am satisfied with their statements as at least an indication of their interest in the scenes.

Thus much for the novels. Turning now to the verse – to myself the more individual part of my literary fruitage – I would say that, unlike some of the fiction, nothing interfered with the writer's freedom in respect of its form or content. Several of the poems – indeed many – were produced before novel-writing had been thought of as a pursuit; but few saw the light till all the novels had been published. The limited stage to which the majority of the latter confine their exhibitions has not been adhered to here in the same proportion, the dramatic part especially having a very broad theatre of action. It may thus relieve the circumscribed areas treated in the prose, if such relief be needed. To be sure, one might argue that by surveying Europe from a celestial point of vision – as in *The Dynasts* – that continent becomes virtually a province – a Wessex, an Attica, even a mere garden – and hence is made to conform to the principle of the novels, however far it outmeasures their region. But that may be as it will.

The few volumes filled by the verse cover a producing period of some eighteen years first and last, while the seventeen or more volumes of novels represent correspondingly about four-and-twenty years. One is reminded by this disproportion in time and result how much more concise and quintessential expression becomes when given in rhythmic form than when shaped in the language of prose.

One word on what has been call the present writer's philosophy of life, as exhibited more particularly in this metrical section of his compositions. Positive views on the Whence and the Wherefore of things have never been advanced by this pen as a consistent philosophy. Nor is it likely, indeed, that imaginative writings extended over more than forty years would exhibit a coherent scientific theory of the universe even if it had been attempted – of that universe concerning which Spencer owns to the 'paralysing thought' that possibly there exists no comprehension of it anywhere. But such objectless consistency never has been attempted, and the sentiments in the following pages have been stated truly to be mere impressions of the moment, and not convictions or arguments.

That these impressions have been condemned as 'pessimistic' – as if that were a very wicked adjective – shows a curious muddle-mindedness. It must be obvious that there is a higher characteristic of philosophy than pessimism, or than meliorism, or even than the optimism of these critics – which is truth. Existence is either ordered in a certain way, or it is not so ordered, and conjectures which harmonize best with experience are removed above all comparison with other conjectures which do not so harmonize. So that to say one view is worse than other views without proving it erroneous implies the possibility of a false view being better or more expedient than a true view; and no pragmatic proppings can make that *idolum specus* stand on its feet, for it postulates a prescience denied to humanity.

And there is another consideration. Differing natures find their tongue in the presence of differing spectacles. Some natures become vocal at tragedy, some are made vocal by comedy, and it seems to me that to whichever of these aspects of life a writer's instinct for expression the more readily responds, to that he should allow it to respond. That before a contrasting side of things he remains undemonstrative need not be assumed to mean that he remains unperceiving.

It was my hope to add to these volumes of verse as many more as would make a fairly comprehensive cycle of the whole. I had wished that those in dramatic, ballad, and narrative form should include most of the cardinal situations which occur in social and public life, and those in lyric form a round of emotional experiences of some completeness. But

> The petty done, the undone vast!

The more written the more seems to remain to be written; and the night cometh. I realize that these hopes and plans, except possibly to the extent of a volume or two, must remain unfulfilled.

October 1911
T.H.

NOTES

p. iii *Vitae post-scenia celant*: (Latin) They hide the back-stage activities of life. This is taken from Lucretius, *De Rerum Natura*, Book IV, l. 1186. The whole line, in R. E. Latham's translation, runs: '[Women] are at pains to hide all the back-stage activities of life from those whom they wish to keep fast bound in the bonds of love.'

p. xxxvi on the stage: Hardy writes in his autobiography that 'a similar situation has been applauded in a play in recent years by Mr Bernard Shaw, without any sense of improbability,' presumably referring to *You Never Can Tell* (1895).

p. 4 Odd nation dang: God, damnation, damn.

p. 4 mullioned and transomed: a mullion is a vertical bar dividing the lights in a window; a transom is a horizontal bar across a mullioned window.

p. 4 moulded parapet: low wall or barrier, placed at the edge of a balcony, roof, etc., with continuous ornamental lines of grooving or projections.

p. 5 boaming: (dialect) travelling.

p. 5 stoor: (dialect) stir.

p. 5 buckle: elaborate, artificial styling of the hair, all crisped and curled.

p. 5 Lord Mayor's Show: an annual procession, featuring great pageantry, in honour of the Lord Mayor of London.

p. 5 Chok' it all: a mild oath; probably from 'May I be choked!' (F. B. Pinion, *A Thomas Hardy Dictionary*).

p. 6 bandy: heavy stick with a bent end, which was once used for spreading manure in the fields.

p. 6 upon my song: (dialect) upon my word.

p. 6 lynes: (dialect) loins.

p. 6 **Work . . . more:** traditional rhyme.

p. 6 **church-hatch:** church gate

p. 6 **nabs:** vain, pretentious person; here a term of jocular familiarity.

p. 6 **canticle:** mistakenly used for 'cant', meaning 'stock phrase'.

p. 7 **duck-hawks:** marsh-harriers or moor-buzzards.

p. 9 **pugree:** (variant of 'puggree' or 'puggaree', meaning an Indian turban) a scarf of thin muslin or a silk veil wound round the crown of a sun-helmet or hat and falling down behind as a shade.

p. 11 **portionless:** without a dowry, penniless.

p. 15 **tire-women:** ladies' maids.

p. 15 **cut:** that is, the pages had been cut open with a paper-knife.

p. 16 **rule-of-three:** (mathematics) a method of finding a fourth number from three given numbers, of which the first is in the same proportion to the second as the third is to the unknown fourth.

p. 17 *vers de société*: (French) light verse dealing with upper-class social life, usually in a playful vein of satire.

p. 17 **justify the ways of girls to men:** adapting Milton's *Paradise Lost*, Book I, l. 26: 'And justify the ways of God to men.'

p. 17 **Sir Thomas Wyatt:** lyric poet (1503–42).

p. 19 **Sappho smiled on Phaon:** the Greek poetess Sappho (born c. 600 BC) was, legend has it, charmed by Phaon, a boatman, who had been made beautiful by Venus.

p. 20 **four large letter X's:** mark indicating the strongest malt brew.

p. 22 **lady-apples:** small apples with red, waxy-looking skins.

p. 24 **pupil-teacher:** a boy or girl preparing to be a teacher was employed during training in an elementary school, also receiving lessons, usually from the head teacher.

p. 24 **their own family game:** skimming the water like a flat stone, as in the boys' game 'ducks and drakes'.

p. 26 **Tussaud complexion:** pink and white, like a waxwork. Madame Tussaud opened the famous London waxwork musuem in 1835.

p. 26 hung higher up on the Academy walls: that is, in the least prestigious place in the annual Royal Academy Exhibition.

p. 26 hand-post: guide-post where roads separated.

p. 27 Egyptian plague of darkness: see Exodus 10: 21.

p. 30 Salamanca: in Spain, where Wellington defeated the French in 1812.

p. 32 Venus knot: coiled and knotted hair like that of Venus in classical statues.

p. 34 transformation scene: instantaneous change of a scene in a pantomime. Here the reference is to the change effected by the use of stage lighting. In the second half of the nineteenth century the usual method was the 'transparency', which 'when lit from the front was as opaque as canvas, but faded from sight when lit from behind' (Phyllis Hartnoll and Peter Found, *The Concise Oxford Companion to the Theatre*).

p. 35 fillet: narrow flat band used for the separation of one moulding from another.

p. 35 quirk: acute hollow between the convex part of certain mouldings and the fillet.

p. 35 arris: sharp edge formed by the angular contact of two surfaces.

p. 35 In shadowy thoroughfares of thought: from Tennyson's *In Memoriam*, LXX.

p. 35 squirrel-coloured: tawny, the colour of the red squirrel.

p. 36 commandments: especially the tenth: 'thou shalt not covet thy neighbour's wife' (Exodus 20: 17).

p. 40 continue harmless ... serpent: see Matthew 10: 16: 'be ye therefore wise as serpents, and harmless as doves'.

p. 43 Anacreontic: lyrical and elegant, in the manner of the Greek poet Anacreon (6th century BC).

p. 43 spondees and iambics: a spondee is a metrical unit consisting of two stressed syllables, an iambic consisting of an unstressed syllable followed by a stressed one.

p. 44 *Seven Days' Review*: a facetious reference to the *Fortnightly Review*, a very distinguished literary journal.

p. 44 **going in for Westminster Abbey**: seeking fame as a poet, and a burial place in Poets' Corner there.

p. 45 **his Ancient**: in Shakespeare's tragedy Iago, the ancient (ensign), deceives Othello into murdering Desdemona.

p. 45 **Sappho**: see note to p. 19 above: here meaning 'a poetess'.

p. 48 **him who can cite Scripture for his purposes**: the Devil. See Shakespeare's *The Merchant of Venice*, I, iii, 93 and Matthew 4: 6.

p. 50 **area-door**: an area is a sunken court, generally at the front of a city house, railed off from the street, approached from ground level by steps, and giving access and light to the basement storey. An area-door is an entrance-door in the basement, used by servants and tradesmen.

p. 52 **What great . . . prattle of**: Shakespeare's *Twelfth Night*, I, ii, 33.

p. 57 **lustrum**: period of five years (from an ancient Roman sacrificial rite performed every five years after a census had been taken).

p. 59 *virginibus puerisque*: (Latin) for maidens and boys. See Horace, *Odes*, Book III, Ode I, l. 4.

p. 63 **'The Shortest Way with the Dissenters'**: a satiric pamphlet by Daniel Defoe (1702), himself a dissenter, in which he ridiculed the Church of England. See also note to p. 82 below.

p. 68 **Naomi . . . Ruth**: in the biblical story, after the death of her husband (Naomi's son), Ruth comes to know Boaz, and marries him.

p. 71 **Come . . . consent**: from Shakespeare's *As You Like It*, IV, i, 65–6.

p. 75 **nitches**: (dialect) bundles.

p. 75 **martel**: (dialect) mortal.

p. 75 **the old feller himself**: the Devil.

p. 75 **chiel**: (dialect) child.

p. 75 **Tom-rig or Jack-straw**: any ordinary man.

p. 76 Gothic style of the late revival: most notably under Augustus Pugin (1812–52).

p. 77 celebrate: mistakenly used for 'celebrated'.

p. 79 Blindman's buff: children's game in which the blindfolded one tries to catch the others.

p. 82 De Foe: Daniel Defoe (1660–1731), novelist and journalist. Interestingly, Hardy himself had an unpublished novel, *The Poor Man and the Lady*, possibly written in the first person, the style of which, as he tells us in his autobiography, had 'the affected simplicity of Defoe's'.

p. 83 tell my tales before a London public: Michael Millgate suggests that here Hardy may have been remembering one Julia Corke, whose story-telling performance 'he had heard of and perhaps seen in the 1860s' in London (*Thomas Hardy: A Biography*, p. 173).

p. 84 apsidal: of the form or nature of an apse, a semi-circular or polygonal recess.

p. 85 snapdragon: a Christmas game in which raisins are snatched from a bowl or dish of burning brandy.

p. 86 brougham: one-horse closed carriage, used chiefly by the socially prestigious.

p. 88 flat tints: matt paints.

p. 88 A wink ... nod: a proverbial expression, meaning 'I can see what you mean. A hint is all that is necessary.'

p. 89 ciphering: arithmetic.

p. 94 drilled-in: sown by an agricultural machine-drill.

p. 94 watering-place: seaside resort, where there are rows of sea-front houses with bow-windows (intended to give the widest possible prospect of the sea).

p. 95 modern critic: Leslie Stephen, in his essay on Defoe, published in 1868, and reprinted in *Hours in a Library*, 1st series, in 1874. As Charles Swann suggests, Hardy 'is making a graceful if private compliment to his editor/friend'. See his article, 'Hardy, Defoe, and Leslie Stephen', *Notes and Queries* (June 1995), 203–4.

p. 95 *vivâ-voce*: (Latin) oral.

p. 97 quiz: regard with an air of mockery, make fun of.

p. 99 bloody sun: an allusion to Coleridge's *The Rime of the Ancient Mariner*, ll. 111–14 (1817 text):

> All in a hot and copper sky,
> The bloody Sun, at noon,
> Right up above the mast did stand,
> No bigger than the Moon.

p. 101 artistic ... present day: this probably refers, as Robert Gittings suggests in his Notes to the New Wessex edition, to the type of design advocated by the 'arts and crafts movement', led by William Morris.

p. 103 As long ... sorrow: from Shelley's *Adonaïs*, XXI.

p. 108 things to dream of, not to tell: an allusion to Coleridge's 'Christabel' (l. 253): 'A sight to dream of, not to tell!'

p. 109 Juliet ... know of it: see Shakespeare's *Romeo and Juliet*, II, ii, 85–106.

p. 113 knots: knotty points, problems.

p. 114 elusions: evading of specific commands or laws.

p. 114 diapason: the interval of an octave; here meaning 'all the notes'.

p. 115 below stairs: in the servants' quarters.

p. 117 calendared saints: saints officially recognized by the Church, whose festive days are included in the Church Calendar.

p. 119 bull's-eye: a lantern with a thick convex lens for concentrating the rays of light; especially used by the police.

p. 122 happy ... debt: an adaptation of a proverbial expression, 'Happy is the country which has no history.'

p. 123 action for breach: under English law it was formerly possible to bring a suit for breach of promise to marry. The most famous fictional example is perhaps the case of Bardell against Pickwick in Dickens's *Pickwick Papers* (1837).

p. 123 flat: simpleton.

p. 124 without her bonnet: that is, with her bridal veil.

p. 125 the University boat-race: the Oxford and Cambridge boat-race, held on the Thames in London. Hardy and his wife attended the race of March 1875.

p. 130 Northern Lights: aurora borealis; bands or arches of coloured light in the night sky seen in the most northern parts of the world.

p. 130 nigger performance: minstrel show with white performers made up as blacks.

p. 131 civil d——: cursing ('damn') under his breath.

p. 132 legitimate drama: straight drama performed at the Patent Theatres of Covent Garden and Drury Lane, as opposed to melodrama, farce, pantomime, etc.

p. 133 too old a bird: an experienced person who is not easily deceived. There is an old saying, 'An old bird is not caught with chaff.'

p. 140 her hermit spirit ... dwell apart: this may be echoing a line from Wordsworth: 'Thy soul was like a Star, and dwelt apart.' Hardy quotes from the same poem in Chapter 27. See note to p. 166 below.

p. 141 dead-reckoner: one who estimates a ship's position from the distance run by the log and the courses steered by the compass, with corrections for current, leeway, etc., but without astronomical observations (*The Oxford English Dictionary*).

p. 142 Enfeoffed ... too much: Shakespeare's *I Henry IV*, III, ii, 69–73.

p. 143 Dryden ... on Providence: an allusion to John Dryden's poem, 'To my Dear Friend Mr Congreve, On His Comedy, call'd, *The Double-Dealer*' (1694), ll. 69–70:

> Unprofitably kept at Heav'ns expence,
> I live a Rent-charge on his Providence:

A. B. Chambers and William Frost gloss this couplet thus: 'kept alive, without benefit to heaven or to myself, by God's grace' (*The Works of John Dryden, vol. 4*, 1974). 'Rent-charge' is an annuity charged by will or settlement on the rents received from an estate, payable to persons named.

p. 143 'Peerage ... 'Baronetage' ... 'House of Commons': publications such as Debrett's *Peerage of England, Scotland, and Ireland* (first published, 1802) and *The Baronetage of England (1808)*, or Edward Walford's annual compilations, *The Shilling Peerage* (first published, 1855), *The Shilling Baronetage* (1857), and *The Shilling House of Commons* (1856).

p. 143 'Landed Gentry': Sir John Bernard Burke's *A Genealogical and Heraldic Dictionary of the Landed Gentry of Great Britain & Ireland*, of which the fifth edition was published in 1875.

p. 143 Doctors' Commons: the everyday name for the College of Advocates and Doctors of Law, which dealt with the probate of wills, the issue of marriage licences, and so on; copies of wills were kept there.

p. 143 gudgeons: small fish; here, credulous, gullible persons.

p. 143 Herald: official of the Heralds' College, which keeps records of the coats of arms of noble families.

p. 143 escutcheon: coat of arms. (More precisely, an escutcheon is a ceremonial shield on which a coat of arms is painted.)

p. 143 Satan ... earth: see Job 1 and 2.

p. 143 ministering angel: a person who helps those who are sick or in trouble (see Mark 1: 13: 'And he was there in the wilderness forty days, tempted of Satan; and was with the wild beasts; and the angels ministered unto him.'); a phrase once commonly used to express the essential feminine nature.

p. 144 rookery: densely populated slum area.

p. 145 like a guilty thing surprised: from Wordsworth's ode, 'Intimations of Immortality', IX, and, of course, *Hamlet* I, i, 143.

p. 147 Atlantean: as strong as Atlas, who in Classical mythology supports the world on his shoulders.

p. 148 Nineveh: capital of the ancient Assyrian Empire, sited in what is now Iraq.

p. 148 Sennacherib: King of Assyria (704–681 BC), familiar to nineteenth-century readers through Byron's 'The Destruction of Sennacherib' (1815). For biblical references see II Kings 18: 7–8, 13–16.

p. 149 the Academy: the Royal Academy. See note to p. 26 above.

p. 149 'Farewell! ... estimate': Shakespeare's sonnet 87, ll. 1–2.

p. 150 'losing a half': losing a half day's pay.

p. 150 Zamzummims: giants. See Deuteronomy 2: 20.

p. 151 **Coryphæus:** leader of the chorus in Greek drama, hence of any sect or opinion.

p. 151 **sons and daughters could prophesy:** see Joel 2: 28.

p. 154 *primâ-facie:* (Latin) based on first impressions.

p. 155 *sangfroid:* (French) coolness, cold blood.

p. 156 **London season:** the period of the year (April to July) which brought fashionable country gentlemen to London.

p. 156 **araucarias and deodars:** one species of the former is familiarly called 'puzzle-monkey' or 'monkey-puzzle', and the latter is a sub-species of the cedar. In fact, they are not really shrubs.

p. 157 **Stygian:** of the Styx, one of the rivers of the underworld in Classical mythology: here meaning 'hellish'.

p. 158 **knacker:** one who buys worn-out or diseased horses and slaughters them for their hides and hoofs, and for making dog's meat.

p. 158 **To see the nakedness of the land:** from Genesis 42: 9.

p. 158 **indifferentist:** one who professes or practises indifference.

p. 159 **Kew:** the Royal Botanical Gardens, commonly called 'Kew Gardens'.

p. 163 **Kamtschatka:** a large peninsula in eastern Siberia.

p. 166 **Milton! . . . need of thee:** from Wordsworth's sonnet, 'London, 1802'.

p. 166 **'Life':** probably David Masson's seven-volume *Life of John Milton* (1859–94), the third volume of which was published in 1873.

p. 169 **Mammon . . . heaven:** Milton's *Paradise Lost*, Book I, ll. 678–80.

p. 169 **changes since this was written:** the church was badly burnt in the Cripplegate Fire of 1897, and in an essay, 'Memories of Church Restoration' (1906), Hardy wrote: 'One would like to know if any note has been kept of the original position of Milton's monument in Cripplegate Church, which has been moved more than once, I believe, and if the position of his rifled grave is now known. When I first saw the monument it stood near the east end of the south isle.'

p. 170 **Oliver Cromwell:** (1599–1658) politician, leader of the Parlia-mentarian army in the Civil War.

p. 171 **Bartimeus:** see Mark 10: 46–52.

p. 174 **Sphinx-like:** inscrutable like the Sphinx in Classical mythology, a monster with the head and breasts of a woman, the tail of a serpent, the wings of a bird, and the paws of a lion, who poses riddles.

p. 175 **common ... as blackberries:** cf. 'plentiful as blackberries', in Shakespeare's *I Henry IV*, II, iv, 234.

p. 175 **when her work ... placid mind:** John H. Schwarz suggests that here Hardy may have had in mind a passage from Newman's sermon, 'Wisdom and Innocence' (1843): 'May He support us all the day long, till the shades lengthen, and the evening comes, and the busy world is hushed, and the fever of life is over, and our work is done! Then in His mercy may He give us a safe lodging, and a holy rest, and peace at last!' See his article, 'An Echo of Newman in a novel by Hardy', *Thomas Hardy Yearbook* (1988), 51–4.

p. 176 **hard-handed order:** working classes.

p. 176 **pet:** fit of ill-humour.

p. 178 **'list:** enlist.

p. 179 **Husbands is rare:** women outnumbered men (according to the 1871 census, there were in England and Wales 11,653,000 females and 11,059,000 males). Added to this, the number of marriages was high, and some eligible males went overseas to the colonies.

p. 179 **sparrowgrass:** (folk-etymology) asparagus.

p. 180 **puss-in-the-corner:** a phrase derived from a children's game with five players, one of whom tries to slip into a corner when the others change places. Here it refers to a person who watches other people unseen by them.

p. 185 **bottle-holder:** the second in a fist fight, who holds a bottle of water.

p. 187 **chip-hat:** hat woven from thin slices of wood.

p. 189 **modern art-workmanship:** see note to p. 101 above.

p. 190 **jew's-harp** small musical instrument made of metal, held between the teeth and played by striking it with one finger.

p. 190 *sotto voce*: (Italian) in a subdued voice, quietly.

p. 191 **Which fashion ... scenes**: from Byron's 'The Waltz', ll. 153–4:

> The fashion hails – from countesses to queens,
> And maids and valets waltz behind the scenes.

p. 191 **unceiled**: not provided with a ceiling.

p. 198 **Guernsey frocks**: thick, knitted, woollen coats which originated in the Channel Islands, of which Guernsey is one.

p. 201 *de rigueur* (French): obligatory, required.

p. 202 **New Jerusalem**: see Revelation 21: 2.

p. 204 **last siege**: see note to p. 207 below.

p. 205 **Mephistophelian**: pertaining to Mephistopheles, the Devil to whom Faust sells his soul.

p. 206 **plate-powder**: powder for polishing silver ware.

p. 207 **history of the castle**: what follows is a history of Corfe Castle, Hardy probably drawing on John Hutchins's *The History and Antiquities of the County of Dorset* (first published, 1774) – he possessed a copy of the third edition (1861), which contains the relevant details: Matilda (1102–67), queen of England, fought her cousin Stephen (1097?–1154) after her father Henry I's death (1135); King John (1167–1216) ascended the throne in 1199, setting aside his elder brother's son Arthur (1187–1203?), Duke of Brittany; Arthur's sister, Eleanor (Alianor), was confined here with the two daughters of Alexander II (1198–1249), from approximately 1209 to 1222; Edward II (1284–1329), after being deposed in 1326, spent a short while in the castle; Elizabeth I reigned 1558–1603. The Castle was besieged by the Parliamentarians in 1645.

p. 209 **Hades**: underworld in Classical mythology.

p. 211 **moved essentially larger mountains**: an allusion to Matthew 17: 20: 'If you have faith as a grain of mustard seed, ye shall say unto this mountain, Remove hence to yonder place; and it shall remove.' See also I Corinthians 13: 2.

p. 212 **To be ... thus**: Shakespeare's *Macbeth*, III, i, 47.

p. 213 **wriggles**: (dialect) sand-eels.

p. 213 vanity and vexation: from Ecclesiastes 1: 14.

p. 214 wonders of the Deep: from Psalm 107, 24.

p. 216 *Le Follet*: a magazine published in Paris, containing elegant fashion plates.

p. 218 Danish fleet: destroyed by a heavy storm off Swanage in 877, when King Alfred was fighting the Danes.

p. 219 re'ching: reaching; sailing a vessel with the sails full and the wind blowing from astern.

p. 221 daw in eagle's plumes: upstart or pretender. In one of Aesop's fables an envious jackdaw unsuccessfully tries to emulate an eagle.

p. 222 clewing up: drawing the clews (lower corners of sails) up to the yard (a long pole that supports a square sail) in preparation for furling.

p. 225 slur in music: a bow-shaped line placed over or under two or more notes to show that they are to be played or sung smoothly and connectedly.

p. 225 cresset: an iron vessel or basket, mounted on a pole or suspended from above, containing a small flame.

p. 226 drops ... sake: see I Timothy 5: 23: 'use a little wine for thy stomach's sake'.

p. 226 table-d'hôte: common table for guests at a hotel.

p. 226 Avernus: entrance to hell in Classical mythology: here the reference is to the fires in the kitchen.

p. 226 v'la!: (French) *voilà!*: here I am.

p. 227 teetotums: toys like small spinning tops.

p. 228 present man-famine: see note to p. 179 above.

p. 228 the cathedral: Hardy visited it and other local sights on his honeymoon trip in September 1874.

p. 229 Hamlet-like ... augury: see Shakespeare's *Hamlet*, V, ii, 215–20.

p. 229 *flèche*: spire.

p. 231 lantern: small erection, open or glazed, crowning a dome or roof.

p. 232 *suisse*: (French) verger; a person who performs small duties in a church.

p. 235 **fable of the well-bonded fagot**: in one of Aesop's fables, a farmer teaches his sons the strength of unity, showing how difficult it is to break sticks bundled together, and how easy to snap a single one.

p. 236 **She shall ... my first**: from Hosea 2: 7.

p. 238 **luggers**: a lugger is a small boat with one or more lugsails.

p. 241 **Bohemianism**: unconventional behaviour typical of artists or actors.

p. 242 **portmantle**: portmanteau, a very large case for a traveller's clothes.

p. 243 **rencounters**: meetings.

p. 244 **spigot on her escutcheon**: a facetious adaptation of the phrase, 'a blot on the escutcheon', which means a cause of shame to a noble family. (See note to p. 143 above.) Here the word 'spigot' is used because Ethelberta is the daughter of a butler, one of whose duties is to take the spigot out when drawing off liquor from casks.

p. 247 **logan-stone**: rocking stone.

p. 248 **well-known treatise on Utilitarianism**: *Utilitarianism* (1863) by John Stuart Mill, whose liberal thinking had a lasting influence on Hardy.

p. 249 **Casuistry**: that part of Ethics which resolves cases of conscience.

p. 249 *disciplina arcani*: (Latin) literally, discipline of the secret: practice ascribed to the early Church of concealing certain theological doctrines and religious usages from the uninitiated.

p. 250 **Satanic school**: a phrase first used by Robert Southey in 1821 against Byron, Shelley, and their imitators, attacking their impiety and immorality.

p. 250 **last infirmity of a noble mind**: that is, Fame: see Milton's *Lycidas*, l. 71.

p. 250 **distorted Benthamism**: Jeremy Bentham (1748–1832), who famously said, 'The greatest happiness of the greatest number is the foundation of morals and religion,' thought human beings were essentially self-interested creatures, always seeking to maximize their pleasures and minimize their pains. This view is 'distorted' by Ethelberta from her reading of Mill, who criticized Bentham and tried to humanize utilitarianism by recognizing such social feelings as altruism.

p. 251 **Tierra del Fuego:** an archipelago south of South America.

p. 251 **minor canon:** a cleric attached to a cathedral who assists in performing the daily service.

p. 256 **jambs:** vertical parts of the masonry or woodwork of a door or window.

p. 256 **rick-staddles:** platforms of timber, stone, etc. on which stacks or ricks were placed.

p. 256 **foliated:** ornamented with leaf-work.

p. 256 **hooded windows:** those with roof-like projections.

p. 256 **string-courses:** projecting horizontal bands along a wall.

p. 256 **ashlar:** square hewn stone.

p. 256 **architraves:** ornamental mouldings around arches, doorways or windows.

p. 256 **fasciæ:** the three parts into which an architrave is divided.

p. 256 **freestone:** sandstone or limestone that can be easily sawn.

p. 257 **double cube:** room of which the breadth is equal to the height and the length is twice the breadth.

p. 257 **Pugin:** see note to p. 76 above.

p. 257 **Escalier de Marbre at Versailles:** the marble staircase in the palace in Paris. When he saw it on his honeymoon trip in 1874 Hardy made a note that it was 'of every colour – marble walls & all' (see Michael Millgate, *Thomas Hardy: A Biography*, p. 165).

p. 257 **King George:** George III, who was on the throne from 1760 to 1820.

p. 257 **poll:** top of the head.

p. 257 **Nine-Elms:** a landing place on the Thames near Battersea.

p. 257 **cramps and dowels:** small bars of metal with the ends bent, and headless pins, used for holding together two pieces of masonry, timber, etc.

p. 257 **White Rose faction:** the Yorkists in the Wars of the Roses (1455–85).

p. 257 **brands:** log fire on the hearth.

p. 258 **love-scenes of Isaac and Jacob:** see Genesis 24, 29.

p. 258 **Reynolds:** Sir Joshua Reynolds (1723–92), portrait painter.

p. 258 **Lely:** Sir Peter Lely (1618–80), portrait painter.

p. 258 **Walpolean scandal:** the letters by Horace Walpole (1717–97) amply record the social events of the day.

p. 259 **Fawkes:** Guy Fawkes (1570–1606), who was involved in the 'Gunpowder Plot' to blow up the Houses of Parliament in 1605. He was deputed to fire the powder, went to watch the cellar by himself, was caught, and hanged.

p. 262 **stanhope:** open, one-seated vehicle.

p. 263 **tabernacle:** body. See II Corinthians 5: 1: 'our earthly house of this tabernacle'.

p. 265 **driving-phaeton:** light four-wheeled open carriage.

p. 265 **fly:** one-horse covered carriage, usually hired by the day.

p. 269 **cherry net:** netting to protect cherries from birds.

p. 274 **hippocras:** cordial drink made of wine flavoured with spices.

p. 275 **Indian fortune:** 'nabobs', Englishmen who acquired wealth and social standing in India and then returned home, were a notable feature of nineteenth-century British society. Joseph Sedley in Thackeray's *Vanity Fair* (1848) is a familiar fictional example.

p. 275 **seneschals:** stewards.

p. 276 **Elzevirs, Caxtons:** books printed by the Elzevir family in Holland in the seventeenth century, and by William Caxton (1422?–91).

p. 276 **Scott:** Sir Walter Scott (1771–1832), poet and novelist.

p. 276 **Lammastide:** Lammas Day (1 August), the day on which, in Anglo-Saxon times, first fruits were offered to God.

p. 276 **diapason blasts:** resounding burst of harmony.

p. 278 **By absence ... miss her:** from an anonymous poem, usually attributed to John Hoskins (1566–1638), 'Absence, hear thou my protestation' (titled 'Present in Absence' in Francis Turner Palgrave's *The Golden Treasury* (1861), which is probably where Hardy read it).

p. 278 **batrachians:** reptiles belonging to the Batrachia, especially frogs and toads.

p. 278 **blower:** one who pumps the organ-bellows.

p. 278 **Choir, Great, and Swell:** stops in an organ.

p. 278 **Dulcianner:** dulciana, an organ stop of a soft, string-like tone.

p. 278 **scrammed:** (dialect) paralysed, numbed.

p. 279 **Miss Hepzibah Pyncheon's chicken:** an allusion to Nathaniel Hawthorne's *The House of Seven Gables* (1851), Ch. 6. For Hawthorne's possible influence on Hardy in this novel and *A Laodicean*, see David W. Jarrett, 'Hawthorne and Hardy as Modern Romancers', *Nineteenth Century Fiction* (1974), 458–71.

p. 279 **hammochrysos stone:** sparkling stone mentioned by the ancients; perhaps yellow micaceous schist.

p. 279 **scot-and-lot freeholder:** owner of a freehold property paying a municipal tax ('scot and lot') on it.

p. 281 **gamesome Curate of Meudon:** François Rabelais (1494–1593), author of *Garguntua and Pantagruel*.

p. 281 **Friar Tuck:** one of Robin Hood's merry men.

p. 282 **hammer-cloths:** cloths covering the driver's seat or box in a family coach.

p. 284 **deals:** planks of pine or fir.

p. 284 **landaus:** a landau is a fancy four-wheeled carriage with a top which can be opened and closed.

p. 285 **multum-in-parvo:** (Latin) much in little: here the phrase refers to a knife with many types of blade and other implements in a small space.

p. 285 **Flemish ladder:** strongly supported set of wooden steps; perhaps a local term in Hardy's youth (F. B. Pinion, *A Thomas Hardy Dictionary*).

p. 285 **exceptious:** disposed to make objections.

p. 291 **consumed:** a malapropism for 'consummated'.

p. 294 **Antipodean . . . murderer:** criminal transported to Botany Bay, in New South Wales, Australia.

p. 299 **Deluge:** see Genesis 6–8.

p. 302 **set-net:** fishing-net set across a stream or channel.

p. 303 **headfast rope:** rope at the head of a vessel, to make her fast to the wharf, etc.

p. 307 **Jack Ketch:** executioner, notorious for his barbarity (d. 1686).

p. 308 **Vandal:** barbarian, destroyer of beauty (from the characteristics of an early German tribe).

p. 310 **knap:** small hill.

p. 310 **law for't:** under English common law an innkeeper or publican is obliged to receive guests who desire accommodation (not just refreshment), no matter how late their arrival may be.

p. 311 **stomachy:** (dialect) ready to take offence, irritable.

p. 312 **rafted up:** (dialect) roused up, disturbed.

p. 312 **larry:** (dialect) confusion, excitement.

p. 313 **fist:** 'to make a fist' means 'to attempt'.

p. 313 **squail:** (dialect) cast, throw.

p. 313 **ekkypage:** equipage; carriage.

p. 313 **purblinking:** (dialect) purblind, dimly lighted.

p. 315 **dogcart:** open vehicle with two seats, back to back.

p. 315 **jinks:** frolics, pranks.

p. 316 **hide-bound:** little but skin and bone.

p. 316 **junks:** (dialect) chunks.

p. 316 **blinking:** (dialect) dimly lighted.

p. 316 pinners: (dialect) pinafores, bibs.

p. 316 tribes of nobodies: this is Hardy's joke about tourists in search of the 'picturesque'.

p. 316 jack-lantern: bluish light flitting over marshy tracts; will-o'-the-wisp.

p. 316 tallet: hayloft over a stable.

p. 321 pitch-and-toss: a game in which each player pitches a coin; the one whose coin lies nearest the mark then tosses all the coins, and keeps those that turn up 'heads'; the one whose coin lies next in order does the same with the remaining coins, and so on.

p. 327 like Abishag beside King David: a young virgin and the king in his old age: see I Kings 1: 1–4.

p. 327 rode upon a cherub: see II Samuel 22: 11 (also Psalm 18, 10): 'And he [Jehovah] rode upon a cherub, and did fly: and he was seen upon the wings of the wind.'

p. 331 A coronet covers a multitude of sins: a variation on 'Charity shall cover the multitude of sins' (I Peter 4: 8); a coronet is a small crown worn by members of noble families.

p. 331 jack-plane: long heavy plane for rough work.

p. 332 barge-boards: boards running along the edges of gables.

p. 332 balconettes: miniature balconies.

p. 339 jib-doors: doors flush with, and designed to be indistinguishable from, the walls in which they stand.

p. 342 balusters: short pillars or columns, forming part of balustrades.

p. 348 Petit Trianon: neo-classical villa in the park at Versailles. Hardy visited it on his honeymoon trip in 1874. See note to p. 257 above.

p. 353 vamp: part of a boot or shoe covering the front of the foot.

p. 353 Bob's-a-dying: (dialect) a great fuss.

p. 356 little finger ... loins: see I Kings 12: 10: 'Thy father made our yoke heavy, but make thou it lighter unto us; thus shalt thou say unto them, My little finger shall be thicker than my father's loins.'

p. 357 **build a hospital for twenty thousand pounds:** as Michael Millgate points out (*Thomas Hardy: His Career as a Novelist*, p. 107), this reflects the London building boom, which Hardy had seen at first hand when he was working for the architect Arthur Blomfield.

p. 357 **made a bishop:** this is Hardy's joke about how a Classical education, necessary training for the ministry, involved familiarity with the dubious exploits of pagan gods.

p. 358 **Walpole's:** see note to p. 258 above.

p. 358 **as poor as Job:** see Job 1: 14–21.

Since its immediate predecessor, *Far from the Madding Crowd*, had been a great success, *The Hand of Ethelberta* was reviewed in more than a dozen journals and newspapers. Most reviews find both weakness and strength in the novel: faults are said to lie in inauthentic dialogue, stylistic clumsiness, the improbability of the whole situation, and in the characterization, particularly, of Ethelberta. On the other hand, the novel is considered amusing and entertaining, and there are tributes to Hardy's 'power' and 'originality'.

The Saturday Review (6 May 1876) is typical: 'one lays down the book with a mixture of feelings'; Hardy is 'capable of making himself a place in the first rank of novelists', but this novel, 'amusing as it is, is hardly worthy of its author's powers'. The reviewer notes Hardy's 'besetting faults of giving incongruous dialogue to his characters, and going far out of his way for laboured similes', 'a certain air of improbability which runs through the book', and the failure 'to inspire a reader with any strong belief in Ethelberta's existence'. R. H. Hutton in the *Spectator* (22 April 1876) declares, 'A more entertaining book than the *Hand of Ethelberta* has not been published for many a year.' No one will read the novel 'without being aware from beginning to end that a very original and a very skilful hand is wielding the pen.' However, 'while Mr Hardy has enough superficial knowledge of human nature to give an air of plausibility and life to all he paints, he has not enough, – or at least, seldom shows enough, – to engrave individual figures on our minds as figures which take leave to live in our memories.' Ethelberta is 'so much of a riddle to us, and so little of a living figure', and other characters, too, are 'vivacious shadows, who amuse us without impressing us'. *The Graphic* (29 April 1876) says, 'This book is unquestionably the work of a true artist and humourist, and yet both the art and the humour somehow miss their effect.' The art is employed in building up a series of situations which are 'well-nigh extravagantly improbable' and the characters who are 'for the most part unreal beings' (Ethelberta is 'throughout a puzzle to us'), while the humour evolving out of such creations, 'amusing as it is, we yet feel to be unsatisfactory'. The reviewer goes on:

> We take it ill of Mr Hardy that he should have abandoned that rustic life which few can portray – for George Eliot concerns herself with farmers, not with farm-labourers – for London drawing-rooms and 'good society', ground on which he seems much less at home. His 'society' talk is clever, but apt to seem strange and unnatural. The wits and the unwise people talk too much alike.... However, in so far as Mr Hardy may have aimed, first of all, at amusing his readers, his book is a brilliant success, for its interest is strong and well sustained to the end.

There are, however, a few points where we find opposed judgements. While some criticize Hardy's style, George Saintsbury in the *Academy* (13 May 1876) notes a 'stylistic improvement' (that is, less laboured eccentricity) in this novel, and the *Atlantic Monthly* (August 1876) says:

> the style everywhere gives token of a sensitive personal touch from the author, where the words ... continually freshen in the quiet dew of thought that the author lets fall upon every detail.... Everything is given in pictures, so far as it may be, and these are always delicately drawn, with a spiritualized force of language, which seems to us uniquely Mr Hardy's among all English novelists.

Hardy's attempt at 'a new direction' in *Ethelberta* was, one suspects, strongly motivated by his wish not to be categorized as a follower of George Eliot. In spite of this effort, when critics blame Hardy for deserting the rural background, or failing thereby to give credible portraits of people, the ghost of Eliot still often hovers behind their judgement. In *The Times* (5 June 1876), where this novel is reviewed side by side with *Daniel Deronda* (then running as a serial), Eliot's genius for 'making everyone in creation, from a Duke to a Dogberry, figure as himself, and not as a puppet' is invoked to make a contrast with Hardy. Yet, the *Westminster Review* (July, 1876), where again the novel is reviewed together with *Daniel Deronda*, considers Hardy equal to Eliot. There is a remark that '[i]t is fortunate, perhaps, for him that it was published before 'Daniel Deronda', or else ill-natured critics would have declared that his principal character was only a copy' (Gwendolen Harleth is also beautiful and strong-minded, entertains an idea of becoming a public performer – a singer – marries without love, and has to face the fact that her husband kept a mistress). But this reviewer is clearly not 'ill-natured', for *Ethelberta*, it is observed, 'will sustain Mr Hardy's reputation', and '[h]e may again, as in *Far from the Madding Crowd*, divide the honours with George Eliot.' After instancing convincing little touches found in lines given to Picotee and London characters, the reviewer says, 'The talk, too, of Mr Hardy's clowns is, we think, more natural than *Far from the Madding Crowd*,' and positively declares that 'the masterpiece in the book is undoubtedly Ethelberta.'

Another interesting area of mixed reactions concerns the question of genre in relation to the 'improbability' of the novel. The *Athenaeum* (15 April 1876) rather condescendingly says:

> Mr Hardy seems, after a preliminary trial of several kinds, to have finally chosen as his branch of fiction that which, for want of a better name, may be called the modern-romantic. That is, he takes the present for his time, and such people as move among us at the present for his characters; but he makes his characters do things, and puts them into positions, which, if not impossible, would at least be thought very remarkable, and worthy of a leading article in every daily paper, if they had really been reported by a living witness. This must be called the second order of fiction, as it is distinctly inferior, in an artistic point of view, to that which produces its effects solely with the materials of everyday life: but in the hands of a master, who is capable of seeing how people might probably act and speak in improbable circumstances, it is by no means unsatisfactory.

The *Examiner* (13 May 1876) takes a directly opposite view:

> Improbability has been the main fault alleged against *The Hand of Ethelberta* in current criticisms of the story. Now we have always been among the enthusiastic admirers of Mr Hardy's work, recognizing in it the very highest artistic purposes and something not far short of the highest powers of execution, and we venture to think that this accusation of improbability as a fault proceeds upon a misapprehension of the writer's intentions.... If the

novelist did not intend his story to be a reflex of real life, he cannot be blamed if it is not, unless we are to lay down a close adherence to the probabilities of real life as an indispensable condition of novel-writing. Mr Hardy seems to us to have deliberately disclaimed being tried by a rigid standard of probability when he adopted as the sub-title of his work 'a *comedy* in chapters'.

This, the reviewer goes on, is 'what may be called ideal comedy, in which fancy is permitted to range beyond the limits of real life'. *Ethelberta* is an admirable success, for '[f]rom whatever point of view we regard the work, we find deliberate artistic aims and unflinching fidelity of execution'. The novel 'shows no falling off in intellectual force', as compared with its predecessor. The review concludes with this observation: 'We doubt whether Ethelberta possesses the popular interest of some of Mr Hardy's previous novels . . . but it is more masterly as a work of art – it reveals a progress in technical excellence which makes us look forward with curiosity to his next publication.'

The *Examiner* reviewer was certainly right in expressing doubt about the fate of the novel, for in critical studies of Hardy in the following decades, *Ethelberta* was most of the time disregarded, or dismissed as of little significance. Albert J. Guerard (*Thomas Hardy*, 1949) typically observes that this novel, like *A Laodicean*, is 'generally regarded as a complete failure'.

Modern critics repeat more or less the same charges against the novel as Victorian reviewers. If anything, they tend to be severer on the comedy: Irving Howe (*Thomas Hardy*, 1966), referring to the subtitle of the novel, tersely comments that 'the chapters are more noticeable than the comedy'. Joseph Warren Beach (*The Technique of Thomas Hardy*, 1922) says, 'After the grave and beautiful work of art of *Far from the Madding Crowd*, Mr Hardy diverted himself with an essay in comedy of rather dubious effectiveness.' Suggesting that here the novelist was aiming at something like Meredith's *Evan Harrington* or *Sandra Belloni*, he points out the failure of Hardy's comedy:

There is no one to correspond to the Countess de Saldar or to the Pole sisters – no one so funny. Ethelberta is not funny at all, in spite of her comic rôle of social climber. She is merely the object of an irony that misses fire. It misses fire because, somehow, the author makes us take her seriously, though without arousing deep interest in her . . . . There is only the most perfunctory suggestion of her being subjected to an ordeal and being found wanting. We cannot feel for her the admiring sympathy we feel for Evan Harrington in his tardy triumph over snobbery, nor the amused scorn we feel for Wilfrid Pole when he succumbs to the seduction of a weak sentimentalism.

A few more recent critics, however, have dealt more sympathetically with the comedy. Richard H. Taylor (*The Neglected Hardy: Thomas Hardy's Lesser Novels*, 1982), also refers to Meredith, particularly to his essay on 'The Idea of Comedy and the Uses of the Comic Spirit' (1877), where it is said that 'the test of true comedy is that it shall awaken thoughtful laughter', and declares that *Ethelberta* 'passes this test well'. He then quotes the letter Hardy wrote (8 August 1927) to J. B. Priestley, who had just published a book on Meredith:

> Meredith was, as you recognize, and might have insisted on even more strongly, and I always felt, in the direct succession of Congreve and the artificial comedians of the Restoration, and in getting his brilliancy we must put up with the fact that he would not, or could not – at any rate did not – when aiming to represent the 'Comic Spirit', let himself discover the tragedy that always underlies comedy if you only scratch it deeply enough.

In the novel, Taylor goes on, 'we do not have to scratch very deeply to discover the potential tragedy; only the author's perspective preserves the comic mode.' In his view, whether employing comic (as in *Ethelberta*) or tragic strategies (as in *Jude the Obscure*), Hardy's fundamental vision remains the same: 'the tragedy (if we conclude, as I think we may, that in a real moral sense Ethelberta's success *is* a tragedy) in each of these novels originates in that most consistent of Hardy's preoccupations: class division.'

According to Paul Ward ('*The Hand of Ethelberta*', in *The Thomas Hardy Yearbook*, 1971), neither the Victorian reviewers nor the modern critics seem to have grasped that 'what the book really has to offer is a fascinating commentary on the relationship between the tragic and comic masks, and on the technique of the artist in establishing and exploring his genre.' Pointing out that a given situation can be treated either comically or tragically, depending upon the manner in which the situation is presented and the character of the persons involved, Ward suggests that here the novelist resolves a potentially serious Hardyesque situation into the comic mode by the use of disinterested observers and inessential details, and through the characterization of the heroine. With regard to the last point, quoting Ethelberta's remarks about life as a game of chess in Chapter 17, he argues:

> Where other major characters in Hardy really *risk* themselves in their encounters to win the highest prize or to lose all, Ethelberta is content to play for smaller stakes. The metaphor of the chess game is significant: where for many of Hardy's characters the pieces are vital parts of their inner souls, for Ethelberta they are façades or poses – not insincere, but as she calls it 'experimental'. What irritates the unsympathetic critics into dismissing the novel as trivial is their inability to accept that with certain people, as with certain buildings, the façade may be the most beautiful or interesting part.

Michael Millgate (*Thomas Hardy: His Career as a Novelist*, 1971) argues that most of the comedy 'can be related, in one way or another, to the question of appearance and reality which provides one of the novel's continuing themes: 'Faith's truth to herself is not matched by Neigh the knacker's heir, nor by other characters who set store by their social pretensions'. He, too, considers the characterization of Ethelberta in relation to the comedy of the novel:

> Hardy seems to have been especially fascinated by the perpetually merging layers of reality and unreality implicit in the pattern of Ethelberta's career. She plays so many superimposed parts before audiences possessed of such differing degrees of initiation into her secrets that her 'true' personality proves finally elusive – perhaps even to Hardy himself, though the deliberate indirection of the final view of her seems not so much an evasion of difficulty as a conscious choice of ambiguity, a decision to rest with the enigma.

Sympathetically responsive to the whole novel, Millgate also locates here Hardy's first serious attempt 'to incorporate architecture more or less systematically as an element in an overall value-system'. This is 'an additional element in that technical adventurousness of *The Hand of Ethelberta* which seems – like the handling of contrasted rural and urban settings and of conflicting class relationships – to demand a higher place for the novel than it has customarily been accorded.' Central to the novel, he argues, is its evocation of great and rapid social change: 'In a world where so much was changing, manners and social attitudes must have seemed ripe for changes on a similar scale, and Hardy treats Ethelberta's career almost as a parable of social revolution.'

Another view of the characterization of the heroine is expressed by John Bayley (*An Essay on Hardy*, 1978), who argues:

> Hardy is here, in fantasy and in projection, completely his own heroine. It is the most singular of his identifications, for as a man who would rather be silent than speak, an observer and not an actor, he projects an extraordinary daydream of *performance*, substituting for his own talent for writing the brilliance of an entertainer, and the daring wit and poise of a social beauty. Nor was that all. As a man whose relations with the world of responsibilities, however shrewd, were passive and unauthoritative, he becomes in the book the arbiter and goddess of a large family, all of whom look to Ethelberta for guidance and support in the shifts of their strange social situation .... And yet Ethelberta remains too much an idea and a daydream ... to engage our interests as Hardy's real heroines can. Hardy is too dispassionate about her, and in a curious way too much in practical earnest about what she might represent for him if he had been in the position of bringing up his own family in the social scale and being responsible for what ensued.

Perceptively Bayley says of the novel as a whole:

> One thing which seems to me certain is that *Ethelberta* is not a failure: and that it does not show, as most Hardy critics assume, that he had no sense of how to handle a social and metropolitan theme. Rather he had too much sense of it. *Ethelberta*, like *Hamlet*, is an imaginative impression of 'court life', about which the novelist is too intrigued to be sure-footed. Yet except for Shakespeare himself no English writer is more naturally a courtier than Hardy. Their attraction towards places where the role is played is a matter of feeling as well as imagination; and they have the art of pleasing both the self-appointed great, and those great

by nature, without forfeiting an essential detachment and an inner amusement.

These sympathetic studies were, as I have said, exceptional cases in the generally indifferent critical response. The situation, however, now seems to be undergoing a kind of sea change, for in the last few years *Ethelberta* has become a focus of much serious attention from materialist and feminine critics. Representative of the former, and indeed most responsible for the current revival of interest in the novel, is Peter Widdowson, whose book, *Hardy in History: A Study in Literary Sociology* (1989), examines the ways in which the idea of 'Thomas Hardy' has been ideologically constructed, first by the author himself, and then by academic criticism, education, publishing, and the mass-media. He devotes a long chapter to *Ethelberta* and discusses it in great detail along these lines:

> I shall show (while avoiding intentionalism) how *Ethelberta* self-consciously foregrounds issues of social class, gender relations, and the artifice of realist fiction writing. And I shall suggest that the exposure of the alienating lies produced by these systems is more readily perceptible in Hardy's other fiction once it has been identified in such uncompromising form in *The Hand of Ethelberta*.

Widdowson shares with critics such as Millgate and Taylor the view that *Ethelberta* is not different from other Hardy novels in its critique of the class system. Yet their reading, as he sees it, has been disabled by the constraints of conventional critical discourse. Theirs is seen as a humanist-realist criticism based on liberal-bourgeois conceptions of 'character' and common-sense 'probabilism'. According to Widdowson, what the novel is really doing is to expose the very artificiality of these conceptions, by its own artificiality and improbability, its use of coincidence, unreal characters, farcical absurdities, and other uncompromisingly fictive contrivances. What is often condemned as the awkward style of the novel is actually an effective device: 'Certainly the novel's style is pervasively self-conscious, but its very consistency makes it more a strategic mannerism – one which intensifies the defamiliarizing ("disproportioning") effect of the whole work – than a failure of control.' Widdowson regards Ethelberta as an inevitably divided character, reflecting as she does Hardy's own 'recognition of the contradictory position in which he was now situated'. He is very good at noticing the shared features of the author and the heroine, showing how Ethelberta's composing an epic poem corresponds to Hardy's own project of *The Dynasts* just started at the time of his writing of this novel. He also discusses, with reference to their use of Defoe, the similarity of Ethelberta's fictional theory and practice to Hardy's own, both of them highly aware of the 'unreal' nature of 'realism'. Widdowson has a number of interesting things to say about the novel, and his is a study no serious reader of *Ethelberta* can ignore, whether to agree or disagree.

Feminist critics mainly focus on the issue of gender in the novel, in an attempt to demonstrate how the text exposes the idea of 'woman' as an ideological construct. Patricia Ingham (*Thomas Hardy*, 1990), for instance, stresses elements which confound patriarchal values, such as Ethelberta's active part in giving her hand in marriage, 'the startling equivalence of the two sexes' (the masculine Ethelberta and the feminine Christopher) which undermines essentialist accounts of women, and the virtual absence of the narrating voice towards the end of the novel which indicates the male narrator's appropriation by the omnicompetent heroine.

Similarly Sarah Davies, in her article, 'The Hand of Ethelberta: De-mythologizing "Woman"' (*Critical Survey*, 1993), argues that the novel, breaking down the facile gender category, redefines the signification of 'woman', in which the heroine is not an inscription by the male pen on a blank page, but a creative writer who can manipulate the 'male gaze'. Hardy's ultimate success lies, in her view, in showing us that 'the feminine figure of the realist novel is a social and therefore male construct, a myth rather than a reality or truth.'

Penny Boumelha ('A Complicated Position for a Woman: *The Hand of Ethelberta*', in *The Sense of Sex: Feminist Perspectives on Hardy*, ed. Margaret R. Higonnet, 1993) observes that

> the novel's manipulation of the plots of social mobility and marriage demonstrates how the ideas of ambition, success, family responsibility and self-fulfilment which must be negotiated in the process of such class transition are specifically inflected through ideologies of gender, in ways which in fact permeated the lives

of Victorian women. And in the figure of Ethelberta as producer of language (writer, story-teller, coiner of aphorisms for the edification of her sister), there is in turn some interrogation of the status of those plots of mobility and stability in their relation to gender.

These recent critics have considered some hitherto unexplored aspects of *The Hand of Ethelberta*. Their efforts are bound to attract new readers to this novel, and will no doubt send seasoned Hardyans back to it with renewed interest.

SUGGESTIONS FOR FURTHER READING

Bibliography and Reference

The standard bibliography is Richard L. Purdy's *Thomas Hardy: A Bibliographical Study* (1954). F. B. Pinion's *A Hardy Companion* (1968) and *A Thomas Hardy Dictionary* (1989) are very useful reference books.

Biography

Michael Millgate's *Thomas Hardy: A Biography* (1982) is authoritative and factually most reliable. Robert Gittings's *Young Thomas Hardy* (1975), covering the period up until (and including) the publication of *Ethelberta*, is also excellent. The most recent, if not the best, biography is Martin Seymour-Smith's *Hardy* (1994). Timothy Hands's *A Hardy Chronology* conveniently provides a day-to-day account of the author's life. Other important sources for biographical information include Hardy's *Collected Letters* in 7 volumes (1978–88), edited by Richard L. Purdy and Michael Millgate, and his autobiography – originally published as a biography by his second wife, Florence – now edited by Millgate as *The Life and Work of Thomas Hardy by Thomas Hardy* (1984).

Criticism

The following is a list of critical material, directly or indirectly dealing with *Ethelberta*, and a brief selection from the vast number of books on Hardy's writings (primarily on his fiction). Items referred to in the section on 'Hardy and His Critics' and the 'Notes' are not listed here.

David Ball: 'Hardy's Experimental Fiction', *English* 35 (1986), 27–36. (Considers the novel in conjunction with *Desperate Remedies* and *A Laodicean*.)

Joe Fisher: *The Hidden Hardy* (1992). (A materialist analysis with a chapter on the novel.)

SUGGESTIONS FOR FURTHER READING   397

Patrick Roberts: 'Ethelberta: Portrait of the Artist as a Young Woman: Love and Ambition', *Thomas Hardy Journal* 10 (1994), 87–94.

John H. Schwarz: 'Misrepresentations, Mistakes, and Uncertainties in *The Hand of Ethelberta*', *Thomas Hardy Journal* 1 (1985), 53–62.

Clarice Short: 'In Defense of *Ethelberta*', *Nineteenth-Century Fiction* 13 (1958), 48–57.

Michael Slater: 'Hardy and the City', in *New Perspectives on Thomas Hardy*, ed. Charles P. C. Pettit (1994).

George Wing: '"Forbear, Hostler, Forbear!": Social Satire in *The Hand of Ethelberta*', *Studies in the Novel* 15 (1972), 568–79.

Penny Boumelha: *Thomas Hardy and Women: Sexual Ideology and Narrative Form* (1982).

Jean Brooks: *Thomas Hardy: The Poetic Structure* (1971).

R. G. Cox: *Thomas Hardy: The Critical Heritage* (1970). (A generally useful selection of contemporary reviews, but reprints none on this novel.)

Ian Gregor: *The Great Web: The Form of Hardy's Major Fiction* (1974).

Robert Langbaum: *Thomas Hardy in Our Time* (1995).

D. H. Lawrence: *Study of Thomas Hardy and Other Essays*, ed. Bruce Steele (1985).

Charles Lock: *Thomas Hardy: Criticism in Focus* (1992). (A useful survey of Hardy criticism.)

Perry Meisel: *Thomas Hardy: The Return of the Repressed* (1972).

J. Hillis Miller: *Thomas Hardy: Distance and Desire* (1970).

Rosemarie Morgan: *Women and Sexuality in the Novels of Thomas Hardy* (1988).

Norman Page: *Thomas Hardy* (1977).

Norman Page (ed.): *Thomas Hardy: The Writer and His Background* (1980). (Contains Merryn and Raymond Williams's essay on 'Hardy and Social Class'.)

J. I. M. Stewart: *Thomas Hardy: A Critical Biography* (1971).

TEXT SUMMARY

Chapter 1

Ethelberta arrives at Anglebury with Lady Petherwin. She takes a walk, gets lost, and then chances upon Christopher.

Chapter 2

Christopher receives an anonymous book of verse. He is disappointed when he locates the sender (Picotee), who refuses to disclose the writer's name. They keep passing each other by on a moorland road.

Chapter 3

In the pouring rain Picotee waits in vain for Christopher; this is observed by Ladywell and others from a hut.

Chapter 4

Christopher, at Ethelberta's suggestion, is asked to play at Wyndway House, where he with revived love observes her dancing.

Chapter 5

Christopher becomes aware that Ethelberta is a widow.

Chapter 6

Picotee is secretly distressed to know that Ethelberta was once in love with Christopher.

Chapter 7

At Doncastle's, Ladywell, Neigh, and others talk about *Meters by E.* Downstairs, Chickerel writes to Ethelberta.

Chapter 8

Christopher goes to see Rookington Park, where Ethelberta is staying. There he sees another man (Ladywell) apparently with the same purpose. He reads in a newspaper that *Meters by E* was actually written by Ethelberta, and sends her a tune he composed to one of her poems.

Chapter 9

Ethelberta sings the tune in a house in London. Having written a letter of thanks to Christopher in which she discloses her family background, she throws it in the fire, and writes another, more formal one.

Chapter 10

Lady Petherwin accuses Ethelberta of having published a book which tarnishes the sacred memory of her son. In a fit of anger she burns her will.

Chapter 11

Christopher, with Faith, moves to London. He calls on Ethelberta, only to find that she has gone off to France. Later, on another call, he is informed of Lady Petherwin's death, and of Ethelberta's current address.

Chapter 12

Christopher visits Arrowthorne Lodge.

Chapter 13

Ethelberta tells Christopher that after Lady Petherwin's death she is now left with nothing but the lease of the London house. She also speaks of her plan to become a professional story-teller.

Chapter 14

Christopher is seen off by Sol and Dan.

Chapter 15

Ethelberta discusses with her family the plan of moving them to the London house.

Chapter 16

Ethelberta's first performance in London. Among the audience are Ladywell, Neigh, Christopher and Faith.

Chapter 17

Christopher calls on Ethelberta. Their conversation is interrupted by Ladywell, to whom she is sitting. Ethelberta receives a letter from Picotee, who is anxious to join the family in London.

Chapter 18

Against Ethelberta's advice, Picotee comes up to London.

Chapter 19

Ethelberta, unaware of her sister's feelings, complains to Picotee about Christopher, who of late has not paid a visit.

Chapter 20

Another performance at Mayfair Hall. Upon returning home, Ethelberta finds that Christopher has called. She sends a letter, telling him not to visit her for some time.

Chapter 21

Ladywell confesses his unrequited love for Ethelberta to Neigh, who unknown to him shares the same admiration for her. Christopher complains to Faith about the way Ethelberta treats him.

Chapter 22

Christopher comes to see Ethelberta, who keeps him waiting. Later when Picotee is sent to him, Christopher, mistaking her for Ethelberta, impulsively kisses her hand. From her reaction he realizes that she is in love with him.

Chapter 23

Picotee confesses to Ethelberta that she loves Christopher. Distressed, Ethelberta tries to talk to her mother and sisters, but comes to the conclusion that it is useless to do so.

Chapter 24

Feeling that her performance is now losing its fresh appeal with the public, Ethelberta discusses with Picotee the idea of an advantageous marriage. Christopher, who is leaving for Melchester, calls. Ethelberta tells him that they are to remain as friends only.

Chapter 25

Ethelberta visits the Royal Academy, where Ladywell's picture in which her face is used is now displayed. There she overhears the rumour that Neigh intends to marry her. Accompanied by Picotee, she goes to see Neigh's estate.

Chapter 26

Having found out about Ethelberta's visit, Neigh proposes to her.

Chapter 27

Ethelberta, Neigh, and others go to Cripplegate Church. Neigh repeats his proposal. Ladywell, who arrives late, realizes that Neigh has been courting Ethelberta.

Chapter 28

Ethelberta becomes aware that Joey is in love with a new maid at Doncastle's. Fearing that this might jeopardize the whole set-up, she consults her father. The woman in question turns out to be Menlove.

Chapter 29

Ethelberta is invited to a dinner party at Doncastle's. Picotee is allowed to come, too, and is shown around by Menlove.

Chapter 30

Ethelberta decides not to marry Neigh, when Picotee tells her that at Doncastle's she overheard him make a joke of their visit to his estate.

Chapter 31

Ethelberta takes her family to Knollsea. Invited by Lord Mountclere, she attends the meeting of the Imperial Archaeological Association at Corvsgate Castle. Neigh is also there, and she says she will give him a definite answer at Rouen.

Chapter 32

Lord Mountclere is informed by his valet that Ethelberta is a butler's daughter.

Chapter 33

Ethelberta, followed by Lord Mountclere, travels to Rouen to visit her aunt.

Chapter 34

Ethelberta receives a letter from her mother, suggesting that she should marry soon since Menlove might expose her any day. She tries to warn Lord Mountclere off from herself.

Chapter 35

Ladywell, encouraged by her mother, comes to see Ethelberta at her hotel. Neigh also calls, closely followed by Lord Mountclere. She asks all three suitors to wait for a month.

Chapter 36

Ethelberta, back in London, tries to decide her course of action with the help of Utilitarian philosophy.

Chapter 37

Ethelberta goes to Knollsea, where she expects a visit from Lord Mountclere. His carriage overturns, and he sprains his ankle.

Chapter 38

Lord Mountclere invites Ethelberta to Enckworth Court. Asked to perform by one of the guests, she tells a story of her own life. When she realizes that Lord Mountclere has been aware of her background, she accepts his offer of marriage.

Chapter 39

Lord Mountclere takes Ethelberta to Melchester, in order to test her as regards her relationship with Christopher.

Chapter 40

Christopher finds out that Ethelberta is going to marry Lord Mountclere. He decides to stop her.

Chapter 41

Edgar visits Sol in London, and informs him of the marriage between his brother and his sister scheduled for the next day. They depart together to prevent it.

Chapter 42

Chickerel, overhearing the Doncastles speak of his daughter's impending marriage, sets off to stop the wedding.

Chapter 43

A strong wind prevents the sea voyage of Edgar and Sol from Sandbourne to Knollsea.

Chapter 44

Edgar and Sol start again from Sandbourne. At Anglebury Christopher picks up an old man (Chickerel) on his way to Knollsea. When their vehicles collide with each other, both parties realize that they are travelling for the same purpose.

Chapter 45

Edgar, Sol, Christopher and Chickerel arrive at Knollsea Church, only to find the signatures of Lord Mountclere and Ethelberta in the marriage-register. Sol and Chickerel go to Enckworth Court, where they glimpse the married couple in a carriage. Ethelberta, through Picotee, asks Sol to see her.

Chapter 46

After being rebuked by Sol, Ethelberta finds a cottage occupied by Lord Mountclere's mistress. She sends Picotee for Sol. Picotee chances upon Christopher, and he decides to rescue Ethelberta when Sol abandons her.

Chapter 47

Christopher's attempt is foiled by Lord Mountclere.

SEQUEL

Two and a half years later. After his sojourn in Italy Christopher visits the Chickerels. He asks Picotee to marry him.

ACKNOWLEDGEMENTS

I wish to thank Edward Costigan and Michael Slater for their invaluable advice. I am also indebted to the late Robert Gittings for information in a number of his notes to the New Wessex edition of *The Hand of Ethelberta* (1975). I benefited from the discussion in the seminar I conducted on the novel at the 1994 Thomas Hardy International Conference in Dorchester and I am grateful to all the participants, in particular to Mary Rimmer. Thanks are also due to Michael Millgate, and to Susan Webb of Dorset County Record Office, who had the patience to answer my queries. Suguru Fukasawa kindly gave me access to the Hardy collection of Chuo University. But my greatest debt is to the series editor Norman Page for his wise and friendly counsel.

CLASSIC NOVELS
IN EVERYMAN

The Time Machine
H. G. WELLS

*One of the books which defined
'science fiction' – a compelling
and tragic story of a brilliant
and driven scientist*
£3.99

Oliver Twist
CHARLES DICKENS

*Arguably the best-loved of
Dickens's novels. With all the
original illustrations*
£4.99

Barchester Towers
ANTHONY TROLLOPE

*The second of Trollope's
Chronicles of Barsetshire,
and one of the funniest of all
Victorian novels*
£4.99

The Heart of Darkness
JOSEPH CONRAD

*Conrad's most intense, subtle,
compressed, profound and
proleptic work*
£3.99

Tess of the d'Urbervilles
THOMAS HARDY

*The powerful, poetic classic
of wronged innocence*
£3.99

Wuthering Heights and Poems
EMILY BRONTË

*A powerful work of genius – one of
the great masterpieces of literature*
£3.99

Pride and Prejudice
JANE AUSTEN

*Proposals, rejections, infidelities,
elopements, happy marriages –
Jane Austen's most popular novel*
£2.99

North and South
ELIZABETH GASKELL

*A novel of hardship, passion
and hard-won wisdom amidst the
conflicts of the industrial revolution*
£4.99

The Newcomes
W. M. THACKERAY

*An exposé of Victorian polite
society by one of the nineteenth-
century's finest novelists*
£6.99

Adam Bede
GEORGE ELIOT

*A passionate rural drama enacted
at the turn of the eighteenth
century*
£5.99

All books are available from your local bookshop or direct from:
Littlehampton Book Services Cash Sales, 14 Eldon Way, Lineside Estate,
Littlehampton, West Sussex BN17 7HE (*prices are subject to change*)

To order any of the books, please enclose a cheque (in sterling) made payable to
Littlehampton Book Services, or phone your order through with credit card details (Access,
Visa or Mastercard) on 01903 721596 (24 hour answering service) stating card number
and expiry date. (*Please add £1.25 for package and postage to the total of your order.*)

In the USA, for further information and a complete catalogue call 1-800-526-2778

CLASSIC FICTION
IN EVERYMAN

**The Impressions of
Theophrastus Such**
GEORGE ELIOT
*An amusing collection of character
sketches, and the only paperback
edition available*
£5.99

Frankenstein
MARY SHELLEY
*A masterpiece of Gothic terror in
its original 1818 version*
£3.99

East Lynne
MRS HENRY WOOD
*A classic tale of melodrama,
murder and mystery*
£7.99

**Holiday Romance and
Other Writings for Children**
CHARLES DICKENS
*Dickens's works for children,
including 'The Life of Our Lord'
and 'A Child's History of England',
with original illustrations*
£5.99

The Ebb-Tide
R.L. STEVENSON
*A compelling study of ordinary
people in extreme circumstances*
£4.99

The Three Impostors
ARTHUR MACHEN
*The only edition available
of this cult thriller*
£4.99

Mister Johnson
JOYCE CARY
*The only edition available of this
amusing but disturbing twentieth-
century tale*
£5.99

The Jungle Book
RUDYARD KIPLING
*The classic adventures of Mowgli
and his friends*
£3.99

Glenarvon
LADY CAROLINE LAMB
*The only edition available of the
novel which throws light on the
greatest scandal of the early nineteenth century – the infatuation of
Caroline Lamb with Lord Byron*
£6.99

**Twenty Thousand Leagues
Under the Sea**
JULES VERNE
*Scientific fact combines with
fantasy in this prophetic tale
of underwater adventure*
£4.99

All books are available from your local bookshop or direct from:
Littlehampton Book Services Cash Sales, 14 Eldon Way, Lineside Estate,
Littlehampton, West Sussex BN17 7HE (*prices are subject to change*)

To order any of the books, please enclose a cheque (in sterling) made payable to
Littlehampton Book Services, or phone your order through with credit card details (Access,
Visa or Mastercard) on 01903 721596 (24 hour answering service) stating card number
and expiry date. (*Please add £1.25 for package and postage to the total of your order.*)

In the USA, for further information and a complete catalogue call 1-800-526-2778

SHORT STORY COLLECTIONS
IN EVERYMAN

The Strange Case of Dr Jekyll and Mr Hyde and Other Stories
R. L. STEVENSON
An exciting selection of gripping tales from a master of suspense
£1.99

Nineteenth-Century American Short Stories
edited by Christopher Bigsby
A selection of the works of Henry James, Edith Wharton, Mark Twain and many other great American writers
£6.99

The Best of Saki
edited by MARTIN STEPHEN
Includes Tobermory, Gabriel Ernest, Svedni Vashtar, The Interlopers, Birds on the Western Front
£4.99

Souls Belated and Other Stories
EDITH WHARTON
Brief, neatly crafted tales exploring a range of themes from big taboo subjects to the subtlest little ironies of social life
£6.99

The Night of the Iguana and Other Stories
TENNESSEE WILLIAMS
Twelve remarkable short stories, each a compelling drama in miniature
£4.99

Selected Short Stories and Poems
THOMAS HARDY
Hardy's most memorable stories and poetry in one volume
£4.99

Selected Tales
HENRY JAMES
Stories portraying the tensions between private life and the outside world
£5.99

The Best of Sherlock Homes
ARTHUR CONAN DOYLE
All the favourite adventures in one volume
£4.99

The Secret Self 1: *Short Stories by Women*
edited by Hermione Lee
'*A superb collection*' The Guardian
£4.99
